# Augmented and M<br>for Commur

*Edited by*

**Joshua A. Fisher, Ph.D.**

Assistant Professor, Immersive Media Columbia College
Chicago, Illinois, USA

**CRC Press**
Taylor & Francis Group
Boca Raton   London   New York

CRC Press is an imprint of the
Taylor & Francis Group, an **informa** business

A SCIENCE PUBLISHERS BOOK

First edition published 2021
by CRC Press
6000 Broken Sound Parkway NW, Suite 300, Boca Raton, FL 33487-2742

and by CRC Press
2 Park Square, Milton Park, Abingdon, Oxon, OX14 4RN

© 2021 Taylor & Francis Group, LLC

*CRC Press is an imprint of Taylor & Francis Group, LLC*

ISBN: 978-0-367-51210-1 (hbk)
ISBN: 978-0-367-51209-5 (pbk)
ISBN: 978-1-003-05283-8 (ebk)

Typeset in Palatino Roman
by Innovative Processors

*Dedicated to*

The pioneers building our XR cities and communities

# Preface

Many years ago, I was working abroad as a teacher. First, I worked in South Korea and then in Turkey. During my time in both beautiful countries, I dreamt about my neighborhoods overlayed with digital information that could help me, an ex-pat, navigate my new world. Sitting at my desk during office hours, I would daydream of city streets where reviews floated in front of restaurants and the work of local artists floated through the air in an invisible gallery. While abroad, I jotted all this down in a leatherbound journal my sister had given me before leaving the United States. When I returned home to Chicago, I discovered augmented and mixed reality. My infatuation with the media was instantaneous. The media allowed me to do what I had been dreaming about. I then dedicated my life to the study of immersive media. I went on to receive my doctorate from the Georgia Institute of Technology. I wrote my dissertation on how augmented and mixed reality can be used in community workshops to bring about social reflection and change. During that time and since, I've published numerous articles on immersive media design, user experience, community impact, and the ethical issues involved. Like me, there are a growing number of scholars, artists, practitioners, and professionals who are all beginning to enter the field of augmented and mixed reality in communities. This collection was organized to gather their scholarship.

My ardent belief is that we are on the precipice of a change in how we interact with our communities and media. In part, this has been prompted by the COVID-19 pandemic. Yet, it is also due to the increased integration of the digital world into our everyday. As the technology that supports augmented and mixed reality develops rapidly, our capacity to analyze what the media is doing in our communities lags behind. To better understand that impact, each chapter in this book ends with an activity. These activities are meant to be integrated into immersive media programs at the college or high school level. They are also perfectly suited to independent scholars and researchers looking to explore these same issues. I hope that this collection's insights spur your own creative thought and critical perspectives.

This collection is only a single step forward. It is part of a larger movement that is exploring immersive media and its impact on our world. From here, reader, I leave it to you to take the lessons in this book and create our new reality.

**Joshua A. Fisher**

# Contents

# List of Tables

# List of Figures

# List of Contributors

**Hank Blumenthal, Ph.D.**

ORCID: 0000-0002-0145-603X; Bowling Green State University

Hank Blumenthal is project manager, academic, and producer His recent work includes producing "The Walk" in Pre-production with Michael Mailer, directed and written by Dan Adams. He is an Assistant Professor at Bowling Green State University, Interactive Media, and Video Production. Before that, he was an Instructor at Georgia Institute of Technology, where he earned a Ph.D. focused on transmedia storytelling, experimental TV, and games. His awards include Webbys for Sputnik7 and Epitonic sites, a Peabody for "The Great Space Coaster," and the Grand Jury Prize for "In the Soup" at Sundance.

**Bill Guschwan**

ORCID: 0000-0001-6924-8408; Columbia College Chicago

Bill Guschwan is a serious digital game designer and field philosopher. He was a founding team-member on Apple's QuickTime, Media Tool, and Newton teams and wrote articles for Apple about graphics, video, and game software. He was on the founding teams of the 3DO Interactive Multiplayer as well as the Sony's PlayStation 1. He wrote important internal game design articles for Sony. He currently teaches at Columbia College Chicago, and writes articles about human transformation and mechanism design using his "gamiformics" framework.

**Anna Wiehl, Ph.D.**

ORCID: 0000-0002-1448-2886; University of Bayreuth

Dr. Anna Wiehl is working as lecturer and research assistant at the University of Bayreuth, Germany, Department for Media Studies. Her research focuses on the interdependencies of audiovisual and digital media, transmedia narratives, (interactive) documentary and the future of television. In 2010, she received her Ph.D. degree (summa cum laude) with her thesis Myth of European Identity. Supranational, national and regional identities in German and French television news. Her current habilitation-project tackles the exploration of new forms of non-fictional audiovisual productions. Apart from her academic career, she has been working for the French-German broadcasting station *arte*, the German public broadcaster ARD and the Bavarian television BR as author for TV, radio and Internet.

**Brian Wassom, J.D.**

ORCID: 0000-0002-6138-9297; Warner Norcross + Judd LLP
Brian Wassom litigates disputes and counsels clients in a wide range of commercial and intellectual property matters. He has developed a particular focus in matters of creative expression, commercial identity, and privacy, which spans the legal doctrines of copyright, trademark, privacy, publicity rights, advertising, journalism, and related fields. A futurist at heart, he has been recognized as a thought leader in the brand-new legal issues raised by augmented reality and other cutting-edge emerging media. He regularly publish, blog, and speak on these topics to industry groups, legal education seminars, and conferences across the country.

**Stylianos Mystakidis, Ph.D.**

ORCID: 0000-0002-9162-8340; University of Patras
Dr. Stylianos Mystakidis is a learning innovator, project manager and researcher at the University of Patras, Greece. He holds a Ph.D. from the Faculty of Information Technology at the University of Jyväskylä, Finland, a MA in Education in Virtual Worlds at the University of the West of England Bristol, United Kingdom and a M.Sc. in Mechanical Engineering at the National Technical University of Athens, Greece. His professional practice and research focus on virtual and augmented reality, e-learning, game-based learning and open education.

**Janíce Tisha Samuels, Ed.D.**

ORCID: 0000-0002-8364-4076; Pepperdine University
Dr. Janíce Tisha Samuels is the founder and executive director of the Chicago, IL based National Youth Art Movement Against Gun Violence, which combines art activism and Augmented Reality technology to provide marginalized youth with the opportunity to be thought leaders in gun violence prevention. Over the past ten years, Janíce has progressed her experience as a higher education and educational technology leader through independent consulting projects, fellowship work, and positions of increasing responsibility. Janíce has received throughout her life numerous awards for her creative writing and, prior to moving to Chicago, proudly served the city of Takoma Park, MD, a sister community to Washington, DC, as an Arts and Humanities Commissioner for three years both as a member of the commission and then as co-chair. Janíce's academic and creative writing can be found in the Journal for Media Literacy Education, in Revelry -- The Voice of the Gwendolyn Brooks Writers Association of Florida and other publications.

**Kelvin Ramirez, Ph.D.**

ORCID: 0000-0001-7618-0886; Lesley University
Kelvin A. Ramirez is a board certified registered Art Therapist with years of experience incorporating art therapy within educational systems to enhance student's personal and academic growth. A Board Member of FNEI, a 501(c)(3) non-profit based in Boston, MA, Dr. Ramirez has taken his expertise and shared it internationally, collaborating with educators, community leaders, mental health professionals and art therapists in Nicaragua, the Dominican Republic, Haiti, Puerto Rico, India and

Mexico. Dr. Ramirez is the Executive Producer of Art Therapy: The Movie (2016), an independent film that explores the healing power of artistic expression through art therapy and Love in the Making (2017), a thought provoking independent film, that examines why we fall in love, what keeps us together, and what pulls us apart? Dr. Ramirez has written a chapter in Kerr (2015) Multicultural Family Art Therapy on identity formation and cultural isolation. Currently, Dr. Ramirez is an Associate Professor in the Division of Expressive Arts Therapies with dual appointments in the Graduate School of Education at Lesley University, Cambridge, MA. Areas of research and activism include incorporating art therapy to support the social and emotional development of adolescent males of color and confronting how art therapy addresses or ignores systemic oppression. Recently, Dr. Ramirez has collaborated with community leaders in Juarez, Mexico developing an initiative, "No Longer Bystanders" which focuses on supporting the complex mental health needs of asylum seekers. For Dr. Ramirez, teaching is an act of service empowering individuals to direct their destinies and author their stories.

**John T. Murray, Ph.D.**

ORCID: 0000-0003-2579-6802; University of Central Florida
Dr. John T. Murray is an Assistant Professor of Games and Interactive Media department at the University of Central Florida, USA. He is co-author of Flash: Building the Interactive Web (MIT Press, 2014) and Adventure Games: Playing the Outsider (Bloomsbury, 2020). His research focuses on interactive narratives and reality media (augmented, virtual and mixed reality). His investigation includes both existing and future computational media platforms, including authoring tools and affordances and measuring and evaluating complex experiences created for them using emerging techniques such as eye-tracking, facial action units, machine learning, and physiological signals.

**Emily K. Johnson, Ph.D.**

ORCID: 0000-0002-5084-1735; University of Central Florida
Dr. Emily Kuzneski Johnson is an Assistant Professor of Games and Interactive Media at the University of Central Florida. She is also core faculty in the Texts & Technology Ph.D. program. Her work focuses on technologically mediated learning environments from interactive narratives to immersive language learning, and just about everything in between. Her interdisciplinary collaborative work includes ELLE the EndLess Learner, a second language acquisition game with versions playable on VR, AR, mobile, and PC; the Middle Passage Experience, a VR simulation designed to promote education and empathy; and Sherlock's Riddles of Biblical Archaeology, a PC game created for Judaic Studies courses.

**Kevin Healey, Ph.D.**

ORCID: 0000-0001-9044-8228; University of New Hampshire
Kevin Healey is an Associate Professor of Communication at the University of New Hampshire. His work focuses on the ethical and religious dimensions of digital culture. His scholarship appears in publications such as the *Journal of Television and New Media* and the *Journal of Media Ethics*. He also enjoys writing creative non-

fiction and poetry, and his creative work appears in venues such as *Salon*, *Huffington Post*, *Religion Dispatches*, *Typishly*, and *Meat for Tea*. He is a co-editor of the book *Prophetic Critique and Popular Media* (Peter Lang, 2013), and is currently working on a new manuscript for Routledge titled *Religion and Ethics in the Age of Social Media: Proverbs for Responsible Digital Citizens*.

### Rebecca Rouse, Ph.D.

ORCID: 0000-0002-3509-8293; University of Skövde
Rebecca Rouse is a Senior Lecturer in Media Arts, Aesthetics, and Narration in the School of Informatics, in the Media, Technology, and Culture research group at the University of Skövde, Sweden. Rouse holds a PhD in Digital Media from the Georgia Institute of Technology (Atlanta, GA), an MA in Communication & Culture from the joint program at York University and Ryerson University (Toronto, Canada), and a BA in Theatre Studies and German Studies from Brown University (Providence, RI). With over a decade of experience working with Augmented Reality (AR) and other interactive media, Rouse's research focuses on theoretical, critical, and design production work with storytelling for new technologies.

### Kelsey Cameron, Ph.D.

ORCID: 0000-0002-3794-4844; Regis University
Kelsey Cameron is an assistant professor of communication at Regis University. She received a PhD in Film and Media Studies from the University of Pittsburgh, and her research and teaching focus on questions of technology, embodiment and infrastructure. Her work has been published in *Participations* and *Transformative Works and Cultures*, and she is currently at work on a book project about the police body camera.

### Jessica FitzPatrick, Ph.D.

ORCID: 0000-0003-0584-5822; University of Pittsburgh
Jessica FitzPatrick conducts research at the confluence of spatial studies, postcolonial theory, speculative fiction studies, and new media creation. She received a PhD in Critical and Cultural Studies from the University of Pittsburgh, where she is a Visiting Lecturer and Assistant Director of the Digital Narrative and Interactive Design program. Her current work includes a book project on postcolonial science fiction and digital humanities ventures like the *Secret Pittsburgh Digital Guidebook*, which exhibits student-generated explorations of Pittsburgh sites and stories.

### Hartmut Koenitz, Ph.D.

ORCID: 0000-0002-3390-831X; University of Amsterdam
Hartmut has studied English Literature and Language, German Literature and Language, Drama, Communications, Information Science, Media Studies, History, and Political Sciences at University of Tübingen, Goldsmiths' College, London, and Freie Universität Berlin. He holds an MA in Information Science, German Literature, and Political Sciences from Freie Universität Berlin. He also obtained a certificate in media research and media pedagogics from the same university. He is currently a Visiting Researcher at the University of Amsterdam.

**Yonty Friesem, Ph.D.**

ORCID: 0000-0002-8463-7660; Columbia College Chicago
Yonty Friesem, PhD, is an Assistant Professor in the Communication Department at Columbia College Chicago and founding director of the MA in Civic Media. With 20 years of experience in media literacy education, Yonty combines his creative work as a media producer with his teaching experience and passionate advocacy for digital empathy every day at Columbia College Chicago. Applying the principles of Human-Centered Design and The Leadership Challenge, Yonty helps his students to develop their creativity and leadership skills and enhance civic engagement.

**David Antognoli**

ORCID: 0000-0002-3000-6580; Columbia College Chicago
David Antognoli is a game developer and Assistant Professor of Game Design at Columbia College Chicago. A game industry veteran with experience in both programming and game design roles, he has worked on projects with companies like Microsoft, Sega, 2K Games, and Nickelodeon. Now he finds creative refuge in independent game development and teaching others how to create amazing games.

# Introduction

## A Call to Explore Augmented and Mixed Reality Experiences in Communities

This collection of essays on Augmented, Mixed, and Virtual Reality in communities may be a bit before its time. The collective vision of an augmented cityscape, one as playful as it is informative, has yet to be realized by technologists, civic media practitioners, scholars, or municipal governments. Nevertheless, the promise is still there. Industry groups like the Virtual Reality Augmented Reality Association (VRARA) hold meetings around the country where practitioners set to blueprinting the augmented city on a hill. At academic conferences all over the world, from the IEEE International Symposium on Mixed and Augmented Reality to the International Conference on Interactive and Digital Storytelling scholars grapple, discuss, and peer into what our collective, augmented future might be. Titans of an emerging industry like Niantic, Vuforia, and Snapchat stand hand-in-hand with Silicon Valley venture capitalists to create and profit from the projected $27.44 billion-dollar industry (Markets, 2020). Meanwhile, artists construct utopian renderings of streets full of eternal play or dystopian hellscapes of mediated confusion.

Beneath these dreams and conjectures, communities across the world are grappling with the COVID-19 pandemic. In the United States, civil unrest and political strife wrack our neighborhoods. In all of this promise and chaos, where the emerging media of augmented, mixed, and virtual reality fit into our communities is unclear. However, the dream will be made real by its adherents, from academia to industry, but how it manifests in our contemporary moment is still unknown. This collection of essays sketches the blurry boundaries of that realization.

### Defining Augmented, Mixed, and Virtual Reality

If you have not experienced augmented, mixed, and virtual reality this collection can be an intermediate first step into the emerging media and discipline. For brevity, the collection refers to these class of immersive media as XR (eXtended Reality) as they all seek to extend reality in one way or another.

A commonly accepted definition of augmented reality (AR), mixed reality (MR), and virtual reality (VR) was established in 1994 by Paul Milgram and Fumio Kishino. In their seminal paper, they define the collective media as "related technologies that involve the merging of real and virtual worlds somewhere along the 'virtuality continuum' which connects completely real environments to completely virtual ones" (Milgram and Kishino, 1994). This broad definition has served industry and academia well in understanding these XR media and what they do.

Milgram and Kishino also helpfully established that all of these media exist on a continuum that bridges reality to virtuality. That Pikachu exists in a liminal state between the virtual space rendered on a device and the physical space in front of a user. If we consider VR, the user may be entirely immersed in a visual experience, but their body is still very much situated in physical reality. As much as immersive media practitioners would like to see the physical world as a springboard they leave behind for their experiences, that same physicality is always present. Whether it be a sidewalk, storefront, or cemetery the physical environment is always connected to the virtual one. When speaking of XR in communities, the physicality of the space and its social, cultural, economic, and political realities, is always present.

Milgram and Kishino present a few other forms of XR along the spectrum, including Mixed Reality (MR) and Augmented Virtuality (AV). These forms can be differentiated by their tendency to involve an equal ratio of physical reality and virtuality, as in MR, or to use more virtuality than physical reality, as in AV. As XR has developed, these distinctions have mainly been papered over by practitioners. Recent scholarship presented at the premier Human-Computer Interaction conference, CHI, found that MR is really whatever its practitioners and designers say it is (Speicher, Hall and Nebeling, 2019). Nevertheless, the ratio of physical reality to virtuality is essential and has consequences on how we perceive our communal spaces.

Maria Engberg, Senior Lecturer at Malmö University in Sweden and Jay Bolter, Professor of Digital Media at the Georgia Institute of Technology have dubbed the spectrum of XR technologies as Reality Media. They provide the helpful definition, "media forms that redefine our perspective of lived experience and of the spaces which we physically inhabit" (Engberg and Bolter, 2020). A running theme in this book is that these physical spaces that we inhabit with our bodies cannot be ignored. When we consider what it means to be a member in a physically situated community, a neighborhood, or a city, we are bound up in the physical materiality of that place. In Chicago, one can play Niantic's AR Harry Potter game, *Wizard's Unite*, and engage in a world of magic far-apart from Wednesday afternoon's banal reality. However, these augmented wizards still play the game on Chicago's sidewalks, with their cracks, litter, graffiti, and history. While the connection between the two may be intentionally obfuscated by the AR rendered for the user, it still exists. For this reason, the definition provided by Bolter and Engberg is particularly constructive. These media redefine our perspective of lived experience, and that includes how we understand our communities.

## Defining Community

The collection takes an intentionally broad definition of community. The authors of the Encyclopedia of Community state, "Communities are indeed the core and essence of humanity, around which everything else is woven or spun" (Christensen and Levinson, 2003). They go on, "Community may be thought of as a geographic place, shared hobbies or interests, a warm sense of togetherness, interaction in a common space such as a chat room, and so forth." Within this nexus, individuals identify themselves as belonging to one or more groups, places, and relations. These might exist for them at a physical level, as in the street they live on or their familial relations; a proximal level, as in in the people nearby; a perceptual level, as in a religious identity or connection to an ethnic group; alternatively, on a digital level, as in the communities formed online through social networks, games, and other mediated experiences. There are communities of practice (as in academics), communities at the pub, and spontaneous communities formed out of necessity. However, even these lists do not do justice to the plurality of communal connections individuals might make or find themselves within.

Within the immersive media world, a shared understanding of community stretches from infrastructures—smart city infrastructure, construction, navigation, urban planning, and architectural preservation to emergency response. While XR certainly offers exciting opportunities to change our perception of these experiences, there is much more that researchers can explore. Another set of experiences uses XR to elevate cultural heritage, location-based gaming, activist efforts, and civic participation. These humanistic experiences cannot be siloed apart from the more technical and engineering focused XR works. The shared technology deeply entrenches one with the other, and the duality is worth exploring.

In a paper on using an AR app as part of a Smart City initiative in Jeddah, Saudi Arabia, the authors state that the technology will help the government, "monitor people inside their city in real time" (Basori, Abdul Hamid, Firdausiah Mansur and Yusof, 2019). A bucolic statement about tourism quickly follows. Later in the paper, they state that their AR app will use a "proposed system [that] will be able to track a person's position and orientation through the accelerometer and gyroscope sensor in [the] suburb[s] by combining geographical data [...] in an area with low GPS signal". This pairing of surveillance with AR is increasingly common and impacts individual liberty and privacy. Compare this work to that of John Craig Freeman's work *Border Memorial: Frontera de los Muertos* (Freeman, 2011).

In Freeman's location-based AR project, skeletons in a Día de los Muertos aesthetic, are situated along the Mexican-United States border. Released in 2012, the AR experience is one of remembrance—marking the thousands of migrants who have died making their way to the United States in search of a better life. When a user points their camera at one of the skeletons, it looks around and then gently floats up into the sky. From Freeman's website:

> In the tradition of Día de los Muertos, Freeman designed the Border Memorial project to honor, celebrate, and remember those who have died. His secondary objective was to vault the immigration issues into public consciousness and American political debate. Freeman intended the project to provide a kind of lasting conceptual presence in an otherwise ephemeral physical environment and cultural discourse.

Critically, this discourse is often obfuscated by the immigration apparatus in the United States with its accompanying oppressive structural injustices. Additionally, as noted by death and dying scholars, in many western cultures, the death act itself is hidden behind medical and religious apparatuses (Stone and Sharpley, 2008). Freeman's work takes these invisible structures, politics, and oppression and makes them visible with XR.

Both the Jeddah project and the one on the United States-Mexico border use XR to make movement visible in different ways. For Jeddah, the invisible is made visible for commercial and surveillance purposes; for Freeman, the invisible is made visible to recognize and critique oppression. To place these experiences within the same discussion is constructive. Both are deeply situated within different kinds of communities and both rely on AR to make the invisible, visible. Just as definitions of community spiral into complex and contradictory structures, so too must our understanding of augmented, mixed, and virtual reality in those communities.

## Organization of the Book

This book contains 13 chapters in which authors address different perspectives, approaches, and frameworks for XR in communities. Each of the authors has their own understanding of community, from a community of learners to physical communities within cities. However, other authors write on their ethical concerns about the individual within the XR community. Authors write of the imperative that XR must be democratic and universally accessible.

With that in mind, each of the authors has included an activity for use in personal research, research groups, or classrooms at the end of their chapter. The collective goal of these sections is to encourage a new generation of scholars, students, designers, and developers to engage with XR in their communities. As several of this collection's authors write, literacy in this emerging media can be liberatory. Each activity is an invitation to help build our augmented futures. Some of the activities may conflict with one another and there is value in this friction as well. Our approach to the creation of AR experiences cannot be monolithic if it is to be democratic. A plurality of perspectives is necessary to build augmented communities that are not oppressive. A brief description of each chapter and its activity follows.

*Rebecca Rouse*, in her chapter **Against the Instrumentalization of Empathy: Immersive Technologies and Social Change,** critiques how XR practitioners understand social change and technology's impact on the process. She complicates the current role designers and developers have for AR and VR in their practices. Rouse ends her chapter with a set of principles for slowing down the design process to draw more realistic insights from work with communities to produce just results. Her proposed activity presents several steps for researchers to undertake as part of her human-centered approach for social change.

*Anne Wiehl,* in her chapter **The Body and the Eye—the I and the Other: Critical Reflections on the Promise of Extended Empathy in Extended Reality Configurations,** disassembles the empathy machine myth in XR into different empirical experiments that practitioners can do as artistic interventions. She reviews

The 'Machine to be Another' to put forward her transdisciplinary theoretical discourse around XR embodiment, empathy, and interventions. Her proposed activity connects cognitive science to XR's affordances to establish compassion and perspective-taking.

*Yonty Friesem*, in his chapter, **The PARIS Model: Creating a Sustainable and Participatory Civic Media with and for the Community through Immersive Experiences,** engages with the myth of the empathy machine and transforms it into a sustainable civic media tool. He combines theories from participatory action research and civic media to encourage XR media literacy. His activity encourages practitioners to elevates principles of diversity, equity, and inclusion through genuine XR collaborations with communities.

*Bill Guschwan* addresses the complexity of truth claims through XR in his chapter **The Philosopher's Stone as a Design Framework for Defending Truth and Empowering Communities**. Guschwan identifies the current obstacles to truth claims that exist in online communities such as Facebook due to mimetic desire. He positions creative mimesis as a solution and utilizes the Philosopher's Stone, from the domain of sacred geometry, as a design framework to achieve it. Guschwan's chapter ends with an activity that guides readers through the Philosopher's Stone framework to design AR experiences that help users make dynamic truth claims.

*Kelsey Cameron* and *Jessica FitzPatrick* provide community engagement practices in their chapter **Designing Lived Space: Community Engagement Practices in Rooted AR**. Bringing together work on critical design and spatial studies, the chapter assesses community engagement in existing AR and offers best practices for future projects. This chapter proposes three levels of AR community engagement: overwriting (pervasive and templeted), tethering (site-specific and brand motivated), and rooted (site- and community-specific). The activity at the end of their chapter encourages readers to use their framework in their own community.

*Kevin Healey* writes on ethics and contemplative media in his chapter, **The Ethics of Augmentation: A Case Study in Contemplative Mixed Reality**. He offers a rubric for assessing MR applications' ethics and provides strategies for developing more ethically and economically sustainable MR technologies. Healy uses Contemplative Media Studies as part of an experiential classroom exercise that uses a combination of nature-based contemplative and arts-based practices and Geospatial and Information Systems applications. Discussion of this case study shows how designers can avoid MR development's common pitfalls in favor of an aesthetic guided by the aspirational virtues of wisdom, integrity, and hope. The chapter's activity puts Healey's framework into practice and provides a guide for students.

*Brian Wassom*, the first lawyer in the United States of America to litigate Free Speech for AR, writes on the case in his chapter **Life, Liberty, and the Pursuit of Pokémon: The Tension Between Free Speech and Municipal Tranquility**. This chapter provides an inside perspective on the origins, motivations, and legal arguments behind *Candy Lab Inc. v. County of Milwaukee*. Wassom explains the technological developments and market-driven serendipity that led to the unprecedented explosion of popularity in location-based augmented reality gaming, and the reactions of citizens and civic leaders who were unprepared for, and mostly unwelcoming of, such a rapid and large-scale change of public behavior. The resulting lawsuit challenged this as an abridgment of free speech rights, leading to a fascinating debate in federal court over how far governments may permissibly limit the time, place, and manner of speech in the XR medium. Wassom's chapter ends with an activity encouraging readers to consider the laws surrounding XR and free speech in their communities.

*David Antognoli*, in the chapter **Reconceptualizing Video Games for Community Spaces,** discusses how AR can continue the legacy of amusement halls and arcades in our communities. He addresses the current physical isolation of games as a consequence of the mainstream gaming industry before turning to a history of public spaces for gaming. Antognoli addresses how these games change the public spaces and encourage the growth of communities of players. He believes that AR provides a new and accessible way to create these experiences in our contemporary civic spaces. Antognoli's chapter ends with a call to action and an activity to encourage designers and developers to begin creating and hosting AR games in their community spaces.

*Hartmut Koenitz* addresses how AR can be used to explore complex histories in his chapter **Reflecting in Space on Time: Augmented Reality Interactive Digital Narratives to Explore Complex Histories**. The chapter positions AR as a platform for public education and discourse as a means to "see through time" to connect past, present and speculative histories. Koenitz engages with questions of complexity and context to point out the importance of narrative as a crucial element to enable sense-making. In the context of AR narrative, this means using Interactive Digital Narrative (IDN) models due to the procedural and dynamic nature of the medium as well as its participatory aspect. He concludes his chapter with an activity for choosing an IDN model for an AR experience that explores the complex histories of locations.

*Hank Blumenthal* and *Joshua A. Fisher* take on the perennial crisis of aura and AR in cultural spaces in their chapter **Augmented Reality, Aura, and the Design of Cultural Spaces**. As defined by Walter Benjamin, aura is a critical aspect of media representations that scholars have argued is in crisis in new media. AR alters the aura of a space by negotiating the original aura with the new mediated aura and the user's perception of both. Building upon previous studies, Blumenthal and Fisher, propose three design models for how AR can engage with aura to enliven, expand, and elevate the existing auratic qualities of cultural spaces. Their chapter ends with an activity that encourages users to perceive the auras of their own cultural spaces and design prototypes through the proposed models.

*Janice Tisha Samuels* and *Kelvin Ramirez* in their chapter **Building a Virtuous Cycle of Activism Using Art & Augmented Reality: A Community of Practice-Based Project** discuss how AR can be used in youth activism movement. Their chapter focuses on developing an out-of-school-time project called the National Youth Art Movement Against Gun Violence. The youth-led project launched an art and AR interactive art tour in the city of Chicago in the fall of 2017. The project provided youth with the ability to use their natural talent in the visual arts to develop and lead a public intervention for gun violence utilizing public spaces enabled with the affordances of XR technologies. Their activity encourages the use of community-based learning with youth to produce liberatory frames of thinking and being through MR.

*John T. Murray* and *Emily K. Johnson* discuss the need for XR students to have capable platforms in their chapter, **XR Content Authoring Challenges: The Creator-Developer Divide**. The chapter builds on the tools provided by platform studies to investigate how current authoring tools support the needs of potential authors and the current barriers to greater participation in the new set of emerging media. Despite these advances, the tools remain out of reach for a wide population of non-computer scientists who wish to create innovative XR experiences relevant to their subject matter expertise. The activity at the end of their chapter asks readers to critically investigate the components of XR authoring platforms and find ways to democratize access to them.

Finally, in *Stylianos Mystakidis'* chapter **Motivation Enhancement Methods for Community Building in Extended Reality,** he discusses how to motivate student engagement through community projects in VR. The chapter presents playful blended learning experiences, gamified distance education courses, and serious game designs in XR community settings. Its main contribution is the discussion of results from multiple studies and the formulation of recommendations for practitioners for building communities of inquiry and practice in XR environments. The activity at the end of his chapter is for interested educators and practitioners seeking to reflect on how to build XR communities that can accommodate the cultivation of positive emotions.

This collection has come together during one of the most catastrophic years in contemporary history. From the forest fires that devoured Australia to the devastating effects of the COVID-19 pandemic, every one of us has been touched by the events of 2020. However, social movements around the globe, such as Black Lives Matter, are organizing within communities to build a more just and equitable world. In the face of all this fear and hope, I am grateful to the contributing authors for their work. It took endurance and tenacity to finish their chapters in this environment. Their effort is a testament to how much each of them cares about the future of communities, augmented or otherwise. It is my sincerest hope and desire that the generation building our XR communities will find these chapters a useful resource for many years to come.

# References

Basori, A.H., Abdul Hamid, A.L. Bin, Firdausiah Mansur, A.B. and Yusof, N. (2019). IMars: Intelligent Municipality Augmented Reality Service for Efficient Information Dissemination based on Deep Learning algorithm in Smart City of Jeddah. *Procedia Computer Science*, 163, 93-108. https://doi.org/10.1016/j.procs.2019.12.091

Christensen, K. and Levinson, D. (Eds.) (2003). Encyclopedia of Community. 1st ed. Thousand Oaks: Sage Publications.

Engberg, M. and Bolter, J.D. (2020). The aesthetics of reality media. *Journal of Visual Culture*, 19(1), 81-95. https://doi.org/10.1177/1470412920906264

Freeman, J.C. (2011). Border Memorial: Frontera de los Muertos. Retrieved from https://bordermemorial.wordpress.com/border-memorial-frontera-de-los-muertos/

MacIntyre, B. (2019). Mirrorworld Bill of Rights? Retrieved from https://blairmacintyre.me/2019/04/05/mirrorworld-bill-of-rights/

Markets, R. (2020). Augmented Reality and Mixed Reality Market – Growth, Trends, and Forecast (2020-2025). Dublin, Ireland. Retrieved from https://www.researchandmarkets.com/reports/4591781/augmented-reality-and-mixed-reality-market?utm_source =dynamic&utm_medium=BW&utm_code=t4zb2z&utm_campaign=1390282+-+Global +Augmented+Reality+%26+Mixed+Reality+Market%3A+Growth%2C+Trends+and+F orecasts+to+20

Milgram, P. and Kishino, F. (1994). Taxonomy of mixed reality visual displays. *IEICE Transactions on Information and Systems*, E77-D(12), 1321-1329. https://doi.org/10.1.1.102.4646

Speicher, M., Hall, B.D. and Nebeling, M. (2019). What is mixed reality? Conference on Human Factors in Computing Systems – Proceedings. https://doi.org/10.1145/3290605.3300767

Stone, P. and Sharpley, R. (2008). Consuming dark tourism: A Thanatological Perspective. *Annals of Tourism Research*, 35(2), 574-595.

# Part 1
# The Body in the XR Community

# Chapter

# 1

# Against the Instrumentalization of Empathy: Immersive Technologies and Social Change

**Rebecca Rouse**
University of Skövde, Kanikegränd 3a, 541 34 Skövde, Sweden
Email: Rebecca.Rouse@his.se

## Introduction: Technology as Solution

> *"It's a machine, but inside of it, it feels like real life, it feels like truth."*
> – Chris Milk (2015)

> *"A continual retreat from the discomfort of authentic racial engagement results in a perpetual cycle that works to hold racism in place."*
> – Robin DiAngelo (2011) p. 66

Technologies have a long history of being sought after as panaceas for complex human problems. Recently, I had a front row seat to this type of thinking at the previous university where I taught. In the midst of a discussion on the development of a new AR/VR lab on campus, the Dean of Engineering asked me, "Could you develop a VR game to teach our faculty diversity and inclusion?" The context for his question was increasingly visible activism from Black student groups on our campus in response to systemic racism, hostile faculty and administrators, and a lack of structural support. It was an open secret that the predominantly white campus lacked in faculty training resources, and that many faculty held racist and other deeply prejudicial views that were expressed in their teaching and interactions with students, negatively impacting the retention rates of students, faculty, and staff of color. While the administration had begun a small effort to provide occasional optional training, the Dean was clearly reacting to the great need with his suggestion to develop a VR game to 'solve the problem.' As an out lesbian (albeit white and cisgendered) I was one of the few 'diverse' games faculty, and the only one actively involved in campus diversity and inclusion work, and therefore an obvious candidate in the Dean's mind to do this work and design a VR game to enlighten recalcitrant faculty members.

After recovering from my initial shock at the question, I did my best to describe why I felt the project would not succeed in the way he seemed to imagine.

My colleague's incredible faith in technology has good company. Think, for example, of the work of immersive journalists and documentary filmmakers such as Chris Milk, Nonny de la Peña, the Be Another research collective, and others. Milk famously described VR as an "empathy machine" in his 2015 TED Talk, stating that by using VR "[...] we become more compassionate, we become more empathetic, and we become more connected. And ultimately we become more human" (Milk, 2015). Milk's claim — which may seem glib at first — has been astutely critiqued by many (Clune, 2016; Murray, 2020; Nakamura, 2020). It is worth further examination, however, because it is emblematic of a pervasive perspective on technology today often encountered in the technology industry, STEM disciplines, and even popular culture at large. The seeming simplicity of this perspective belies the many layers of assumption underneath, many of which I believe hamper designers in achieving meaningful impact with their works. In this chapter the layers of assumption in the empathy machine perspective are examined, and an alternative way of structuring the human-technology relationships that occur in the design process is suggested.

First, let us examine the tacit assumptions that underlie statements about VR as an empathy machine. There are two main parts to this larger claim. One part is a claim about what empathy is, and how it can influence people and society. A second claim centers on the nature of interactive, immersive media as particularly conducive to fostering this specific type of empathy in viewers. What is meant by empathy in the usage from Milk and other journalists and documentary makers working in immersive media today should be made explicit. Empathy in this case is used to denote a positive outcome in the viewers, due to change in attitude or belief, with a likelihood that this change may result in pro-social behavior and even actions advancing justice. It is worth examining how this colloquial understanding of empathy holds up against scholarship on the topic, which will be discussed below. More deeply embedded in this definition is an implied mental model of how social change works, and so the question also arises as to whether not this empathy-based model of social change is accurate. At the foundation of this set of assumptions is an idea about the ontology of technology itself, as a labor saving device that is capable of simplifying complexity.

Viewed from this perspective, it becomes easy to see why this idea of the 'empathy machine' could be so attractive to many across the technology industries, STEM disciplines, and popular culture in the West. The reasoning may go something like this: if only we can use AR/VR to unlearn prejudice and inspire action, then the hard, painful work of the emotional and intellectual labor of coming to terms with prejudicial beliefs and attitudes could be made easier. There is a connection to be made here with Robin DiAngelo's concept of white fragility as discussed in her original paper (2011). DiAngelo developed the concept of white fragility to understand and name the defensiveness, fear, misdirected anger, and inaction often displayed by white people when confronted with their participation and complicity in perpetuating oppressive racist systems and these systems' devastating costs to others. The idea of using a technology, such as AR or VR, to 'change minds' via empathy (understood as an almost involuntary, emotional response) plays into a fantasy that neatly aligns with a privileged positionality, seeking quick, easy, and relatively painless methods of mitigation that fall far short of actual change.

This perspective on technology as labor-saving device fits well with dominant so-called common-sense but wrongheaded ideas about technologies as neutral tools that can take on the burden of labor from humans and increase efficiency, notably critiqued by Langdon Winner (1980), Susan Leigh Star (1999) and others. Other methods for prejudice reduction, such as in-person intergroup dialogue training, require many resources (mostly trained practitioners and teachers, who must be paid) and quite a lot of time—even years. The technological fantasy of the immersive media empathy machine imagines a mass medium that can seamlessly reach scores of individuals, necessitate no actual interpersonal contact with the 'others' these individuals seek to empathize with, and smoothly and easily change minds in minutes. Unfortunately, these foundational ontologies of both technology and social change are at odds with key concepts in scholarly research on social change, and the media artifacts produced within this imaginary are more likely to serve to assuage the privileged person's guilt and enrich the artifact's creators (through money or social capital, or both) rather than effect true social transformation. This ironic moral pitfall is discussed in depth by Kate Nash (Nash 2018), in her examination of the difficulties of designing an effective experience in VR for witnessing the suffering of others.

De la Peña's 2012 *Hunger in Los Angeles* provides just one example of the many immersive media projects that function in this manner and fall prey to what Nash describes (Nash, 2018). In De la Peña's 2012 piece, a spatial 3D rendering created in the Unity game engine displays a reenactment of people standing in line at a food bank in L.A., using actual audio recorded from the real food bank line. The situation becomes increasingly stressed as one man succumbs to a diabetic seizure and collapses on the sidewalk. The VR interactor, however, is prevented from taking any action let alone an ethical one to help the man and can only continue as a passive voyeur in the scene. But, the question is opened, even if the interactor could make choices to help the sick man or the many hungry people, how meaningful would that be? Ultimately, the work presents a simulation with little functional connection to reality, transforming the very real suffering of people struggling with poverty and disease into a simulated spectacle.

In an interview with Lizzy Goodman (2012) de la Peña discusses interactors' reactions to the piece as emotionally intense, citing interactors' tears and aggrieved facial expressions following the experience. Remarkably, de la Peña expresses her complete surprise that interactors would want to help the stricken man, stating "It's shocking to me the number of people who were so upset that they couldn't help this guy." This statement reveals far more about de la Peña's understanding of people than the reactions of the interactors who experienced the VR piece. It is also important to note that throughout the interview de la Peña refers to the sick man as "this guy" and "some guy," but never by name, which suggests she does not know the man and made no effort to involve him in the design of the work, or seek his consent. In terms of the value of the VR work, the article mentions it was prominently exhibited at the prestigious Sundance film festival, and de la Peña discusses the need to "think about experience as part of your overall business plan [...] The idea of commodifying experience is not new but this is like commodifying emotion" (Goodman, 2012). No positive impacts for the actual people struggling with hunger and illness are mentioned, and so it seems the largest positive impact of the work was for de la Peña herself. As discussed by Joshua Fisher (2017) it is all too common in the case of this genre of VR work that the interactor ends up empathizing most closely with the VR designer, and not the subject (Fisher, 2017). This brings to mind the many examples of mediated witnessing that lack authentic or meaningful engagement with the person suffering but bring value to the designer, such as photographer Dorothea Lange's cursory interaction with and ultimate exploration of Florence Owens Thompson, better known as 'Migrant Mother' (1936).

## Empathy, Ethics, and Social Change

> *"What [white Americans] see is a disastrous, continuing, present condition which menaces them, and for which they bear an inescapable responsibility. But since, in the main, they appear to lack the energy to change this condition, they would rather not be reminded of it."*
>
> – James Baldwin (1966) p. 173

What exactly is empathy? Is it an emotion, a media-induced response, a personality-based positioning, or something else? There is a wealth of scholarship on empathy and related phenomena such as compassion, identification, and transference. Steve Larocco's research provides an important perspective on the ethical complexity of empathy, which is relevant to our discussion given the focus on social change. Larocco understands empathy as a type of positioning of the self towards the other, as opposed to an emotion or feeling (Larocco, 2018). Larocco underscores the uncertainty around the potential of this empathic positioning, as there are many possibilities along a spectrum, all the way from authentic identification with another to selective empathy that seeks to misconstrue the other as similar to the self, or identifies only with aspects of the other perceived as similar to the self. Larocco points out that due to this wide range of empathic responses, it is a mistake to draw a causal relationship between empathy and compassion.

While empathy is commonly thought of as a positive, warm emotional response, it can also be directed and instrumentalized or used as a tool in a predatory manner. A fictional example that nicely illustrates this usage of empathy is the interrogation scene in *Star Wars: The Force Awakens* (2015). The villainous Kylo Ren seeks to understand resistance fighter Rey in order to probe for weaknesses in her psyche so that he may more easily defeat her. This capacity to weaponize empathy has been important in the development of early VR systems, which were first designed to facilitate military training and simulation. In these systems, such as *FlatWorld* (Pair et. al., 2003), *America's Army* (Zyda et. al, 2005), *Living Worlds* (Zielke et. al.,2009) and *HuSIS* (Schubert et. al., 2016), soldiers are trained to empathize with an other, characterized as an enemy, in order to anticipate their actions so that they may be more efficiently killed. Indeed, one of the earliest immersive interactive systems, Frank

Waller's gunnery trainer designed for the US Army during the Second World War, was declassified after the war and commercialized as *Cinerama*, an early immersive cinema format that presaged IMAX and later VR cave technologies. VR and game technologies have a long history of entanglement in military simulation, which cannot be discounted when seeking to understand the embedded values designed into such systems even as they are repurposed for entertainment today (Zyda et. al., 2005; Smith, 2010).

Empathy's invasive potentials have been noted by several theorists, such as bell hooks (1992) and Lisa Nakamura (2020) as particularly evident in technological systems that seek to provide the viewer or interactor with an empathic response experience. Hooks' discussion of supposedly empathy-inducing films draws out the absence of the actual 'other' who is represented, meaning the direct experience of empathy, which normally involves a process of consent and negotiation from all participants, cannot take place since the filmic 'other' is absent. This total absence of the other persists in immersive media, neatly preserving a privileged interactor's safety and comfort over the consent and agency of the 'others' represented. Why is the other's story more palatable as a mediation, as opposed to in direct human interaction? Hooks further unpacks this unilateral gaze at the representational other as colonizing and racist, as 'taking' voice more than giving it, and at the core of cultural appropriation. There is a connection to be made here between the twin logics of the racist colonizing gaze and Laura Mulvey's theorizing of the filmic 'male gaze' (Mulvey, 1975). After all, white supremacy and misogyny are old bedfellows. Nakamura bridges this argument with a discussion of capitalism, and delves into the dubious motivations of technology companies who in the face of their industry's morally bankrupt history of systems that instrumentalize empathy for exploitation and violence, now find it expedient to recast their systems as in service of the social good in an opportunistic but ultimately empty gesture (Nakamura, 2020).

Philosopher Paul Bloom's research further critiques empathy as a dangerously ambiguous compass for moral decision making. Bloom points out that studies of empathy are based on individuals identifying with other individuals, but not situated within the large social contexts that surround us all and make actual social problems complex (Bloom, 2016; p. 85). Examples are discussed such as the funds directed toward the Make-A-Wish foundation, which provides a wonderful personal experience to terminally ill children, versus funds directed to the Against Malaria foundation, which supplies mosquito netting to children in need, saving many hundreds of children's lives. Bloom points out that because Make-A-Wish so effectively leverages empathy in its solicitations, it is able to garner far more funding than the malaria foundation. Empathically, donors feel connected to the promises and pathos of Make-A-Wish. But morally and rationally, it must be agreed that saving many children's lives is a better goal than providing a single child with a wonderful experience, no matter how deserving the child or emotionally fulfilling for the giver.

Bloom also reminds us of the uneven legacy of empathic artifacts in spurring social change that advances justice. He notes that while novels such as Dickens' *Oliver Twist* and Beecher Stowe's *Uncle Tom's Cabin* have been cited as helping to motivate social change, they also misfire badly in many ways, exploiting and appropriating those who they hope to support. And, we must also remember there are counterpart works of social significance that have advanced causes furthering oppression and domination through empathy, such as Ayn Rand's novels or Adolph Hitler's memoir, in which the reader is encouraged to empathize with beleaguered protagonists who fend off others characterized as social spongers and degenerates, to rise above, victorious. Certainly, these empathic artifacts have also functioned as their creators intended, inspiring many to join oppressive and violent causes.

Shifting our focus to immersive media more specifically, the problems found in older media discussed above persist in many of the AR and VR experiences designed today for empathic response. *Clouds Over Sidra*, Chris Milk's 2015 VR documentary about the Syrian refugee crisis falls into this category. Milk promoted the VR experience as successful due to the medium's ability to fill the viewer's field of view, thus creating a virtual sense of presence for the viewer, who feels 'as if' they are co-located in a Syrian refugee camp with the film's protagonist. However, this conflation of simulated co-location with empathy and social change has been astutely critiqued by Clune (2016), who noted that while VR may virtually place the viewer in another space, the viewer is still themselves, with their own subjectivity and positionality. Clune points out that other peoples' consciousnesses are not simply 'other spaces,' and highlights that the 'as if' of VR is not at all the same thing as the lived reality of fleeing to a refugee camp. The VR viewer can simply remove the HMD when they tire of the experience; leaving a refugee camp is more complex, difficult, and dangerous by many orders of magnitude.

This myth that merely by entering an immersive simulation of another person's environment you can understand their perspective has insidious effects even for well-intentioned viewers. In the case of white viewers seeking empathy with the perspectives of people of color, there is a long, racist history of whites donning Blackness that must be considered. The ongoing legacies of minstrelsy and blackface persist, as does the equally misguided impulse toward what Alisha Gaines describes as cross-racial identification, with seemingly well-intentioned white people seeking to become 'black for a day' to advance their own personal understanding of racism (Gaines, 2017). Gaines' research highlights that even when whites may approach such an ill-advised project with the aim of advancing social justice, this outcome has yet to materialize from these types of appropriative, invasive moves. In the end, the people who benefitted most were the white impersonators, both monetarily and in terms of social capital. This type of instrumentalized empathy functions in the same manner as the colonialist rhetoric of extraction, allowing the white oppressor to mine a Black other for value, knowledge, and power.

The narcissistic qualities of the VR medium may make the technology predisposed to the creation of these types of extractive, exploitive experiences. In the case of VR works that are designed for a single interactor to access via a head-mounted display, the interactor is hermetically sealed inside a mediation with only their own reactions and responses. Echoing the narcissism of one of VR's media ancestors, video, as discussed by Rosalind Krauss (1976) this solitary isolation stands in the way of any true dialogue, active listening, or meaningful witnessing that could have the potential to lead to impactful, co-consensual exchange. This narcissistic nature of VR perpetuates the centering of white perspectives that DiAngelo (2011) discusses as a key factor in the development of white fragility and maintenance of racially unjust social structures. As Kate Nash (2009) identifies in her analysis of failed attempts at global cosmopolitan human rights movements, "The creation of feeling for the suffering of distant people, which can generate a collective understanding of moral obligation to act to relieve that suffering, always risks degenerating into an emotionally indulgent admiration of one's own sensitivity, sincerity and strength of will" (Nash 2009, p. 153). Next, we will examine scholarship on the nature of social change, its many actors and processes, and discuss what role, if any, immersive media can play.

Just as empathy is complex, so too is social change. Two major camps of thought could be described as the prejudice reduction model, and the collaborative social action model. The scholarship on prejudice reduction dates from the post Second World War era (interestingly, during the same period when we see the birth of VR) and centers on individuals in society who hold positions of power and prejudicial opinions about those they oppress. The focus in this scholarship is on reducing prejudice among these individual actors by providing corrective information that counters negative stereotypes. The aim is to reduce conflict and mitigate harm (Devine & Levine, 2012). A second camp of research on social change focuses on coalition building and intergroup relations, with the aim of facilitating collaborative social action. The focus here is the disruption of existing systems and structures, which may indeed necessitate conflict, and even, in some cases, violence (Wetherell, 1992/2012). Both models of social change are necessary, with focus at times on individuals and the mitigation of harm, and at times on coalitions and the overhaul of systems, but the question is how to balance these two perspectives.

However, it must be pointed out there is a potentially dangerous alignment between the focus on individualism in the prejudice reduction model of social change and the emphasis on white individualism as discussed by DiAngelo (2011). This emphasis on individualism can act to thwart meaningful change by providing absolution for members of oppressive groups such as white people who feel they have already 'done the work' or are 'woke enough,' and because they 'aren't racists' individually they do not need to work actively to dismantle the logics and structures of whiteness. Nevertheless, there is a place for individual focus and learning in terms of examining one's own biases and prejudices. Sociologist Bobbie Harro's scholarship (Harro, 2000) provides a useful graphic model of how these two perspectives on social change can operate in confluence in her conception of the cycles of socialization (ie., oppression) and liberation. Harro provides insight into how oppression may be disrupted through the cycle of liberation, opening up opportunities (but not guarantees) for shifts toward social justice. In Harro's models, we see that media participate as just one node among many that work in collaboration and sometimes opposition to shift any one individual's attitudes, beliefs, and actions. There is no research showing that it is possible to use a single technology to circumvent the complex and arduous labor of the cycle of liberation.

# Persuasive Media

*"But to substitute monologue, slogans, and communiqués for dialogue is to attempt to liberate the oppressed with the instruments of domestication."*
– Paulo Freire (1970/2005) p. 65

So how do media participate in these cycles of socialization and liberation as described by Harro? While a single media artifact functions as just one node among many, the role of media in aggregate is still significant. Even media that are not explicitly designed to teach or persuade will carry some embedded values of the society they are created within, and therefore do the important work of reinforcing dominant narratives. Dominant narratives are not necessarily bad; for example, 'treat your neighbor as yourself' could be considered a dominant narrative that encourages pro-social behavior and even kindness. Other dominant narratives, however, include oppressive ideas that target marginalized groups such as women, trans and non-binary people, people of color, people with disabilities, people struggling in poverty, and immigrants. These oppressive dominant narratives reinforce negative stereotyping about these groups and function to maintain or even worsen these groups' marginalized status and hamper access to power.

But within media at large there are also examples explicitly designed to teach, persuade, or even coerce. We might discuss this subset as 'persuasive media.' Communication technologies, broadly understood as encompassing speech, books, images, and mechanical and digital technologies have long been implemented in service of persuasion. Some of these efforts have proved successful, others have not. Often it may be difficult to disentangle one media artifact's role in a large social shift and determine the precise ways in which it may have helped or hurt a particular cause. Some of the most persuasive media artifacts that have successfully instigated or cemented social change are understood as propaganda. A recent example of this propagandistic use of media was the 'pizza-gate' conspiracy of 2016 designed to cast then presidential candidate Hillary Clinton as the leader of a satanic child trafficking ring run out of a Washington DC pizza restaurant (Robb, 2017). This example of propaganda against Clinton is particularly clear as it exhibits a key characteristic of classic propaganda, serving to reinforce existing attitudes, solidify them as beliefs, and ignite action. Leveraging empathy for the nonexistent child victims of the alleged scheme, this propaganda campaign was successful enough to convince a man from North Carolina to travel to the Washington DC restaurant and fire several rounds from his AR-15 in what he described as an attempt to liberate the captive children.

Another illustrative example is Leni Riefenstahl's 1935 Nazi propaganda film, *Triumph of the Will*. Watching this film alone will not convince you to become a Nazi, but if you are already a Nazi it will help to cement and celebrate those beliefs and attitudes. Watching it while steeped in a culture and mediascape that also celebrates and normalizes the values of National Socialism might indeed convince you to join the cause, particularly if other nodes in the cycle of socialization such as friends and family members have already bought into the ideology. As Harro's model depicts, media participate as just one node among many in the powerful forces of socialization that work to instruct us, from the youngest age, as to how we should behave to maintain the status quo in social structures of power (Harro, 2000).

How media are received and interpreted by viewers has been the subject of study of many fields for more than a century, from psychology to communications and cultural studies. Of particular importance are Stuart Hall's theories on reception that recognize the creative agency of the viewer in the interpretive act (Hall, 1973). While Hall's focus was mostly television, his perspective remains relevant for understanding media reception today. The core of Hall's reception theory describes a range of possibilities for the viewer as part of what Hall terms the encoding/decoding process of communications. While media creators seek to encode messages in their artifacts, viewers engage in a decoding process to interpret these artifacts. Hall describes three broad types of decoding that viewers may participate in, even shifting between modes at times. These reception modes are: dominant/hegemonic (in which the viewer accepts the canonical or intended meaning encoded in the artifact by the creator); negotiated (in which the viewer accepts some parts of the canonical message but takes issue with other aspects); and oppositional (in which the viewer disagrees with the canonical message and/or may creatively appropriate and re-interpret intended meanings to shift them to fit their own value system) (Hall, 1973).

Shifting to examine the experiences of interactive, immersive media, as opposed to television, it must first be noted that while the terms 'immersion' and 'interactivity' are commonly used to denote good or pleasurable experiences, this is not a default. Interactivity can be generative and engaging, but it can also be tedious—hence the concept of decision fatigue. Immersion, too, is not necessarily a good thing. The 1965 Michael Caine film *The Ipcress File* provides a compelling fictional illustration of the unpleasant side of immersion, with its portrayal of a proto-VR cave system utilized as a torture device. And, real life architectures of immersion, such as Governor Nelson Rockefeller's Empire State Plaza in Albany, New York also provide good counterexamples to arguments that essentialize immersion as pleasurable. The Plaza is a seamless white marble monstrosity, constructed at giant scale, and often unacknowledged human cost. The state had to forcibly displace several neighborhoods with thousands of inhabitants to create this fantasy of seamless modernity and power (Paley, 2014). Experienced in person the Plaza feels more like a suffocating enclosure, a horror of whiteness, in which participation is only possible as texture, as one of a crowd.

Pleasurable or not, media interactors today experience interactive, immersive artifacts in a variety of ways. Scholar Jay David Bolter has identified two main modes of interaction for contemporary media; catharsis and flow (Bolter, 2014). Bolter discusses the aims of more traditional media, such as the novel and Hollywood cinema, as evoking catharsis or an emotional release in the viewer. Interactive media, on the other hand, he argues work to perpetuate a state of flow for the interactor. Flow is a concept developed by psychologist Mihaly Csikszentmihalyi (1991) and describes an individual state that differs quite a bit from catharsis. Bolter describes this disjunction as follows: "Catharsis aims at the achievement of a desired emotional state, whereas the state of flow wants to continue forever, with minor variations in the intensity of involvement. Flow is the negation of desire [...] because it does not move toward its own repletion" (Bolter, 2014, p. 123). Bolter goes on to identify a third mode of reception as reflectivity, citing the modernist avant-garde's strategy to disrupt aesthetics of immersion and flow, with the aim of shifting the viewer into a position of critical distance from the work, in which reflection may be possible.

This tripartite taxonomy of media aesthetics and reception (catharsis - flow - reflectivity) is very useful for mapping the majority of media experiences available today. Most do indeed fit within this scope, and many do make use of all three aesthetics to lesser or greater degrees. Interestingly, these three modes of reception are largely characterized as individual, not only by Bolter but by other theorists as well including Csikszentmihalyi, Raymond Williams, Stuart Hall, and others. This individualist focus is useful and necessary for understanding how a single interactor may experience a work, but it is less useful for examining how a work may function in terms of reception if the work aims to instigate social change. Social change, after all, must happen in the realm of the social—in other words, with other actual humans as opposed to mediated representations of others. Acknowledging the co-constitutive nature of the social, it is necessary to push past the individualist focus of the concepts of catharsis, flow, and even reflectivity, to discuss an aesthetic and reception mode that centers the relationships and communication between multiple humans. Dialogue is a good possibility for this and may provide a way forward as an interaction mode that has potential to foster conditions necessary to enact social change.

Dialogue, as described by David Bohm, functions in many ways that are opposite from persuasive media (Bohm, 1996). As a communication practice that is distinct from discussion or debate, dialogue prioritizes active listening, attention to process, and questioning for understanding. While a dialogue is often established within a framework of co-designed guidelines, these guidelines are not rules and may be changed as participants' needs shift and emerge. Unlike a game, a dialogue has no winners or losers, and as Bohm states, "Everybody wins if anybody wins. There is a different sort of spirit to it. In a dialogue, there is no attempt to gain points, or to make your particular point of view prevail. Rather, whenever any mistake is discovered on the part of anybody, everybody gains" (Bohm, 7). In my own collaborative research with Amy Corron, we have already seen positive results in the application of a critical feminist pedagogy based in dialogue in the transformation of game design curriculum (Rouse & Corron, 2020). Considering the aesthetics of dialogue and the modes of reception and interaction in dialogic communication practices may be a promising way for AR and VR designers to begin to rethink approaches to creating immersive interactive media intended to support social change.

## Conclusion: Against the Instrumentalization of Empathy

*"[...] cultural, ethnic, and racial differences will be continually commodified and offered up as new dishes to enhance the white palate [...] the Other will be eaten, consumed, and forgotten."*

– bell hooks (1992) p. 39

Defined in terms of aims, many in contemporary culture have instrumentalized empathy as a means to an end. Instrumentalization refers to the characterizing of something as a tool or instrument, mistakenly viewed as neutral and unproblematically not entangled in culture and politics, in a fantasy of separation. A shift away from the instrumentalization of empathy in interactive immersive media design will not be easy. The empathy-centric approach has strongly entrenched for at least the past twenty years and has had far-reaching consequences. To examine these consequences, it is helpful to return to Lisa Nakamura's work to understand her explanation of how instrumentalized uses of empathy cross over into a kind of violence, which she describes as "toxic empathy" (Nakamura, 2020). She further identifies the cathartic experience of empathy, often accompanied by tears from a privileged viewer, as actually serving as a kind of 'alibi' for the viewer by supplying a surfeit of feeling as a way to overwhelm the senses and avoid the labor of taking constructive action.

Disturbingly, empathy has also been explicitly instrumentalized as a design tool. This has been done to make the design process more efficient and easier, by providing the designer with a more seamless way to access the other, who is being designed *for,* as opposed to *with*. The commercial design firm IDEO has published a set of cards intended to assist designers by sharing approaches and methods. One such card is the 'Empathy Tools' card, which describes the shallow, appropriative methods used by the designers to claim access to the subjectivities of potential users of their products who are disabled. The card describes the method as follows:

"HOW: Use tools like clouded glasses and weighted gloves to experience processes as though you yourself have the abilities of different users.

WHY: This is an easy way to prompt an empathic understanding for users with disabilities or special conditions.

IDEO designers wore gloves to help them evaluate the suitability of cords and buttons for a home health monitor designed for people with reduced dexterity and tactile sensation" (IDEO, 2003).

Similar to the well-intentioned but ultimately racist and misguided moves by white people to experience empathy for Black people by 'blacking up' themselves (Gaines, 2017), this instrumentalization of empathy as design tool suggests the designer can access the experience of disability in a meaningful way by putting on a pair of gloves or glasses. This reduction of disability to a single mechanic, like the reduction of Blackness to skin color, and the refugee experience to (virtual) presence in a location all rest on twisted notions of empathy, technology, and social change that have little basis in scholarly research or reality, and utterly fail to take into account the designer's own positionality. More recent work from the fields of co-design, participatory design, and socially engaged art provide helpful contributions for moving away from this approach of designing for others and shifting toward designing with and in communities (Helguera, 2011; Friedman & Hendry, 2012; Bardzell & Bardzell, 2013; Cipolla & Bartholo, 2014; Sanders & Stappers, 2014).

Focusing again on the category of works discussed at the opening of the chapter, VR experiences like de la Pena's *Hunger in Los Angeles* (2012), *One Dark Night*

(2015), and *Out of Exile: Daniel's Story* (2017), projects from the *Be Another Lab* research collective (2012 - ongoing), and Milk's *Clouds Over Sidra* (2015) have so many layers to unpack, revealing these works as actually functioning to re-inscribe the oppression they claim to push back against. Beyond the aesthetics and ontology of the particular technology and underlying assumptions regarding the empathic mode of reception, there is also the ethically fraught issue of telling someone else's story, no matter the medium (Shuman, 2005; Parvin, 2018; Rouse, 2019). In the realm of nonfiction, as all these examples are, this issue is particularly charged. These examples are rife with serious missteps such as the taking of voice as opposed to giving it, cultural appropriation, and colonizing moves to extract things of value from the oppressed. These problems are particularly highlighted in the case of others' stories of pain, oppression and violence, when the designer and interactor are not part of the community experiencing these horrors (Baker, 2015; Fisher & Schoemann, 2018). This extraction and remediation as safe simulation can provide viewers with a perverse sense of pleasure in the suffering of others, even if that pleasure is construed as morally 'good' in the name of providing information for the aim of prejudice reduction.

Where does the landscape of instrumentalized empathy leave immersive technologies like AR and VR in the quest for social change and justice? First, designers must find our own place in the conversation, and then consider technology. This means designers must first work to cultivate critical self-awareness and understanding of their own positionality as always already culturally and politically entangled. The neutral designer is a myth. This self-knowledge is necessary as a foundation to be able to critically assess how one's own creations participate in the cycles of socialization and/or liberation. In addition, in the journey to develop self-awareness, it is necessary to maintain the humility to know and hopefully enjoy the fact that we never stop learning and this journey is never complete. Never-ending learning means continually finding out that previously held ideas are wrong. This is a fact of life; the only alternative is willful ignorance.

With this in mind, I suggest a set of dichotomous qualities that are intended to help designers think towards an anti-instrumentalist design approach. This approach is centered on dialogue as opposed to any particular media technology, and prioritizes human-to-human interaction as opposed to simulation.

The qualities associated with human dialogue are counterintuitive for many design processes. The process of dialogue is not quick, its outcomes are not disposable, its work is never finished, and it is not productive in the capitalist sense nor easy to monetize. This approach can be, however, transformative, as opposed to informative. While a dichotomy is certainly reductive, its value is in the structure it can provide as a frame for supporting inquiry. There is an interesting middle space, a third possibility, between human dialogue and media simulation, that is inhabited by mixed reality. This blended space may provide the most fertile ground for experimentation in the work of socially engaged immersive design moving forward.

In practice, the type of process suggested by the above qualities takes place over multiple years. Pushing back against the language of speed so common in industrial design terms, such as the design "sprint" (Knapp et. al., 2016), a design process

**Table 1.1:** Comparison of Dialogue-based versus Media-based design approaches to aid anti-instrumentalist thinking

| Human Dialogue | Media Simulation |
|---|---|
| Not efficient, requires considerable labor and time | Efficient, Labor-saving, Quick, fast |
| Outcomes are not disposable (you can't un-know what you learn in dialogue) | Outcomes are disposable, can become obsolete, may even be designed to include planned obsolescence |
| Not interchangeable | Every interactor accesses the same core experience |
| Not productive in the capitalist sense | Productive and able to be commercialized |
| Never finished | Discreet |
| Characterized by intimacy | Characterized by performativity |
| Necessitates risk, discomfort, and conflict | Provides comfort and safety |
| Shares agency among participants, de-centering power | Continually re-asserts authorial and system control over participants through the absence of or constraining of choices, even while under the guise of interactivity |
| Transformative | Informative |

centered in dialogue could be described as a slow approach to design, or design in real time, as opposed to machine time. If the ultimate goal is to develop an AR or VR project that will be truly transformative, the first step is for the designer or designers to engage in learning about and examining their own social identities, and practice being in dialogue with others who have different social identities than their own. This step might take a few months, or even a year, or more. It certainly cannot be accomplished in a five-day design sprint. Many resources for this first step of self-examination and dialogue with others are discussed in Rouse & Corron (2020).

Following this first step, a second step is for the designer to spend time in their own community, considering who—including the designer themselves—needs to learn what. This step may also take a year or so, and the resources needed will depend on the particular qualities of the community in which the designer finds themselves, and how they are positioned within that community. This second step should also include developing genuine relationships in the community that are naturally pertinent to the design aim. For example, if the aim is to design for middle school children, consider becoming a volunteer homework tutor at the local middle school or public library; if the aim is to design applications for cultural heritage, visit local museums and heritage sites and get to know the curators and patrons there. Following these first two steps, designers will be armed with invaluable resources of knowledge and connections that elude many designers who seek to skip ahead.

In a third step, the designer should work with their now-developed network of contacts to create a series of community roundtables and participatory design workshops to begin to explore the design space of their own community with fellow community members. These events should be designed to facilitate knowledge sharing between the designer, their network, and others. The designer might find themselves in the position of educating others on the how-to's of AR technology, for example, while learning from others about the spaces and history they care about most in the community. For some examples of projects developed in this manner see Rouse (2019). This third step may take several months. Finally, a fourth step involves gathering a more formalized design team, and working toward a functional prototype that can be shared with the community in a participatory fashion at iterative stages, leading to a finished project. Many designers begin with this fourth step, and it is easy to see why the projects that result are often informational only, and not transformational.

This is the crux; if social transformation is the true goal, designers must seek methods that truly transform themselves and participants through co-constituted, consensual, collaborative means that result in transformational knowledge production and meaningful experience. Continuing to cosset designers and interactors in simulation can only result in the perpetuation of systems of oppression.

## Acknowledgements

The author thanks Professor Nassim Parvin for her insightful and generous mentorship on this research.

## Put it Into Practice

Taking the lessons from this chapter, envision a multiyear project that uses XR for social change but does not seek to do so through the instrumentalization of empathy.

1. Engage in learning about and examining your own social identities, and practice being in dialogue with others who have different social identities than your own.
2. The designer must then spend time in their own community, considering who— including the designer themselves—needs to learn what. This second step should also include developing genuine relationships in the community that are naturally pertinent to the design aim. Following these first two steps, designers will be armed with invaluable resources of knowledge and connections that elude many designers who seek to skip ahead.
3. The designer should work with their now-developed network of contacts to create a series of community roundtables and participatory design workshops to begin to explore the design space of their own community with fellow community members.
4. The fourth step involves gathering a more formalized design team, and working toward a functional prototype that can be shared with the community in a participatory fashion at iterative stages, leading to a finished project.

# References

Baker, C.R. (2015 ). *Humane Insight: Looking at Images of African American Suffering and Death*. Chicago, IL: University of Illinois Press.

Baldwin, J. (1966). Unnameable objects, unspeakable crimes. pp. 173-183. *In: The WHITE Problem in America*. Chicago, IL: Johnson Publishing Company.

Bardzell, J. and Bardzell, S. (2013). What is "Critical" About Critical Design? pp. 3297-3306. *In:* Proceedings of the SIGCHI Conference on Human Factors in Computing Systems.

Bloom, P. (2017). *Against Empathy: The Case for Rational Compassion*. New York, NY: Random House.

Bohm, D. (1996). *On Dialogue*. London and New York: Routledge.

Bolter, J.D. (2014). The aesthetics of flow and the aesthetics of catharsis. pp. 121-136. *In:* Gaafar, R., Schulz, M. (eds.). Technology and Desire: The Transgressive Art of Moving Images. Bristol and Chicago: Intellect.

Cipolla, C. and Bartholo, R. (2014). Empathy or inclusion: A dialogical approach to socially responsible design. *International Journal of Design*, 8(2), 87-100.

Clune, M.W. (2016). Virtual reality reminds users what it's like to be themselves. *The Atlantic Magazine*, April 20, 2016.

Csikszentmihalyi, M. (1991). *Flow: The Psychology of Optimal Experience*. New York, NY: Harper Perennial.

Devine, J. and Levine, M. (Eds.) (2012). *Beyond Prejudice: Extending the Social Psychology of Conflict, Inequality, and Social Change*. Cambridge and New York: Cambridge University Press.

DiAngelo, R. (2011). White fragility. *International Journal of Critical Pedagogy*, 3(3), 54-70.

Fisher, J.A. (2017). Empathic actualities: Toward a taxonomy of empathy in virtual reality. *Interactive Storytelling*. Lecture Notes in Computer Science 10690, Cham, Germany: Springer International. pp. 233-244.

Fisher, J.A. and Schoemann, S. (2018). Toward an ethics of interactive storytelling at dark tourism sites in virtual reality. *Interactive Storytelling*. Lecture Notes in Computer Science 11318. Cham, Germany: Springer International. pp. 577-590.

Freire, P. (1970/2005). *Pedagogy of the Oppressed: 30th Anniversary Edition*. London and NY: Continuum.

Friedman, B. and Hendry, D. (2012). The envisioning cards: A toolkit for catalyzing humanistic and technical imaginations. pp. 1145-1148. *In:* Proceedings of the SIGCHI Conference on Human Factors in Computing Systems.

Gaines, A. (2017). *Black for a Day: White Fantasies of Race and Empathy*. Chapel Hill, NC: University of North Carolina Press.

Goodman, L. (2012). Hunger in L.A. immerses viewers in an interactive journalism experiences (and a food line). *Fast Company*, January 31, <2012. https://www.fastcompany.com/1679530/hunger-in-la-immerses-viewers-in-an-interactive-journalism-experience-and-a-food-line> accessed June 28, 2020.

Hall, S. (1973). *Encoding and Decoding in the Television Discourse*. Birmingham, UK: Centre for Contemporary Cultural Studies.

Harro, B. (2000). The cycle of socialization. pp. 15-21. *In:* Readings for Diversity and Social Justice: An Anthology on Racism, Sexism, Anti-Semitism, Heterosexism, Classism, and Ableism, Second Edition. New York, NY: Routledge.

Harro, B. (2000). The cycle of liberation. pp. 52-58. *In:* Readings for Diversity and Social Justice: An Anthology on Racism, Sexism, Anti-Semitism, Heterosexism, Classism, and Ableism, Second Edition. New York, NY: Routledge.

Helguera, P. (2011). *Socially Engaged Art.* New York, NY: Jorge Pinto Books.

Hooks, B. (1992). Eating the other: Desire and resistance. pp. 21-39. *In:* Black Looks: Race and Representation. Boston, MA: South End Press.

IDEO. (2003). *Method Cards: 51 Ways to Inspire Design.* Palo Alto.

Knapp, J., Zeratsky, J. and Kowitz, B. (2016). *Sprint: Solve Big Problems and Test New Ideas in Just Five Days.* New York, NY: Simon & Schuster.

Krauss, R. (1976). Video: The aesthetics of narcissism. *October*, 1, 50-64.

Larocco, S. (2018). Empathy as orientation rather than feeling: Why empathy is ethically complex. pp. 2-15. *In:* Exploring Empathy: Its Propagations, Perimeters and Potentialities. Leiden and Boston: Brill Rodopi.

Milk, C. (2015). How virtual reality can create the ultimate empathy machine. TED Talk, April 22,2015. <https://www.ted.com/talks/chris_milk_how_virtual_reality_can_create_the_ultimate_empathy_machine/> accessed June 4, 2020.

Mulvey, L. (1975). Visual pleasure and narrative cinema. *Screen*, 16(3), 6-18.

Murray, J.H. (2020). Virtual/reality: How to tell the difference. *Journal of Visual Culture*, 19(1), 11-27.

Nakamura, L. (2020). Feeling good about feeling bad: Virtuous virtual reality and the automation of racial empathy. *Journal of Visual Culture*, 19(1), 47-64.

Nash, K. (2009). *The Cultural Politics of Human Rights: Comparing the US and the UK.* Cambridge and New York: Cambridge University Press.

Nash, K. (2018). Virtual reality witness: Exploring the ethics of mediated presence. *Studies in Documentary Film*, 12.2, 119-131.

Pair, J., Neumann, U., Piepol, D. and Swartout, B. (2003). FlatWorld: Combining hollywood set-design techniques with VR. *IEEE Computer Graphics and Applications*, January/February 2003, 12-15.

Paley, M. (2014). *The Neighborhood that Disappeared.* Film.

Parvin, N. (2018). Doing Justice to stories: On ethics and politics of digital storytelling. *Engaging Science, Technology, and Society*, 4, 515-534.

Robb, A. (2017). Anatomy of a fake news scandal. *Rolling Stone*, November 16, 2017. < https://www.rollingstone.com/politics/politics-news/anatomy-of-a-fake-news-scandal-125877/ > Accessed June 28, 2020.

Rouse, R. (2019). Someone else's story: An ethical approach to interactive narrative design for cultural heritage. *Interactive Storytelling*, Lecture Notes in Computer Science 11869, Cham, Germany: Springer International. pp. 47-60.

Rouse, R. and Corron, A. (2020). Levelling up: A critical feminist pedagogy for game design. *MAI: Journal of Feminism and Visual Culture*, 5.

Sanders, E.B-N. and Stappers, P.J. (2014). Probes, toolkits, and prototypes: Three approaches to making in codesigning. *CoDesign*, 10(1), 5-14.

Schubert, R., Welch, G., Daher, S. and Raij, A. (2016). HuSIS: A dedicated space for studying human interactions. *IEEE Computer Graphics and Applications*, November/December 2016, 26-36.

Shuman, A. (2005). *Other People's Stories: Entitlement Claims and the Critique of Empathy.* Chicago, IL: University of Illinois Press.

Smith, R. (2010). The Long History of Gaming in Military Training. *Simulation & Gaming*, 41(1), 6-19.

Star, S.L. (1999). The ethnography of infrastructure. *American Behavioral Scientist*, 43(3), 377-391.

Winner, L. (1980). Do artifacts have politics? *Daedalus*, January 1980, 121-136.

Wetherell, M. (1992/2012). The prejudice problematic. *Beyond Prejudice: Extending the Social Psychology of Conflict, Inequality, and Social Change.* Cambridge and New York: Cambridge University Press. pp. 158-178.

Zielke, M.A., Evans, M.J., Dufour, F., Christopher, T.V., Donahue, J.K., Johnson, P., Jennings, E.B., Friedman, B.S., Ounekeo, P.L. and Flores, R. (2009). Serious games for immersive cultural training: Creating a living world. *IEEE Computer Graphics and Applications*, March/April 2009, 49-60.

Zyda, M., Mayberry, A., McCree, J. and Davis, M. (2005). From Viz-Sim to VR Games: How we built a hit game-based simulation. *Organizational Simulation.* Hoboken, NJ: John Wiley & Sons. pp. 553-589.

Chapter

# 2

# The Body and the Eye—The I and the Other: Critical Reflections on the Promise of Extended Empathy in Extended Reality Configurations

**Anna Wiehl**

University of Bayreuth, 95440 Bayreuth

Email: anna.wiehl@uni-bayreuth.de

## Introduction: The Hype and the Hope of VR as "The Ultimate Empathy Machine"

In 2015, Milk got the ball rolling when he referred to Virtual Reality (VR) as "the ultimate empathy machine" (Milk, 2015)[1]. This was an early promise of VR, and presented a testable premise for immersive and transformative affective experiences in non-fiction. Milk's conviction was that "through providing viewers with the means of standing in the shoes of the filmmaker's subjects—[…] VR non-fiction could allow audiences to experience and connect to 'the real' in ways beyond what could be achieved with traditional two-dimensional film" (*ibid*). The often-repeated supposition was that users—or rather user-interactors[2]—would no longer be restricted

---

[1] The myth of the "empathy machine" was first used in the context of film criticism by Roger Ebert in 2005. He used this metaphor to describe the potential of cinema to allow the viewer to "live somebody else's life for a while", to "see what it feels like to be a member of a different gender, a different race, a different economic class, to live in a different time, to have a different belief". In Ebert's eyes, this experience could have "a liberalizing influence", give one "a broader mind" and help "to identify with the family of men and women on this planet".

The claim that VR allows one to walk in the shoes of someone else even more and as a consequence promotes a change in one's social attitudes or even behaviour positively has been true with the 'old' media ever since and especially with the 'new' media, promising insight into the lives of others.

[2] In *Inventing the Medium: Principles of Interaction Design,* new media and literary scholar Janet Murray argues that the term 'interactor' should be preferred to 'user' which was the

(*Contd.*)

to being passive observers of a story unfolding before their eyes. VR would now allow them to stand in the situation as if they were there, *in situ,* in person, in real time. Milk believed that a sensation of physical presence and a feeling of embodiment would lead to an immersion that would induce deep, immediate emotional reactions. This belief sparked a hype-fueled-hope that VR, AR, MR and XR[3] configurations[4] could enhance mutual understanding, profound affective connections, pro-social behavior and transformative experiences. Held loftily above these valued effects was the promise of greater empathy with others.

Empathy is one of the most important human emotions. Vignemont and Singer propose two 'major roles' for empathy: "its epistemological role is to provide information about the future actions of other people, and important environmental properties. Its social role is to serve as the origin of the motivation for cooperative and prosocial behavior, as well as help for effective social communication" (Vignemont and Singer, 2006, p. 435). As such, other empathy-related phenomena such as perspective taking, respect, empathic concern and altruism are crucial for successful social interactions. In many ways, "the ability to share other people's emotional experiences and to react to them in a fine-tuned manner might facilitate social communication and create social coherence. For example, in action imitation, the chameleon effect—the tendency to adopt other people's postures, gestures and mannerisms—was found to create affiliation and fondness. Similarly, perceiving another person's empathy for oneself is likely to increase affiliation and strengthen

---

more common term up to then. As the main reason for this re-thinking also in terms of concepts digital media must not be seen as 'tools' which require a 'user' (Murray 2012, p. 426) but rather as artefacts that invite an engagement of—namely—'interactors' Murray explains.

[3] In contrast to the currently frequent terms of VR (VR—placing the interactor in a purely virtual world) and augmented reality (AR—putting a virtual layer over a physically real environment), XR will be understood as a more comprehensive and flexible term. XR can thereby be defined as any form of "mixed reality environment that comes from the fusion of [...] ubiquitous sensor/actuator networks and shared [...] virtual worlds" (Paradiso and Landay 2009, p. 14). The *"Machine to be Another"* discussed later qualifies as such as an XR configuration as its working principles are much more multifaceted than simply adding a virtually generated surplus of information over 'reality'. Moreover, it allows us to bring the example in the case study closer to concepts of virtuality as suggested for example by Deleuze (1966) or Lévi (1998) which positions the virtual as not opposed to the real, nor is the digital positioned as the opposite of the biological. This enables us to disentangle the complex relationship in which virtuality actualizes real, bodily effects and emotions and therefore can be said to become 'real'.

[4] In the following, the terms 'configuration' and 'assemblage' (as coined by Deleuze and Guattari and also adopted by Actor Network Theory, e.g. Latour, 1996; Law, 1992) will be used synonymously to delineate not only technological environments but techno-cultural and socio-psychological interdependencies within complex interrelated, fluid, dynamic and hybrid settings comprising human and non-human agents such as technological features and protocols.

the emotional bond with that person" (Vignemont and Singer, 2006, p. 440).[5]
From this, it follows that empathy allows us to learn from and better understand
to collaborate and support each other. In short, empathetic feelings are crucial for
societies to evolve and prosper (cf. Decety, 2010; Singer and McCall, 2013).[6]

Given the promise that VR configurations could enhance empathy, educational
scenarios and training protocols were developed to stimulate pro-social behavior.
Indeed, non-profit organizations saw the possibility of reaching and moving passive
audiences to support their cause. Projects like *"Clouds over Sidra"* (Milk, 2015)
tried to give a first-hand experience of what life in a refugee camp is like; the project
*"iAnimal"* (Valle, 2016), commissioned by Animal Equality, positioned the user-
interactors behind the curtains of a dairy business and exposed what happens in
slaughterhouses, for example; Greenpeace takes the user-interactors on *"A Journey
to the Arctic"* (MediaMonks, 2016), where they encounter endangered species; and
*Charity: "Water about a watering project"* (Burmeister and Ismall, 2016) in which
user-interactors are allowed to accompany local children profiting from a well during
the tour of a village in Ethiopia.

In this sense, VR allows the user-interactors to visit and explore places which
are normally hidden from the public, which they probably would never be able to
'in real life', and experience living through situations which only a limited few are
exposed to.[7]

In 2020, the excitement around VR and empathy has cooled down, but VR and
XR still inspire experimental-experiential configurations in non-fiction storytelling

---

[5] Also noteworthy with regard to the following discussion of *"The Machine to be Another"*,
is the possibility of Vignemont and Singer proving that prior mirroring of other people's
postures and gestures stirs empathy in both functional magnetic resonance imaging
measuring brain activity and experiments.

[6] Nonetheless, though one usually has some kind of common-sensical notion of 'empathy',
it is difficult to define its concept in scientific terms (depending on the discipline, various
definitions exist) – and it is even more difficult to measure it (cf. among others Bevan, 2019;
Fisher, 2017). As follows, it will be referred to as "feeling the emotions of another individual
under observation without mixing them with our own" (Bertrand et al., 2018, p. 2; cf. also de
Vignemont and Singer, 2006; Decety and Meyer, 2008; Decety, 2010).
As will be seen later, this differentiation between one's own emotions and the re-lived
feelings of someone else is crucial. Moreover, it is necessary to distinguish between empathy
and sympathy, though the first often comprises the second, as Fisher notes: As opposed
to empathy, sympathy is considered to be a feeling of care for someone in need. For these
experiences to do justice to the subjects they represent, it is assumed that the VR designer has
had a direct experience with them that resulted in both cognitive and emotional empathy."
(Fisher 2017, p. 238.)

[7] VR configurations are even supposed to allow user-interactors to become more sensitive
to diseases. There is the promise to enhance comprehension beyond mere cognitive
understanding and knowledge gain, which are on the fore front in many other documentary
projects. It is different in VR: *"A Walk Through Dementia"* (Visyon, 2016), is for example,
a VR-experience produced for Alzheimer's Research UK, which not only explains facts, but
it tries to simulate and induce the symptoms people are suffering from when afflicted by the
disease.

which go beyond a merely functional use of technologies as in educational and training contexts, and also beyond entertaining pastimes in virtual worlds. While maturing as a technology and medium, VR practitioners have been fathoming its socio-cultural affordances, like art, artistic research and experiential non-fiction storytelling discover and XR exploration. This movement towards configurations is accompanied by critical discourses. Among others, Rose (2018), Sutherland (2015), Nash (2019), Bailenson (2019), Bevan et al. (2019), McRoberts (2018) and Farmer (2019) discuss the potentials and the challenges that VR in non-fiction offers.

Most often, this endeavor is a transdisciplinary enterprise. Considerations from neurosciences, individual and social psychology, education, medicine, art history, and production of activist interventionist media are brought into dialogue with media theory, and ecological media discourses especially. Particularly thrilling is the experimental research and artistic interventions in XR that simultaneously probe into what the media configurations already *are* and what they might *become theoretically and practically.*

This chapter will focus on a set of interrelated issues. Basic reflections about XR and concepts of embodiment will be discussed in relation to its applications in the field of empathy-building. These considerations will be subjected to a media-ethical analysis framed by the myth of XR as 'the ultimate empathy machine'.

The argument unfolds in three stages: moving from the eye to the body, from the body to the mind, and finally from experience to experiment—or in other words: from artistic intervention to artistic research. The work's guiding questions are:

- Which paradigm shifts are implied in the movement from visual to embodied experiences, beyond the ocular centrism, and in terms of extended 'perspective taking' especially?
- What happens when XR not only affords an illusory swap of bodies but also aspires a swap of mindsets?
- How far are our conceptualizations of others, as well as of ourselves, altered when mediated in XR assemblages?

To explore these points, the XR project *"The Machine to be Another"* (BeAnotherLab, 2014) will be analyzed. *"The Machine to be Another"*[8] is an XR embodiment system and an exemplary assemblage. The results from empirical studies on the project by the "BeAnotherLab" research group[9] and the Virtual Human

---

[8] One disclaimer should be put ahead: Though the nature of XR implies writing about experiencing the act is thus necessarily accompanied by a loss of vivacity and immediacy, I will try my best to be as plastic and accurate as possible—always navigating on the narrow ridge between scientific intersubjectivity on the one hand and what stands in the focus of this chapter on the other hand: feelings—namely empathy, probably one of the most complex and subjective emotions.

[9] The "BeAnotherLab" research team comprises among others Philippe Bertrand, Daniel Gonzalez-Franco, Christian Cherene, Arthur Pointeau, Jérôme Guegan, Léonore Robieux, Cade Andrew McCall, Franck Zenasni, Elen Collaco de Oliveira, Marte Ernesto Roel Lesur, Priscila Palomo, Marcelo Demarzo and Ausias Cebolla; cf. Bertrand et al., 2013; 2018; cf. Oliviera et al., 2016.

Interaction Lab of the Stanford University will guide this chapter's transdisciplinary theoretical discourse around XR.

## "The Machine to be Another"

*"The Machine to be Another"* is an especially ambitious project in the field of artistic research that probes the potential of VR, AR, MR and XR at the intersection of neurosciences, theatrical practices and new media art. The experience is quite complex, as its configuration comprises two participants, both equipped with Oculus Rift headsets and headphones, a flexible script which leaves room for improvisation, and in some instances physical objects. In contrast to VR games, there is neither a task nor a plot that unfolds. Instead, the participants are put into a physically concrete, virtually extended situation. The participants are meant to swap perceptual systems with each other, and they mirror whatever the other is doing. If one person lifts her/ his hand, the other lifts his/her hand as well, but if person A looks at 'her/his' hand, the headset shows her/him the hand of person B as if it was their own. This *visually* illusory body-swap is enabled through a camera set above the oculus rift headset which transmits whatever the other sees.

**Figure 2.1:** The coupling of 'human—machine (VR-technology)—human' in *"The Machine to be Another"*. Combining a body swap with a gender swap
Screenshot from the IDFA-trailer of *"The Machine to be Another"*, online: https://www.youtube.com/watch?v=_Wk489deqAQ

As discussed elsewhere (Wiehl, 2020), this makes *"The Machine to be Another"* a special exploration of VR and XR configurations. In contrast to fully pre-scripted narrative experiences, *"The Machine to be Another"* can be more accurately described as a "protocol" or "embodiment system" (Bertrand et al., 2013). In this context, "embodiment systems" are complex configurations in which the experience is a formalized, structured interaction with 'an other'. The interplay has cues, but it is not fully scripted. Like in happenings—a form of expression extremely *en vogue* in the Fluxus movement—the framing of the interplay is roughly planned, but the actual interaction is improvisational, requiring creative user-interactor participation. This makes each experience a unique experimental-experiential encounter.

Usually, the experience begins with the participant being fitted with an Oculus headset and led into a room where 'the other', who will be sharing the experience, is already waiting. Then, the participant is invited to open her/his eyes and to slowly start moving. This is the moment when looking down at herself/himself, she/he for the first time discovers the body of 'the other'. Typically, the first impulse is to touch one's self and to physically examine one's own 'new', strange body—for example a body of a different skin color, sex or disabilities.

As a socio-technological complex the assemblage feels fragile—movements are usually very tentative—especially at the beginning. Eyes and bodies must be tuned together, and movements must be agreed upon with 'the other'. If gestures are performed too abruptly, the invisible 'bond' which develops between the two user-interactors, is broken. This makes the encounter of one's self with 'the other', but also with one's self and with one's new (visually illusory) self, a precarious experience that requires cooperation[10].

This factor of liveness is crucial in the context of empathy-building. For example instead of a filmed situation which is then rendered as a 360° video (such as in *"Clouds over Sidra"*), *"The Machine to be Another"* is based on real-time interaction with a physically present "other". This increases empathetic reactions, as both the spatial and temporal distance are minimal—the participants sit back to back or, in other scenarios, even face to face. This VR is characterized by immediacy, wherein, "Real time tuning to the mental states of others is necessary to generate an accurate empathy response" (Bertrand et al., 2018, p. 4). What also distinguishes *"The Machine to be Another"* from experiences such as *"Clouds over Sidra"* is that the taking perspective includes a first-person experience of really 'walking in the shoes of someone else' being in the body of that person and not merely being a passive uninvolved spectator like a rather indifferent bystander.

## From the Eye to the Body: Paradigm Shifts from Ocular Centrism and Tactile Visuality to Physical Embodiment and Interaction

*"The Machine to be Another"* is based not only on the *visual* illusion of being in another person's body; it also affords illusory *agency* over this body—or rather the coupling of one's own body and the other's body, as movements with 'the other' need to be coordinated and harmonized. This shifts the visual perception and tactical visuality to the perception of physical embodiment.

One key word in this context is 'embodiment' with respect to the 'body ownership illusion'. There are two major stimuli to induce embodiment: first,

---

[10] This fact that sets *"The Machine to be Another"* apart from single-user VR/XR configurations only reminds one more of collective VR experiences such as CAVE-live VR theatre experiences as described by Layng et al. (2019), for example.

there is visuo *motor* synchronicity which is linked to physical moves—that is, seeing one's self in the body of someone else that mirrors or mimics one's own *movement* in real time; second, their visual *tactile* synchronicity which relates to the sense of *touching* an object, seeing tactile stimuli applied to one's illusory XR body which are simultaneously applied to one's own physical body (cf. for example, Maselli and Slater, 2013; Tsakiris, 2007). All this stimulates a sense of presence, i.e. the "subjective experience of 'being here' in the moment as one moves along the time-space trajectory of everyday life" (McRoberts, 2017, p. 103). This 'being here' implies that the mind consciously perceives bodily senses and experiences the external world. Most importantly the cognitive and embodied experience implied by a sense of presence enables one to *interact* with the world as they expect to experience it. This comprises their social interactions wherein a sense of *social* presence comes into play.

In this sense, when both participants *touch* their bodies an experience which is even more complex[11] is induced. Their hands feel their bodies, and their bodies feel the touch, but their eyes see something different—the body of the other.[12]

**Figure 2.2:** Further complication of the hybrid configuration in *"The Machine to be Another"*: participants touching their own bodies
Screenshot from the IDFA-trailer of *"The Machine to be Another"*, online:
https://www.youtube.com/watch?v=_Wk489deqAQ

---

[11] As the researchers of the SEL (Social and Emotional Learning) research group, underline, that the experience of situations in their complexity is key in the field of emotional and social learning, oversimplification can lead to the formation of new biases and prejudices—which in fact ought to be overcome. Thus, to train compassion and empathy, liveness, "realistic and plausible stimuli for understanding another's point of view, cooperative tasks and contextualization are essential rather than abstract instruction, pre-scripted narratives, or predetermined instructional sequences since they enable context and content, and dependant knowledge construction" (Betrand et al., 2018, p. 5).

[12] At this point it should be remarked that the discussion of the haptic quality of vision already originated around the year 1900. Among others, German art historians like Adolf Hildebrand and Alois Riegl explored the extent of existence of phenomena such as "visual touch".

The notion of 'tactile' or 'haptic visuality' as coined by Marks (2002) is then extended. For Marks, 'tactile vision' regards both the qualities of visual perception and the haptic qualities that are assigned to the *images* of the objects represented. As Huhtamo underlines, this implies that "in actual practices of *looking*, the 'optical' and the 'haptic' can never be entirely separated" (Huhtamo, 2007, p. 73; emphasis A.W.). In this paradigm, however, one still resides in the realm of ocular centrism:

The idea of 'haptic visuality' implies the transposition of qualities of touch to the realm of vision and visuality. It confronts the issue of the physicality of touch indirectly, through a corporeal operation involving the eyes and the brain. The hands are not part of it, except as an imaginary 'projection.' (*ibid*)

In *"The Machine to be Another"*, in contrast, the eyes do *not* see what the tactile senses submit, but the other way round: the eyes see someone else's hand touching them, and still, they do not only feel it *'as if'* it were their own hand, but they actually have the physical sensation of that touch because their own hand touches their body too.

This haptic visuality serves the purpose of empathetic learning, as Bertrand et al. (2018), Tsakiris (2007), Suzuki et al. (2013) and other researchers in the fields of body cognition, neuroimaging and social psychology suggest. The basic idea behind these processes is that one's awareness about one's own body is based on the interdependency and the constant exchange of bottom up brain phenomena (from the body to the brain) and top down processes (from the brain to the body). This means that information of interoceptive states (such as physical perceptions which are connected with emotions, e.g. proprioception, breathing, heart rate and general arousal) and exteroceptive sensations (such as vision and touch) form the brain's predictions of the perception of the self. As Bertrand et al. put it, "the regulation between internal bodily states, external environment information, and mental concepts give us the sense of ourselves and the space that surrounds us" (Bertrand et al., 2018, p. 9).

However, *The Machine to be Another* comprises of more than the basic tactile exploration of one's new but familiar body. The experience, through different protocols, makes it possible to bring people of different genders and racial backgrounds, and of different physical conditions, together to experience body swaps. *"The Machine to be Another"* allows participants to 'stand in the shoes' of groups of people who are often discriminated against because of their skin color, cultural background or a physical disability. In one script, for example, the user-interactors swap bodies with Youssoupha, a young immigrant from Senegal. In "In Merce's wheels", user-interactors with no disabilities participate in what Bertrand et al. describes as a, "functional diversity exchange" (Bertrand et al., 2013). User-interactors exchange a body with Merce, a young woman in a wheelchair, while listening to Merce's experiences. They are then able to temporarily experience what it means to face the everyday challenges of sitting in a wheelchair, specifically from the situated perspective of Merce. Such experiences are intended to have a transformative potential as they stimulate a physical response, a reconstructive-cognitive emphatic reaction, and an immediate-emotional reaction.[13]

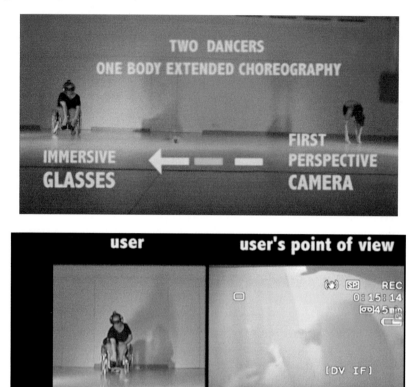

**Figures 2.3 and 2.4:** In different protocols, *"The Machine to be Another"* enables participants to experience what Bertrand et al. (2013) describe as "functional diversity exchange"—i.e. virtual body-swaps with individuals of a different gender, a different socio-cultural background or with a physical challenge.
Screenshot from the IDFA-trailer of *"The Machine to be Another"*, online: https://www.youtube.com/watch?v=_Wk489deqAQ

## From the Body to the Mind—Virtual Body Swap and Swap of Mindset?

The role of audio in combination with vision and bodily experiences makes the configuration of *"The Machine to be Another"* more complex. The participants do not only *see* themselves embodied as 'the other' and haptically *feel* what the other probably feels as movements are mirrored (e.g. in the setting with an apple). In

---

[13] Other scripts included asylum seekers in a detention centre in Israel, Iraq veterans in the USA and victims of police brutality in Brazil.

addition to the visual impression, the participants can also listen to the 'thoughts' of 'the other' like a stream of consciousness. For example, while exploring an object or while touching themselves, the mirroring participants speak their thoughts aloud. By doing so, they do not only describe haptic sensation; they posit their emotional states in the actual situation. Thus, the idea is not only to probe into the potential of a virtual-visual body swap but to also inquire into the possibilities of a mindset swap. In turn, this helps to extend the working of the mirror neurons beyond mere vision. This is even more prominent in the experiences featuring narratives from minority groups experiencing discrimination—as in the case of Youssoupha. These stories, created by the participants themselves, are based on their personal views and experiences, and range from social stigma to stories of forgiveness.

However, "BeAnotherLab" does not aspire to create a complete reconstruction or representation of the subjective experience of 'an other', nor are they interested in only "straightforward social perspective-taking", as Sutherland (2015) notes. Rather, they are fathoming the potential of XR to enhance extended empathy through extensive embodiment. Apart from making the participant experience another person's body, the assemblage is used "to stimulate pro-social behavior and to overcome intergroup social barriers" (BeAnotherLab, 2019). While the interactor 'listens' to another person's often very intimate emotions, the bond that is created through tentative cooperative movement is further fostered.[14] Hence, one of the crucial aspects in *"The Machine to be Another"* is that it shifts the focus from a rather ocular centrist paradigm to embodiment *and* cognition and affect. In this context, embodied simulation mechanisms, in conjunction with the simulation of actions and physical corporeal sensations and sharing of emotions as well, have deep implications for understanding the perception of one's body and social cognition[15]. In this manner, *"The Machine to be Another"* provide[s] a unique way for the exploration of identity and how it is related to embodiment and narrative in a deeply immersive way (Bertrand et al., 2013).

Empathy is meant to be fostered through the perception of one's new body and the accompanying social cognition. The *Be Another Lab* defines empathy as, "the ability of one individual to feel another individual's emotional state *while preserving the knowledge about its personal origin*" (BeAnotherLab, 2019; Emphasis A.W.). Empathy in this sense is based on an understanding of the other and possible differences between that other's experiences and one's own at the same time.[16] 'Taking

---

[14] For further experiments in the field of pro-social behaviour stimulated through VR non-fiction cf. among others Betrand et al. 2018; 2013.

[15] Social cognition is the forming of empathy through what psychologists describe as "neural plasticity" and the formation of concepts (cf. Bertrand et al., 2013; Gallese and Lakoff, 2005).

[16] For a detailed survey of the origins of different notions of empathy, especially in terms of emotional and cognitive empathy cf. Fisher, 2017. In this context, Fisher underlines that "emotional empathy is the instantaneous and somatic reaction to a subject's emotions without the conscious intentionality of that subject. Emotion is seen as a contagion that colonizes the observers with feelings which are not their own" (Fisher, 2017, p. 236) whereas cognitive empathy is a "primary epistemic perceptive mode" which results in taking perspective (*ibid*, p. 237).

perspective' in this context is employed both in the literal and the metaphorical senses to promote "pro-social behavior such as altruism and compassion" (*ibid*)— this is the intention of the producers of *"The Machine to be Another"* in the least.

This intention can be regarded (cf. below) as a prerequisite for a better sympathetic, and empathic feeling, for an other through an embodied experience that engages one's sense of presence, body agency, embodied narrative, and physical immersion. Bertrand et al. (2018) present an illuminating comparison between an interventionist-media-experience perspective and a scientific-experiment understanding of *"The Machine to be Another"*.

> 'Try to walk a mile in another person's shoes.' This proverb, found in many cultures in the world, suggests a way to help us understand each other better, and relates to several empathy-related responses. Imagine if we try to follow this proverb literally and walk a mile in the shoes of someone in need. First, we would (a) move our own body, copying the other person's movements. Then we would (b) feel distressed for walking in their place and facing their needs. Doing so, we would (c) understand what the other person is going through and would (d) understand what they are feeling. Also, we would (e) feel the emotions that the other feels on their path. After doing so, we may feel the (f) desire to help this person. This desire could (g) drive us to actually help the other, regardless of the cost to self.
>
> In the same order, under a psychological or neuroscientific perspective we can identify the following empathy-related phenomena in this proverb. (a) *Mimicry* is a tendency to synchronize the affective expressions, vocalizations, postures, and movements of another person. (b) *Empathic Distress* is when one is personally distressed by the distress of another person. (c) *Taking perspective* is the cognitive ability of imagining that of others. (d) *Online simulation* is the ability to predict other people's emotions. Perspective taking and online simulation are sub-factors of cognitive empathy. (e) *Affective empathy* (or simply "empathy") means experiencing an isomorphic feeling in relation to others with a clear differentiation between self/other, knowing that the origin of the emotion comes from the other. Therefore, affective empathy is related to the emotional engagement of the observer with the situation of the emoter. (f) *Compassion* is an emotional and motivational state of care for the wellbeing of the other. Finally, (g) *altruism* is characterized by the prosocial behavior of helping others at a cost to the self. (Bertrand et al., 2018, p. 2)

Applying these thoughts to *"The Machine to be Another"* we can say: a) *Mimicry* is one of the requisites for the XR-experience to be possible: without tuning one's movements to the movements of the other, the connection between the two performers will be broken. b) *Empathic Distress* happens when listening to the encounter with Youssoupha, the young immigrant from Senegal, and his recollection of his flight. (c) *Taking perspective* comes into play by the very nature of the experience's configuration that combines an illusory body-swap with a change of visual perspective in the literal sense. (d) *Online simulation* is not that obvious in *"The Machine to be Another"*. However, it is necessary to predict the other person's emotions in order to coordinate parallel action-taking during the improvised part of the encounter. (e) *Affective empathy* stands at the center of *"The Machine to be Another"* whereby the important factor is that one distinguishes one's own emotions from those of the other (f) *Compassion* and (g) *altruism* finally are most prominent in thematic protocols as they enhance an understanding beyond cognitive comprehension and potentially affect one's own reaction to physically challenged others. This is exemplified in "In Merce's wheels".

Essential to this context is that affective empathy seems to be key to the other dimensions of empathetic response. As McCall and Singer found out (2013), enhancing abilities in one domain can have a ripple effect of benefits to others. Another factor that seems to be crucial is the reduction of differences between me and 'the other'. Socio-psychological research (Decety, 2010 among others) has shown that one is inclined to feel greater empathy toward familiar individuals or individuals whom one perceives as similar to one's self. Two aspects need to be noted in this context: first of all, the differentiation between 'me' and 'the other', between 'us' and 'them' is neither static nor is it always explicit. What is called 'group affiliation' and 'in group empathy' is often influenced by so-called phenotypes: i.e. gender, age, skin color, race, but implicit biases also have some subtle influences on whom one feels closer to. Thus, *"The Machine to be Another"* tries to create a situation by means of XR and the perceptual body-swap in combination with the stream of consciousness enhances in-group affiliation. Once one has literally and metaphorically changed perspective with someone, the person is not only familiar in a cognitive but also in an emotional sense.

All this shows, that, what at first sight seems to be a thrilling artistic *intervention* gives way to artistic *research*. In this sense, new media, namely XR, are used to gain deeper insight into the process of empathy to prove hypotheses, and, in turn, reflect empirical findings in order to modify that same empathy-motivating configuration.

## From Artistic Intervention to Artistic Research—Backing Things Up and Moving Things Forward

*"The Machine to be Another"* can be described as an 'artistic research' or 'public experiment'. Whereas the first concept has gained a standing as an interdisciplinary practice, the latter calls for more explanation. Reflections by Nowotny, Scott and Gibbons (2001), Born and Barry (2013) suggest exploring issues of scientific and social relevance in the form of a 'public experiment' consisting of settings where improvisational artistic productions offer new options for research and helps to discover connections, and sets the agenda for future initiatives. These new avenues comprise of both scientific work *and* its artistic realization *for* and *with* a public. Public experiments are deeply embedded in transdisciplinary endeavors that challenge Snow's hypothesis of 'two cultures' specifically being arts on the one hand, and 'hard' sciences on the other (Snow 1959). "We consider alternative ways of knowing equally valid in our processes: the fundamentals being, qualitative, bodily, and

affective knowledge, but quantifying for generalizing knowledge is also given value and importance ..." (BeAnotherLab, 2019). This bridge between social psychology, ethnography, anthropology, interventionist art performance and the opening up of spaces for intersubjective encounters simultaneously characterizes *"The Machine to be Another"*. The members of "BeAnotherLab" explain that through their position as artists, they can work more swiftly and with greater improvisation than in a traditional research setting.

With the authors suggesting that their artistic interventions provoke specific changes in attitudes and bias, the project is subject to a contemporary public expectation of scientific validity. For this reason, "BeAnotherLab" flanks their interventions with qualitative research in the form of questionnaires and in-depth interviews with participants. Apart from empathy, participants were asked to answer a questionnaire concerning their feeling of presence[17] which is one of the prerequisites not only for a body-swap but also for a swap of mind and enhanced empathy. One experiment measured the sense of presence and the impact of feeling in-another-body in two groups with one group being confronted with a Second Life virtual tour without a real 'other' but represented with a computer-generated avatar. The other group was given the experience of *"The Machine to be Another"* and a 'real other' with whom they swapped bodies.

In both cases, the user-interactors were leaving 'their own' worlds and bodies and getting immersed in another reality. The key difference was that in the setting of the Second Life, there was only immersion through a first-person perspective and the exploration of a virtual space. Whereas, in *"The Machine to be Another"*, the experience included seeing another body through the first-person point of view. Questions regarding a sense of acting in the other person's body (rather than operating something from outside), awareness of one's own body, being captured by the body swap (mentally and affectively), and the realism of the experience were asked. The questions were measured on a 7-point Likert scale ranging from -3 ('I completely disagree') to +3 ('I completely agree'), with 0 corresponding to 'I neither agree nor disagree'. The evaluation of the data collected showed significant differences between the experience of *"The Machine to be Another"* and the virtual tour in the Second Life environment. As Oliviera et al. (2016) report, the setting of *"The Machine to be Another"* promoted high levels of presence (M = 1.80, SD = .62; compared to the Second Life experience which rated moderately in comparison (M = .21, SD = 1.37)).

However, not only did *"The Machine to be Another"* induce a high perception of presence, but participants stated that they "felt closer to the other person especially in the narrative step" (quoted in *ibid*, p. 85), that they were drawn to vis-à-vis their

---

[17] There exist various approaches to measure and evaluate presence in literature. Generally speaking, there are two kinds of approaches: objective and subjective approaches. Where the former are based on physiological data to *quantify* presence such as e.g. changes in skin conductance, heart rate and blood pressure, muscular tension, respiration rate and depth, as well as neurologic data (e.g. Lombard et al., 2009), the latter work qualitatively and try to survey subject opinions (e.g. Oliviera et al., 2016, p. 82).

virtual and even started fusing their self-perception and mental conceptualization with the other. Participants repeatedly reported it was confusing to be me and, at the same time not to be me!" (quoted in *ibid*, p. 85). This motivated the transdisciplinary team of "BeAnotherLab" to conclude that the configuration has a stimulating effect regarding empathy and mutual understanding. Further, that this empathy and mutual understanding occurred across cross-cultural differences, genders, and physical abilities.[18] Moreover, the participants reported not only a heightened awareness for the feelings and emotions of the *other*, but for their ability to access their own emotions as well. In fact, their sense of self was transformed.

This phenomenon which is called the 'Proteus Effect' (Bem, 1972) is based on "self-perception principles under which the individual explains his [sic!] attitudes and internal states based on observation of external cues" (Bertrand et al., 2018, p. 11). Listening to the stream of consciousness for example of Youssoupha, the young immigrant, while embodying his physicality, the user-interactor is induced to make implicit inferences about her/his own personal dispositions, of bringing back memories of similar (even if less distressful and menacing) experiences for example that she/he has already experienced. We have come a full circle. An awareness of self is a prerequisite for an awareness of the other. The eye and the body, the I and the Other are perceived in new, unfamiliar ways, and empower the imagination.

## Conclusion: (Im-)proper Distance, *Dis*immersion and the Issue of 'Making the Familiar Strange'

As such, with regard to a critical discussion of *"The Machine to be Another"*, one summarizing point should be made. Maybe it is not so much the *immersion* afforded by the configuration, but rather a form of dis-immersion that takes place which is a feeling of *ostranenie* or estrangement in the Brechtian sense which makes *"The Machine to be Another"* such an interesting configuration for theoretical and technical discussion. The encounter with a physical 'other', with the tactile sensations, and the HMD's 'enclosed' setting enhances a feeling of immersion. Immersion in this context comprises three dimensions: spatial, narrative and interactive.[19] In *"The Machine to be Another"*, all three dimensions achieve considerable results. Spatial immersion is achieved by the physical setting of the encounter, narrative immersion is achieved through the audio stream of consciousness, and the degree of agency

---

[18] For a detailed statistic evaluation, qualitative data and a critical discussion of the results of the experiment conducted by researchers from "BeAnotherLab", the Polytechnic School of the University of São Paulo, Paris Descartes, University of Valencia and University of Zürich, cf. Oliveira et al., 2016; Bertrand et al., 2013.

[19] Building on both the theoretical conceptualisations of presence and immersion drawing on the philosophical tradition of phenomenology and existentialism on the one hand and rather practical issues on the other as to the design of HCI, XR applications investigate how a 'sense of presence' is mediated by technologies. This has led to a rich output of empirically based immersion and presence studies by HCI designers, new media researchers and psychologists (cf. among others Young, 2007).

and interactive immersion is extremely high through the coordination of improvised movements.[20]All this results in a high degree of immersion and creates a bond between the participants. At the same time, this effect attracts attention to Nash's apprehensions about the moral risk of 'improper distance'.

Drawing on the work of Chouliaraki (2011), Nash describes this risk as "a form of ironic morality in which 'truths about ourselves' are elevated above the experiences of others" (Nash 2018, p. 120). In many non-fiction VR settings, the user-interactors start putting *their* feelings over those experienced by the protagonists of the 'story', a phenomenon known as contagion (cf. among others de Vignemont and Singer, 2006). User-interactors start confounding *their* emotions for those of *the other*[21].

In this context, Fuchs differentiates between three forms of empathy: primary, intercorporeal empathy, extended empathy ( empathy that is based on what one's self thinks that the other feels), and fictional empathy ( empathy with fictitious persons) (Fuchs 2014, p. 152). And indeed, one of the arguments for VR as an 'empathy machine' is that self-contained VR configurations tend to foster fictitious empathy—which is a rather shallow feeling in terms of a transformative moment—and which can even become abusive regarding the respect one should give to the other and their feelings.

*"The Machine to be Another"* is important because it moves beyond many other self-contained VR non-fiction experiences. The experience achieves its exemplary status by evoking a feeling of immersion and presence while simultaneously enabling self-reflexive experiences to bridge the gap between 'primary empathy' and 'extended empathy'. This self-reflexivity can be described as critical *dis*immersion (cf. Weidle, 2018), moments in which the user-interactors become aware that they are *different* from the other, though they perceptively swap bodies, and that they have *different* feelings, but are readily trying to feel *with* the other without imposing their own feelings. One can conclude that there are different dimensions of empathy here at play: reconstructive-cognitive, immediate-emotional, personal-individual, and social forms too.

In relation to emotional engagement, Ryan (2005) distinguishes three levels: an emotional reaction to 'the other' (such as sympathy, like, dislike etc.), the imagination of the emotions probably felt by 'the other' (empathy), and the emotions felt for one's self. As McRoberts notes, "VR has the ability to incorporate all three levels of emotional engagement, but the medium in its uniqueness approaches higher levels of presence as the second and third levels overlap" (2017, p. 109)—or to put it differently: these two levels in *The Machine to be Another* are co-present to alternating extents. It is this very paradox of immersion and disimmersion, empathy for the other and one's own emotions, that *"The Machine to be Another"* productively uses. The configuration subtly oscillates between different sets of feelings and

---

[20] For detailed data on the actual scores cf. Oliviera et al., 2016, Bertrand et al., 2013, BeAnotherLab, 2019.

[21] Though 'seeing through the eyes of someone else' as a visual illusion does not automatically imply seeing things and perceiving them exactly as the other one does despite the metaphorical usage of 'point of view' and 'perspective-taking'.

different impulses. The first set, is the one of bodily presence and sensations versus the virtuality of one's projected body on the other; the second set, is one's own experience and subsequent inner monologue versus/while listening to 'the other's' experiences and thoughts; and the third set, is the impulse to exert body agency and the need to coordinate one's movements with those of 'the other'.

One of the greatest potentials of XR experiences to be explored is that of playing with the oscillation of presence and distance, immersion and disimmersion, empathy and critical self-reflection. The ability to make the familiar strange, and the strange familiar at the same time, can promote a better understanding of not only 'the other' but of one's self.

## Put it Into Practice

Collect factors that enhance empathy. How can XR technology be used to enhance these factors?

- Take a concrete educational, medical, psychological or social situation or what you think of as an urgent issue, for example, immigration, racial conflict or climate change. Develop a protocol that enhances different dimensions of empathy with those concerned by the condition. When setting up the concept, keep key factors such as body ownership illusion, illusion of presence, agency illusion, visuo *tactile* and visuo *motor* synchronicity, familiarity and estrangement and others in mind.
- Which measures would you advise to be taken in addition to the VR/XR protocol so that emotional contagion and uncritical immersion are countered by critical disimmersion? How would you embed and contextualize the XR experience (e.g. by accompanying the experience with workshops etc.)?
- Can you imagine other contexts in which XR can stimulate artistic research?

Discuss:
- Can the Proteus effect be used to enhance feelings of compassion and altruism?
- Can a virtual body swap, including agency illusions and a first-person perspective and narrative, be used to induce self-attribution of compassionate actions targeting 'outgroup members' or 'strange others' (such as immigrants, and individuals from different socio-cultural backgrounds, for example)?

## References

BeAnotherLab (2019). The Machine to be Another. http://beanotherlab.org/home/work/tmtba/

Bem, D. (1972). Self-perception theory. pp. 1-62. *In:* L. Berkowitz (ed.). *Advances in Experimental Social Psychology.* Vol. 6. Academic Press, New York, USA.

Bertrand, P., Gonzalez-Franco, D., Cherene, C. and Pointeau, A. (2013). The Machine to Be Another: embodiment performance to promote empathy among individuals. Retrieved from https://pdfs.semanticscholar.org/3c49/68463c596f58d0915ff3013681752e263003. pdf.

Bertrand, P., Guegan, J., Robieux, L., McCall, C.A. and Zenasni, F. (2018). Learning Empathy Through Virtual Reality: Multiple Strategies for Training Empathy-Related Abilities Using Body Ownership Illusions in Embodied Virtual RealityVRFront. *Robot. AI*, 5, 1-18.

Bevan, C., Green, D.P., Farmer, H., Rose, M., Cater, K., Stanton Fraser, D. and Brown, H. (2019). Behind the Curtain of the 'Ultimate Empathy Machine': On the Composition of Virtual Reality Nonfiction Experiences Association for Computing Machinery. CHI Conference on Human Factors in Computing Systems. Glasgow: 1-12.

Born, G. and Barry, A. (2013). Art-Science: From public understanding to public experiment. pp. 247-272. *In:* A. Barry and G. Born (eds.). Interdisciplinarity. Routledge, London.

Chiao, J.Y. and Mathur, V.A. (2010). Intergroup empathy: how does race affect empathic neural responses? *Current Biology*. CB 20(11), R478-480.

Deleuze, G. and Guattari, F. (2011) [1980]. *A Thousand Plateaus: Capitalism and Schizophrenia.* Reprint. Continuum, London.

Chouliaraki, L. (2011). Improper distance: Towards a critical account of solidarity as irony. *International Journal of Cultural Studies*, 14(4), 363-381.

Decety, J. (2010). The neuro development of empathy in humans. *Developmental Neurosciences*, 32, 257-267.

Decety, J. and Meyer, M. (2008). From emotion resonance to empathic understanding: A social developmental neuroscience account. *Development and Psychopathology*, 20, 1053-1080.

Deleuze, G. 1988. *Le Bergsonisme.* Translated by H. Tomlinson and B. Habberjam. Zone Books, New York.

Ebert, R. (2005, June). Ebert's Walk of Fame remarks. https://www.rogerebert.com/roger-ebert/eberts-walk-of-fame-remarks

Farmer, H. (2019). A Broken Empathy Machine? Immerse. https://immerse.news/a-broken-empathy-machine-can-virtual-reality-increase-pro-social-behaviour-and-reduce-prejudice-cbcefb30525b.

Fisher, J.A. (2017). Empathic actualities: Toward a taxonomy of empathy in virtual reality. pp. 233-244. *In:* N.J. Nunes, I. Oakley and V. Nisi (eds.). *Interactive Storytelling.* Springer, Cham.

Fuchs, T. (2014). The Virtual Other: Empathy in the Age of Virtuality. *Journal of Consciousness Studies*, 21(5-6), 152-173.

Gallese, V. and Lakoff, G. (2005). The brain's concepts: The role of the sensory-motor system in conceptual knowledge. *Cognitive Neuropsychology*, 22(3), 455-479.

Huang, S.A. and Bailenson, J. (2019). Close relationships and virtual reality. pp. 49-65. *In:* T.D. Parsons, L. Lin and D. Cockerham (eds.). *Mind, Brain and Technology: Learning in the Age of Emerging Technologies.* Springer, Cham.

Latour, B. (1996). On actor-network-theory: A few clarifications and more than some complications. *Soziale Welt*, 47, 369-381.

Latour, B. and Woolgar, S. (1986). *Laboratory life: The Construction of Scientific Facts; with a New Postscript and Index by the Authors.* Princeton University Press, Princeton, New Jersey.

Layng, K., Perlin, K., Herscher, S., Brenner, C. and Meduri, T. (2019). CAVE: Making collective virtual narrative. *Leonardo*, 52(4), 349-356.

Lombard, M., Ditton, T. and Weinstein, L. (2009). Measuring presence: The temple presence inventory. *Proceedings of the 12th Annual International Workshop on Presence.* pp. 1-15.

Lévy, P. (1989). *Qu'est-ce que le virtuel?* La Découverte, Paris.

Magnor, M.A., Theobalt, C., Sorkine-Hornung, O. and Grau, O. (eds.) (2005). *Digital Representation of the Real World. How to Capture, Model, and Render Visual Reality.* Taylor and Francis, Hoboken.

Marks, L. (2002). *Touch: Sensuous Theory and Multisensory Media.* University of Minnesota Press, Minneapolis and London.

Maselli, A. and Slater, M. (2013). The building blocks of the full body ownership illusion. *Frontiers in Human Neuroscience*, 7, 1-15.

McRoberts, J. (2017). Are we there yet? Media content and sense of presence in non-fiction virtual reality VR. *Studies in Documentary Film*, 21(5), 101-118.

Milk, C. (2015). How virtual reality can create the ultimate empathy machine. TED talks. https://www.ted.com/talks/chris_milk_how_virtual_reality_can_create_the_ultimate_empathy_machine

Murray, J.H. (2012). *Inventing the Medium: Principles of Interaction Design as a Cultural Practice*. Cambridge, MIT Press.

Nash, K. (2018). Virtually real: Exploring VR documentary. *Studies in Documentary Film*, 12(2), 97-100.

Nowotny, H., Scott, P. and Gibbons, M. (2011). *Re-thinking Science: Knowledge and the Public in an Age of Uncertainty*. Polity Press, Cambridge.

Oliveira, E.C. de, Bertrand, P., Lesur, M.E.R., Palomo, P., Demarzo, M. and Cebolla, A. (2016). Virtual Body Swap: A New Feasible Tool to Be Explored in Health and Education. pp. 81-89. 18th Symposium on Virtual and Augmented IEEE.

Paradiso, J.A. and Landay, J.A. (2009). Guest editors' introduction: Cross-reality environments. *IEEE Pervasive Computing*, 8(3), 14-15.

Rose, M. (2018). The immersive turn: Hype and hope in the emergence of virtual reality as a nonfiction platform. *Studies in Documentary Film*, 12(2), 132-149.

Ryan, M.L. (2015). *Narrative as Virtual Reality 2: Revisiting Immersion and Interactivity in Literature and Electronic Media*. Johns Hopkins University Press, Baltimore, MA.

Singer, T. and McCall, C.A. (2013). Empathy and the brain. pp. 195-213. *In*: S. Baron-Cohen, H. Tager-Flusberg and M. Lombardo (eds.). *Understanding Other Minds: Perspectives from Developmental Social Neuroscience*. Third edition. Oxford University Press, Oxford.

Snow, C.P. (1959). *The Two Cultures*. Cambridge University Press, Cambridge.

Sutherland, A. (2015). The Limits of Virtual Reality: Debugging the Empathy Machine. MIT OpenDocumentaryLab 2015. http://docubase.mit.edu/lab/case-studies/the-limits-of-virtual-reality-debugging-the-empathy-machine/.

Sutherland, A. (2017). No, VR Doesn't Create Empathy. Here's Why. BuzzFeed News 2017. https://www.buzzfeed.com/ainsleysutherland/how-big-tech-helped-create-the-myth-of-the-virtual-reality?utm_term=.nc9bE2rYQ#.axmqVAw9B.

Suzuki, K., Garfinkel, S.N., Critchley, H.D. and Seth, A.K. (2013). Multisensory integration across exteroceptive and interoceptive domains modulates self-experience in the rubber-hand illusion. *Neuropsychologia*, 51, 2909-2917.

Tsakiris, M. (2017). The multisensory basis of the self: From body to identity to others. *Quarterly Journal of Experimental Psychology*, 70, 597-609.

Tsakiris, M., Schütz-Bosbach, S. and Gallagher, S. (2007). On agency and body-ownership: Phenomenological and neurocognitive reflections. *Consciousness and Cognition*, 16(3), 645-660.

Vignemont, F. de and Singer, T. (2006). The empathic brain: How, when and why? *Trends in Cognitive Sciences*, 10(10), 435-441.

Weidle, F. (2018). How to reconcile that flinch: Towards a critical analysis of documentary situations in 360° and VR environments. *Participations*, 13(1), 412-426.

Wiehl, A. (2020). What if me were another? Extended Realities, extended bodies and the challenge of extended empathy. pp. 231-245. *In*: J. Sieck et al. (eds.). *Kultur und Informatik—Extended Realities*. Werner Hülsbusch, Glückstadt.

Youngblut, C. (2007). What a Decade of Experiments Reveals about Factors that Influence the Sense of Presence: Latest Findings. Institute for Defense Analyses, Virginia.

# The PARIS Model: Creating a Sustainable and Participatory Civic Media with and for the Community through Immersive Experiences

**Yonty Friesem**

33 E. Ida B. Wells Dr. Chicago, Il 60605
Email: yfriesem@colum.edu

## Introduction

In the summer of 2015 at the Museum of the Moving Image in New York City, I walked through an exhibition called Sensory Stories that showcased new narrative experiences. As I put on the Oculus Quest and the headphones, I witnessed the 360 degree experience of an abstract animated story, "*Evolution of Verse*" (Milk, 2015), an interactive game called "*Way-to-Go*" (Morisset, 2014), and the documentary *Herders* (Lajeunesse and Raphael, 2014) about Mongolian peasants in the mountains. This experience introduced me to the power of Virtual Reality (VR) as an immersive experience that takes your sensory senses and stretches your perception of reality. However, these three videos did not prepare me for the emotional experience of "*Clouds Over Sidra*" (Milk and Arora, 2015), a short VR movie that follows a day in the life of a young Syrian refugee girl. The audience has a glance at Sidra's routine at The Za'atari Refugee Camp in Jordan as she eats with her family, visits the bakery, visits the computer lab inside a large container converted into a classroom, plays football with her friends and goes back to sleep in her tent. Born and raised in Israel, this was the closest I had been to visiting a Syrian refugee camp. Although the video lasted for less than 9 minutes, the impression of this immersive experience is vivid in my mind and heart five years later. As my Israeli friends and I stepped out of the museum into the hot and humid streets of Queens, I was still under the influence of this sensational experience. And yet, I was not certain if I actually learned anything new about the lives of the refugees at the Za'atari Camp or Sidra. There was no mention about what happened to Sidra after the 2013 filming. At the end of the day, this experience did not change my way of understanding Syrian refugees living in a camp in Jordan.

**Figure 3.1:** Sensory Stories exhibition on the Museum of the Moving Image webpage

*"Clouds Over Sidra"* co-director, Chris Milk (2015) offered a TedTalk showcasing VR as the ultimate empathy machine. Milk claims that by using VR the audience can feel and empathize in a deeper way, and that VR filmmakers can change its minds with this machine. With the endorsement of the United Nations, World Economic Forum in Davos, the film successfully raised 3.8 billion US dollars for Syrian refugee education. Further, Secretary-General Ban Ki-Moon experienced the humanitarian need and recognized that more donations were necessary to support the Syrian refugees (United Nations Virtual Reality, N.D.). In addition, Bujić, Salminen, Macey, and Hamari (2020) found that immersive journalism can positively change attitudes toward human rights. They address the misinterpretation of the term *empathy machine* caused by the criticism of the use of VR for inducing the emotion. Bujić and his colleagues highlight the effectiveness of using VR to better relate to others and change attitudes.

As a civic media educator, I argue that the powerful tool of immersive media can be used for causes way beyond a change of attitude and fundraising. Instead, the media can be used to address issues of social justice as part of a sustainable participatory process of co-design. Unlike the premise of VR as a simulated environment, Augmented and Mixed Reality (AR/MR) offer a more complex and therefore more genuine experience for users mediating between their reality and a digital augmentation. This is why civic media practices align better with AR/MR which elicit a genuine empathic response that addresses a community's needs as opposed to the emphatic concern generated by sympathy used in an exploitative way by VR creators. Civic media frameworks support the scaffolding process of media literacy in a participatory way by which the community is fully included and equal in the co-production process. Using digital media such as AR/MR promotes a greater empathic effect and contributes to the fight for social justice.

## The Digital Empathy Oxymoron

The term empathy has evolved over the years starting with ancient Greek perception of emotional connection up to its modern re-introduction by Robert Vischer's 1873 German interpretation of imagining yourself *"feeling into"*. Currently, many in the field of psychology use dichotomous evaluations of cognitive empathy as the ability to understand and predict behavior and emotions vs emotional empathy as the ability to sense others' feelings. Batson's (2009) division into eight related but distinct phenomena helps demystify this complex human experience of knowing or feeling another person's state of mind and what leads to sensitivity and care.

- Cognitive Empathy (Empathic accuracy) – Knowing what another person thinks or feels.
- Facial Empathy – Adopting the physical/neural responses of an observed other.
- Affective Empathy (Emotional contagious) – Coming to feel as another person feels.
- Aesthetic Empathy – Projecting oneself into another's situation.
- Psychological Empathy (Perspective-taking) – Imagining how another person thinks or feels.
- Projective Empathy – Role-playing how one would think and feel
- Empathic Distress – Feeling distress at witnessing another person's suffering
- Empathic Concern (sympathy) – Feeling for another person who is suffering

This taxonomy is helpful to better understand how Milk, Arora and the enthusiastic policy-makers in Davos perceive *Clouds Over Sidra* as an empathic experience while others called out the exploitations of the Syrian refugee girl for humanitarian fundraising (Irom, 2018, Sutherland, 2017).

Gabo Arora, the co-director of *Clouds Over Sidra*, claims that "empathy is a catalyst for action" (Traldi, 2017, Para 6) and he thinks that immersive storytelling

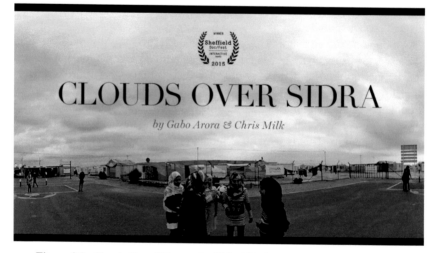

**Figure 3.2:** *Clouds Over Sidra* on the United Nations Virtual Reality's webpage

can help decision-making based on facts in an empathic way. I do not disagree. What is missing in the marketing and distribution of the VR experience of *Clouds Over Sidra* is not the voice of Sidra that narrates the short video, but her agency. As I researched data on the video and interviews of the filmmakers, I could not find any data about Sidra, whether she was part of the production process or how she was even chosen. It was disappointing that she may never have learned about the impact that her story has had. However, the most concerning thing was that I could not find any information on where she is now, or even if she is alive and well.

The basic ethics of research and journalism do not seem to be applied to the two filmmakers calling their work an empathy machine. One of the most notoriously known acts of exploitation is the famous photo of the "Migrant Mother" taken by photographer Dorothea Lange during the great depression in 1936. The subject of the photo, Florence Owens Thompson, expanded in a letter how she felt exploited forty two years earlier (Pruitt, 2020). While the filmmakers designed their creation to evoke sympathy of the audience toward their movie subjects, there is no evidence that their process demonstrated empathy toward their human participants.

While some might be looking at the effects of *Cloud Over Sidra* as empathic concerns and maybe aesthetic psychological and projective empathy, they miss what Segal (2011) calls social empathy. The lack of a courageous decolonizing lens prevents the VR experience from becoming a holistic empathic experience beyond the sensory, cognitive and emotional response to the short video that may result in a donation or policy change (Nash, 2018). This does not undermine the value of donations and policy changes that are welcome and needed. On the contrary, Segal's call for empathic action is also self-reflective and social justice oriented.

Empathy in all its various definitions and usages is about human connection. While digital media can advance communication it also can create miscommunication or oppression through mediation. I have tried previously to bridge this oxymoron (Friesem, 2016) using the concept of digital empathy for media production, but I have realized that the range of definitions for empathy creates misconceptions about how to use empathy with digital media. Historically storytelling uses empathy to impact audiences. The tradition of telling a narrative, and immersing the audience in a human experience they did not have, goes back to the inception of culture. Storytelling allows humans to experience what they might not be able to, or cannot, or have not yet been through. Consuming narratives allows us to learn about other cultures, examining one's own opinions and emotions as well as debate moral dilemmas. However, as Fisher (2017) explains it, immersive media successfully embrace an almost "real live experience" that promotes the cognitive and emotional empathy along with sympathy toward the characters. This cognitive and emotional experience is more a projective and psychological empathy according to Batson (2009) than a real human connection—what Segal (2011) calls social empathy. Irom (2018) analyzed the representations of refugees in *Cloud Over Sidra* and finds that the voice over and story eventually reinforce gender roles. Further, the experience acts as if time, history and movement do not exist off screen. This problematic representation contributes to the suppression of the real world as it immerses the audience in a narrow and constructed reality (Fisher, 2017).

To go beyond the superficial empathetic experience of VR, like in the case of *Clouds Over Sidra*, an immersive experience must be truly empathic and courageous, produced through an equitable participatory process. AR/MR offers an immersive experience that requires one to reconstruct the experience of reality with the added digital platform but situated within a physical environment. This reflective practice includes cognitive, emotional, sensory and kinetic aspects that can get the audience one step further into a holistic empathic experience. The user is grounded in a liminal space between both a digital and physical reality: the former controlled by the whims of producers and the latter by forces outside the producers' control. The media ecologist, Marshall McLuhan (1964) said that the medium is the message, arguing that each medium has its characteristics and therefore impacts the audience differently. Following that logic, AR/MR offer the audience an immersive experience that, unlike VR, situates them within the real world. This is a crucial difference in the immersive media and produces a different empathic experience. While VR immerses you completely into a projected world, AR/MR offers users an opportunity to cognitively, emotionally, sensationally and kinetically bridge between real spaces in communities and their digital augmentations (Sharma, Alharthi, Dolgov and Toups, 2017).

Genuine and holistic empathic experience occurs when Batson's (2009) characteristics are activated all together with Segal's (2011) social action as a compassionate and courageous process toward social justice. Empathy as a human connection has to be reciprocal to avoid oppression. If media producers want to use digital tools such as immersive media to evoke empathy, they need to remember to reflect on their position, one that might be patronizing toward their participants and audiences. Empathy is based on the ability to listen and embrace another person's state of mind and experience. This includes the participants of the production and the audience. Whereas the US media industry is based on individualistic rewards and acknowledgement, digital empathy calls for a more participatory approach.

## Designing a Participatory Immersive Production

By engaging the community members in an equal process of research, design, production, editing and distribution, the immersive experience creates digital empathy via the media and not just a superficial sympathetic response for audience catharsis but encompass the social, cognitive, and emotional aspects all together as a digital experience. Participatory design according to Devisch, Huybrechts, De Ridder and Martens (2018) is a collaborative effort to redistribute political and economic power through "a never-ending process of making public new marginalized aspirations and needs" (p.3). They state that media can be useful in order to gather a collective guide through the process and make sure it is sustainable "on the condition that they (the media) are open enough to allow for collective experimentation" (p. 7).

McLuhan (1964) argues that consuming and analyzing media is not enough to be media literate. Especially today as a digital citizen, as Rushkoff (2010) modified the idea to the digital era, you choose to either program or be programmed. Although immersive media more than traditional TV or radio consumption is a whole sensory

**Figure 3.3:** *Project Portland* (Designed by Cameron Collis in 2019 as a speculative project)

experience, the audience is led by the designers of the media and the message. While the user can move and have various decisions about how to proceed with the narrative, these limited options have been designed and coded by someone else. For example, Collins (2019) offers on his professional website a speculative design project he calls *Project Portland*. This suggested immersive experience would have the user help the city to reimagine its public spaces using AR mobile technology. As the user navigates the map of Portland and captures video of the real public space they have the decision to add a tree, a bench, a playground, etc. However, they cannot choose to comment or to suddenly add a feature that is not included in Collins' app. This experience would allow the audience to contribute to public discourse about the redesign of Portland public spaces, but as community members, this does not help them address their own issue.

Decolonizing the use of immersive media for community engagement can come in the form of a participatory design. The idea of working with a community instead of working for a community has been a contentious debate, especially in the humanitarian field (Gregory, 2016). On one hand, the effectiveness of immersive media for raising money for humanitarian causes has been proven to be highly effective, e.g. *Cloud over Sidra*. On the other hand, members of the community that participate in the production of the immersive media often do not benefit from the fundraising, and more so, their social issues in the community are not resolved (Gregory, 2016). Participatory design can help media producers to work with the community to first assess the needs, co-design a prototype and test it, co-produce and edit the media, and lastly decide collaboratively how to distribute the media. Patronizing community members and their social issues by producing for them will not solve social issues, but rather reinforce the inequalities.

Design processes such as Human-Centered Design (HCD) developed by IDEO.org as well as the Design Thinking model by Stanford University's d.school position empathy at the beginning of the design thinking process. Prioritizing listening to a target audience is crucial to develop a product that will benefit the audience. However, the model is used for commercial intent and economic profit. Empathy is exploited to provide a customized experience that persuades an audience to buy a product. One example is the beautifully designed work of Isobar.com that helps commercial companies use immersive media to connect with their consumers' needs. While they refer to it as augmented humanity (CMO.com, 2019), their higher-ed design products are made with state-of-the-art equipment and professional immersive media designers, and not as part of a participatory work.

In an effort to revisit the model of design thinking, David Clifford (2017) and Stanford's d.school built a framework where the beginning of the process included the practice of noticing and, at the end, a reflection. The HCD process of design thinking is moving between two major processes where researchers begin with noticing and then move toward the regular design thinking process as researchers reflect on the process. Similarly, Stanton, Kramer, Gordon, and Valdez (2016) offer an additional decolonizing process to include with reflection, contextualizing, and democratizing as part of the empathic stage prior to defining, ideating, prototyping and testing.

Notwithstanding the challenges of group dynamics and working as a team with multiple community members on a project, democratizing the process of making immersive media with a community is the only way to genuinely become an empathy machine with the potential for being a social justice machine. In the example of *WRLDCRAFT BLOCKS LEGENDS* (Castro, 2019) users can see how participatory

**Figure 3.4:** *Wrldcraft Blocks Legends* (Developed by Alfio Lo Castro in 2019)

action research with various players creating a community are redesigning spaces anywhere on earth with what looks like real world scale Minecraft blocks. The immersive experience allows the audience to collaborate around the globe in an attempt to use the AR experience to add digital augmentation to the visual space on their mobile device. The purpose of the application is to design and build AR experiences. At the same time it can be used as a participatory action research tool where each one of the users can add Minecraft objects to test alternative structures in real spaces inside or outside. Furthermore, this immersive experience was designed by a professional developer, Alfio Lo Castro and can be played by anyone who downloads the application and contributes their own digital and augmented structures and designs.

One example of a genuine immersive media working to drive social change is Skwarek (2011) AR Occupy Wall Street. The AR experience allows the user to digitally add a protestor or art to the reality on mobile devices. Skwarek, the founding director of New York University's Mobile Augmented Reality Lab, created the app in 2011 as part of the Occupy Wall Street movement when police did not allow protesters to get near the New York Stock Exchange. He filmed protesters and had their digital representations be augmented near the buildings. In similar political works, Skwarek uses AR to challenge the perception of borders, for example erasing all elements of the border between North and South Korea, or Palestine and Israel.

Unlike the commercial process of designing an immersive experience using models of HCD, the design process of a community co-produced media should add a learning curve for the non-professional media producers. Professional producers have experience and knowledge of their craft where they can directly dive into the design process. When working with community members in order to co-design, the whole participatory process should include educational aspects that benefit the community participants as well as the finished product. While some professional media producers might find it burdensome, this is the only democratic and non-patronizing path to take if they genuinely come to the community to listen, empathize and offer their support.

## Media Literacy Practices along Participatory Design

Hobbs (2021) defines media literacy as the ability to access information, analyze and evaluate media messages, create your own media, reflect on your consumption, and be socially responsible when using media. Working with community members, all five competencies (access, analyze and evaluate, create, reflect and act) are part of the co-design process of a participatory immersive media production. Table 3.1 aligns the media production process with HCD and media literacy competencies. Each competency is part of a practice to learn to be more digital and media literate. In the following section, I provide examples for each competency and practice and how to incorporate them into the participatory design and co-production process.

**Table 3.1:** Aligning the production process with design thinking and media literacy

| Production Process | Design Thinking | Media Literacy |
|---|---|---|
| Research | Note | Access |
| | Empathize | |
| Design | Define | Analyze and evaluate |
| | Ideate | |
| Pre-production | Prototype | Create |
| | Test | |
| Production | | |
| Post-Production | Reflect | Reflect |
| Distribution | | Act |

Note: Revised HCD and Design Thinking (Clifford, 2017); Media Literacy Competencies (Hobbs, 2021).

## Access

Learning about the multidimensions of accessibility is the gateway for community members toward a more inclusive community. With rising concerns about misinformation, accessibility in media literacy refers to not only the physical access to media, but also to the validation of information and assessment of its accuracy. When working on a participatory design project within the community, the process of data accuracy and availability of tools to research, design, produce and distribute are critical to the lives of the community members. While immersive media allow cell phones to download an application and start the experience, the co-producers should inquire and test the various requirements of cellular data, devices, operating systems, and user experience as part of the research on accessibly. Social change can be done with informed citizens who can access the tools they need to drive the social change in their communities.

When designing an immersive experience, the issues of accessibility include two different practices. First, a responsive design that allows for all community members and users to be able to use the app. Part of this inclusion is the ability of community members to join the design process, and as a form of crowdsourcing, contribute to the way the immersive media will be produced and distributed (Foth et al., 2013). Second, the community action research looks for accurate information about the social issue that the community wants to address. Since many commercial immersive media do not address the needs of a community, community members can help validate relevant information and provide access to their own needs (Antognoli, 2021). For example, in Taos, New Mexico a 6th grade class did research with the local homeless shelter to better understand what it means to be homeless in Taos. The kids raised awareness to support the shelter with a series of three podcasts that included interviews with the Mayor, local journalists, social workers and people at the homeless shelter. The students not only provide access to all community members including young kids to learn about homelessness in Taos, but they also learn to validate the information and strategically use reliable data to inform the community.

## Analyze and Evaluate

The process of deconstructing media messages is inspired by the Marxist claim that liberation comes by uncovering the mechanics of production. Therefore, learning to analyze media messages and evaluate their purpose, values, agenda, biases, interpretations, and omissions reveals the ideologies and techniques to reinforce them. A community project should look into both external and internal forces and how they use ideology via the media to maintain their power. Working on a participatory design to address a social issue will evoke a response from people and institutions who want to maintain the status quo. Being informed about the various rhetorical uses of media can help address social issues as the community members co-design their immersive media (Fisher, 2019).

In the case of immersive media, the analysis and evaluation can come as part of the research and design as well as part of the immersive experience. As we discuss social issues of the community, members of the community will look into the information about the issue and will need to determine what is relevant, what was done before to fight the status quo and what was successful or not. As described in Healey's (2021) chapter of this book, immersive media can be used as a source of analysis and evaluation to better understand the complexity of a problem. Healey's rubric provides a better sense of ethical considerations and offers a better-informed discussion in the issue the community wants to address. It also leads the way toward a more sustainable solution based on community members analysis and evaluation.

## Create

As the core of the participatory design is to co-produce the immersive media, the community members need to learn to be part of the creation. The main competency of creation is the ability to convey your message effectively to a specific target audience. Identifying the audience and the intended impact is the first step to plan the creation. As the community members learn the production techniques, they can choose to take a role and its responsibilities. Not all roles in a media production demand technical skill by being the script writer, director, actor, producer, distributor, etc. Immersive media has many roles beyond coders, cinematographers and editors. Looking at the end goal of driving social change in the specific community can support the diverse, equal, and inclusive process of co-creating the media.

As mentioned by Murray and Johnson (2021) in another chapter of this book, readers can see the challenges of having non-professional designers create immersive media. While there is a lack of options currently to design immersive media by non-professionals, there are some opportunities to collaboratively develop media that will address various needs of the community. One example is CoSpaces EDU (Delightex, 2016) that provides an online platform for kids to design their own immersive media collaboratively. The students choose their space and characters, then design it and create scenes that the audience can move through. The affordances of the platform allow the educators to focus on educational purposes of creating an immersive scene. Metaverse (GoMeta, 2016) is a free AR platform where any community member can create their own scavenger hunt, quizzes, or augmented pictures. These educational platforms are encouraging more educators and community leaders to use immersive media for non-commercial purposes.

**Figure 3.5:** *CoSpaces EDU* (Developed by Delightex in 2016)

## Reflect

Digital media has become a major component of daily life and it is vital to be able to stop and examine its intended and unintended effect. Many times, the planned goal is not the actual outcome. While many factors impact the process and the final results, it is always important to reflect on the process. Reflection can include many practices ranging from written self-reflection to videotaped peer feedback. It allows us to halt the action in order to observe what was the initial aim of the message, how it was produced and delivered and what is the tangible result. The idea of reflecting in a participatory design is to allow various voices to be heard in order to modify the process and product. This democratic practice of group evaluation along the production process teaches about the ways in which each member of the group can share their interpretations of the trajectory of the process and the anticipated product.

Hidalgo (2015) describes the way immersive media can be helpful to have community members reflect as part of what she defines as augment scholarship: "a collaborative process between researchers and oppressed communities to produce alternative narratives and reveal erased histories using AR to inform, educate, raise public consciousness, elicit community action, and social change, thus bridging the gap between communities and academia" (p. 301). Having a collaborative work to allow for each community member to tell their stories and narrative uses their

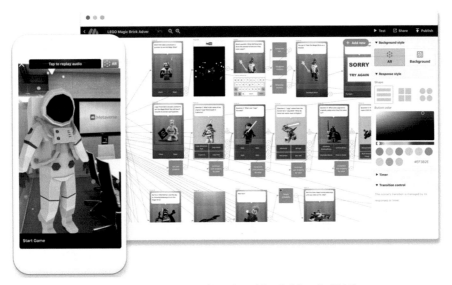

**Figure 3.6:** *Metaverse* (Developed by GoMeta in 2016)

reflection as part of the immersive experience to address issues of social justice. As Wiehl (2021) describes in her chapter in this book, immersive media should provide a place to reflect on the mind-body empathic experience. The complex experience of VR/XR between the reality and the digital additions needs to allow the user the possibility to reflect on their own participation. An effective way to use simple practice of reflection with media is by applying peer feedback that is based on empathic exchanges (Friesem and Greene, 2020). The one who provides feedback is using first person and their own perspective to summarize, praise, suggest and inquire. With immersive media, this four-sentence feedback can be done digitally as a collaborative exchange.

**Figure 3.7:** Peer Empathic Feedback

## Act

The last practice of media literacy is to actively be socially responsible. The practice ranges from being mindful of sharing online information, representing diverse voices, or producing media to drive social change. Along the whole production process being socially responsible means to be inclusive and respectful of multiple voices. As a participatory project, the community members are part of the decision-making in every step from the research, design, production and especially the distribution. How the message is going to be delivered usually depends on the media and the traditional conduit to channel the message to its target audience. This practice of media literacy action is challenging the traditional practices of sharing media to allow the community members to be part of the process to not only determine the distribution but also to contribute. With cellular usage and social media each community member is their own distributor. However, the community members should also be attentive as they consider the digital economics of free labor and the monetization of social media with their own content (Duffy, 2017).

Samuels and Ramirez (2021) portray in their chapter in this book, how the National Youth Art Movement Against Gun Violence with teenagers from Chicago used an immersive experience as a public intervention for gun violence. In 16 locations across the city youth created murals that portray their civic art against gun violence. Using the Vamonde app, each mural came to life with augmented digital features to raise awareness of gun violence. The adolescents not only learn to access, analyze, evaluate, create and reflect, but they take it a step further by actively engaging in civic and public discourse on a vital issue in the community. Whereas media literacy offers the various practices to ensure the learning of community members along the participatory design process, it is also beneficial to look at civic media principles to ensure the diversity, equity and inclusion of the process and its outcomes.

## Civic Media Principles for Participatory Designers

Civic media as a framework can help to apply media literacy practices within a participatory design of an immersive media with the community. According to Jenkins (2007), civic media is "any use of any medium which fosters or enhances civic engagement" (Para 4). For the purpose of this chapter, civic media is defined as the participatory process in which community members collaboratively research, design, produce, and distribute immersive media to drive social change for their community. The immersive media can be used only within the community to address a specific social issue. At the same time, it can also target a larger audience to influence policy change or create societal awareness. Civic and community engagement have many shapes and forms, but the work of Ersoy (2017) suggests a model of co-production that allows community engagement to fight for social justice. The civic part of the media co-produced by the community is where there is a place for diversity, equity and inclusion of multiple opinions and control over the process and product.

In a professional production of immersive media, the producers have not only the control over the format, content, distribution and access, but also the prior professional

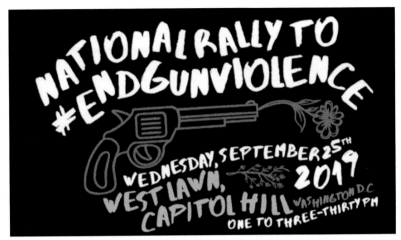

**Figure 3.8:** Youth Art Movement Against Gun Violence

knowledge to exclude ideas and contributions from community members. In order to ensure the democratic and sustainable process benefits the community, five civic media principles can be helpful. While media literacy practices help us better understand the guidelines, these civic media principles help us frame the values and ethics of working collaboratively with a community. I developed the PARIS model with the five civic media principles as I examined the work of my graduate students with five vulnerable communities in Chicago during the COVID-19 pandemic. The following section introduces each principle along with a leading question to guide the journey of professional media producers working with the community.

## How Do You Share the Control Over the Format, Content and Distribution?

*Participatory*

As stated in the chapter, the most important factor of working with a community is being with the community as a partnership with its members and not just for the community. While we know where we can get with well-meaning intentions, only an inclusive and equitable process that invites diverse voices from within the community will really serve the community. The prior knowledge of the professionals will get producers as far as the technicalities but will not allow us to know what the history is, causes are, and current internal and external forces are part of the social problem to address. Unlike the sense of empowerment where producers would control the format, content and distribution, the participatory process of civic media promotes the equity of control by the collective of the community and the external producers. Social justice challenges the status quo by revealing the structural power that prevents change. The participatory process, as difficult as it might be, needs to be transparent and open to changes to support the same ethics as it preaches to others (Devisch, Huybrechts, De Ridder and Martens, 2018).

Although Khan and Loke (2017) provide many examples of participatory methods to create collaboratively immersive media, they also acknowledge the challenges and barriers to be genuinely inclusive. One of these examples is the work of the NGO Project for Public Spaces that promoted the project to reshape cities such as Baltimore, San Antonio, Denver, and NYC. By having community members participate in a challenge to map changes in public space, together the community was able to visualize how it could look. While the immersive media can intimidate participants that feel a lack of confidence in their coding and design abilities, being participatory is about sharing ideas and being inclusive, not about having everyone code. The strength of diversity is in the different skills and opinions that each individual brings to the table, and not having everyone do the same part. The idea of participatory design and participatory action research is just like team work where everyone shares the goal but contributes in different ways.

## How Do You Include and Invite Others to Produce and Use the Media?

*Accessible*

Inclusion in the media and process of production ranges from understanding universal design, responsive design and enabling any user to consume the media no matter their barriers. The participatory process needs to be open and available to any community members who want to join. Issues of inclusion are not only about having physical access, but also about having the skills, usages, and motivation (Van Dijk, 2020). Related to the questions of control and the practice of being participatory, there needs to be an open dialogue that is inviting and is open to hearing what barriers exist in the community project. After all, the community is a co-producer of the experience. Being inclusive is about not letting biases and assumptions lead the research, design, production and distribution. Shared responsibility and open dialogue are key to commitments to the accessibility of the community.

Thevin et al. (2019) showcase how a participatory action research of people with visual impairments helped develop an immersive technology that would allow them to draw digitally with the movement of their fingers as if they were holding a paintbrush. The five integrations allowed the participants to be included in the design, and to implement a tool that would benefit them by providing more access. This work addresses the two parts of inclusion: being included in the research, design, production and distribution as well as having responsive media for any user to access. When looking to create an immersive experience, including diverse voices is the only way to ensure an effective responsive design. Genuine accessibility is achieved through both the making process and the eventual usage.

## How Do You Keep Yourself Accountable?

*Reflective*

Having a process that lets participants reflect on their experience increases accountability. If goals are set to reach a certain social change in the community, then along the process there needs to be a way to keep track of how it is reached, whether it proceeds toward that goal, and if there are any modifications needed. Holding these tenets, all participants during the process of research, design, production and distribution will ensure alignment with the intended goal. This is the third principle since it is built upon the principles of participatory culture and accessibility that allow the participants to reflect and share their thoughts, concerns and ideas through the process. Since immersive media is a community-based project for and with the community, its producers should be held accountable for and by the community.

Immersive media offer many ways to reflect on its usage to ensure the accountability of its purpose. *Building Bridges* is a digital board game where LGBTQIA+ seniors and youth play together as part of a reflection on their identity. Strauss and Arena (2020) designed the game after going through a participatory action research with the members of the LGBTQIA+ community. While going through various iterations as part of their practicum of the MA in Civic Media at Columbia College Chicago, they received a lot of feedback and changed platforms to make the game more accessible. As they worked on the design with their participants, they realized that participants wanted a place to reflect during the game that encouraged intergenerational dialogue on issues of the LGBTQIA+ community. And so, the reflection in their project was two-fold: reflection to modify the creation process and offering various places of reflection for users during the game. One of the most powerful examples is the exhibition #NoKidsinPrison (Performing Statistics, 2018) that uses a large space with immersive media to introduce an audience to the disproportionate amount of black kids who are sentenced to jail. As the audience travels through the various immersive experiences they have the ability to reflect on using art as they learn about youth incarceration. The exhibition ends in a large space where the audience is welcome to reflect on their ideas on how to invest in community

**Figure 3.9:** #NoKidsinPrison exhibition by Performing Statistics (2018)

youth. The project was a participatory design effort that involved multiple voices of young people impacted by the youth justice system.

## What is Your Intended and Unintended Change?

*Impactful*

It is important to remember that the creation of the immersive media with the community is designed to bring social change and address a specific issue. Designing and producing media is a pleasurable and demanding task for those who take part in it. This is why the practicality of its use should be in the core of the process. Following the process of participatory action research to find the issue together with the community members, that goal is the beacon of the project while remembering to be inclusive and reflective to allow this goal to be achieved. The challenges of a production always hinder the theoretical end goal. Therefore, when deciding on the intended change in the community, the co-designers and co-producers should not only consider the practicality of the immersive media but its unintended effects.

**City Tech Collaborative**
@CityTech_

For youth, by youth, yes! Read up on the #expungeio youth-led design session we led in June bit.ly/1Mv2HCQ

**Sonja Marziano** @ssmarziano · Nov 11, 2015

Today, @MCJJustice visited @Literacenter to film messages about Expunge.io from youth to youth. We had so much fun!

10:08 AM · Nov 12, 2015 · Twitter Web Client

**Figure 3.10:** Expunge.oi by Mikva Challenge (2014)

Augmented reality can be highly impactful like in the case of Indian PM Modi that had used AR to appear in simultaneous rallies during election year (Nelson, 2014). But the impact was more about his campaign messaging, while according to Nelson sole viewers were disappointed when Modi's hologram disappeared and they recognized that he was not really there. And so, impact is not about persuading the masses using immersive media, but rather together with the community members to make the intended social change. In 2013, the Knight Foundation gave $35,000 to build a prototype of an interactive digital platform that would engage young adults to expunge their juvenile records. With over 8,000 hits and a growing interest in how a digital platform could better reduce recidivism in Cook County, Illinois, the state legislature decided in 2014 to pass a bill that implemented auto-expungement state-wide (Mikva Challenge, 2014). In Chicago, 17,000 records have been expunged per year since the bill was passed. The digital platform impacted the legislation and reversed the lack of engagement by young adults to expunge their juvenile records.

## What Measures Do You Take to Keep the Project Relevant without Your Involvement?

*Sustainable*

The last civic media principle is also the most difficult one to achieve. In a world of foundation money that provides for a one-time project and the declining support for non-for-profit organizations, it is almost impossible to ensure the sustainability of a project. It is hard to keep the media updated and maintain constant improvements of platforms when the technology changes constantly. This is why the principle of sustainability is not so much about if the project will survive the next software update or budget cut, but rather the intention to set up mutual responsibility where multiple people can continue the endeavor. The design of the process and product should look at the collaborative aspect beyond the process of research, design, production, and distribution. Going back to the previous principles, sustainability continues the logic where the process is participatory, everyone has access and can reflect on the intended impact while planning on keeping the work alive until the social change has been achieved.

It is very difficult to keep an immersive project running for years. Most of the social justice oriented projects that use immersive media are funded by grants for a limited time and once the grant ends the updates to software stop and therefore the media cease to work. In summer 2019, Facebook opened its SparkAR platform for any user to use various ways of augmented reality with their account. While the new feature provides more accessibility to use and design your own AR, it also continues Facebook's problematic use of data for its company profit not to mention the lack of participatory design of its users. As part of the response of Seattle Design festival in summer 2020 to BlackLivesMatter protests and the COVID-19 pandemic, they offered residents to download the application named *Amp'Up Seattle*. The AR experience allowed users to see augmented art at eight locations in the city that represent the "art that is gone" (Vansynghel, 2020, para 4). Although people practiced physical distancing because of the pandemic and the protests were still ongoing, the application is on the personal device that allows for a collective memory to be sustainable through the discovery of the protests through the augmented view.

**Figure 3.11:** *Amp'Up Seattle* by Seattle Design Festival (2020)

The PARIS (participatory, access, reflection, impact, and suitability) model of civic media offers a framework that ensures the decolonizing of the research, design, production and distribution process as professional producers work with community members. As stated before, making the process inclusive, equitable and diverse is very challenging, especially if the desire is to produce professional immersive media. Unlike the professional process, the goal of working with the community toward social justice is to make social change and challenge the status quo. Applying the media industry hierarchical production models and practices perpetuate the inequalities and disparities that the project aims to fight against.

At this moment, there are not many immersive media that have been produced as part of a community-participatory design to address social issues. There are many examples of professional producers of immersive media that work for the community and provide services to the community. However, having a slick media that was done for the community and not with the community can have successful short-term effects such as fundraising, but does not provide a long-lasting and sustainable path toward social justice. The limitations of budgeting, proficiency of design and production, group dynamics, and the actual fight with external and internal powers that want to keep the status quo, prevent most genuine participatory media production from failing. It is my hope that this chapter provides clear and feasible guidelines of the practices (of media literacy) and the principles (of civic media) to make the production of an immersive experience sustainable as part of a participatory experience with a community.

## Sustainable Impact of Immersive Media

In recent years, more calls for diversity, equity and inclusion influence the media industry. Some creators of immersive experiences are making superficial changes to pay lip service and claim that they are inclusive, empathetic to their audience and want social change. But only grassroots production powered by the community members will provide genuinely space for diversity, equity, and inclusion to drive social justice. If the authentic goal of a community-based immersive media is to work with and for the community, being open and inclusive to diverse voices is the way toward a deep and sustainable change. This is not a magic wand. It takes resources that are beyond a financial commitment. The challenge of fighting the status quo has a personal price that not everyone is ready to pay. The invitation to participate in a participatory process toward social justice, should include the terms of personal commitment to ensure that everyone is heard and acknowledged. Then, the practice of constant reflection will keep all involved accountable as the process progresses.

Reality keeps changing, people evolve, and so does the technology. The ability to adapt and modify as a group can allow sustainable impact with and for the community. Future research should examine the level of community engagement and social impact on the participants rather than looking at the level of empathy of the spectators. In order to use immersive media with and for the community, co-creators should embark on a genuine, non-patronizing, transparent and fully collaborative endeavor with their participants. This is a challenging task since collaboration occurs with the professional producers and the community members as together they co-research, co-design, co-produce, and co-distribute.

I want to circle back to the problematic rhetoric of immersive media as an empathy machine. In his TedTalk, Milk (2015) proudly explained how screening *Clouds Over Sidra* helped policy-makers who attended the Economic Forum in Davos, Switzerland to change the lives of the people in the film from the Syrian Refugee camp in Lebanon like Sidra. Milk's enthusiasm for the VR machine to enhance human connection is omitting the agency of his film's subjects. If media producers are truly empathetic to the humans they work with, their participants should have a say in the research, design, production, and distribution of their civic media. While VR and similar immersive stories made by filmmakers like Milk can enhance sympathy for their subjects, using immersive media as a participatory civic machine can not only change policy and increase donations, but also drive change toward social justice.

## Put it into Practice: Creating a Civic Media Machine with Community Members

As you plan your civic media project as a collaborative and creative process, try to answer these guiding questions to have a better understanding of your plan, your values and the execution of this complex community partnership that will result in an immersive media experience:

## PARIS Model of Civic Media Principles

Participatory - Who will have the control over the content, format and distribution of the media?

Accessible - Who is included or excluded from the process and usage of the immersive media?

Reflective - How will participants provide feedback to ensure accountability?

Impactful - What is the practical goal toward social change?

Sustainable - What mechanisms are in place to ensure the adaptability and continuity of the community project as an immersive media experience?

Together with your community partners, answer these questions as you design and plan your immersive media project:

## Media Literacy Practices

Access: What accurate data is available to better inform us on our project?

Analyze and evaluate: What has been done and how it was successful or not in addressing power structures and bringing more diversity, equity and inclusion?

Create: How can we design an immersive experience that would build upon previous attempts to make social change and be inclusive?

Reflect: What are the effects of the immersive media on moving toward social justice?

Act: How can each one of the participants contribute to the effort to research, design, produce and distribute the immersive media to bring social change?

# References

Antognoli, D. (2021). Reconceptualizing Video Games for Community Spaces. *In*: J.A. Fisher (Ed.). Augmented and Mixed Reality in Communities. CRC Press.

Batson, C.D. (2009). These things called empathy: Eight related but distinct phenomena. pp. 3-15. *In*: J. Decety and W. Ickes (Eds.). The Social Neuroscience of Empathy. MIT Press. https://doi.org/10.7551/mitpress/9780262012973.003.0002

Bujić, M., Salminen, M., Macey, J. and Hamari, J. (2020). Empathy machine: How virtual reality affects human rights attitudes. Internet Research. https://doi.org/10.1108/INTR-07-2019-0306

Castro, A.L. (2019, May). *Worldcraft Blocks Legends – Build, Dig, Explore, Fight. Everywhere, Forever, for Real* [AR]. Wrldcraft.Com. https://www.wrldcraft.com/

Clifford, D.H. (2017). *K12 Lab Liberatory Design Deck MASTER* [Presentation]. D.K12 Lab Network. https://docs.google.com/presentation/d/1S-7fZojfgGs3M3T110vaXZFztRvjm MdkCjJ4UiIQ5i0/edit?usp=embed_facebook

Collis, C. (2019, August 28). *AR Community App—Case Study*. Medium. https://uxplanet.org/ case-study-ar-community-app-fa7a6f93e4bd

CMO.com. (2019, February). *What is Augmented Humanity—And Why You Should Care* [Blog]. CMO. Adobe.Com. Retrieved August 15, 2020, from https://cmo.adobe.com/articles/2019/2/augmented-humanity-isobar.html

Delightex (2016). *CoSpaces Edu: Make AR & VR in the Classroom.* AR/VR. https://cospaces.io/edu/

Duffy, B.E. (2017). *(Not) Getting Paid to Do what You Love: Gender, Social Media, and Aspirational Work.* Yale University Press.

Ersoy, A. (ed.) (2017). *The Impact of Co-Production—From Community Engagement to Social Justice.* Policy Press.

Fisher, J.A. (2019). Interactive non-fiction with reality media: Rhetorical affordances [Doctoral dissertation, Georgia Institute of Technology]. https://smartech.gatech.edu/handle/1853/61274

Fisher, J.A. (2017). Empathic actualities: Toward a taxonomy of empathy in virtual reality. pp. 233-244. *In*: N. Nunes, I. Oakley and V. Nisi (Eds.). Interactive Storytelling. Springer. https://doi.org/10.1007/978-3-319-71027-3_19

Foth, M., Parra Agudelo, L. and Palleis, R. (2013). Digital soapboxes: Towards an interaction design agenda for situated civic innovation. Proceedings of the 2013 ACM Conference on Pervasive and Ubiquitous Computing Adjunct Publication. pp. 725–728. https://doi.org/10.1145/2494091.2495995

Friesem, Y. (2016). Empathy for the digital age: Using video production to enhance social, emotional, and cognitive skills. pp. 21-45. *In*: S. Tettegah and D. Espelage (Eds.). Emotions, Technology, and Behaviors. Vol. 1. Academic Press. https://doi.org/10.1016/B978-0-12-801873-6.00002-9

Friesem, Y. and Greene, K. (2020). Tuned in: The importance of peer feedback with foster youth creating media. *Reflective Practice.* https://doi.org/10.1080/14623943.2020.1798919

GoMeta. (2016). *Metaverse* [AR]. Metaverse Studio. https://studio.gometa.io

Gregory, S. (2016, August 2). Immersive witnessing: From empathy and outrage to action [Blog]. *Witness.Org.* https://blog.witness.org/2016/08/immersive-witnessing-from-empathy-and-outrage-to-action/

Healey, K. (2021). The ethics of augmentation: A case study in contemplative mixed reality. *In*: J.A. Fisher (ed.). Augmented and Mixed Reality in Communities. CRC Press.

Hidalgo, L. (2015). Augmented fotonovelas: Creating new media as pedagogical and social justice tools. *Qualitative Inquiry*, 21(3), 300-314. https://doi.org/10.1177/1077800414557831

Hobbs, R. (2021). *Media Literacy in Action: Questioning the Media.* Rowman & Littlefield.

Irom, B. (2018). Virtual reality and the Syrian Refugee Camps: Humanitarian communication and the politics of empathy. *International Journal of Communication*, 12, 23.

Jenkins, H. (2007, October 2). What is Civic Media [blog]. *Confessions of an ACA-FAN.* Retrieved from http://henryjenkins.org/blog/2007/10/what_is_civic_media_1.html

Jones, S. and Dawkins, S. (2018). Walking in someone else's shoes: Creating empathy in the practice of immersive film. *Media Practice and Education*, 19(3), 298-312. https://doi.org/10.1080/25741136.2018.1520538

Khan, M.A. and Loke, L. (2017). Locative media interventionism: A conceptual framework for critical review of augmented reality applications in the participatory spatial design context. *Archnet-IJAR: International Journal of Architectural Research*, 11(1), 181-209.

Lajeunesse, F. and Raphael, P. (2014). *Herders* [VR]. https://docubase.mit.edu/project/herders/

McLuhan, M. (1964). *Understanding Media: The Extensions of Man.* Signet Books.

Milk, C. (2015, March). How virtual reality can create the ultimate empathy machine. [Video]. *TedTalk*.https://www.ted.com/talks/chris_milk_how_virtual_reality_can_create_the_ultimate_empathy_machine

Milk, C. and Arora, G. (2015). *Clouds Over Sidra* [VR]. https://docubase.mit.edu/project/clouds-over-sidra/

Milk, C. (2015). *Evolution of Verse* [VR]. https://www.with.in/watch/evolution-of-verse

Mikva Challenge (2014, September 24). *Program Impact Spotlight: Expunge.io*. https://mikvachallenge.org/blog/program-impact-spotlight-expunge-io/

Morisset, V. (2014). *Way to go* [VR].http://a-way-to-go.com/

Moroz, M. and Krol, K. (2018). VR and empathy: The Bad, the Good, and the Paradoxical. *2018 IEEE Workshop on Augmented and Virtual Realities for Good (VAR4Good)*, 1-4. https://doi.org/10.1109/VAR4GOOD.2018.8576883

Murray, J.T. and Johnson, E.K. (2021). XR content authoring challenges: The creator-developer divide. *In*: J.A. Fisher (ed.). Augmented and Mixed Reality in Communities. CRC Press.

Nash, K. (2018). Virtual reality witness: Exploring the ethics of mediated presence. *Studies in Documentary Film*, 12(2), 119-131. https://doi.org/10.1080/17503280.2017.1340796

Nelson, D. (2014, May 2). *"Magic" Modi uses hologram to address dozens of rallies at once—Telegraph*. https://www.telegraph.co.uk/news/worldnews/asia/india/10803961/Magic-Modi-uses-hologram-to-address-dozens-of-rallies-at-once.html

Performing Statistics. (2018). *#NoKidsinPrison* [Installation]. https://www.performingstatistics.org/nokidsinprison

Pruitt, S. (2020, May 8). *The Real Story Behind the 'Migrant Mother' in the Great Depression-Era Photo*. HISTORY. https://www.history.com/news/migrant-mother-new-deal-great-depression

Ramachandran, V. (2015, August 7). *Knight Prototype Fund winner Expunge.io inspires change in Illinois law*. Knight Foundation. https://knightfoundation.org/articles/knight-prototype-fund-winner-expungeio-inspires-change-illinois-law/

Rushkoff, D. (2010). *Program or Be Programmed: Ten Commands for a Digital Age* (1st edition). Soft Skull Press.

Samuels, J.T. and Ramirez, K. (2021). Building a virtuous cycle of activism using art and augmented reality: A community of practice-based project. *In*: J.A. Fisher (Ed.). *Augmented and Mixed Reality in Communities*. CRC Press.

Segal, E.A. (2011). Social empathy: A model built on empathy, contextual understanding, and social responsibility that promotes social justice. *Journal of Social Service Research*, 37(3), 266-277. https://doi.org/10.1080/01488376.2011.564040

Sharma, H.N., Alharthi, S.A., Dolgov, I. and Toups, Z.O. (2017). A framework supporting selecting space to make place in spatial mixed reality play. Proceedings of the Annual Symposium on Computer-Human Interaction in Play, 83-100. https://doi.org/10.1145/3116595.3116612

Skwarek, M. (2011). *AR Occupy Wall Street* [AR]. https://docubase.mit.edu/project/ar-occupy-wall-street/

Staton, B., Kramer, J., Gordon, P. and Valdez, L. (2016, June). *From the Technical to the Political: Democratizing Design Thinking*. From CONTESTED_CITIES to Global Urban Justice. Madrid, Spain.

Strauss, D. and Arena, S. (2020). *Building Bridges* [Online Game]. https://tabletopia.com/games/building-bridges

Sutherland, A. (2017, October 12). *No, VR Doesn't Create Empathy. Here's Why*. BuzzFeed News. https://www.buzzfeednews.com/article/ainsleysutherland/how-big-tech-helped-create-the-myth-of-the-virtual-reality

Thevin, L., Jouffrais, C., Rodier, N., Palard, N., Hachet, M. and Brock, A.M. (2019). Creating accessible interactive audio-tactile drawings using spatial augmented reality. Proceedings of the 2019 ACM International Conference on Interactive Surfaces and Spaces, 17-28. https://doi.org/10.1145/3343055.3359711

Traldi, L. (2017, March 1). Gabo Arora: VR as a tool to create active empathy. *Design @ Large*. https://www.designatlarge.it/gabo-arora-vr-active-empathy/?lang=en

United Nation Virtual Reality. (N.D.). *Syrian Refugee Crisis*. http://unvr.sdgactioncampaign. org/cloudsoversidra/#.XzML-BNKhTY

Van Dijk, J. (2020). *The Digital Divide*. Polity.

Vansynghel, M. (2020, August 14). *Augmented Reality App Reveals Seattle Protest Art In Surprising Places*. Crosscut. https://crosscut.com/culture/2020/08/augmented-reality-app-reveals-seattle-protest-art-surprising-places

Wiehl, A. (2021). The Body and the Eye—The I and the Other: Critical Reflections on the Promise of Extended Empathy in Extended Reality Configurations. *In*: J.A. Fisher (ed.). Augmented and Mixed Reality in Communities. CRC Press.

# Chapter

# 4

# The Philosopher's Stone as a Design Framework for Defending Truth and Empowering Communities

**Bill Guschwan**

916 S Wabash Ave, Chicago, 60605
Email: WGuschwan@colum.edu

Augmented Reality (AR) is a technology, that when integrated into social media platforms, can help avoid their systemic issues. The technology also enables new affective experience but it is critically important to consider how it can ethically benefit users and society. Facebook's and other social platforms' use of mimetic desire provides a mechanism for powerful entities to use massive cloud computing resources against users and community. Thus, this paper proposes a model to fight against the leverage caused by the problematic design of social platforms. Rebecca's Adams idea of (Barfar, 2019) creative mimesis provides some insight (Neufeld and Thomas, 2014) when paired with Martin Heidegger's 20th-century definition of truth and clarity. To account for the dynamism of this conception of truth, an equally mutable framework is necessary. The Philosopher Stone uses sacred geometry to provide a visual geometric model that moves beyond dualities and mimetic desire. The shape of the framework allows for multiple logics to exist simultaneously, which provide a personalized manifestation of truth. This has particular value for AR as it moves designers away from the traditional dichotomy of augmented and physical reality to a multiplicity of realities in which meaning is made.

## The Problem of Truth-as-Correspondence in Social Media

AR is an emerging mainstream technology that is already being integrated into social media platforms such as Facebook, Instagram, and Snapchat. Yet, the inclusion of this technology occurs even as they provide a troubling affective experience. Facebook continues to be a divisive political tool use for disinformation (Barfar, 2019) and promoting authoritarianism (Cadwalladr, 2020). The platform has also been cited for enhancing depression (Moreno et al., 2011) and creating a venue for racism (Matamoros-Fernández, 2017). Similar issues are shared across social media platforms, but due to their demographics, teenagers on Snapchat are particularly vulnerable (Charteris, Gregory and Masters, 2018). (Charteris, Gregory and Masters, 2018). Even though these ills are recognized, social media platforms such as Facebook are able to maintain engagement due to the addictive quality of the resulting affective experiences (Blackwell, Leaman, Tramposch, Osborne and Liss, 2017; Tang, Chen, Yang, Chung and Lee, 2016; Błachnio, Przepiorka and Pantic, 2016). This is problematic from a platonic sense of correspondence as truth.

Correspondence as truth can be understood as a scholar making a statement about an observable reality. A statement is true, "if it corresponds with states of affairs in an outer reality (which is objective, that is, not affected by the subject)" (Huttunen and Kakkori, 2020). By example, when Galileo Galilei observed that the earth and other planets orbited around the sun, his observation had correspondence with the natural physics of the universe. Even though his contemporaries in the Roman Catholic Church dismissed him and considered him a heretic, we now recognize that his observation was true, indeed. Hubert Dreyfus observed, "Plato took Good to be the pure present ground of everything, and truth to be the correspondence of theoretical propositions to an independent reality (Dreyfus, "Being and Power" Revisited). Plato's theory (and "eidos"), asserts that some ideal forms exist, and that truth is their correspondence to real things. In short, real things that correspond to these ideal forms are true.

Since posts on Facebook are performative this understanding of truth is problematic. It connects users to an addictive relationship to a truth that they cannot realize. There is an apocryphal story about the pitch, founder of Facebook, Mark Zuckerberg, made to the venture capitalist Peter Thiel. At the time, Facebook was gaining traction as a start-up, but it wasn't guaranteed to be a huge success. Peter Thiel was one of the first investors to see the huge upside on Facebook (Wearden, 2010). Peter Thiel went to Stanford and René Girard was one of the professors to have interacted with him. Girard had a very notable theory on "mimetic desire" according to which readers of literary works identified their desires with those of literary characters (Girard, 1994). Girard extends this philosophy to those outside of literary circles as well (Richard Feloni, 2014).

We are drawn to our desires through others by what they already possess or what they desire too indeed. Girard refers to this other as a mediator. The mimesis of this desire is mediated by them, to that of the subject through their actions and personhood. Critically, this aspiration to fulfill the other's desires through one's own actions is never attainable. It is illusory and ever shifting. Facebook, by allowing users to share images and pictures, feeds right into mimetic desire: it is a digital platform for it. (Shullenberger, Mimesis and Facebook Part 2: Harnessing Violence, 2016).

Mimetic desire is a genuine part of human nature that the platform leverages to maintain a dominance in the social media space (Shullenberger, Mimesis and Violence Part 1: Peter Thiel's French Connection, 2016). In a positive light, the same mechanism is part of the structures that give rise to many of the platform's benefits—such as fostering a sense of community and togetherness across the world (Tracy, 2020). However, transposing the desires of others onto users enables the platform's addictive nature (Ghose, 2015). This has far-reaching consequences when issues of truth, politics, and identity come into play. Mimetic desire can upset the situated knowledge of individual users on a social network due to the performative nature of social media posts (Hogan, 2010). These performances are mistaken for actual reality even though they are fictionalized. This is akin to Girard's original conception of mimetic desire and make them even more difficult, if not impossible, to fulfill in reality.

It is perhaps, then, apparent that Facebook's understanding of truth is problematic. The company's general policy about truth is that it is relative, and that one organization should not be its arbiter (Levy, 2020). In relation to misinformation propagated by hate groups and others, Mark Zuckerberg, the CEO of Facebook, had this to say:

> 'I just believe strongly that Facebook shouldn't be the arbiter of the truth of all that people say online,' Zuckerberg told Fox News. 'Private companies, especially these platforms probably should not placed in a position to do that' (McCarthy, 2020).

Other companies like Twitter have been a bit more aggressive in policing and providing a policy about content that stretches the truth (Sherisse Pham, 2020). In response to COVID-19 misinformation, the company wrote this in a May 2020 blogpost:

> Depending on the propensity for harm and type of misleading information, warnings may also be applied to a Tweet. These warnings will inform people that the information in the Tweet conflicts with public health experts' guidance before they view it.
>
> Helpful definitions of their labels are:

- Misleading information—statements or assertions that have been confirmed to be false or misleading by subject-matter experts, such as public health authorities.
- Disputed claims—statements or assertions in which the accuracy, truthfulness, or credibility of the claim is contested or unknown.
- Unverified claims—information (which could be true or false) that is unconfirmed at the time it is shared.

The difference between these two social media platforms perspectives highlights the issues emerging from truth, desire, and the realization of both in reality. Facebook does not consider itself accountable for the mistruths and false statements published on its platforms; Twitter attempts to make some efforts to protect users from such damaging disinformation. However, as designers we must move away from these dual-logic understandings of correspondence as truth. The truth is more dynamic than dualities and as designers we require a deeper understanding.

# Actualizing Heidegger's Truth as a Design Goal

Martin Heidegger believed that *truth as correspondence* is its limited view[1]. Heidegger counter proposed that while truth is related to the original translation of the Greek term, *Aletheia,* it also involves the cognition of the subject. Heidegger understood Plato's use of *aletheia* as "unhiddenness" but found its lack of subjectivity dissatisfying. He does state that this understanding of aletheia is still present in Plato's Cave allegory. The truth is still hidden in the cave and must be "unhidden", but that is not all that is occurring. Critical to Heidegger's understanding of truth is how the subject reaches that recognition. Heidegger's refers to this as a "correctness of vision" and focuses our attention back on the individual doing the understanding or rather, realizing the truth.

He develops his work around the notion that truth is "revealing" showing both hidden and unhidden things (Rauno Huttunen, 2020). This means that the platonic conception of original truth is not attainable. The visual conception of truth as a light that eliminates the shadows of falsity does not take into account what cannot be seen. Heidegger is quoted here as "A clearing in the forest is still there, even when it's dark. Light presupposes clearing. There can only be brightness where something has been cleared or where something is open to light" (Royle, 2018). For Heidegger, there must be a subject "clearing" space for light and darkness simultaneously as part of this work. Heidegger makes a proposition about a clearing as something that provides the stage for things to show up and for things to show up as truth in the form of a revelation. The "clearing" is all around the subject because it is an integral part of human cognition. As we seek the truth, humans create a "clearing" wherein present understandings recede and make future understanding possible. Thus, truth is a very dynamic process and the "clearing" makes a new meaning visible while being invisible itself.

## Utilizing Heidegger's Conception of Clearing in Design

While science has benefited greatly from the positivist concept of truth as correspondence it closes off dynamism and change (Alawa, 2013). Heidegger's

---

[1]  According to Heidegger, the ignorance of the "clearing" in Western philosophy has been since the days of Plato and this ignorance has adversely affected society as a whole. Since society is focused on truth as correspondence, this limited view of truth has ramifications in society as a whole. The riots around the death of George Floyd has renewed a focus on the notion of white privilege, fragility and supremacy amongst other terms used to describe the framework for systemic racism. Using Heidegger's view of Plato's notion of truth dominates society, white privilege and fragility can be seen as an "ideal form" against which truth corresponds. The negative effects of the Platonic static clearing are now in society. White privilege can be considered a "clearing". Like any "clearing", white privilege recedes or withdraws in its role in truth. It conceals its presence, while providing an oppressive and stabilizing sense of truth for the powerful in society. People's identities are formed within this static clearing of white privilege and the accompanying oppressive injustices follow.

"clearing" is more expansive and promotes the dynamic nature of time and space in the role of truth (Morrison, 1997)[2]. Any new technology in the 21st-century should account for clearing as a design policy. In other words, tools for dynamic clearing should be built in as a fundamental aspect of a technology platform, otherwise those in power will be able to control people through manipulation by making a "clearing" static. Twitter, by correcting factually incorrect tweets, makes people aware that although a subject may want to promote a "clearing" as static and authoritative that it is in fact dynamic. A user must engage in its own clearing and can only be made aware of it in the moment of its realization with the platform's helpful labels. Facebook's position on truth is tragically ironic considering Heidegger's "clearing". By not correcting factual errors, the platform is in some sense supporting the position that truth as correspondence is problematic. However, by failing to check facts, they preserve the self-concealing and authoritative nature of the proposed "clearing", preserving truth erroneously as static. By doing so, they fall short of Heidegger's definition of truth.

The design of user experiences impact our communities. The static aspect of a "clearing" can be thought of as an ideology and ideological process. The static "clearing" is a hidden background against which truth is manifested for users. Consequently, the platform can manipulate communities by inducing events such as meddled election campaigns which impact them through the hidden agendas of static clearings (Andriole, 2019). That said, future platforms that replace mechanisms of static clearings with new ones supposedly with better values are not a solution. While it is not necessarily wrong for platforms to be ideologically aligned, it is not right to put the power of computers in the hands of the platform without allowing users to have tools to counter it. Twitter's work getting rid of static clearings by correcting factual errors is a step toward dynamic clearing, but it is still stuck in a dual logic. While it is progress to point out the static clearing manipulations, it still has not addressed the core design problem caused by them as a mechanism for manipulation. The overwhelming and radical power of computers to flood the static clearing can only be defeated by using the same power to maintain the personal dynamic clearing of users. For future platforms, the static clearing should be replaced with a mechanism or tool such as artificial intelligence to maintain their personal dynamic clearing mechanisms using multiple logics. Multiple logics is a hallmark of dynamic clearing. Users need to be empowered with tools to make the "clearing" dynamic for themselves or to retain the dynamic nature of "clearing". Controlling the clearing

---

[2]  The impact of Heidegger's reconfiguration of truth can be seen on other philosophers. Michel Foucault's work on discourse and power is one example. He was indebted to Heidegger, as he said his "entire philosophical development was determined by [his] reading of Heidegger" (Rayner, 2007). James Gee's big "D" discourse is another conception that accounts for time, space, and history in truth, and his notion of affinity space (Gee, n.d.). George Herbert Mead generalized that the "other" could be taken as an example of a static clearing and the concept of self can be seen in line with Heidegger's notion of truth (Malhotra, 1987). A rereading of natural law by Bernd Belina and Iris Dzudzek as forms of discourse rooted in societal practices that are forgotten or concealed by subjects can be seen as influenced by Heidegger (Schnelzer, 2017)

is an ethical issue for any new social media platform and the user should be given tools to fight for its control. Twitter gives you some control of the static clearing by making you aware when facts are erroneous, since it has not been built with a dynamic clearing kept in mind. Tools need to be built into the platform to support users ability to manifest truth as a dynamic clearing. As Steve Jobs reminds us, "man is a tool maker [...man] has the ability to make a tool to amplify an inherent ability that he has" (Jobs, 1980). Our tools should amplify our natural ability for a dynamic clearing of truth that combats the current manipulations on platforms.

### Realizing Heidegger's Clearing in Augmented Reality Design

While early Heidegger's notion of Being and truth was focused on time, he later integrated conceptions of space as well (Dreyfus, Later Heidegger Lectures, 2014). Truth is a clearing situated both within space and time (Arisaka, 1995). For AR, this conception of truth has overlapped. AR is situated within space and time, not just time. It also makes claims about the truth of what immediate physical reality is (Fisher, 2019). It is constructive, for design purposes, to use Mikhail Bakhtin's notion of the Chrono tope to understand how AR can give way and enable clearing (Guschwan B., RPGs as Knowledge Creating Chronotopes, 2014). Bakthin defines the Chronotope as under:

> In the literary artistic chronotope, spatial and temporal indicators are fused into one carefully thought-out, concrete whole. Time, as it were, thickens, takes on flesh, and becomes artistically visible; likewise, space becomes charged and responsive to the movements of time, plots and history. This intersection of axes and fusion of indicators characterizes the artistic chrono tope (Bakthin, 1981).

While Bakhtin is speaking specifically about literature, the observation can be remediated for AR (Engberg and Bolter, 2015). The rendered images of AR are situated on location, viewed at a particular time, and perceived by the user making representations "artistically visible". AR affords designers an opportunity to encourage dynamic clearing by making a plurality of truths available to the user in real time and in their immediate presence. Within this augmented space, a user may be actively engaged in clearing its own situated representations of truth and meaning.

Pokémon Go demonstrates these qualities of AR as a chronotope. Using a mobile phone and its applications, players are able to find virtual creatures and collect them in the environment of the real world. These creatures are placed in the real world by game developers and players can virtually collect them by flicking a Poke Ball at the creatures. The Pokémon "take on flesh" by their rendered presence in both space and time[3]. Another example is a project that the author worked on called the Walk-

---

[3] While Pokémon Go is entertainment, what if Pokémon Go was repurposed to collect experiences of rapport with your neighbors? Maybe your neighbor needs help with their computer. They could register their request on a data beacon that uses Ultra-wide band (UWB) that has a broadcast distance of 10 meters (Jeff Foerster, 2001). Apple is currently building UWB chips into the iPhones (Shankland, 2019).

In Brain. In that project, MRI data of the brain vasculature was processed to make a geometric model (Hartung, Alaraj and Linninger, 2016). The model of the vasculature was then brought into a game engine and then interacted with users with the use of "Microsoft HoloLens".Users could then walk into the projected hologram of the brain to view its vasculature at different angles. Usually invisible to human visual perception, (Vern Neufeld Redekop, 2013) the brain's vasculature "takes on flesh" through the rendered imagery, the user's embodiment, and its immediate presence in real time. Virtual interactions which are spatial and immediate with augmented environments and objects are powerful examples of presenting representations for dynamic clearing.

## Utilizing Creative Mimesis to Challenge Dwelling and Motivate Clearing

In the Wizard of Oz[4], Dorothy experiences clearing in a way that is constructive for designers. When Dorothy is knocked out, she enters Oz and is unaware that she is in a dream world. The truth is only unconcealed through her journey. Her life, literally and figuratively, was black-and-white: the truth was presented as correspondence and the clearing was static in Kansas. In that static clearing, Dorothy perceived that Auntie Em treats her poorly because she is cruel. However, when she wakes up at home after returning from the multi-colored world of Oz, in possession of a new understanding—a dynamized clearing—she realizes that Auntie Em is complex. Dorothy realizes that the truth is not so static. Auntie Em loves her dearly.

For Dorothy to arrive at the dynamic clearing, and its expression of truth, she was put through tests on the yellow brick road in Oz. She had to deal with the Wicked Witch, the scarecrow, tinman and lion, and finally Oz. These were tests that helped her grow. She grew in her understanding and it eventually lead to a different view of truth. Heidegger's notion of clearing as a space time is captured here. She says of Oz, "It wasn't a dream, it was a place…A real, truly live place! . . .". It could be rewritten with the dynamic clearing in mind: "Truth wasn't a dream, truth was a place!"

Since clearing is both a place and an action, a dynamic clearing gives way to what Heidegger referred to as a dwelling. Jeff Malpas explains dwelling as "We are not 'in place' only when in the throes of wonder. Just as, to use Heidegger's terminology, dwelling in the surroundings is a human mode, so a human being is essentially a being in place, just as it is also one in the world (Malpas, 2012)." As clearing is both embodied within an individual and enacted spatially over time, it happens in a state of dwelling. A subject dwells within and on its environment even as it works to develop clearings within that environment to create meaning. The land of Oz is a dwelling within Dorothy that expresses itself through her perception of Kansas as a land of wonder, not dreariness.

The titular Willy Wonka in Charlie and the Chocolate Factory experiences a similar dwelling. Like Dorothy, Wonka has his own disillusionment with his

---

[4]  The author is discussing the movies for both the Wizard of Oz and Willy Wonka and the Chocolate Factory.

dwelling. His disillusionment is cynically expressed when he devises a challenge to find a child to take over his factory. He has a static understanding of adults as cruel and seeks the innocence of a child to run his factory. Enter Charlie, an idealistic child. As is the case with Oz, the factory is colorful and surreal. That is where Willy lives, figuratively and literally: where he dwells. He seeks to pass on this colorful, innocent, and joyous world to Charlie. When he recognizes Charlie as his successor, he has a way to extend his clearing. Malpas writes that Heidegger viewed this kind of realization as, "a mode of seeing that, against his own admonitions, can easily be read as seeing through or beyond—but rather seeing that remains, allowing things to shine in their very presence, and in the process shining to light up the structure of the world that shelters and sustains them" (Malpas, 2012).

At the beginning of both stories, Willy and Dorothy exist in dwellings that make their clearings static and authoritative. They each suffer from a mimetic desire that cannot be realized by the initial situations. Dorothy desires a fun fantasy world of color and joy like those in her stories; Wonka desires a heir that has his own childlike curiosity and wonder. The environments they inhabit make these realizations difficult, if not impossible, from the initial clearings. It is only after a journey and adventure that the initial clearing becomes dynamic and their initial dwellings are shifted. Designers and developers should consider their users as approaching their experiences with an established dwelling. How to use an interface and technologies that will allow them to shift from a static clearing based in this dwelling to one more active, creative, and dynamic is the challenge.

## Creative Mimesis to Challenge Clearing

Instead of Facebook's mimetic desire, a new AR social platform would account for creative mimesis. Professor of Sociology Rebecca Adams challenged Girard's conception of mimetic desire because of its inherent reliance on a textual artefact. She viewed this reliance as a way of scapegoating the worst of human impulses and placing accountability with the artefact—not the individual actors. Instead, she proposed that creative mimesis is a pro-social alternative. Creative mimesis is a beneficial desire motivated by love and appreciation for subjects, in terms of who they are, what they have, and what they might desire. It is not a violent form of desire, but one born of mutual respect. Instead of coveting, creative mimesis encourages dialogic co-construction wherein the subjects get what they need—but with no immediate and direct loss of value to themselves or others.

Facebook cannot achieve creative mimesis because its foundational mechanisms exist to exploit the desires of users. Advertising being the company's main source of revenue, creates a dwelling for users wherein their participation is predicated upon that same exploitation. Even while using advertisement blocking software, the stripping and monetization of user data occurs as part of the dwelling. As already stated, even while the content of Facebook may appear dynamic, it maintains an authoritative and static clearing. Users are bound by the code and procedures of the system (Graham, Zook and Boulton, 2013). For the users to achieve creative mimeses on Facebook they would need a third-party system that enables them to compete, dynamically, with the dwelling of the social media behemoth. One might imagine a machine learning agent that could help a user dynamically clear a way to meaning. Users need a Toto or even moralizing Oompa Loompas which helps them find a preferable dwelling with dynamic clearing.

# The Philosopher's Stone as a Design Framework for Creative Mimesis and Dynamic Clearing

Adams' great contribution is opening a discussion on an alternative to mimetic desire. She knew that Girard's solution to mimetic desire as giving up desire to God was problematic. Adams asserted that mimetic desire was not tenable for societally disadvantaged people (Taylor, 2018). Much has been written about her solution of creative mimesis (Vern Neufeld Redekop, 2013). Various expressions of creative mimesis include aphetic mimesis, which implies letting go and being responsively submissive to the agency of the other (Ryba, 2014). Girard's model is stuck in the dual-logic mentality that keeps truth and clearing static. Adam's model to improve on mimetic desire is about being receptive to its control, and leveraging it to create a space for agency "as the capacity to participate fully in a loving dynamic relationship of giving and receiving in relation to others (Taylor, 2018)." This capacity results in more than dual logics as individuals act and relate to more than singular perceptions of one's self and others.

Unfortunately, Adams' model is not constructive for designers because it is not properly visualized. The author believes that a visual representation of a non-dual logic framework is necessary. Adams proposed the need for such a non-traditional logic in creative mimesis, "the dual emphasis of both acting, yet also being acted upon; of desiring, yet also being receptive to other people's desire (Moore, 2014)." To support Adams' model, the Philosopher's Stone introduces the use of a non-traditional logic that allows for both acting and being acted upon by desire simultaneously from multiple perspectives.

## Mapping the Nondual Logics of Creative Mimesis

Before moving into the Philosopher's Stone, it is helpful to understand the relationship between traditional dual logics (i.e. correspondence as truth) and dynamic nondual logics (dynamic clearing as truth). Table 4.1 will be referenced.

**Table 4.1:** Mapping logics

| Dual Logic (Intrinsic) | | Nondual Logic (Extrinsic) | |
|---|---|---|---|
| I desire | I desire my neighbor's garden. | I both desire and don't desire | I desire the garden because my parents had one; I don't desire it because it is beyond my means. |
| I don't desire | I don't desire my neighbor's garden. | I neither desire nor don't desire | I neither desire the garden nor not desire it because I rather have a new car which will raise my status in comparison to my neighbor. |

In Table 4.1, the first row defines different logics: dual and nondual. Critically, dual logic is conceptualized as internally motivated: the individual is acting out of embodied motivations. The nondual logic, is an extrinsic logic, since it is developed in a system consisting of others: the individual is acting in response to a system or society. Adam's creative mimesis demands a framework that encompasses acting and being acted upon—both through dual and nondual logics[5]. For designers to achieve creative mimesis through dynamic clearing in their AR experiences, they must engage with such nondual logics. The Philosopher's Stone is a recommended guide for designing the same.

## The Philosopher's Stone's Dual and Nondual Logics

The Philosopher's Stone, presented in Figure 4.1, is a geometric figure that represents dual and nondual logics visually. Its different shapes comprise of multiple intersecting lines and points which can be used to map nondual logics. It has four geometric figures: a circle in the middle, a square around the circle, a triangle around the square, and then a larger circle encompassing the triangle.

**Figure 4.1:** Philosopher's Stone
(https://en.wikipedia.org/wiki/Philosopher's_stone#/media/File:Squaredcircle.svg)

### The Innermost Circle

Symbolically, the innermost circle is the self (see Figure 4.2). The self is engaged in dual logics of I desire and I do not desire. It is Heidegger's dwelling from which an individual acts. In AR, this innermost circle might be represented with access to an experience that critically reflects the self. Filling out a profile of preferences for an AR experience is a rudimentary actualization of the innermost circle. However, this is an approximation of the self that may in some instances be performative.

---

[5]  The author has argued elsewhere that these 4 axioms mirror Aristotle's four causes and that it provides a model of decision making (Guschwan P.Z., 2014).

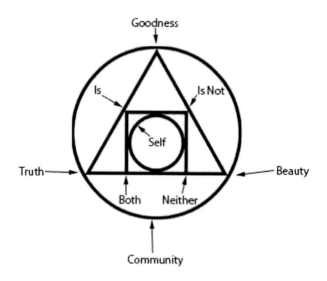

**Figure 4.2:** Annotated Philosopher's Stone

## The Square

The square represents the future self or the gnomic self. Michel Foucault defines the gnomic self as "where force of the truth is one with form of the will [...] A permanent superposition, in the form of a memory, of the subject of knowledge, and of the subject of the will [...] constituting an ontological unity, the knowledge of the soul and the knowledge of the being" (Foucault and Blasius, 1993). This is an evolution of the self beyond dual logics into nondual logic. This is the self that is engaged with its agency and its place in a system of space and time in which desires are either fulfilled or not. Thus, the small circle and the square represent your two selves, the present-self and the future-self. The future gnomic self must be willed and thus is not a guaranteed expression of the self.

In a VR experience, the same profile of preferences might be filled out with expectations users have for themselves in the system. For example, for a social VR experience like AltspaceVR a user might fill out the form in order to get a particular response from others in the system. They are relying upon their understanding of the system to fulfill a desire. They may not be successful. However, in this moment they are attempting to merge their intrinsic desires with those of the community. This attempt is an opening up of the self to the community. Once done, the self may be rejected or formed by the community it has been exposed to.

## The Triangle

These two shapes, the small circle representing the self and the square representing the future-self, sit within a triangle. The triangle acts as a bridge to a larger community. Each point of the triangle is a dimension of dynamic clearing as exercised by an individual in relation to the community. The author refers to these three points as truth, beauty, and goodness. The first point is truth which is the Heideggerian act of revealing the self to the community. The second point is beauty which is the light of the clearing that makes the product of uncovering possible. Hans Gadamer explains: "The beautiful […] reveals itself in its being: it presents itself. […] Beauty is not radiance shed on a form from without. Rather, the ontological constitution of the form itself is to be radiant, to present itself in this way (Gadamer, 1999)." The third point goodness is the effected movement of the self in the configuration of society. A powerful definition of this conceptualization of the Good comes from Jason M. Wirth's summary of F.W.J. Schelling: "The idea of Good is clearly equated with the idea of Freedom (Wirth, 2003)."

Turning back to an AltspaceVR community, the points of the triangle can be explored. For the first point, the truth, the users' forthright dialog and desires embodied in VR space in the form of interactions, leads to uncovering their selves. As users engage with one another they will naturally encounter challenges to their positions which fosters the process of revelation. For the second point, when other users in the VR space recognize and elevate the user for their actions in the community, they are shining light on that user's self. Finally in the third point, when users enter the VR world they are partaking in goodness, by participating in the configuration of that VR community and space and changing it by their presence.

### The Circle

The larger circle represents the system in which the individual is situated. It is beneficial to think of that system as a community in which the individual acts. Based on the Philosopher's Stone framework, an individual can only access that space through participating in logical processes represented by the previous shapes. Individuals who do not participate would have limited agency in the community: they would not be validated for their personal truth through a revelation; they would not receive the awe and sublime glory of community; and they would not be exposed to the fruitful opportunities born of dynamic relationships in that community. Individuals who participate can practice nondual logic to access the broader community in which they operate.

Consider an individual who does not have access to AltspaceVR in a world where political deliberations occur utilizing the platform. They are cut off from participating in that space and community. Their lack of participation results in a denial of their personal truth and hence the circumstances for a revelation can never occur. Without being embodied in that VR space they can never feel the light of the community and cannot take advantage of relationships in it. In many ways, they are denied full participation in the society they are part of.

# A Proposed Prototype Using the Philosopher's Stone Framework: The Rapport

By using the above framework, and what has been discussed about clearing and creative mimesis, a design prototype called The Rapport is proposed. The Rapport would be a type of decision engine that takes data in and provides challenges in the form of connection opportunities. The decision engine (Figure 4.3) would have an inference engine for generating future possibilities and machine learning algorithms for building a causal model of the dynamic self.

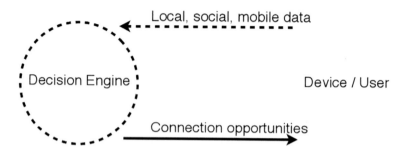

**Figure 4.3:** Decision engine for challenges

For example, we will use a well-known machine learning algorithm called the Actor/Critic. It was chosen as it can support the tetralemma of decision making.

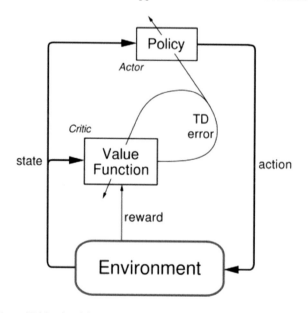

**Figure 4.4:** Actor/Critic algorithm (https://towardsdatascience.com/reinforcement-learning-w-keras-openai-actor-critic-models-f084612cfd69)

The algorithm represents an actor who takes the input of the current state, computes it against a policy, and gives an output in the form of an action (Karagiannakos, 2018). In this case, the actor is the Philosopher's Stone self. In the algorithm, the self must have a policy to decide what action to take (Patel, 2017). It can be calculated using the Philosopher's Stone square.

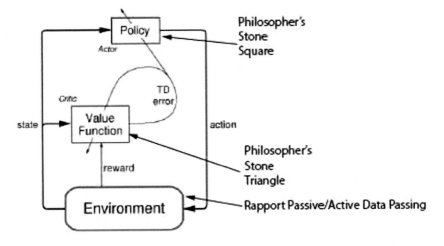

**Figure 4.5.** Annotated actor/critic algorithm

For example, a person is deciding which event to attend an opera or a movie. It is a date. The state includes the preferences of both him and his date. The state is your self. The Policy will be modelled by the Square, where you define what you want ("It is"), what materially limits what you want ("It is not"), what is possible to do where you are both able get what you want while accounting for the material limitations ("It is both"), and identifying imaginative possibilities that transcend your perceived options ("It is neither"). The action in this example will be the experience of the date that is chosen using the Squared policy.

The second representation is the critic and the triangle from the Philosopher's Stone which will be used to generate the Value Function. After the date, the Critic evaluates the response of the date against the 3 aspects of the triangle: (1) was it validating of the truth of self, (2) did events occur that were spontaneously radiant, and (3) was there activity that afforded good feelings. The Value Function outputs a ranking that reflects the value of the decision and this can be stored for possibly updating the policy of the algorithm. In this case, updating the Policy will be updating the Philosopher's Stone's square.

Finally, the Environment can be accomplished by using active and passive data passing. A simple technology like Ultra Wideband (UWB) hardware can be used to collect the data using an iPhone (Mearian, 2019). Machine learning can collect data in the long run and become better optimized to make suggestions or inferences for the user in alignment with the Philosopher's Stone. The date, in this example, acts as a challenge, and the algorithm identifies strategies for the users to use to achieve their goals in alignment with their gnomic selves (square) and Philosopher's Stone. Thus, experiences are organized into goal-oriented campaigns based on a gnomic self. The technology aggregates and shapes experiences into challenges that maximize emotional experience of life in line with the person's truth as represented by Truth, Goodness and Beauty of the Philosopher's Stone. The tool will synthesize the emotion of rapport in real-time by prioritizing connections and facilitating decisions for optimal pleasure and goal-seeking in alignment with harmonizing with the Community.

## Conclusion: Achieving Dynamic Clearing with the Philosopher's Stone Design Framework

Grappling with nondual logics is critical to AR design in communities. The Philosopher's Stone framework is a tool for thinking through these different intersecting logics. AR tools should amplify dynamic truth to increase connections for users within communities. Contemporary mimetic desire has been shown to be a static clearing for social media platforms that stunts dynamic truth in communities through its manipulations by various powers. Creative mimesis is a better model as it provides for a plurality of logics and truths to exist simultaneously. Maintaining these multiple truths is critical in AR as digital and physical reality do not exist in a dual logic state. Ways of perceiving reality exist on a gradient of multiple constructions and logics, each subjective and situated but connected to a broader community. The Philosopher's Stone Framework provides designers with a tool to explore these intersecting nondual logics. The Rapport prototype was presented as an example of an implementation. It is meant to inspire other implementations in the battle for truth. The power of computing must be put to use to defend the user's truth in the face of the computing power used by powers to manipulate the truth. In the end, a new AR platform that amplifies social good through protecting each user's truth could be possible.

## Put it into Practice: A Philosopher's Stone Design Activity

Using lessons from this chapter, envision a social AR platform that keeps the user from falling into a single static and authoritative clearing. Consider words that begin with the prefix "en". The prefix "en" is used for words that: (1) express entry into a particular state; (2) express conversion into a state; and (3) go in or into a thing. Each of these states exist in a dual logic. Either one is *enamored* or not in love, one can *envision* or not have a vision, and an item can be *encrusted* or not covered in crust. Yet, we might extend this to nondual logics. Consider, for example, an AR ball that both *enlivens* physical reality but does not exist in physical reality. Or, consider, a group of Pokémon Go users who both *engage* with a physical space but also do not utilize the physicality of that space for anything other than a stage for AR. In these instances, the nondual state of AR is present. Using the Philosopher's Stone framework, address these nondual logics in the design of your experience and try to "square your circle" by being "enamored", "engaged", and "envisioned" in your own life.

# References

Alawa, P. (2013, July). Martin Heidegger on Science and Technology: It's Implication to the Society. Retrieved from *IOSR Journal of Humanities and Social Science*: http://www.iosrjournals.org/iosr-jhss/papers/Vol12-issue6/A01260105.pdf

Arisaka, Y. (1995, December). *On Heidegger's Theory of Space: A Critique of Dreyfus.* Retrieved from Inquiry 38:4 P, 455-467: http://www.arisaka.org/dreyfus.pdf

Błachnio, A., Przepiorka, A. and Pantic, I. (2016). Association between Facebook addiction, self-esteem and life satisfaction: A cross-sectional study. *Computers in Human Behavior*, 701-705.

Bahktin, M. (1981). Forms of time and of the chronotope in the novel. pp. 84-85. *In*: M. Bahktin (ed.). In The Dialogic Imagination. Austin: University of Texas Press.

Bambach, C. (2013). Thinking the Poetic Measure of Justice: Hölderlin-Heidegger-Celan. SUNY Press.

Barfar, A. (2019). Cognitive and affective responses to political disinformation in Facebook. *Computers in Human Behavior*, 173-179.

Blackwell, D., Leaman, C., Tramposch, R., Osborne, C. and Liss, M. (2017). Extraversion, neuroticism, attachment style and fear of missing out as predictors of social media use and addiction. *Personality and Individual Differences*, 69-72.

Bryn Farnsworth, P. (2020, April 14). *How to Measure Emotions and Feelings (And the Difference Between Them).* Retrieved from Imotions: https://imotions.com/blog/difference-feelings-emotions/

Cadwalladr, C. (2020, July 26). If you're not terrified about Facebook, you haven't been paying attention. Retrieved from The Guardian: https://www.theguardian.com/commentisfree/2020/jul/26/with-facebook-we-are-already-through-the-looking-glass

Charteris, J., Gregory, S. and Masters, Y. (2018). Snapchat', youth subjectivities and sexuality: disappearing media and the discourse of youth innocence. *Gender and Education*, 205-221.

Dreyfus, H. (n.d.). "Being and Power" Revisited. Retrieved from Berkeley: https://goldberg.berkeley.edu/courses/S06/IEOR-QE-S06/being.power_hubert.dreyfus.pdf

Dreyfus, H. (2014, November 29). Later Heidegger Lectures. Retrieved from Youtube: https://www.youtube.com/watch?v=ywuNea7-1Q8

Engberg, M. and Bolter, J.D. (2015). MRx and the aesthetics of locative writing. *Digital Creativity*, 182-192.

Etherington, Darrell. (2020, July 9). Elon Musk sets update on brain-computer interface company Neuralink for August 28. Retrieved from TechCrunch: https://techcrunch.com/2020/07/09/elon-musk-sets-update-on-brain-computer-interface-company-neuralink-for-august-28/

Eyal, N. (2012, February 26). Habits Are The New Viral: Why Startups Must Be Behavior Experts. Retrieved from TechCrunch: https://techcrunch.com/2012/02/26/habits-are-the-new-viral-why-startups-must-be-behavior-experts/

Fisher, J.A. (2019). *Interactive Non-fiction with Reality Media: Rhetorical Affordances.* Atlanta: Georgia Institute of Technology.

Foucault, M. and Blasius, M. (1993). About the beginning of the hermeneutics of the self: Two lectures at Dartmouth. *Political Theory*, 198-227.

Gee, J. (n.d.). *Discourse, Small-d, Big D.* Retrieved from James Gee: http://jamespaulgee.com/pdfs/Big%20D,%20Small%20d.pdf

Ghose, T. (2015, January 27). What Facebook Addiction Looks Like in the Brain. Retrieved from Live Science: https://www.livescience.com/49585-facebook-addiction-viewed-brain.html

Girard, R. (1994). *When These Things Begin: Conversations with Michel Treguer.* Lansing: Michigan State University Press.

Graham, M., Zook, M. and Boulton, A. (2013). Augmented reality in urban places: Contested content and the duplicity of code. *Transactions of the Institute of British Geographers*, 464-479.

Guschwan, B. (2008, August 26). Bill Guschwan: A History of Video Game Development. Retrieved from Youtube Google Tech Talk: https://youtu.be/9NVvrYIOBBk?t=2807

Guschwan, B. (2014). RPGs as Knowledge Creating Chronotopes. Intelligent Technologies for Interactive Entertainment. pp. 118-122. Springer.

Guschwan, P.Z. (2014, January). Aristotle's Fourfold Causality, Tetralemma, and Emergence. Retrieved from Questia: https://www.questia.com/read/1G1-375211796/aristotle-s-fourfold-causality-tetralemma-and-emergence

Hakkarainen, K., R.G.-H. (n.d.). *Epistemic Mediation, Chrontope, and Expansive Knowledge Practices.* Retrieved from Academia: https://www.academia.edu/363695/Draft_of_Hakkarainen_K._Ritella_G._and_Seitamaa-Hakkarainen_P._submitted_Epistemic_mediation_chronotope_and_expansive_knowledge_practices

Hartung, G.A., Alaraj, A. and Linninger, A.A. (2016). Walk-In Brain: Virtual Reality Environment for Immersive Exploration and Simulation of Brain Metabolism and Function. Retrieved from Semantic Scholar: https://www.semanticscholar.org/paper/Walk-In-Brain%3A-Virtual-Reality-Environment-for-and-Hartung-Alaraj/b09a5cfcd53c6257e551935de95311d70cd019b9

Hogan, B. (2010). The presentation of self in the age of social media: Distinguishing performances and exhibitions online. *Bulletin of Science, Technology & Society*, 377-386.

Huttunen, R. and Kakkori, L. (2020). Heidegger's Theory of truth and its importance for quality of qualitative research. *Journal of Philosophy of Education*, 1-13.

Jeff Foerster, I.A. (2001, Q2). Ultra-Wideband Technology for Short- or Medium-Range Wireless Communications. Retrieved from *Univeristy of Colorado, Intel Technology Journal*: https://ecee.colorado.edu/~ecen4242/marko/UWB/UWB/art_4.pdf

Jobs, S. (1980). Steve Jobs rare footage conducting a presenation on 1980 (Insanly Great). Retrieved from Youtube: https://youtu.be/0lvMgMrNDlg?t=555

Karagiannakos, S. (2018, November 18). The idea behind Actor-Critics and how A2C and A3C improve them. Retrieved from The AI Summer: https://theaisummer.com/Actor_critics/

Levy, S. (2020, June 5). Mark Zuckerberg is an arbiter of truth—Whether he likes it or not. Retrieved from Wired: https://www.wired.com/story/mark-zuckerberg-is-an-arbiter-of-truth-whether-he-likes-it-or-not/

Lifton, R.J. (1989). *Thought Reform and the Psychology of Totalism: A Study of 'brainwashing' in China Paperback.* University of North Carolina Press.

Lisa Eadicicco. (2020, July 10). Apple is reportedly producing lenses for what could be its next major product: an augmented reality headset. Retrieved from Business Insider: businessinsider.com

MacAvoy, M. F. (2003). *Terrence Malick's Heideggerian Cinema.* Retrieved from Closeup Film Centre: https://www.closeupfilmcentre.com/vertigo_magazine/volume-2-issue-5-summer-2003/terrence-malick-s-heideggerian-cinema/

Malhotra, V.A. (1987). A Comparison of Mead's "Self" and Heidegger's "Dasein": Toward a Regrounding of Social Psychology. Retrieved from JStor: Human Studies 10(3/4): https://www.jstor.org/stable/20009008?seq=1

Malpas, J. (2012). *Heidegger and the Thinking of Place: Explorations in the Topology of Being.* Cmbridge: MIT Press.

Matamoros-Fernández, A. (2017). Platformed racism: The mediation and circulation of an Australian race-based controversy on Twitter, Facebook and YouTube. *Information, Communication & Society*, 930-946.

McCarthy, T. (2020, May 28). Zuckerberg says Facebook won't be 'arbiters of truth' after Trump threat. Retrieved from The Guardian: https://www.theguardian.com/technology/2020/may/28/zuckerberg-facebook-police-online-speech-trump

Moore, S. (2014). Seeding Reconciliation in a Theater of War. *In*: T. Ryba (ed.). René Girard and Creative Reconciliation. Maryland: Lexington Books.

Moreno, M.A., Jelenchick, L.A., Egan, K.G., Cox, E., Young, H., Gannon, K.E. and Becker, T. (2011). Feeling bad on Facebook: Depression disclosures by college students on a social networking site. *Depression and Anxiety*, 447-455.

Morrison, J.D. (1997). Heidegger, Correspondence Truth and the Realist Theology of Thomas Forsyth Torrance. Retrieved from Digital Commons Liberty University: https://digitalcommons.liberty.edu/cgi/viewcontent.cgi?referer=https://www.google.com/&https redir=1&article=1099&context=lts_fac_pubs

Neufeld, V. and Thomas, R. (2014). Introduction: René Girard and the Problem of Creativity. pp. 1-37. *In*: V. Neufeld and R. Thomas (eds). René Girard and Creative Mimesis. Plymouth: Lexington Books.

Patel, Y. (2017, July 31). Reinforcement Learning w/ Keras + OpenAI: Actor-Critic Models. Retrieved from Towards Data Science: https://towardsdatascience.com/reinforcement-learning-w-keras-openai-actor-critic-models-f084612cfd69

Porter, L. (1991, Fall). Bakthin's chronotope: Time and space in a touch of the poet and more stately mansions. Retrieved from Project Muse: Modern Drama University of Toronto Press: https://muse.jhu.edu/article/499334/summary

Rauno Huttunen, L.K. (2020, April 25). Heidegger's Theory of Truth and its Importance for the Quality of Qualitative Research. Retrieved from Wiley Online Library: https://onlinelibrary.wiley.com/doi/full/10.1111/1467-9752.12429

Rayner, T. (2007). No eBook available A&C Black Amazon.com Barnes&Noble.com Books-A-Million IndieBound Find in a library All sellers » Front Cover 0 Reviews Write review Foucault's Heidegger: Philosophy and Transformative Experience. A&C Black.

Richard Feloni (2014, November 10). Peter Thiel explains how an esoteric philosophy book shaped his worldview. Retrieved from Business Insider: https://www.businessinsider.com/peter-thiel-on-rene-girards-influence-2014-11

Royle, A. (2018). Heidegger's Ways of Being. Retrieved from Philosophy Now: https://philosophynow.org/issues/125/Heideggers_Ways_of_Being

Rushdie, S. (1992, May 4). Out of Kansas. *New Yorker*. https://www.newyorker.com/magazine/1992/05/11/out-of-kansas.

Russ Mason, M. (2002, April). Magnets, meridians, and energy medicine: An interview with William Pawluk, M.D., M.Sc. Retrieved from Infomed: ALTERNATIVE & COMPLEMENTARY THERAPIES: http://www.sld.cu/galerias/pdf/sitios/mednat/magnetos,meridianos_y_medicina_energetica.pdf

Sawh, M. (2020, July 1). The best AR glasses and smartglasses 2020: Snap, Vuzix and more. Retrieved from wareable: https://www.wareable.com/ar/the-best-smartglasses-google-glass-and-the-rest

Schnelzer, N. (2017). Libya in the Arab Spring: The Constitutional Discourse since the Fall of Gaddafi. Springer VS.

Shankland, S. (2019, September 14). Apple built UWB into the iPhone 11. Here's what you need to know (FAQ). Retrieved from CNET: https://www.cnet.com/news/apple-built-uwb-into-the-iphone-11-heres-what-you-need-to-know-faq/

Sherisse Pham. (2020, June 3). Twitter says it labels tweets to provide 'context, not fact-checking'. Retrieved from CNN Business: https://www.cnn.com/2020/06/03/tech/twitter-enforcement-policy/index.html

Shullenberger, G. (2016, August 9). Mimesis and Facebook Part 2: Harnessing Violence. Retrieved from The Society Pages: https://thesocietypages.org/cyborgology/2016/08/09/mimesis-and-facebook-part-2-harnessing-violence/

Shullenberger, G. (2016, August 2). Mimesis and Violence Part 1: Peter Thiel's French Connection. Retrieved from The Soceity Pages: https://thesocietypages.org/cyborgology/2016/08/02/mimesis-and-violence-part-1-peter-thiels-french-connection/

Tang, J.-H., Chen, M.-C., Yang, C.-Y., Chung, T.-Y. and Lee, Y.-A. (2016). Personality traits, interpersonal relationships, online social support, and Facebook addiction. *Telematics and Informatics*, 102-108.

Taylor, M. (2018). Rebecca Adams' Model of "Loving Mimesis": An Overview and Assessment (Draft). Retrieved from Academia: https://www.academia.edu/38790661/Rebecca_Adams_Model_of_Loving_Mimesis_An_Overview_and_Assessment_Draft_

Tracy, T. (2020, June 9). Facebook's Advantage Over Other Social Media. Retrieved from Investopedia: https://www.investopedia.com/articles/company-insights/070216/what-facebooks-advantage-over-other-social-media-fb.asp

Wearden, G. (2010, August 25). Shareholder trading values Facebook at more than $33bn. Retrieved from The Guardian: https://www.theguardian.com/technology/2010/aug/25/facebook-value-flotation

# Part 2
# Situating XR in the City

# Chapter
# 5

# Designing Lived Space: Community Engagement Practices in Rooted AR

**Kelsey Cameron[1] and Jessica FitzPatrick[2]**

[1] Regis University
  Email: kcameron@regis.edu
[2] University of Pittsburgh
  Email: JLF115@pitt.edu

When AR developers augment a location, they automatically enter into a relationship with the communities inhabiting that space. However, that relationship is often unrecognized or underdeveloped. Space is, in part, lived—it is made through inhabitation and use—and that should matter to AR. This chapter theorizes what can be gained by "rooting," a more attentive practice of AR design. Bringing together work on design justice and spatial studies, it explores how ethical AR can approach public communities not only as settings, but as project partners. Working with communities allows practitioners to approach locations as places of lived experience affected by hierarchies of difference.

This chapter assesses community engagement in existing AR projects and offers better practices for future projects. It proposes three levels of spatial attunement, working through examples to illustrate each. Level one, *overwriting*, covers community context with digital augmentation. The popular mobile AR game *Pokémon GO* is an example of overwriting, for its success and ability to scale depends on indifference to community histories (Niantic, Inc., 2016). Level two, *tethering*, includes titles like *[AR]T Walk*, a collaboration between Apple and New York's New Museum that curates site-specific artworks (Apple, 2019a). Although tethering distinguishes particular locations, it is still less attentive to communities. Rather, this level of engagement operates at the scale of larger organizations, institutions, and brands. Level three, *rooting*, attends to the geographies being augmented and invites local partners as collaborators. This level is largely aspirational, but the examples in this section (*Village LIVE, Mariposa AR, Still Here*) show the range of ways rooting is beginning to happen (David et al., 2017; Code the Dream, 2020b; Al Jazeera Contrast, 2020). Looking towards future work, a final section outlines steps for rooted AR development, based on the principles of collaboration over appropriation, historical awareness, and ethical community outreach. This chapter demonstrates that ethics are not just about technical execution in relation to AR: they start with conceptualizing a project and imagining collaboration in the midst of complex power relations.

## Reconsidering Design: Justice and Community

Before turning to examples, it is necessary to work through why uniting design and spatial studies is useful to reconceiving AR development. Design fields tend to figure their work as politically neutral, unaffected by dynamics of race, gender, and ability (Costanza-Chock, 2020, pp. 36-7).[1] In this narrative, design experts make things— applications, buildings, devices—that serve a universalized user: if a product works, it is assumed to work for everyone, across identity categories and social distinctions (Papanek, 1974). However, there is a growing body of scholarship pushing back against this assumption (Benjamin, 2016; Escobar, 2018; Khalil and Kier, 2017). As Ruha Benjamin (2019) puts it: "social biases get coded, not only in laws and policies, but in many different objects and tools we use in everyday life" (p. 5). To use her example, a public bench produces discriminatory effects if it has armrests preventing users from lying down: "the inconvenience is negligible" for someone just walking by, but "for a person who is homeless, it is another concrete reminder of one's denigrated status" (pp. 5-6). In this way, designed objects can, and often do, reinforce patterns of systemic oppression even as they proclaim their own neutrality.

This lesson is important for augmented reality design. Like built environments, augmented ones also make choices about which users and perspectives matter (Graham et al., 2013). Drawing on critiques of design's tendency to reproduce inequality, this chapter works toward an ethical, community-driven process of augmented reality design. It takes cues from Sasha Costanza-Chock's concept *design justice*, a term they define as follows:

> Design justice is a framework for analysis of how design distributes benefits and burdens between various groups of people. Design justice focuses explicitly on the ways that design reproduces and/or challenges the matrix of domination (white supremacy, heteropatriarchy, capitalism, ableism, settler colonialism, and other forms of structural inequality). Design justice is also a growing community of practice that aims to ensure a more equitable distribution of design's benefits and burdens; meaningful participation in design decisions; and recognition of community-based, indigenous, and diasporic design traditions, knowledge, and practices. (Costanza-Chock, 2020, p. 23)

Significant here is the double function of design justice: it is both framework for analysis and roadmap for practice. Thus, not only is critiquing existing design objects important, so too is articulating a better process for design. The end goal –

---

[1] There are many definitions of design, but this chapter understands it to mean intentionally and creatively intervening in the world. A number of fields involve the practice of design, including but not limited to graphic design, game design, architecture, industrial design, and product design.

"a more equitable distribution of design's benefits and burdens" (Costanza-Chock, 2020, p. 23) – is as much about how design happens as what is being designed.

This chapter works toward an AR-specific conception of design justice. Costanza-Chock (2020) suggests that the design justice framework is "applicable to all activities that fit under the rubric of design," but also acknowledges that, "in practice, little can be accomplished without more field specificity" (p. 217). Costanza-Chock's background is in software development, and their main examples come from this field. Other design realms raise different questions for justice-oriented practice. For example, space tends to be a secondary concern in software creation: a crime prediction algorithm might assign different neighborhoods different criminality scores, but here space is one variable among many rather than the focus of design work. In centering AR–a field structured by questions of spatiality and representation–this chapter takes up Costanza-Chock's (2020) call to "elaborate a spatial theory of design justice" (p. 233).

To build this theory, the chapter draws on the community emphasis already found within design justice practice (Algorithmic Justice League, 2020; Creative Reaction Lab, n.d.; Design Justice Network, 2018). Historically, design work tends to happen in professionalized domains insulated from the concerns of real-world communities: there is abstract talk of an end user, but there is rarely space for meaningful input from the people meant to benefit from design solutions (Costanza-Chock, 2020, p. 77). In a design justice approach, this changes: "the most valuable ingredient in design justice is the full inclusion of, accountability to, and control by people with direct living experience of the conditions designers claim they are trying to change" (p. 25). This community focus is a valuable intervention for AR practitioners, encouraging inclusion of and accountability to the people with 'on-the-ground' experience of spaces being augmented. However, even design justice can ignore the fact that that 'ground' is not just a background setting. In order to expand design justice into locative fields like AR, spatiality must be a vital register of community.

## Reconsidering Space: Communities of Place

Spatial theory underpins this chapter's claim that there are particular ethical stakes in the connections between space, place, and community in AR. After all, location-based media define communities by their physical location. AR not only augments spaces but organizes the movements of users through them—sometimes through arenas they would not otherwise inhabit. This impetus to travel in non-habitual ways makes the concepts of place and community particularly important.

Definitions of *place* often combine physical or scientific specifics (size dimensions, building materials, geographic coordinates) with a sense of the intangible or experiential (New York City's connotations as "The Big Apple", a neighborhood garden where your grandmother taught you how to pick strawberries). Human geographer Yi-Fu Tuan suggests that a place is distinct from other spaces, existing as an anchor of personal emotional attachment and involvement where humans "pause" in an otherwise highly mobile existence (1977, p. 6). For Tuan, place is what brings meaning to human lives; place is intimate. A place is meaningful, and AR design benefits from recognizing the multiplicity of that meaning. Using this lens of place requires prioritizing lived experiences, working in what spatial theorist Edward Soja called the register of "lived space" (1996, p. 63). This spatial understanding engages both the physical and the experiential, attending to the inhabitants whose intangible experiences make the location a place.

This effort of place-making is not always legible. For example, the Freedom Corner memorial in Pittsburgh has multiple inscriptions of lived experience, some of which are more visible than others. Pedestrians following Google Map directions may be routed by Freedom Corner, but, passing by that space on the way to their final destination, they would not have access to the corner's meaning as a place. This is where residents of the Hill District neighborhood halted city 'beautification' efforts that bulldozed half their community (Dyer, 2001), but also where parishioners of St. Benedict the Moor church, across the street, come by every Sunday, pausing to speak with friends and neighbors. Even places with an official designation, like the Freedom Corner memorial, have everyday alternatives, and multiple registers of lived space.

With these definitions in mind, this chapter reconceives community as a spatial term. This *community of place* consists of people who share a place, even when they engage that place in very different ways. A community of place can encompass different identity groups and perspectives. As human geographer Doreen Massey suggests the relationship between place and community can be fraught:

> If it is now recognized that people have multiple identities then the same point can be made in relation to places. Moreover, such multiple identities can either be a source of richness or a source of conflict, or both.
>
> One of the problems here has been a persistent identification of place with 'community'. Yet this is a misidentification. [...] the instances of places housing single 'communities' in the sense of coherent social groups are probably—and I would argue, have for long been—quite rare. Moreover, even where they do exist this in no way implies a single sense of place since people occupy different positions within any community. [...] I'm sure a woman's sense of place in a mining village—the spaces through which she normally moves, the meeting places, the connections outside—are different from a man's. Their 'sense of place' will be different (Massey, 1994, pp. 153-154).

A place-defined community is not necessarily as exclusive as one would imagine it to be—it is not limited to "coherent social groups" (Massey, 1994, p. 153). As Massey points out in her example of gendered space, both men and women in the mining village inscribe meaning through lived experience. However, women's place-making is historically invisible; only the man's lived experiences—and so his conceptions of the village—anchor political and economic systems. This narrower understanding of place results in erasure. In opening up the ideas of place and community away from stagnant colloquial use, Massey restores the power of often marginalized community members to place-make.

By combining Massey, Soja, and Tuan, this chapter contends that places have their own communities—ones united by the lived space of that place, even as that place is experienced from multiple lived social positions. Just because communities of place are anchored by the same experienced location, they are not uniform. Lived experiences, and therefore places, are also, as both Massey (1994; 1999) and David Harvey (1993; 2012) point out, constructed within systems of power (e.g. capitalism, white supremacy). Communities of place "may meet up and affect each other, may repel each other, may overlap in indifference. They coexist in a continuous dance of space-time configurations. But they are not all equal" (Massey, 1999, p. 160).

AR designers should recognize that places are socially created and subject to systems of power. Doing so protects rooted AR makers from mistakenly viewing a place as unchangeable, frozen in time, or universal. This framing also makes commodifying a place for profit difficult (Cresswell, 2015). It is a perspective that allows AR practitioners to design more justly.

## Design + Space = Spatial Design Justice

Spatial theory teaches us to value lived dimensions of space (Massey, 1994; Soja, 1996; Tuan, 1977). Critical design teaches us to orient practice around questions of justice (Costanza-Chock, 2020; Benjamin, 2019). Bringing them together is a step towards a spatial theory of design justice and offers an understanding of community that enriches AR design—in particular, it gives practitioners tools for exploring the connection between people and a place. Those invested in the theory and practice of AR are beginning to grapple with the contested, political nature of place. Sharma et al. (2017) suggest that AR creation is an act of 'place-making,' arguing for the importance of "select[ing] physical spaces to make places" (p. 83). In this, they make space specificity an important design choice in making place, since "mixed reality systems render spaces meaningful (even if their setting already has place-ness)" (Sharma et al., 2017, p. 85). Graham et al. (2013) point out that augmented "place-ness" is never neutral: "the seeming innocence of augmented realities hides uneven constellations of power relations that help shape everyday practices and the cultural and political meanings of particular places" (p. 471). Projects like *Invisible Cities* (Fisher et al., 2018) activate this more nuanced understanding of place-based power relations. Emphasizing a group's right to impact digital augmentations within their geographic bounds, *Invisible Cities* deliberately ties content moderation to community membership (Fisher et al., 2018, p. 425).

However, even AR theorists who acknowledge the importance of "place-ness" (Sharma et al., 2017) can sideline communities. Part of the problem is the tendency to approach place through Walter Benjamin's concept of aura, applied to AR as "the personal and cultural significance that an object or place holds for an individual or group of viewers" (Bolter et al., 2006 p. 23). Aura turns attention away from how, and who, produces significance--objects and places come already endowed with meanings, rather than being sites of contestation or meaning-remaking. As such, it is difficult to account for the contributions of everyday lived experiences or embrace community partners as participants in AR design. To remedy this erasure, this chapter offers communities of place as a conceptual reorientation. The sections that follow reconsider existing AR projects by asking questions like: How is community conceived? How is place incorporated? Who gets to participate, and on what terms?

# Level 1: Overwriting & Pokémon GO

The most visible mode of AR engagement with community is *overwriting*. When AR designers overwrite, they use digital augmentation to cover a place. This level prioritizes a designed experience that offers a distinct, self-contained sense of user-community. As such, it de-emphasizes communities of place. *Pokémon GO* is an example of overwritten AR because the game is everywhere and nowhere: you can play it most places in the world, but it only superficially acknowledges human geography.

*Pokémon GO* adapts the successful transmedia Pokémon universe from previous movies, television series, and card and video games. It brings the Pokémon universe into the new arena of AR while still activating existing name-recognition and nostalgia. As the most successful mobile AR game, there are high stakes to *Pokémon GO*'s understanding of space. Similar to mapping, AR produces a necessarily partial portrait of geography, highlighting certain landmarks, uses, and histories while relegating others to invisibility or insignificance. In *Pokémon GO*, specific elements of the player's environment are transformed into templated features (Sharma et al., 2017) of the Pokémon Universe: routes marked in-game are actual roads and trails; pokéstops are anchored at nearby landmarks; spawn points depend on types of real terrain like oceans and open/wooded areas; and Pokémon type availability depends on that day's weather.[2] Although these features come from the player's 'real world' environment, their inclusion motivates players to enter further into the narrative world of Pokémon, not to consider the world around them. *Pokémon GO* thus creates a community of play, a sense of shared sociality that only exists within and because of the game. Players trade Pokémon, battle, and move through space with friends to get to pokéstops. The game does not open outwards; players have no incentive to access, learn about, or even acknowledge the existence of people who are not playing and landmarks that are not incorporated into the game. Players' motivation to explore spaces around them (Evans and Saker, 2019) is therefore difficult to leverage into a deeper consideration of place (Stokes, 2019; Grant et al., 2019).

However, the place where play occurs cannot be fully discounted. AR's spatiality is importantly different from, say, a filmic or virtual reality representation of a location: *Pokémon Go* requires play in public. Consequently, ignoring place can be dangerous, especially for players who are 'safe' only in the digital world of Pokémon, not their actual playing location. Infamously, vehicles hit players immersed in the game (Reilly, 2016). The game must warn players not to lose connection with their surroundings before the map screen opens, since the 'real' place of the player is not actually included into the game in a sustained way (Heldman, 2016).

---

[2] *Pokémon GO* builds from the prior Niantic AR game *Ingress* (2013), a lineage clear in the game's map and interface mechanics. For example, anchors crowdsourced through *Ingress* become pokéstops. In this way, *Pokémon Go* also overwrites the world of *Ingress*.

This speaks to *Pokémon GO*'s overall relationship with place: the digital overwrites everything. The function of the AR camera reinforces this overwriting. When the game uses the camera AR feature to bring specific visual details of a player's place into the game, like during Pokémon capture or buddy-play sessions, they enter without specificity or consequence. At best, the place of the player becomes a photogenic background for Pokémon encounters; at worst, it is a distraction. Moments blending a player's surroundings and the Pokémon universe are intended to be celebrated—often these screens have in-game camera capture options, which you can then circulate on social media. However, limiting spatial meaning to physical appearance makes lived space more difficult to access. Token deployments of place can seem innocuous, but overwriting has the potential to do actual harm. The process of grafting digital overlays onto physical space can create conflict between existing, community-based inhabitations of space and new, AR-encouraged patterns of use.

Because *Pokémon GO* became so popular, there are visible, documented instances of conflict between communities of place and play. For example, in Occoquan, a small, riverfront town in northern Virginia, *Pokémon GO* radically disrupted existing patterns of social and economic life. Before the game's release, Occoquan was known for historic sites and an upscale shopping district: resident and artist Lauren Jacobs described it as a "sleepy town" where "it was very comfortable walking around on these picturesque historic streets and it was...this very relaxed kind of outing" (Mars, 2020). However, because of the way *Pokémon GO* augments physical space, the town became a gameplay hotspot. Occoquan's many historic sites turned into pokéstops, locations where Pokémon are plentiful and ripe for capture. Since the town is on a river, players can capture both land and aquatic Pokémon. Thus, the history and terrain of Occoquan made it a particularly compelling location for play in *Pokémon GO*'s augmented world, attracting many more people than Occoquan is accustomed to holding. As mayor Elizabeth Quist said in 2016, "I get in traffic jams coming home from council meetings on Tuesday nights now. I can't think of another time on a weeknight I've been six deep at a stop sign waiting for other people to go" (Stein).

One might imagine that *Pokémon GO* players would have been a boon for a small town and its businesses. However, the opposite was true. Occoquan's shopping district depended on pedestrians willing to spend several hundred dollars on distinctive items for sale. *Pokémon GO* players did not fit into this consumer category, and the crowding resulting from their presence drove away previous customers. So, despite the increased foot traffic, Jacobs saw a decline in her art sales: "Not only were we not seeing people in the gallery, the wealthy residents weren't shopping in their neighborhood anymore, period. And we had this huge influx of people and instead of revitalizing the town, it completely destroyed commerce" (Mars 2020). She tried to adapt to the new demographics populating Occoquan, selling smaller, cheaper, more mainstream pieces, but eventually the gallery closed. A number of Occoquan's small businesses met the same fate, demonstrating that *Pokémon GO*—despite happening in an augmented digital world—has material consequences.

At the core of Occoquan's troubles are incommensurate imaginations of community: *Pokémon GO*'s community–filled with predominantly young players who travel in groups and do not have the financial resources to buy a $200 painting–is very different from the kind Occoquan previously cultivated. This difference has consequences: *Pokémon GO* players transform the town through inhabitation, remaking its public spaces to suit their needs at the expense of a preexisting community. Such is the danger of overwriting, for it is indifferent to the lived realities it sends players into.

In addressing overwriting, it is important to note that effects are unevenly distributed. Scholars have pointed out how AR development can re-inscribe social inequalities (Akil, 2016; Kooragayala, 2016; Hjorth, 2017). Occoquan is a publicized example in part because of the privilege it has as a relatively wealthy, white, picturesque town in an affluent region. It is a place privileged by systems of power, and so national media like the *Washington Post* paid attention to the harm overwriting caused it. Many marginalized communities do not get that same level of public recognition, or trust that speaking out about experiences would do them any good. For example, to return to the Hill District in Pittsburgh, city officials discounted lived experience and community perspectives when razing the 'Lower Hill' portion of the neighborhood in 1956. Hill residents celebrated their community's long-held importance as a center of jazz and the arts, though many hoped redevelopment plans would address Lower Hill "housing, streets, and sanitary conditions" that had grown "reprehensible" (Whitaker, 2018; Glasco, 2011, p. 38; General Committee on the Hill Survey, 1930). However, the city's Urban Redevelopment Authority framed the Hill as irreversibly "decayed" (Crowley, 2005, p. 82). They feared "property values of the [downtown would be] suppressed by the proximity of a 'slum'" and so targeted the entire Hill for redevelopment even as displaced Lower Hill residents struggled without access to long-promised new housing (Crowley, 2005, p. 82; Sala Udin in Glasco, 2011, p. xviii). By invalidating the neighborhood's self-assessment, the city devastated the Hill economically and socially (Fullilove, 2004; Hazzard, 2019; Wilson, 1997/2003, *Jitney*, 2.2). For communities like the Hill District, overwriting AR can compound the trauma of discounted lived experience.

## Level 2: Tethering

As the most successful mobile AR engages in overwriting, it may seem like this is the default mode for AR design. However, whereas *Pokémon GO* aims to be playable everywhere, many AR experiences are limited in geographic scope. They are tethered— tied to particular points in space rather than a way of transforming and gamifying space in general. Tethered AR opens up possibilities for site-specific experiences, for augmentations that build on where a user is and what they are seeing in a less categorical way. Where overwritten AR applies the same augmentation to an entire category of real world locations (for example, all Starbucks become Pokémon gyms (Kharpal, 2016)), tethered AR picks a particular, individual site as anchor for tailored augmentation (for example, the wall of one Starbucks becomes the backdrop for a digital art exhibit). Tethering does not necessarily translate into valuing place. Rather, it is a form of branding, remaking augmented space as a corporate property at the expense of lived experience.

Consider *[AR]T Walk*, an AR experience launched by Apple in 2019 in cooperation with New York's New Museum. *[AR]T Walk* pairs sites in five cities (San Francisco, New York, Tokyo, Hong Kong, and London) with work by seven artists (Nick Cave, Nathalie Djurberg and Hans Berg, Cao Fei, John Giorno, Carsten Höller, and Pipilotti Rist) to create guided AR public art tours. Each two-hour "experiential walk" features the same art works but attaches them to unique anchors within the different cityscapes (Apple, 2019b). This is an important difference from overwritten AR: tethering is geographically contained, augmenting a series of curated locations rather than the world as a whole. For example, in the San Francisco iteration of *AR[T] Walk*, users must go to a particular city park (Yerba Buena Gardens), stand at a designated point, and use an iPhone camera to access each piece of AR art.

Apple's branded, managerial presence looms large in the design and experience of *[AR]T Walk*. Each walk uses proprietary Apple technology and begins at an Apple store, and Apple employees orchestrate the experience as it is happening. *Wired*'s Peter Rubin (2019) describes the San Francisco *[AR]T Walk* as follows:

> Two employees from Apple's in-store events staff […] lead each group. One carries an iPad that controls the private *[AR]T Walk* app on the Apple-furnished XS Pluses attendees use; the other acts as a behavioral model, demonstrating at each location exactly how to trigger the AR experience.

The priority here is branded technology, and the meanings and possibilities of AR are tightly controlled: "The whole thing feels very Apple: incredibly polished and incredibly stable, as long as you did things exactly the way Apple told you to" (Rubin, 2019).

A question then arises: what kind of community do *[AR]T Walk* and tethered AR engage? It is not a community of place: tethering purposefully chooses locative anchors, but only for the benefit of the brand. For example, in Nick Cave's *Soundsuits,* a giant brightly fashioned AR being perches atop a New York City skyscraper visible from Central Park. The location here becomes a backdrop: the surroundings serve as a frame emphasizing the power of Cave's figure and Apple technology. *[AR]T Walk* uses a depopulated version of locations in all five cities, appropriating distinctive physical details of each anchor spot in a way that is detached from history or lived experience. The experience keeps user-location interactions targeted since Apple consumers are there to watch the technological spectacle as part of a sales pitch. Place-based meaning is deliberately overwhelmed by consumption.

The only community *[AR]T Walk* acknowledges is the Apple consumer base. Deirdre O'Brien, Apple's senior vice president of Retail + People, describes the walk as "a window into the creative arts made possible by our products and customers" (Apple, 2019b). This phrasing is not incidental: Apple's vision of sociality is premised on socioeconomic status and brand loyalty, and on having the money and desire to buy in to Apple's product catalogue. *[AR]T Walk*, then, routes community through commodification. That this is a branded community as opposed to a community of place is also clear in the fact that Apple stores across the United States demonstrated a scaled-down version of *[AR]T Walk* (Apple, 2019b): the Apple name and technology is its essential ingredient.

Tethered AR feeds into the broader trend of branded digital ecosystems. Corporations like Apple, Microsoft, and Google seek to create their own walled off worlds in digital systems: proprietary hardware, software, applications, and services serve every possible need a user could have without breaking the flow of profits. Augmented reality is an increasingly visible—and well funded—part of branded ecosystems (Carman, 2020; Linder, 2020; Stein, 2019). With Apple, even AR creation gets absorbed into Apple's profit-generating machine: after completing an *[AR]T Walk*, customers can sign up for training on Apple's exclusive suite of AR tools.

In tethered AR, place becomes a casualty, rendered irrelevant to AR development. *[AR]T Walk* enacts the branded enclosure of physical space through digital means. It creates Space, by Apple. Another way of engaging a place exists. When AR designers make communities of place foundational to their AR projects, they create new opportunities for process and storytelling.

## Level 3: Rooted AR

Rooted AR exhibits an awareness of the place being augmented and invites local partners as collaborators. In this level, design processes prioritize communities of place. In doing so, rooted AR respects community desires, whether affirming existing understandings of a place or imagining new ones. It is not universalizing: it acknowledges that working with one community's sense of place does not provide access to all possible ones.

Rooting is necessary because roots have not always been respected. Social psychiatrist Mindy Fullilove (2004) writes of displaced communities experiencing the emotional trauma of "root shock", of having their places "ripped away" by natural disasters or urban gentrification (p. 11). Even something that can seem inconsequential can result in community trauma if it happens without consent, "as happened in Brooklyn when the Dodgers moved to Los Angeles" (Fullilove, 2004, pp. 11-12). Technology can appropriate places in ways that do similar harm. Consider the Microsoft mapping application that routes users away from high crime areas to "avoid the ghetto" (Keyes, 2012) or the erasure of abortion clinic locations in Siri responses (NPR, 2011). Both orient users to specific, normative versions of space that foreclose local understandings. When AR is "imposed upon the community" (Fisher, 2018), it can damage communities of place. Rooted AR, in contrast, strives to treat communities respectfully, and ethically. This means not just avoiding damage, but actively trying to remedy it. Thus rooted AR conceives rooting as growth—an action of potential expansion and change, that can be terrain breaking, as well as anchoring.

Rooted AR does not have to be formulaic. In the following three case studies, we explore how rooted processes can engage different scales of production and distinct registers of community. Even when project goals like restoring historic neighborhood presences or interrogating the idea of 'progress' seem similar design outcomes and priorities are diverse.

## Village LIVE

The first example of rooted AR is *Village LIVE*, an AR mobile application that layers one perspective of queer history on to New York City's Greenwich Village. It uses the Nelson Sullivan Video Collection at New York University's Fales Library, an archive documenting the 1980's NYC queer club scene. This project prioritizes the experience of the neighborhood's physical spaces as places of queer community; it also works with community history in a way that emphasizes the relevance of archived lived experiences.

In this project, community of place is both contemporary and historical. The queer community is at the heart of the project's design, an investment that pre-dates the team's decision to work in an AR medium. As design team Shir David, Anne K. Goodfriend, and Jordan Frand explain, they were brainstorming a final project for a Design for Social Change graduate course, and they kept returning to

> the idea of safety for queer people in New York. This was 2015, and there were statistics that had shown a sharp increase in reported hate crimes or incidents against people based on sexuality in New York City. It was something that was close to us personally and we wanted to do something about that. We were also just really inspired by this archive (David et al., personal interview, 2020).

Even as the project shape shifted away from contemporary violence into historical recovery, the queer community remained at its focus. In the final version, the team set out to close a personally experienced "disconnect between the previous generations and the generations coming after us" (NowThis Future, 2018). In order to achieve this goal, they used an existing archive of video footage from iconic queer videographer Nelson Sullivan, who preserved protests, performances, and everyday moments with fellow club scene figures like RuPaul and Dean Johnson, anchoring video clips to the geographic locations where Sullivan originally filmed (Colucci, 2014). The team "wanted to see [the archive] in the world," so they anchored Nelson's footage to NYC locations in a joyful restoration of queer history (David et al., personal interview, 2020).

Since Nelson passed away in 1989, he cannot be an active community partner and design participant. The design team decides which locations, and clips, form the AR experience. However, they base their decisions on those Nelson made when alive, and include him as he positioned himself: a guide to his everyday places. To achieve this, *Village LIVE* anchors its experiences only in locations discernible from archival footage and prioritizes moments when Sullivan appears on the scene, active as both cameraman and actor, narrating his feelings about his community and gentrification of his city spaces. The deference to Nelson's agency is clear from the outset. Users are welcomed into the app with a self-introduction from Nelson's footage, proclaiming his original intention for his recordings: "Hi, I'm Nelson! I want to take you walking with me, wherever I go" (David et al., 2017).

In this way, *Village LIVE* centers around retrieving Nelson's lived experiences and restoring those past inscriptions of place to the cityscape. This intention is visible in the application's interface design. The main screen is a map with tour points, offering brief descriptions and walking directions. When at a point, users scan their surroundings, matching an in-app photo to its physical counterpart (details unlikely to change anytime soon, like The Stonewall Inn's historic plaque). Doing this plays a clip from Nelson's archive, letting users see that place from Nelson's time. This connection between a location's physical materiality (Stonewall Inn's plaque) and lived experiences (Nelson recounting his arrival in NYC during the Stonewall riots) is distinctive of rooted AR, which anchors to and through a place. Unlike in overwritten AR, the photo-capture feature of *Village LIVE* is crucial for users to access content; you cannot fully use the app if you are not physically in the same place Nelson filmed. In this way, the design team roots their project to Nelson, taking their design cues from the cityscape Nelson captured and how he narrated those places.

*Village LIVE* allows users to encounter places in Greenwich Village through a new layer of meaning. As the design team said,

> it is one thing to read about someone's experience in New York, it is another thing to stand in the place where they stood and watch what they saw. AR presented the opportunity to situate someone in the same physical location and experience this view (David et al., personal interview, 2020).

With promises that users will "never look at these streets the same way again after you've seen them through Nelson's eyes", this venture uses AR to make queer inscriptions of place accessible (David et al., 2017). *Village LIVE* shows one way that rooted AR can circulate preserved community understandings of place.

## Mariposa AR

The next example of rooted AR enables community access and self-narration. *Mariposa AR* anchors stories of community migration to two murals ("I Am My Own Muse" by Argentinian artist Cecilia Lueza and "Juchari Ziranhua / Nuestros Raices / Our Roots" by Mexican-American artist Cornelio Campo) commissioned by the North Carolina Museum of Art (*Frieda Khalo,* 2019-2020; Lueza, 2019; Campos, 2019). *Mariposa AR* also offers a different organizational model for rooted AR—one where the design process explicitly includes training for community-based practitioners. In this project, the Code the Dream (CTD) design team operates within and for the local community as a way of making the design community more inclusive (Code the Dream, 2020a).

CTD's model is ethically aligned with the idea of rootedness. It brings community collaboration into the design process by offering a way for "students from diverse backgrounds to build real apps to launch their tech careers" (Code the Dream, 2020a). In this way, CTD projects equalize access to design education and experience for students from low-income backgrounds, creating what Costanza-Chock calls a more "equitable distribution of benefits" (2020, p. 23). Designing the *Mariposa AR* project served as an AR development training experience for two CTD student developers, Irene Serrano and Jorge Rodriguez, who worked with a CTD supervisor to realize the project. Their training was prioritized as both an intended contribution-to and outcome-of the project; their training was part of the project's design goals. This is visible in the structure of *Mariposa AR*'s launch, where Serrano and Rodriguez introduced the project to journalists and were recognized as the designers (Russom, 2020). Through projects like *Mariposa AR*, CTD then brings students from backgrounds historically excluded from design positions into the role of designers. Rooting not only lowers barriers of entry into design communities, but also invites community members into projects where their expertise is relevant. Serrano and Rodriguez both migrated from Mexico; they have lived experience relevant to this project about Mexican art and migration.

In addition to expanding access to design training, *Mariposa AR* engages in place-making. Its AR experiences are anchored to the Durham convention center, a location built for events like conferences and conventions. Although this space hosts experiences that matter to groups of people (fans, employees, competitors), its communities of place are fleeting, and often non-local. *Mariposa AR* adds local meaning to this location. In an act of place-making, the AR experience brings crowdsourced stories of migration to Durham and anchors them to the walls of the convention center.[3] Users scan the mariposa (butterfly) in the mural "Juchari Ziranhua" to access crowdsourced stories of migration plotted on a 3D globe. Each story is attached to a monarch butterfly that can 'migrate' as a kaleidoscope of butterflies, landing at home in Durham, symbolizing the building of Durham's migrant community. By attaching these stories to the Durham convention center, a public space designed to accommodate foot traffic, *Mariposa AR* does not negatively affect community understanding of the AR location. Instead, it builds meaning, and transforms the convention center into a place. This was evident during the launch where, as a member of CTD described:

> People were finding new ways to engage with art. Downtown Durham was more dynamic as a result of the app, promising unique ways for people to be a part of their city. And perhaps most importantly, immigrants and their stories were being celebrated, both by the app and by the media […] launch day reminded us of our connections to art, to our city, and to each other (Russom 2020).

*Mariposa AR* proclaims the importance of migrant experiences by making a place for migrant community.

## Still Here

Although *Mariposa AR* is student-designed, professional storytelling practices also benefit from rooting. *Still Here* (2020), an AR project by AJ Contrast (a division of

---

[3] *Mariposa AR* is different from much crowdsourced AR, which can seem like meaningful community inclusion but often prescribes an already defined software and narrative framework. Another example of meaningful crowdsourcing is Mark Skwarek's *OccupyAR* (2011), which solicited "AR activists" to augment Wall Street in conjunction with Occupy Wall Street protests. Participants without AR design experience could send Skwarek videos and photos of themselves posing as though they held protest signs—Swarek then layered signs into their images and added them to the augmented occupation.

media conglomerate Al Jazeera), immerses users in the experiences of women of color navigating life post-incarceration. This critically acclaimed piece prioritizes community control of place and representation, showing that rooted AR does not have to foreclose wide circulation and award recognition.

Besides acclaim, *Still Here*'s rooted process results in a better relationship with community collaborators. Nine formerly incarcerated women of color were invited into the project very early, "with workshops on immersive storytelling, storyboarding the VR and AR scripts," and their collaboration continued through "feedback during the post process" (Al Jazeera Media Network, 2020). Notice how AJ Contrast not only established community connections, but also dedicated time to negotiate different fields of expertise between their media production team and Women's Prison Association collaborators. This process allowed community members to affect, challenge, and change the project design priorities and choices from the beginning. One collaborator, Elaine Daly, suggests AJ Contrast's approach is "unique," as "more often, we are approached by storytellers looking to check boxes, but with this platform, we drew the boxes ourselves, and the team filled them in with their own creativity and amazing technology" (Al Jazeera Media Network, 2020). This rooted process of collaboration approaches formerly incarcerated collaborators like Daly as "experts in our own stories" instead of experiences to be mined without agency.

Drawing from these lived experiences, *Still Here* follows a previously incarcerated character (Jasmine) as she returns to a gentrified Harlem. Users begin on a virtual street covered with flickering visuals of now-missing-but-vividly-remembered homes, people, and businesses. These figures of Black Harlem temporarily reclaim their places from the ubiquitous cafes and white-washed inhabitants that replaced them. Their flickering presence mimics the physical overwriting that has uprooted Jasmine's place; by experiencing this erasure of Black community, users are confronted with the emotional trauma of having a place "ripped away" (Fullilove, 2004, p. 11). Notably, the AR experience that allows community partners to make their own boxes values community control over lived experiences and places.

This is one reason why *Still Here*'s users are not physically in Jasmine's neighborhood. *Still Here* is community-specific and built through rooted design, but it does not require on-location viewing. This design choice allowed the project to debut at the prestigious Sundance film festival in Utah. It also avoids further invasion of Black community spaces that have already suffered from being commercialized, recoded, and dismantled for outside use. By making even the geographic connection to the places of Harlem digital, *Still Here* brings questions about racist urban gentrification to all audiences, including the people who gentrify.

## Spreading Roots

Rooted AR is as much about the process of community involvement and relationship about place as it is about project outcomes or mechanics. Consider how these examples of rooted AR evoke communities of place. *Still Here* engages how personal anchors of lived experience, like home and neighborhood, become unrecognizable for previously incarcerated women. *Mariposa AR* is an equity-focused educational opportunity that enacts place-making. *Village LIVE* provides access to one queer community member's experiences of place to users distanced in time.

As each example suggests, there is interest for rooted AR across different kinds of institutions. *Village LIVE* won university-based grants and was a finalist in an entrepreneurship competition (David et al., personal interview, 2020). *Mariposa AR* was designed in partnership with a prominent museum (North Carolina Museum of Art) and commissioned by Google Fiber.[4] City officials also expressed interest in further AR collaborations after seeing the finished product (Russom, 2020). *Still Here* debuted at Sundance and won at the Telly Awards and the Drum Awards (Al Jazeera Media Network, 2020). The variety of support and recognition should encourage AR practitioners about the viability and opportunity of rooted AR. Though *Village LIVE, Mariposa AR*, and *Still Here* show potential ways forward, the category of rooted AR is still largely aspirational.

**Table 5.1:** Levels of Community Engagement in AR

| Level | Design Process | Relationship to Place | Community Type | Example |
|---|---|---|---|---|
| Overwriting | Resource rich, industry-based development Can incorporate crowdsourced content in limited way | Pervasive reach; everywhere but nowhere Category-based engagement with environment (e.g. bodies of water) | Community of Play | *Pokémon GO* |
| Tethering | Brand and technology-driven development Managed user experiences | Site-specific; anchored to one or multiple locations Incorporates physical characteristics of individual sites (e.g. a specific building) | Branded Community | *[AR]T Walk* |
| Rooting | Collaborative design including community partners Community determines project priorities | Site- and Community-specific; anchors to and through place Connects physical details of spaces to lived experience | Community of Place | *Village LIVE* *Mariposa AR* *Still Here* |

# Roadmap for Rooted AR

As the examples above show, community engagement and spatial attentiveness occurs across a scale of intensity, from overwriting, to tethering, to rooting (see Table

---

[4]  Here, Google's position as background financier is different from the branded community seen in Level 2, Tethering.

5.1). All have their uses for specific AR projects. However, this chapter particularly encourages AR designers to consider the possibilities of rooted design. What follows is a roadmap, distilled from the above case studies, for those who aspire to build AR that nurtures communities of place. These steps are loosely sequenced for AR development, but can be rearranged and remixed according to project needs.

- Approach communities as experts by *listening* as both a value and a inciting procedural move. Search for existing community organizations and talk with them about their goals, worries, and existing projects. Who does it make sense to partner with for your particular project?
- Ask community partners to share their lived spatial experiences of the sites to be augmented—and value their expertise. Pay attention to both the everyday uses and presentations of place for outside audiences. How can you continue, expand, or challenge those experiences through AR?
- Be sensitive that relationships of place can be emotional, even traumatic. Can your project engage them without being extractive or creating more trauma?
- Define the scope and goals of your project. Find ways to ethically balance the needs of various stakeholders, prioritizing those of the community whenever possible. What is each stakeholder, including you, unwilling to compromise? Why are these elements so important?
- Formalize collaboration with community partners by establishing parameters for communication, ownership, and maintenance. Agree upon the benefit of the project to everyone involved. Is this partnership equitable?
- Spend time in the locations you want to augment and observe how they function as lived spaces. How do people interact with that place and with each other? How will your project affect those interactions?
- Seek out additional narratives of the place being augmented. Community organizations have situated, experiential knowledge of a place, which is always partial. Where are the gaps or conflicts in this place's story? What histories are buried or overwritten?
- Make feedback and iteration integral. Ideally, community partners have the power of veto throughout the design process. How will you create opportunities for reevaluation and revision? Who are you inviting to offer feedback?

## Conclusion: Rooting the Future

Orienting questions of design, justice, and place around AR newly activates these concepts. As the examples of overwriting, tethering, and rooting AR have shown, AR design always contends with communities of place—even when it chooses not to prioritize them. This chapter argues that AR practitioners need to engage communities of place and offers rooting as an AR-specific theory and practice of design justice.

Though this chapter focuses on AR, it also has broader applications. For spatial studies, emerging mixed-reality technologies add layers to our understanding of place, complicating frameworks of community formation. This offers both opportunities and challenges in imagining equitable place-making, opening new ways to undermine systems of power. For design, this chapter shows how practitioners can combine a spatial orientation and a commitment to equity. It hopes that other design fields invested in spatiality, from mapping to architecture to urban planning, take up and elaborate similar justice-oriented practice for their own fields.

As design fields face pushback from historically excluded groups, this is a moment of reevaluation and change. As a new medium, AR has the potential to establish ethical development practices from the outset. Upcoming AR designers will decide who design serves, who gets to design, and who gets credited for it. Rooting AR in communities of place helps answer these questions while minimizing harm. Rooting as a method hopes to "prevent further damage by nurturing the world's neighborhoods instead of destroying them; we who care about community are many" (Fullilove, 2004, p. 7). By joining Fullilove's "we," designers have the opportunity to change the ethos and process of design.

## Put it Into Practice: Cultivating Roots in AR

1. In small groups, imagine a new narrative-driven mobile AR game set in your local area.
2. Pick three physical locations to use as anchors for your narrative. Map them on Google Maps. Describe how and why you would augment your chosen sites. How would these locations be used in your game's narrative?
3. Present your group's AR game to the class.
4. As a class, discuss any patterns in the locations you chose. Where do your stories happen? How do these new gameworlds mobilize or ignore place? Are you overwriting?
5. Break back into your groups. Discuss the communities that have a lived stake in your chosen locations. (Research if necessary!) Make a list of possible groups, organizations, or individuals you could work with if you were to develop your AR game as a rooted practitioner. How would your game generate conflict with existing uses of place? What in your design idea needs to change to make these potential partnerships more viable?
6. *Optional:* As a class, discuss how the AR games changed in Step 5, when groups specifically took communities of place into account.

## Acknowledgements

Much of our thinking about community engagement results from collaborations with Terri Baltimore of the Hill House Association; Ervin Dyer, Paul Ellis, and Christopher Rawson of the August Wilson House Organization; and Kirk Holbrook of the University of Pittsburgh Community Engagement Center in the Hill District.

# References

Akil, O. (2016). Warning: Pokemon GO is a death sentence if you are a Black man. Medium. https://medium.com/dayone-a-new-perspective/ warning-pokemon-go-is-a-death-sentence-if-you-are-a-black-man-acacb4bdae7f

Al Jazeera Contrast. (2020). Still Here (Version 1.1). https://ajcontrast.com/watch-stillhere

Al Jazeera Media Network. (2020). About Still Here. https://ajcontrast.com/about-stillhere

Algorithmic Justice League. (2020). Mission, team, and story. https://www.ajl.org/about

Apple (2019a). Apple offers new augmented reality art sessions. https://www.apple.com/ newsroom/2019/07/apple-offers-new-augmented-reality-art-sessions/

Apple (2019b). [AR]T Walk [Private augmented reality application].

Benjamin, R. (2016). Catching our breath: Critical race STS and the carceral imagination. *Engaging Science, Technology, and Society*, 2, 145-156.

Benjamin, R. (2019). *Captivating Technology: Race, Carceral Technoscience, and Liberatory Imagination in Everyday Life*. Duke University Press.

Bolter, J.D., MacIntyre, B., Gandy, M. and Schweiz, P. (2006). New media and the permanent crisis of aura. *Convergence: The International Journal of Research into New Media Technologies*, 12(1), 21-39. https://doi.org/10.1177/1354856506061550

Cave, N. (2019). *Soundsuits* [Augmented Reality Artwork]. New York, NY, United States.

Campos, C. (2019). Juchari Ziranhua/Nuestros Raices/Our Roots [Public mural]. Durham Convention Center. The North Carolina Museum of Art and the City of Durham Cultural and Public Arts Program, Durham, NC, United States. https://durhamnc.gov/3245/Public-Art-Collection

Carman, A. (2020). Google buys AR glasses company North. *The Verge*. https://www.theverge.com/2020/6/30/21308281/google-north-focals-glasses-purchase-acquire

Cresswell, T. (2015). *Place, an Introduction*. Wiley Blackwell.

Code the Dream. (2020a). About. Code the Dream. https://www.codethedream.org/about/

Code the Dream (2020b). Mariposa AR (Version 1.04). https://www.codethedream.org/ mariposa-ar/

Costanza-Chock, S. (2020). *Design Justice: Community-led Practices to Build the Worlds We Need*. The MIT Press.

Colucci, E. (2014). Remembering New York's Downtown Documentarian Nelson Sullivan. *Vice*. https://www.vice.com/en_us/article/8gdv3v/ remembering-downtowns-documentarian-nelson-sullivan

Creative Reaction Lab. (n.d.) Our Approach. https://www.creativereactionlab.com/our-approach

Crowley, G. (2005). *The Politics of Place: Contentious Urban Redevelopment in Pittsburgh*. University of Pittsburgh Press.

David, S., Goodfriend, A. and Frand, J. (2020, June 18). Personal Interview. (Since an interview did not put et al.)

David, S., Goodfriend, A. and Frand, J. (2017). *Village Live*. https://annekgoodfriend.github.io/Bootstrap_villageLIVE/

Design Justice Network. (2018). *Design Justice Network Principles*. https://designjustice.org/read-the-principles

Dyer, E. (2001). Freedom Corner dedicated in Hill District: Memorial marks battle for civil rights. The Pittsburgh Post-Gazette. http://old.post-gazette.com/regionstate/20010423freedomreg2.asp

Escobar, A. (2018). *Designs for the Pluriverse: Radical Interdependence, Autonomy, and the making of Worlds*. Duke University Press.

Evans, L. and Saker, M. (2019). The Playeur and Pokémon Go: Examining the effects of locative play on spatiality and sociability. *Mobile Media and Communication*, 7(2), 232-247.

Fisher, J., Shangguan, L. and Crisp, J.S. (2018). Developing a platform for community-curated mixed reality play spaces [Abstract]. CHI Play '18, Melbourne, Victoria, Australia. https://doi.org/10.1145/3270316.3271513

Frida Kahlo, Diego Rivera, and Mexican Modernism from the Jacques and Natasha Gelman Collection [Exhibition] (2019-2020). The North Carolina Museum of Art, Raleigh, NC, United States. https://ncartmuseum.org/calendar/series_parent/frida_kahlo_diego_rivera_and_mexican_modernism_from_the_jacques_and_natasha

Fullilove, M.T. (2004). Root shock: How tearing up city neighborhoods hurts America, and what we can do about it. One World/Ballantine Book.

Graham, M., Zook, M. and Boulton, A. (2013). Augmented reality in urban places: Contested content and the duplicity of code. *Transactions of the Institute of British Geographers*, 38, 464-479. https://doi.org/10.1111/j.1475-5661.2012.00539.x

Glasco, L.A. and Rawson, C. (2011). *August Wilson: Pittsburgh Places in his Life and Plays*. Pittsburgh History & Landmarks Foundation.

Grant, G., Della-Bosca, D., Patterson, D., Prenzler, S. and Roberts, S. (2019). Explorations in mixed reality with learning and teaching frameworks: Lessons from Ludus and the Vulcan Academy. pp. 103-125). *In*: V. Geroimenko (ed.). *Augmented Reality Games II: The Gamification of Education, Medicine and Art*. Springer.

Harvey, D. (1993). From space to place and back again. pp. 3-29. *In*: J. Bird, B. Curtis, T. Putnam, G. Robertson and L. Tickner (eds.). Mapping the Futures: Local Cultures, Global Changes. Routledge.

Harvey, D. (2012). *RebelCcities*: *From the Right to the City to Urban Revolution*. Verso.

Hazzard, K. (2019). The first responders: The Black men from Pittsburgh who made up America's first paramedics corps wanted to make history and save lives—starting with their own. *The Atavist Magazine*, 92. https://magazine.atavist.com/the-first-responders-paramedics-pittsburgh-civil-rights-ems

Heldman, B. (2016). Pokemon Go adds new safety warnings. *Entertainment Weekly*. http://ew.com/article/2016/07/31/pokemon-go-new-safety-warnings/

Hjorth, L. and Richardson, I. (2017). Pokemon GO: Mobile media play, place-making, and the digital wayfarer. *Mobile Media & Communication*, 5(1), 3-14.

Keyes, A. (2020). This app was made for walking, but is it racist? *NPR*. https://www.npr.org/2012/01/25/145337346/this-app-was-made-for-walking-but-is-it-racist

Khalil, D. and Kier, M. (2017). Critical race design: An emerging methodological approach to anti-racist design and implementation research. *International Journal of Adult Vocational Education and Technology*, 8(2), 54-71.

Kharpal, A. (2016). Starbucks is launching a 'Pokémon Go Frappuccino' as its stores become gym locations. CNBC. https://www.cnbc.com/2016/12/09/starbucks-pokemon-go-frappuccino-stores-become-gym-pokestop-locations.html

Kooragayala, S. and Srini, T. (2016). Pokémon GO is changing how cities use public space, but could it be more inclusive? Urban Institute. https://www.urban.org/urban-wire/pokemon-go-changing-how-cities-use-public-space-could-it-be-more-inclusive

Linder, C. (2020). Everything we know about Apple's smart glasses. Popular Mechanics. https://www.popularmechanics.com/technology/gadgets/a33022469/apple-augmented-reality-smart-glasses/

Lueza, Cecilia (2019). I Am My Own Muse [Public mural]. Durham Convention Center. The North Carolina Museum of Art and the City of Durham Cultural and Public Arts Program, Durham, NC, United States. https://durhamnc.gov/3245/Public-Art-Collection

Mars, R. (Host) (2020). Map quests: Physical, political, digital (No. 393) [Audio podcast episode]. In 99% Invisible. https://99percentinvisible.org/episode/map-quests-political-physical-and-digital

Massey, D. (1994). A Global Sense of Place. pp. 146-157. *In*: Space, Place, and Gender. University of Minnesota Press.

Massey, D. (1999). On Space and the City. pp. 157-176. *In*: Doreen Massey, John Allen and Steve Pile (eds.). City Worlds. Routledge and The Open University.

Niantic, Inc. (2016). Pokémon GO (Version 1.145.2). https://www.pokemongo.com/en-us/

NowThis Future (2018). 'VillegeLIVE' app highlight queer history in New York. Facebook. https://www.facebook.com/NowThisFuture/videos/2166546536719848/UzpfSTM1MjYyOTg0NTI1NDUzODo0MjY2OTU1NjQ1MTQ2MzI/

Papanek, Victor (1974). *Designs for the Real World.* Paladin.

Reilly, K. (2016). Pennsylvania Teenager Hit by Car While Playing Pokémon Go. Time. https://time.com/4405221/pokemon-go-teen-hit-by-car/

Rovener, Julie (2011). Siri's Position On Abortion? A Glitch, Not Conspiracy, Apple Says. NPR. https://www.npr.org/sections/health-shots/2011/12/02/143067993/siris-anti-abortion-tendencies-a-re sult-of-technology-not-apple-conspiracy

Rubin, P. (2019). Apple puts the AR in 'art' (and in 'transparent sky-being'). Wired. https://www.wired.com/story/apple-ar-art-walk/

Russom, R. (2020). Launch Day at Code the Dream. Code the Dream. https://www.codethedream.org/launch-day-at-code-the-dream/

Sharma, H.N., Alharthi, S., Dolgov, I. and Tuops, Z. (2017). A framework supporting selecting space to make place in spatial mixed reality play. *CHI PLAY*, 83-100. https://doi.org/10.1145/3116595.3116612

Skwarek, Mark (2011). AR Occupy Wall Street. https://aroccupywallstreet.wordpress.com/join-participate/

Soja, E. (1996). *Thirdspace: Journeys to Los Angeles and Other Real-and-imagined Places.* Blackwell Publishers Inc.

Stein, P. (2016). Pokemon Go's augmented reality is augmenting the reality of this small town. Washington Post. https://www.washingtonpost.com/local/pokemon-gos-augmented-reality-is-augmenting-the-reality-of-this-small-town/2016/08/13/b39cd6f2-5e1d-11e6-8e45-477372e89d78_story.html

Stein, S. (2019). Facebook is making AR glasses and is mapping the world for them to work. CNET. https://www.cnet.com/news/facebook-is-making-ar-glasses-and-is-mapping-the-world-for-them-to-work/

Stokes, B., Hill, A. and Dols, S. (2019). City tactics for Pokémon GO: Remixing commercial platforms for local events [Conference paper]. ICA Conference 2019: Communication Beyond Boundaries, Washington, D.C., United States.

Sullivan, Nelson (1976-1989). Nelson Sullivan Video Collection (MSS.357), Fales Library and Special Collection. New York University Special Collections Center, NY, United States.

Tuan, Y. (1977). *Space and Place: The Perspective of Experience.* University of Minnesota Press.

Whitaker, Mark (2018). *Smoketown: The Untold Story of the Other Great Black Renaissance.* Simon & Schulster.

Wilson, A. (2003). *Jitney.* The Overlook Press (1997).

# Chapter
# 6

# The Ethics of Augmentation: A Case Study in Contemplative Mixed Reality

**Kevin Healey**

Associate Professor of Communication, University of New Hampshire
2 Hoitt Drive, Durham, NH 03824
Email: Kevin.Healey@unh.edu

## Introduction: Augmentation of What?

To develop ethical guidelines for AR and MR design, the technical and philosophical assumptions of standard definitions of augmented reality (AR) need to be questioned. Consider for example the following definition from Milgram and Kishino (1994, p. 4):

> As an operational definition of Augmented Reality, we take the term to refer to any case in which an otherwise real environment is "augmented" by means of virtual (computer graphic) objects.

The technical assumption in this definition is that augmentation takes the form of digital or computerized media. This is clearly too narrow a definition, as the history of media aesthetics includes, and should continue to include, specific attention to analog as well as digital formations. Long before HoloLens, Vive, or mobile AR applications, artists developed the technique of linear perspective "for the purpose of creating the illusion of three dimensions in their work" as part of a broader project "to make the painting a window on to a world" (Engberg and Bolter, 2014, p. 4). Nineteenth-century panoramic displays similarly aimed to create an immersive experience, essentially representing an earlier, analog form of virtual reality (Bolter et al., 2013, p. 42).

The philosophical assumption in the above definition is that augmentation is a process of expanding or adding to an existing environment, with the implication that the original 'real' environment remains essentially the same. More recent discussions carry the same assumption, as in the suggestion that AR portends "a future in which our physical surroundings are *enhanced* or *overlaid* with digital visualizations" (Cowling et al., 2017, p. 43, emphasis added). In these frameworks, AR adds virtual objects to a pre-existing set of objects in a particular space. A similar assumption persists regarding VR environments, where augmentation is understood to be adding 'real' objects to an immersive virtual space.

While these definitions are technically useful for developing platforms and systems, they are ineffective in terms of understanding the social implications of such systems. This is not a criticism per se, but a reminder that working definitions reflect particular intentions and purposes, and therefore have ideological implications in addition to technical ones. In fact, technically-focused definitions of AR contain an implicit ethical assumption, that is, empirical knowledge about the physical environment can, and perhaps should, precede any ethical assessment of a particular technology. A related implication here is that questions of ethics ought to be addressed after the fact, since design and development are assumed to be morally neutral processes.

The framework proposed here turns this technical assumption on its head, following Levinas' (1969) insistence that ethics "precedes ontology" (p. 43). In this formulation, human experience is driven primarily by questions of ethics, and secondarily by questions of knowledge. The definitions above are helpful as far as they go, provided they are understood within a broader ethical context. In this chapter, the 'ethics of augmentation' therefore refers to the question of what is being augmented socially, politically, and ideologically through the introduction of new forms of mediation.[1] As Jafari Naimi (2015) explains:

> The key question at the forefront of design and criticism as we deploy and employ such technologies is: What vision of social interaction is sought and advanced through this design and does it appropriately characterize and address the problematic situation at hand? (p. 10)

From this perspective, augmentation is not simply additive but transformative—a process by which an environment is changed in a holistic and ecological sense. The mediated presence of virtual objects and images does more than append or supplement an existing environment; instead it generates a new social and ethical environment altogether. Media studies have long understood there is "a feedback loop in which our view of the world changes our designs, and our use of new artefacts and designs changes how we perceive the world" (Bolter et al., 2013, p. 39). This iterative and holistic process is a consistent theme within Science and Technology Studies (STS) and the narrower field of Medium Theory.

Technologies tend to augment or amplify pre-existing social conditions in ways that artists, designers, business leaders, and politicians fail to anticipate, or which they avoid acknowledging. Augmentation may imply distortion, imbalance, or instability if the systemic impact is undesirable. In this case something valuable is lost or diminished. Alternately, augmentation may lead to greater balance and more stability, if its impact over time is desirable and something valuable is restored, recaptured, or increased. In either case a transformative, systemic effect is nearly certain, which is why media scholars insist that technologies are never morally neutral, contrary to the assumptions embedded in most technical definitions of AR. Technologies tend to

---

[1] I would go so far as to say that ethics itself, as a method and endeavor, is a technology of augmentation in the sense that it creates a virtual presence for people who are absent, underrepresented, or who do not yet exist.

amplify or augment specific social and ethical issues, making some more pressing than others and in need of attention. The moral landscape changes along with the physical and technical one. With these premises in mind, this chapter aims to place questions about the ethics of augmentation at the center of any discussion of media aesthetics.

## Design Aesthetics as Ethical Practice

Against more limited, traditional definitions, the term "aesthetics" has evolved to refer to "the study of our perception of our whole environment, not just objects of beauty" (Bolter et al., 2013, p. 38). Since media technologies play an increasingly central role in perception, aesthetics must of necessarily include "a range of emotional, affective, and even tangible relationships with technology" (Bolter et al., 2013, p. 38). This chapter suggests that, in aiming to move beyond 'beauty' to address these types of relationships, media aesthetics actually aims to capture a range of concepts from virtue ethics. Chief among these are wisdom, integrity, and hope. Introducing these virtue terms and their accompanying vices moves the discussion beyond what is aesthetically pleasing (visually or otherwise) to what is worth pursuing socially and technologically. This approach asks, for example, whether emergent systems augment wisdom or ignorance; authenticity or disingenuousness; courage or cowardice.

On reflection it is apparent that media aesthetics is fundamentally an ethical endeavor. As a program of research, media aesthetics extends beyond observation and reflection to involve active participation in the production of new forms and structures of technical mediation. In this sense it is a form of "productive theory" whose goal is not merely to critique but to improve or otherwise transform technically-mediated experiences (Bolter et al., 2013, p. 38). Insofar as scholars aim to "guide designers as they explore new forms of digital media" (Bolter et al., 2013, p. 37), such guidance must include attention to the immediate social context of design as well as its potential long-term implications. New technical systems tend to reflect, and therefore to augment, whatever ideologies, worldviews, and assumptions are already present. Each such worldview, in turn, has its own moral center of gravity—its own ecology of vice and virtue.

The lay public has an implicit understanding of this basic premise, as evidenced by recent public debates about Google Glass and police body cameras, both of which broadly qualify as MR (the former legitimately qualifying as AR) (see Healey and Stephens, 2017). Research on those debates demonstrates that the public understands intuitively how MR and AR platforms augment not just information but institutions and systems of social power. By making these ethical concerns explicit, we broaden the term 'augmentation' to refer not simply to a description of the technical features of specific environments, but to an assessment of their broader political and economic impacts.

To summarize, the ethics of augmentation proceeds from the premise that systemic transformation is part and parcel of MR development. Its charge is therefore twofold: first, to understand the extent and type of transformation we can reasonably expect from new devices and platforms; second and perhaps more importantly, to ask before design begins what we intend to amplify, augment, or increase socially and ethically, not merely informationally. The analog pre-history of Human-computer Interaction (HCI) research is important in underscoring these concerns about ethical universals like wisdom, compassion, and integrity. At the same time, the increasing intensity of mediation in our technical environments (its immersiveness and fidelity of reproduction) makes these ethical questions more pressing and urgent (see Engberg and Bolter, 2020).

## Making the 'Spatial Turn'

The unique affordances of mobile devices and mapping applications provide scholars and designers "the opportunity to redefine the relationship between information and our physical and built up environments" (Bolter et al., 2013, p. 39). To develop such technologies ethically, it is important to put this opportunity in historical perspective. In recent decades, scholarship in the humanities and social sciences has witnessed a "spatial turn"—that is, a shift in thinking about the importance of place and space (Warf and Arias, 2009, pp. 1-2). This shift involves not just a renewed emphasis on geography, but an upheaval of the modernist assumptions that have traditionally accompanied geographic and cartographic thought. Modernity espouses a fantasy of "absolute space" in which "static places" each serve as "an inert container" for social reality (Warf, 2009, p. 75). Further, modernist thought understands geography as "a homogenous plane that pre-exists coherent, well-ordered societies" and consequently modern Cartesian geographies "create a false dichotomy between the local and the global" (Warf, 2009, p. 75). The spatial turn upends these assumptions.

Contrary to modernist notions, social life is embodied and situated, unfolding in "interconnected sets of places" (Warf, 2009, p. 75). In this view, "relational geographies are always dynamic, incomplete, forever coming into being, and perpetually in flux, giving rise to ever-changing patterns of centrality and peripherality" (Warf, 2009, p. 75). Scholarship in this critical vein understands that space and place are not simply found, discovered, or described; they are co-created, and ongoingly reconstructed, in ways that reflect shifting power relationships. Information technologies are part of this spatial turn insofar as they disrupt traditional techniques of map-making and historical understandings of space and time. GIS technologies provide tools to "analyze spatiality" in a way that "is not simply reflective of the new importance of space, but also constitutive of it" (Warf and Arias, 2009, p. 6).

While such affordances represent a potential transformation toward more equitable map-making, it is important to avoid naïve optimism regarding the long-term impact of GIS. As noted above, technologies tend to reflect and augment existing ideologies. GIS is no different in this regard, being tethered to a positivist ideology that defines 'truth' in a narrow way that historically has privileged some social groups while marginalizing others. In other words, there is real potential for a colonizing ideology to drive GIS technologies in a way that displaces its potential for social empowerment of marginalized groups.

As early as the mid-1990s, scholars argued that GIS textbooks tend to support a "myopic vision" or "technocratic myopia" where GIS is understood as the domain of the military or commercial strategists (Pickles, 1995, p. 16) while displacing potentially disruptive uses for "local action groups" and state counter-surveillance (Pickles, 1995, p. 17). More recently, scholars have argued that AR and MR applications often reflect outdated and techno-centric assumptions about the purpose of emergent technical systems. Consider this forward-thinking question about the so-called Internet of Things (IoT):

> What would the world look like if the IoT wasn't about rendering our physical world tractable to computational systems and was instead about the preservation of the unique personal meanings that accumulate around our material objects? (Cowling et al., 2017, p. 44)

Such questions highlight the ideological assumptions embedded in development, underscoring the need for examples of "best practices" (Cowling et al., 2017, p. 42) that place user- and citizen-centered experiences of meaning and value above more utilitarian goals, whether commercial, military, or otherwise. The spatial turn thus represents more than the mere possibility of injecting more information into, or deriving more information from, our built environments. As a guide for technical development, spatial thinking offers the opportunity to transform structures of power, whether physical or ideological, into "an ethically-responsive and economically-sustainable architecture of human flourishing" (Healey, 2014, p. 208).

## Ethics as a Form of Cognitive Mapping

In the ethics of augmentation outlined in this chapter, 'mapping' will serve as a driving metaphor. Here this term refers to two processes: the literal act of creating physical maps of the 'real' world, whether analog or digital; and the metaphorical process of creating mental or 'cognitive' maps of social and emotional reality. Physical and cognitive maps are clearly interdependent and, as noted above, neither are morally neutral. One draws from and depends upon the other in terms of both accuracy and sophistication. Leading an ethical life involves developing a capacity for mapping, i.e. the ability to perceive, understand, and navigate the complexities of our physical, social, and emotional lives. An ethically-informed design aesthetic should yield technologies that enhance, rather than undercut, this quintessentially human 'mapping' capacity.

A map is always/already ethical whether or not it is articulated in physical form. In the narrowest sense of the term, a cognitive map is a simple and practical representation of physical space—a mental heuristic that allows us to get from home to work and back again (see Downs and Stea, 1977). Yet even such seemingly benign day-to-day maps represent both physical and social value. People tend to be myopic in their geographic knowledge, forming cognitive maps that are self-serving if not narcissistic (Sinton and Bednarz, 2007, p. 20). Good citizenship, such as knowing how to respond to environmental catastrophes, depends on forming cognitive maps that are both accurate and inclusive (Sinton and Bednarz, 2007, pp. 20-21).

Beyond the day-to-day lives of individuals, questions of "cartographic power" on a collective scale long preceded digital applications (McHaffie, 1995, p. 115). The drive to "put something on the map" (McHaffie, 1995, p. 115) speaks directly to the relations of power involved in physical map-making, for sure, and also to questions of culture and ideology. Commonplace metaphors, as when a social group aspires to "put us on the map" (McHaffie, 1995, p. 115), underscore the inseparability of social-emotional reality from the embodied, technically-mediated world. Movements from women's suffrage to civil rights and Black Lives Matter are efforts to put those who have been devalued by cultural norms and political ideologies 'on the map'.

Two key principles emerge from the use of 'mapping' as a conceptual foundation for the ethics of mixed-reality applications. First, ethically sustainable MR allows for flexibility and growth in users' physical and social environment cognitive maps. To put it simply, ethical MR encourages creativity and imagination with regard to participants' understanding of themselves in relation to the world. Second, it brings intentionality to this creative flexibility, imbuing it with a sense of meaning and purpose. Since Aristotle, philosophers of virtue ethics have held that the experience of meaning and purpose is inseparable from the pursuit of higher-order character traits like integrity and wisdom. The pursuit of such virtues involves a willingness and a capacity to question one's sense of self and one's place in the world. Ethical MR should therefore encourage moments of "spatial uncertainty" (Downs and Stea, 1977, p. 212), leveraging such moments for personal and social transformation.

The upshot of these two principles is that ethical MR allows participants to "learn *how* to learn" (Downs and Stea, 1977, p. 213, emphasis original), creating a culture of curiosity and capability. It is active rather than passive. Over time, across different platforms and applications, ethical MR should encourage users to develop a sort of meta-map that represents a wide range of places, persons, and perspectives around the world. Such a comprehensive 'map of maps' is a defining characteristic of more advanced stages of ethical and moral development (Labouvie-Vief, 2000, pp. 110-111). In fact, an important aspect of post-conventional moral thought is the capacity to understand the relationship between different and conflicting maps, i.e. worldviews or ideologies, held by others. Such a capacity allows individuals to facilitate civil discourse, turning cross-cultural conflicts into opportunities for social change.

## Mapping the Ethics of Mixed Reality

In order to leverage the affordances of MR for their potential long-term benefits to the public good, we have to move beyond technical typologies of MR (types of environments) to ethical rubrics that actively assess, diagnose, and prescribe their social impact, for better or worse. This section argues therefore that an ethics of augmentation must include two analytical axes. The virtuality continuum, commonplace in technical discussions of AR, is one of these. It refers to mediated representations ranging from entirely 'real' to entirely 'virtual' environments. This is represented in Figure 6.1 on a radial axis measuring the intensity of technical mediation from low (center) to high (periphery).

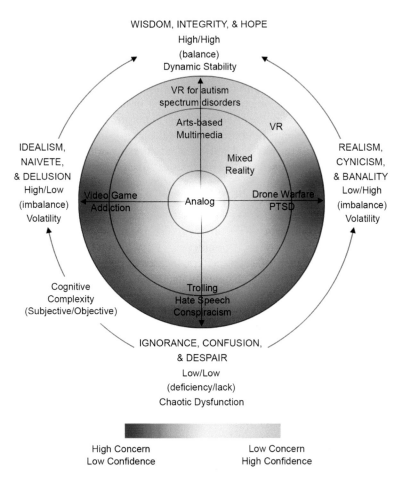

**Figure 6.1:** Ethics heat map for mixed-reality environments

While the virtuality continuum is useful for addressing technical questions, it is flawed from an epistemic perspective. The distinction between 'real' and 'virtual' takes on different meaning when we position ethical questions as primary, and technical questions as secondary. Milgram and Kishino's (1994) taxonomy distinguishes between a "real" world defined epistemically as one that is "unmodelled" and one that is "completely modelled" (p. 9). In terms of the cognitive mapping of our everyday lives, however, there is no such thing as a world that is 'unmodelled'. Except during experiences of flow or heightened perception, which are relatively infrequent (for example spiritual crises or altered states), our normal experience is filtered through a cognitive map of the world and our place within it. This model of the world is rarely complete, and arguably cannot be.[2] In other words, even if we set aside questions

---

[2] Descriptions of mystical experiences as 'ineffable' would seem to support this view, suggesting that 'ultimate' reality cannot be mapped or described, only directly experienced.

of technology and media, and look only at unmediated human experience, we are always/already living in a state of mixed reality involving some elements that are real and others that are virtual.

While humility reminds us that we can never enjoy a complete model of the world, we can nevertheless aspire toward more *wisdom* and *integrity*, both terms suggesting cognitive maps which are sophisticated in terms of both accuracy and creative flexibility. The more important axis here, therefore, is the cognitive mapping continuum. This continuum refers to the mental pictures or heuristics that guide users' understanding of the physical and social-emotional world around them. In the spirit of Levinas' (1969) understanding of ethics as "first philosophy," the framework outlined here situates cognitive mapping as the foundational axis. The virtuality continuum is a secondary axis, the primary effect of which is to amplify or augment the cognitive context that gives rise to technical design.

The cognitive continuum is sub-divided into two dimensions, subjective and objective, representing the relative complexity of social-emotional and real-world heuristics. This continuum of cognitive complexity is represented as the angular axis of Figure 6.1, meaning that complexity increases as one moves away from the bottommost point of the circle. Using a ratio-type layout, this axis encompasses four different zones. In Zone 1, both subjective and objective heuristics are low in complexity (a ratio of 0:0 at the bottommost point). Zones 2 and 3 respectively feature low versus high ratios of subjective to objective cognitive complexity. Zone 4, labeled as the 'Green Zone' (top-center of Figure 6.1) represents an ideal one-to-one ratio of subjective to objective cognitive complexity.

In other words, the Green Zone of the AR ethics heat map represents a range of mediated scenarios, from purely analog to fully-immersive VR, which tend to enhance participants' capacity for understanding *both* their social-emotional *and* physical environments. The other Zones are problematic for reasons described in the following sections. It is sufficient to say that the four zones represent different types and levels of ethical concern, as indicated by the legend. We can move with confidence in the Green Zone, though even here we must proceed judiciously, ensuring that development reflects and embodies an intention to cultivate wisdom, integrity, and other virtues. In each zone, the further we move from the center towards more intensely-mediated environments, the more powerful the design aesthetic becomes—for better or worse. Zones that are relatively imbalanced or otherwise lacking are danger zones or 'red' zones.

## Red Zone 1: Augmented Ignorance

Zone 1 represents systemic deficiency in both subjective and objective heuristics, meaning that individuals have little or no understanding of basic geography and history, or of their own (let alone others') socio-emotional reality. With regard to MR technologies like GIS, the risk is that users who lack spatial intelligence are more easily misinformed and manipulated. People tend to make false assumptions when viewing maps and other visual information (Sinton and Lund, 2007, pp. 4-6). Various types of "cartographic distortions" can take place (Monmonier, 1996, p. 184), including everything from unwitting or sloppy misinformation (for example by placing aesthetic concerns over accuracy) to deliberate manipulation and propaganda. As Monmonier (1996) warned, "If not harnessed by knowledge and honest intent, the power of maps can get out of control" (Monmonier, 1996, p. 186).

Zone 1 carries broader risks beyond such issues of mapping and spatial thinking. If understanding of our social-emotional worlds and objective reality are both deficient, we may sink into ignorance and despair. Emotion may be weaponized to "lubricate reason" in a way that renders individuals vulnerable to manipulation (Slovic et al., 2007, p. 1349, quoted in Sivek 2018, pp. 132-133). Technical augmentation of this underlying lack leads to enactment of anger and desperation, stereotyping and cross-cultural animosity. In an online context, this may manifest as cyberbullying, hate speeches, trolling, and conspiracies. While this ethos may appear on the surface as transgressive, it is not the kind of intentional and purposive transgression described above. As Cresswell (1996) suggests, "constant transgression is permanent chaos" (p. 166). Individuals situated in the chaos of Zone 1 may experience a semblance of agency, but in fact are vulnerable to the political-economic and technical systems represented by the volatile extremes of Zones 2 and 3 (right- and left-most areas in Figure 6.1).

*Red Zone 2: Augmented Cynicism*

Zone 2 represents a volatile imbalance where objective heuristics are untethered to socio-emotional reality. In other words, the ethos of this zone prioritizes information, knowledge, and data as an end unto itself, with little regard for the subjective, emotional, or spiritual dimensions of wisdom and well-being. From a contemplative perspective, as this ethos takes hold "we often remain trapped in what we call normalcy," a state of complacency and complicity where life "revolves around problem-solving, fixing, explaining, and taking sides with winners and losers" (Rohr, 2016). If individuals have a sophisticated map of the objective world around them, but a relatively simplistic map of social and emotional reality, they run the risk of cynical complicity with the banal manifestations of evil (Zone 2, right-most area of Figure 6.1). Life may be experienced as meaningful and purposeful, but in a way that is morally bankrupt and destructive.

Silicon Valley culture is especially prone to this type of imbalanced thinking, as exemplified by the corporate mottos of Facebook and Google, both of which implicitly assume that unrestrained data collection and algorithmic processing is an inherently progressive endeavor. This ideology assumes falsely that information equals wisdom, that processing equals judgment, and that data connectivity equals social intimacy (see Healey and Woods, 2019). Though often framed in democratic and egalitarian rhetoric, this perspective tends to generate an attitude of cynicism towards users' concerns about privacy and surveillance. As this attitude informs policy and design decisions, the result is the construction of "architectures of contempt" (Healey, 2015, p. 958) that reinforce the power and authority of technical and political elites. By the same token, this distortion often manifests somatically in users, as exemplified by reports of post-traumatic stress disorders (PTSD) from front-line workers in commercial social media and the military (Newton, 2019, Press 2018).

## Red Zone 3: Augmented Delusion

In Zone 3, the prevalent cultural ethos is characterized by highly complex social-emotional maps, but relatively simplistic or inaccurate maps of the 'real' world. Individuals in this zone harbor complex and emotionally meaningful political ideologies, religious mythologies, or fantasy lives which are ungrounded in accurate information and untethered to relevant knowledge about the objective world. Such individuals run the risk of becoming naïve and idealistic or trapped in an escapist fantasy. Life may be experienced as meaningful and purposeful, but in a way that is at best inaccurate and misleading, and at worst a dangerous and self-destructive delusion. In pre-digital eras, this imbalance manifested in a range of dysfunctional religious beliefs, from unhealthy medical procedures based on superstition to violent campaigns based on fantasies of racial superiority.

The digital economy has augmented such imbalances in a number of ways. As suggested with regard to the risks in Zone 1, social media can augment ignorance about everything from vaccines to race, leading to dangerously naïve beliefs and behaviors. Paradoxically, Silicon Valley is prone to naïve idealism even as it is prone to cynical realism. Here it may manifest as a quasi-religious belief in the coming Singularity, wherein digital systems are expected to render death itself obsolete. Among users, such imbalances may manifest in the form of compulsive online gaming. Whether such behavior is technically a form of addiction is still controversial among health experts, although the World Health Organization (2019) has officially recognized "gaming disorder" as a mental health condition.

## Green Zone (Zone 4): Augmented Wisdom

Zone 4 represents a technical environment that reflects, and cultivates complex and well-integrated understandings of our socio-emotional and physical worlds.[3] The driving virtues here are wisdom, integrity, and hope—which, as noted before, are special forms of cognitive mapping. Some psychologists posit integrity as the ultimate virtue, defining it in terms of a synthesis of wisdom, hope, purpose, and the other key virtues from each developmental stage (see Hampden-Turner, 1981, p. 135). Importantly, such definitions see integrity as relational in nature, meaning that it requires knowledge and empathy of people "of distant times and of different pursuits" (Erikson, 1980, p. 104). It is thus not self-centered, but rather "involves a willing sensitivity to the needs of the whole" (Beebe, 2000, p. 12). As indicated by its location in Zone 4 of Figure 6.1, integrity in this view involves both subjective and objective heuristics or, as Stevens-Long (2000) explains, "the integration of the events of the external world into an ongoing story about the self" (Stevens-Long, 2000, p. 163).

---

[3] This framework is not intended to suggest a binary between analog/digital or subjective/objective, where one is better than the other. The most desirable environments integrate technical and ethical concerns into a holistic design aesthetic where such binaries are transcended altogether. Nor does the framework assume that every application must augment social-emotional and real-world heuristics at once. The goal instead is a general synergy between various applications that individuals may use over time.

Wisdom and hope derive from this integration. Hope is a unique capacity afforded by integrity, namely "understanding what one's society is and imagining what it could be" (Babbitt, 1997, p. 118). Wisdom, meanwhile, entails "knowing and understanding not merely the proximate goods but the ultimate ones, and seeing the world in this light" (Nozick, 1989, p. 276, quoted in Emmons, 1999, p. 154). Together, wisdom and hope involve perception, understanding, and responsibility. These are creative and imaginative capabilities, but ones that must clearly be grounded in the realities of the world around us—not self-serving and myopic, but holistic and visionary. In other words, hope should not be understood cynically as mere wishful thinking, but as an imaginative response to clearly-perceived and thoughtfully-understood reality. It is for this reason that hope is positioned on the heat map in the position where subjective complexity and objective complexity are both at their highest. These capacities are indeed opposite in character to the ignorance and despair of Zone 1; but they also avoid the volatility of Zones 2 and 3, generating a kind of dynamic stability in which sustainable growth emerges over time.

The contemplative and arts-based practices described in the following sections are practical implementations of this approach to ethical MR development. They begin with an intention to understand and to embody wisdom and empathy and proceed dialectically by gently tacking back-and-forth between analog and digital, local and global, informational and expressive. More immersive applications are already yielding promising results for individuals, as seen in early trials of virtual reality assisted cognitive behavioral therapy (VR-CBT). Such applications leverage the immersive affordances of VR to address social anxiety in autistic persons, for example (see Maskey et al., 2019). These applications integrate real-world circumstances with "emotional literacy training," exemplifying the main goals of Green Zone development. In both practical and educational arts-based applications, and in clinical-therapeutic applications, MR technologies "produce new codings and practices, and with them new possible geographies" (Pickles, 1995, p. 226). Restated more expansively, what ethical MR technology charts are new geographies of heart and mind which re-orient us to a future that is more ecologically, technologically, and politically connected.

## Design Aesthetics for the Green Zone

While the previous section outlines general high-level principles for ethical development, this section (and the following case study) returns to the discussion of media aesthetics by answering the call to "guide designers" (Bolter et al., 2013, p. 37) with a set of "best practices" for design aesthetics (Cowling et al., 2017, p. 42). The method described here adds to ongoing efforts to articulate "a vocabulary for thinking and talking about designs that include such subjective terms as *affect*, *empathy*, and *enchantment*" (Bolter et al., 2013, p. 38. Emphasis original). The meaning of the first two terms should be apparent from the previous sections, while the third warrants special consideration. Murray (2017) defines enchantment as the sense of "dwelling in an augmented space adjacent to the real world where contrary-to-reality things—things that we wish for or fear in real life—fill our senses, and we are given powers contrary-to-reality to create effortless transformations" (n.p.). This is part of what Murray (2017) calls "mature media," which we can achieve by following certain standards and conventions and avoiding common design mistakes (n.p.).

In the framework proposed here, Green Zone development can better encourage such maturity by incorporating insights from the scholarly field of contemplative studies, which aims at "cultivating individual and collective forms of enhanced intelligence, wisdom and well-being" among students, scholars and citizens (Gunnlaugson et al., 2014, p. 4). Building on three decades of medical and psychological lab research on practices such as meditation and yoga, contemplative studies have expanded to include the application of contemplative principles to research in education, economics and music performance. Much of this work focuses on "mindfulness," defined as "paying attention in a particular way: on the purpose, in the present moment, and non-judgmentally" (Kabat-Zinn, 1994, p. 4; see also Gethin, 2011, p. 269).

In a previous work the present author outlines a subset of contemplative scholarship termed Contemplative Media Studies (CMS), defined as "the application of contemplative practices and principles to the critical analysis of media technologies, content, and institutions" (Healey, 2015, p. 954; Healey, 2013). A key component of CMS is contemplative practice, a good working definition for which includes the following (from Oman, 2010, pp. 8-9):

- Set-aside time for "a disciplined activity or exercise that has a comparatively powerful effect on training attention."
- Additional practices through-the-day for stabilizing attention and recovering "a sense of inner strength and balance."
- A focus on specific virtues and character strengths, such as wisdom, courage, and integrity.
- Exemplars or models of these virtues and character strengths.

By placing affect at the center of attention, contemplative practice cultivates empathy as one among several cross-culturally recognized virtues. It also cultivates an ongoing predisposition toward enchantment with one's environment, where it is taken to mean "a fleeting return to childlike excitement about life" (Bennett, 2001, p. 5). Such enchantment allows individuals to exercise critical, yet generous and good-humored, judgment about the subject matter at hand (Kinane, 2013). This type of even-handedness is precisely the goal of virtue ethics. In sum, while contemplative practice develops the capacity for maintaining such even-handedness ongoingly, CMS harnesses this capacity for the targeted purpose of evaluating and guiding technical development. When put into practice, development along these lines may be referred to as contemplative design aesthetics.

There are several reasons why CMS (as a pedagogical and research methodology) and GIS as a technical domain are especially suited to one another. As economic, environmental, and political crises become increasingly transnational and global in character, map-making and spatial thinking skills also increase in importance (Sinton and Lund, 2007, pp. ix-x). While social science and humanities scholarship has long aimed to cultivate critical thinking skills, the above-mentioned spatial turn and the growing availability of mapping tools like ArcGIS generate new possibilities for expanding critical thinking to include "thinking spatially" (Sinton and Lund, 2007, pp. x). Indeed, with regard to the critical cognitive skills it generates, map-making is similar to writing. Moreover, map-making and map-reading are more than "mechanical activities," since they "entail discernment, understanding, and communication" while "allowing an extensive range of expression" (Sinton and Lund, 2007, p. xvii).

Mapping is a powerful tool because students' visual capabilities, for example, their ability to remember a complex image, often exceeds their analytical understanding of the meaning of the image (Sinton and Lund, 2007, p. 1). Exercises that use mapping and visual elements leverage this visual capability to develop other skills. CMS adds additional benefits insofar as it strengthens concentration and attention. Environmental learning, in the sense of creating a mental or cognitive map of an environment, often takes place unintentionally or with a lack of awareness (Downs and Stea, 1977, p. 212). Much environmental learning and spatial problem solving occurs while people are doing other things, and therefore this type of learning "operates largely outside of the realm of conscious awareness" (Downs and Stea, 1977, p. 219). To the extent that contemplative practices cultivate attention and judgment, CMS can make this type of learning much more effective. Beyond its obvious practical benefits (for example learning to drive or walk through a foreign city), environmental learning has wide applicability given that so much of our daily life involves skills like categorizing and interpreting. Mapping "forces us to abstract, discriminate, generalize, and simplify reality" (Sinton and Bednarz, 2007, p. 23). In fact, mapping and contemplative studies are well-suited to one another because, as argued above, exemplary virtues like wisdom and integrity are quite literally a special form of cognitive mapping.

CMS and mapping tools (both analog and GIS) are also well-suited to one another because their combination facilitates non-linear (holistic/systems) thinking. Even in analog modes, spatial thinking can be non-linear. As Staley (2007) notes, "the map can concisely convey the relationship between wholes and parts" (p. 41). Digital mapping techniques augment this non-linear potential since GIS applications do not merely add supplemental forms of representation, but instead act as a primary means for interacting with and understanding data (Staley, 2007, p. 37). Arts-based GIS applications can help students understand social, political, and ethical relationships more deeply.

Finally, CMS and GIS together encourage participatory modes of learning that readily translate into new forms of civic engagement. In contemplative photo-mapping, each participant serves as a "procedural author" or "co-creator of the story of the map," working collaboratively to build a "customizable cartographic space" (Staley, 2007, p. 44-45). This process allows for a "participatory narrative" in which participants maintain "a certain power over what they see" (Staley, 2007, p. 45). When applied in a pedagogical context focused on news literacy, this form of MR has the potential to sharpen students' embodied perception and understanding of international developments. In this way, analog experience informs digital use, which then feeds back into our flesh-and-blood encounter with the world, augmenting our innate capacity for compassion and wisdom.

## Contemplative Photo-mapping: A Green Zone Case Study

This section provides a description of an exercise facilitated by the author in two seminars at University of New Hampshire (Media and Ethics and Contemplative Media Studies, both offered through the Department of Communication). It is known informally as the College Woods exercise since it usually takes place in the campus College Woods. However, it is readily adaptable to other settings, and has even been conducted within the confines of a conference hotel (Healey, 2018).

The exercise consists of two main phases. Phase 1 begins in an analog mode, using printed materials, and ends with production of digital photographs. Phase 2 involves low-level methods of digital augmentation, using mobile GIS applications to layer photographs and digitally-edited collage pieces onto participants' local spaces. This combination of arts-based, contemplative experiences with mixed-reality mobile applications makes news consumption an emotionally-aware and embodied process. The exercise leverages the wisdom of a hyper-local environment (for example, sitting under a particular tree in a local forest) to engage international news events with greater compassion and empathy (for example, a photo of a person or persons from another part of the world). In summary, participants reconnect with their local, natural environment to engage with global news images more mindfully.

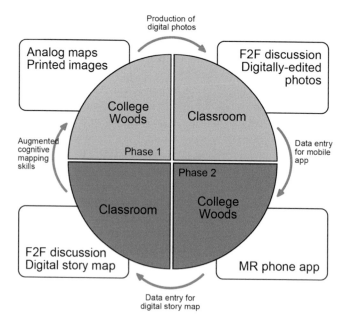

**Figure 6.2:** Process diagram for Phases 1 and 2

The exercise's long-term goal is to encourage participants to 'steer the ship' of the digital economy in a more sustainable direction. This goal reflects concerns within critical media studies about citizens' ability to understand and interpret information; to appreciate complex transnational and cross-cultural relationships; and to recognize the role of commercial social media in exacerbating socioeconomic inequalities. In keeping with the conventional aims of media studies pedagogy, the exercise cultivates a critical orientation to digital media, so participants can break out of habitual patterns of use especially with regard to news consumption. Unlike conventional media studies approaches, it incorporates experiential and arts-based methods and puts analog and digital materials into productive conversation. By integrating contemplative practices (mindfulness and walking meditation) and arts-based methods (photo-journalism and collage), the exercise offers a framework for participants to engage the emerging digital media environment in their capacity as consumers and citizens. The overall experience moves beyond cynical media criticism toward positive forms of engagement that emphasize user agency, creativity, and empathy.

## Phase 1

### Step 1

Participants arrive at a chosen location, ideally a natural setting like a forest or park, though the exercise can be adapted to other contexts. Upon arrival, each participant chooses a sealed envelope with instructions attached or printed on the outside. The envelopes contain a few key items. There is a printed map of the local area, a printed world map (or another larger geographical region), a push pin, and extras like printed quotes related to the course content. Importantly, the two maps are printed on either side of one sheet of paper, or are stapled together. The quotes should represent key virtues and character strengths, and ideally should be sourced to a moral exemplar (whether a scholar, artist, musician, or activist).

### Step 1 (Variation)

Participants who live in separate locations can begin with different maps of local, 'natural' spaces that are convenient to them. For example, during the summer of 2020 just after the global coronavirus pandemic caused a nation-wide lockdown in the U.S., the author created a new walking path through the wooded area in his backyard in New Hampshire (shown in Figure 6.6). He worked collaboratively with Karolyn Kinane, Associate Director of Pedagogy and Faculty of Engagement at the Contemplative Sciences Center at University of Virginia. Karolyn happens to live on a property adjacent to a large county park in Virginia. This type of arrangement adds a level of complexity, layering the same global map onto two natural spaces located at a distance from each other.

### Step 2

With their phones turned off, participants enter the local space, find a quiet spot, and become accustomed to the natural setting. Ideally, participants will have read about the practice of *shinrin-yoku* (also known as forest bathing), or other nature-based contemplative practices (see Aubrey, 2017). At this point participants open their envelopes to view and reflect upon news images the facilitator has selected and printed. Here again, it is helpful if participants have read about a contemplative practice such as "beholding," a form of mindful engagement with art or other imagery (Barbezat and Bush, 2013, pp. 47-48).

## Step 3

Using their phones if necessary, participants identify the location of the event featured in the printed news image. Pressing the push-pin into the world map simultaneously marks a corresponding location on the hyper-local map. This corollary location becomes the virtual destination for a walking meditation exercise.

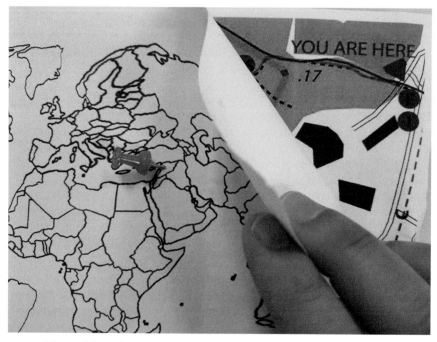

**Figure 6.3:** Analog process for identifying local/global corollary locations

## Step 4

This step combines contemplative practice (walking meditation) and arts-based methods (photography and collage). Participants begin a virtual journey toward the destination featured in their news image. On their virtual journey to a newly-identified destination in the woods, participants look for visual elements in the natural scenery that represent an emotional and/or metaphorical response to their news image. In the iteration of this exercise shown in Figure 6.4, the set of news images were from Jinan, China; Dallas, Texas; Baton Rouge, Louisiana; and Aleppo, Syria.

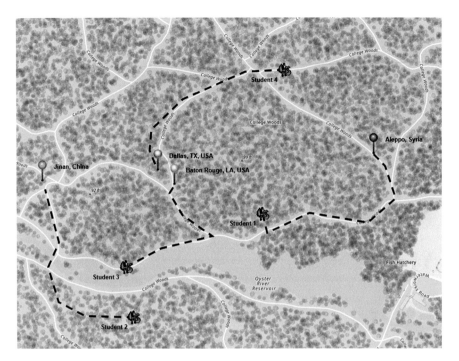

**Figure 6.4:** Paths of student journeys to corollary locations

After viewing a news image from Aleppo, Syria, a student wrote the following about her photo-response (see Figure 6.5):

> This contrast of a smile in a forest where there are dead trees and the destroyed remains of a habitat of many animals, plants and life forms, accurately exemplifies the image of a child in Syria who's home has been destroyed, and who is struggling to obtain a sense of youth.

## Step 5

Participants exit the local area at the same point where they entered. The instructor or facilitator, who ideally will have walked through the area to engage and assist participants as necessary, should return to the entry point at a designated time for debriefing. Participants will have taken numerous photographs on their virtual journeys and will need time to review and reflect on their experience. This review process may include additional research on the news events from participants' envelopes. Two or three digital photographs of the local environment should be chosen, and participants may elect to edit them or create more elaborate collage pieces. The final product for discussion should be a set of blog posts that feature all of the key visual elements: the news image prompt; the original photographs taken during the exercise; and any final collage pieces or edited images. These should be accompanied by a reflective essay on participants' experiences. These become the raw materials for Phase 2.

**Figure 6.5:** Envelope contents and participant's photo-response

## Phase 2

*Step 6*

After completing Phase 1 in their respective local spaces, participants create an interactive map of their local space using Google Earth or ArcGIS. The interactive map includes several elements: first, the basic features of the local space (paths, ponds, streams, etc.); second, a superimposed map of the global region where the news images are located. The first two elements are basically a digital version of the printed corollary maps from Phase 1, but here the maps are layered digitally, with the global map set at a lower opacity (see Figure 6.6). Additionally, the interactive maps include the news images themselves and the user-generated photo-responses from Phase 1. While viewing the interactive map, participants can see themselves geo-located in real-time on both the local and global corollary maps.

*Step 7*

Participants enter their local space again using the same starting locations from Phase 1. Relying this time on Google Earth or ArcGIS to guide their journey, participants travel to the corollary locations in the news images. On their mobile applications, these destinations now additionally include the user-created images or collages created in response to the news images. In the instance conducted in summer 2020, Kevin and Karolyn had selected three destinations: Turin, Italy; Quetta, Pakistan; and Asuncion, Paraguay. Arriving at these virtual destinations, they were able to tap the element on their screen to view the news image as well as each other's photo-

**Figure 6.6:** Google Earth view of backyard path with layered global map

responses. For example, as Karolyn moved to each destination, she could tap a push-pin icon (see Figure 6.7) to view the news image as well as Kevin's photo-response.

## Step 8

The final piece of the exercise involves building an interactive digital story map with the elements produced in Phases 1 and 2 (photographs, reflective essays, etc.). While story maps include interactivity such as described in Steps 6 and 7, they afford a more comprehensive narrative of an idea or event. The ArcGIS StoryMaps platform offers such an interactive narrative, combining geospatial mapping with text, imagery, and other multimedia elements in a sequential beginning-middle-end format (for a functional example see Healey, 2020). The creation of a digital story map provides participants with an interactive platform for reflecting on their overall experience. The process of curating materials and assembling them into a sequential narrative facilitates integration of participants' local

**Figure 6.7:** View of layered maps in ArcGIS mobile app (Karolyn's location)

experiences with their thinking about broader issues of news literacy and cross-cultural understanding. This method generates increased capacity for complex cognitive mapping skills as participants re-enter their local environments under normal circumstances, outside of the context of the exercise (see Figure 6.2).

## Discussion and Analysis

The opening sections of this chapter sought to re-frame the concept of augmentation by prioritizing social and ethical definitions over technical ones. Recall that the central question for design aesthetics is what ought to be augmented socially, politically, and ideologically through new forms of mediation. Augmentation through various political-economic and technical systems long preceded the digital era. The goal of an ethically-sensitive aesthetic design is to identify, critique, and re-imagine the 'regimes of augmentation' in which users live.

Effective design exploits the unique affordances of MR applications to enhance users' originality and complexity of thought. Design aesthetics which creatively integrate analog and digital modalities can have the surprising effect of making digital affordances more powerful. Spatial layering is one such affordance. Simple forms of layering are possible in analog modalities, as the case study makes clear. Mixed reality applications bring such layering more clearly into users' conscious awareness. Another key affordance of MR is what Staley (2007) calls procedural authorship, referring to the kinds of creative engagement that interactive applications promote. Procedural agency of this sort is important given the risks associated with the red Zones of Figure 6.1, where technical systems presume or dictate points of view. Creative engagement disrupts systems of informational and sociological propaganda, which are typically characterized by unconscious, taken-for-granted, or unquestioned beliefs.[4]

In conjunction with analog and arts-based work, the case study above leverages these affordances of MR to disrupt established regimes of augmentation. The process challenges common-sense assumptions about analog versus digital media, local versus global spaces, natural versus built environments. Layering international news events onto local space has the effect of displacing modern Cartesian geographies with "a progressive sense of place that links places to other places" (Warf, 2009, p. 75). As Warf (2009) explains:

> A relational politics of place calls into question easy distinctions like inside/ outside, near/far, space/place, and global/local, artificial differentiations that are always embedded in each other and mutually constituted (p. 75).

Participants move beyond the assumption that these concept pairs are opposite and mutually exclusive, seeing them instead as relational and complex. Contemplative practices enable this view since, as Zajonc (2014) notes, such practices are adept at enhancing "the ability to engage with paradox or contradiction" (p. 19-20). By

---

[4] Here 'propaganda' refers not only to discrete instances of misinformation but, via Ellul (1973), to complex technical and sociological processes that coerce citizens into complicity with a dehumanizing ideology.

whatever method, contemplative or otherwise, the ability to question commonplace binaries is a key element in Green Zone design aesthetics.

The following sections offer three basic, high-level strategies for effective MR design in the 'Green Zone.' A focus on the key aspirational virtues of wisdom, integrity, and hope serve as a common thread. While the case study in contemplative photo-mapping serves as a touch-point, these three strategies can be readily applied in a variety of contexts and in different technical forms.

## Denaturalizing Space, Naturalizing Wisdom

Through primarily analog means, Phase 1 in the above case study develops participants' capacity for "spatial relations," an aspect of spatial thinking which contributes to "global awareness" (Sinton and Bednarz, 2007, p. 30). As we begin to understand spatial relations, we recognize similarities and differences across space and time, including the relationship between information and events. We also gain a self-reflective ability to ask whether the correlations we perceive in and across space are accurate (Sinton and Bednarz, 2007, p. 29). From a media and news literacy perspective, this capacity is important because journalistic news framing, especially algorithmic personalization in social media, tend to reinforce a false dichotomy between local and global. As writer Brian Jay Stanley (2012) notes:

> We cannot easily believe that people distant in time or space are real like us. If our next-door neighbors' house burns down, we rush to their aid with pity… Yet if some unpronounceable village in Cambodia burns down… many of us vaguely suppose that calamity is natural where they live, and grief there stings less than here. The superficiality of news coverage encourages such prejudices.

Bringing global news images into a serene, hyperlocal setting is disruptive because we typically use natural settings as tools to relax or de-stress. As the quotation above suggests, that kind of normative use of space absolves us of ethical responsibility for global events that are deemed 'natural' for the foreign spaces where strangers live. As Karolyn (2020) notes, bringing news into a local, natural space seems counter-productive:

> I felt uncomfortable with the idea that I would be belittling the plights of others as I sought some weak comparison to my own experiences.

This discomfort is appropriate because it signals an awareness of the boundedness and inequitable distribution of social justice through 'real' geographic space. By including elements of environmental learning, a Green Zone design aesthetic leverages local, analog space to disrupt and reimagine cognitive maps in more complex and inclusive forms. Environmental learning has important socio-political implications since the cognitive heuristics it develops are readily transferable from one place to another across time and distance. In learning the intricacies of one local space and recognizing its correlations with another, participants are "learning to learn" in a way that permanently impacts their understanding of themselves in relation to the world around them (Downs and Stea, 1977, p. 228). As Cresswell (1996) notes, "social power and social resistance are always already spatial" (p. 11).

One way that contemplative photo-mapping cultivates resistance to "geographical orthodoxy" or "the geography of normality" (Cresswell, 1996, p. 95) is by calling into question the dualism of natural and built worlds. Consider Karolyn's (2020) self-report from Phase 1 of the exercise:

> My mind was—with some mild resentment—playing over this narrative: "I go into the woods to leave the world behind and to get grounded, not to 'engage' with the world…" I was uncomfortable with the idea that I would be engaging in a human-centered use of the "natural" world—using trees and moss as a means to understand or make sense of human experiences.

Ironically, common assumptions about the restorative power of 'natural' spaces are actually expressions of socially-constructed or 'built' ideologies which tell us how to think about, and within, certain spaces. In fact there are very few if any spaces that are 'natural' in the sense of being physically or socially untouched. Even 'natural' spaces like county parks or college woods begin and remain as such through a social process of identification, legal protections, and cultural norms. In this sense, the mental or cognitive 'space' they provide is actually quite structured and bounded, and typically serve to reinforce the political-economic ideologies that privilege 'built' environments over 'natural' ones. Design aesthetics that call such structures into question have the effect of "denaturalizing" space (see Cresswell, 1996, p. 164-165).

Paradoxically, by disrupting the false dichotomy between natural and built environments, nature-based contemplative practices like walking meditation and *shinrin-yoku* (forest bathing) allow us to move beyond socially-privileged constructions of 'nature' as a respite from everyday life—a source of relaxation and stress-reduction that allows us to maintain daily routines. While contemplative practices understand nature as a source of wisdom, in the long term they help us recognize that ecological wisdom is, or ought to be, distributed throughout 'natural' and 'built' spaces simultaneously in a coherent whole.[5] Thus while the case study above frames nature as a sacred space, it does so not just literally but metaphorically, drawing attention to inequitable access to spaces where empowering plays a role and imagination emerges 'organically' (see Louv, 2008). 'Nature' is not so much a thing or a place, but a possibility for more coherent ways of being regardless of one's location. From this perspective, Green Zone design aesthetics encourage an understanding of the deeper, systemic sources of stress that draw people to so-called 'natural' spaces in the first place. In a manner of speaking, effective design denaturalizes normative space in order to re-naturalize virtues like wisdom and compassion as necessary, foundational elements of our shared technical and social environments.

---

[5] As Cresswell (1996) suggests, architecture and landscape can both be read as texts, and both are ripe for critical interpretation (p. 13). In the case study exercise, students are provided with supplementary readings on the distributed intelligence of trees (see Wohlleben, 2016) and discernment exercises where they are asked to identify virtue and vice in both natural and built objects. Such readings and exercises cause students to question their habitual ways of thinking about 'natural' versus 'built' objects and spaces.

*Designing for Integrity*

Spaces are always normatively structured, and therefore tend to enable taken-for-granted social realities (Cresswell 1996, pp. 8-9). Yet space and place can also be used to engage in transgression—questioning what is normative or understood as "common sense" (Cresswell, 1996, p. 21):

> Place links ideas to actions in an ideological fashion and makes us all practical philosophers. Most of the time we obey taken-for-granted rules of place as proper. By the repetition of our actions we reinforce the established norms of behavior in space. But since our behavior in space is linked to ideas, this behavior also has the seeds of rebellion in it (Cresswell, 1996, pp. 164-165).

Denaturalizing space creates opportunities for conscious engagement with issues of social ethics. In the photo-mapping case study, for example, global news seems 'out of place' in spaces like forests and woodland preserves because its presence reveals and calls into question the normative construction of natural spaces. The photo-mapping exercise augments the transgressive potential of natural settings by calling attention to the political character of such spaces.

As described above with reference to Zone 1, chaos results when transgression becomes an end in itself. However when intentionality is present transgression becomes resistance (Cresswell, 1996, pp. 22-23), which is to say it clears a path to social transformation. Politically mindful engagement in any space requires recognizing unacknowledged intentions and replacing them with conscious ones. As Karolyn (2020) explains in her reflection on photo-mapping:

> I realized that until this exercise this day I had been going into these Virginia woods with unacknowledged intentions: I had been walking through these woods to clear my head, yes, but also to cover ground—to get exercise, burn calories... At the start of this walk I had believed I "usually" went into the woods with no intentions. This practice made me realize that I have had them, after all.

In the context of contemplative practice, intentionality involves aspiration toward a clearly-defined virtue like wisdom. Once a space is denaturalized in this way, with participants having realized their unspoken intentions, a new cognitive space opens up in which to build a more expansive map that transcends geopolitical boundaries. Thus the question for participants in the photo-mapping exercise becomes: How can I live more wisely and responsibly here, in this place, knowing that the suffering and injustice I see in this news image is occurring there, in that place?

In a sense, effective design creates opportunities to integrate the binary concepts noted above: local and global, natural and built, analog and digital. Participants bring these elements together, synthesizing them into a coherent whole. In other words, Green Zone design catalyzes integrity, personally and collectively. The case study exercise makes *our* space into *their* space; it layers *that* place onto *this* place; it brings events happening over *there* into the spaces we treat as special and sacred *here*. In this way participants understand that differences in location are not necessarily differences in meaning, importance, or relevance. They redraw cognitive maps to be more inclusive geographically, politically, and socially.

From a media and news literacy perspective, this kind of MR experience runs counter to commercial regimes of augmentation driven by algorithmic personalization. Such commercial regimes are exemplified by Facebook CEO Mark Zuckerberg's suggestion that "a squirrel dying in front of your house may be more relevant to your interests right now than people dying in Africa" (Kirkpatrick, 2010, p. 181). By contrast, the case study exercise provides an embodied process of integrating local and global events into a meaningful and coherent whole. People dying in Africa, children suffering in Syria, become newly relevant in the construction of participants' literal and cognitive maps. As Karolyn (2020) notes, the effect of this process transforms our ongoing experience of local space:

> I walked in the woods again today and was somewhat surprised to find the images from yesterday still with me: Images of the scavenging boy, the palm-toting medical staff, the protesting doctors, and my thoughts about each of them arose at various points as I climbed hills, turned corners, and climbed rocks. By carrying these images in my mind yesterday as I walked with open awareness and attention to my surroundings, today I carry the impressions of these images with me the way I carry memorized bits of poetry and song lyrics with me. These images have become part of my inner landscape and part of the way I see and interpret the world.

Commercial interests prioritize a consumerist understanding of relevance which tends to reinforce preconceived tastes and established social identities. By contrast, a Green Zone design aesthetic intentionally places within users' awareness objects that seem out of place or even inappropriate. It does so not because it sees transgression as an end in itself, but because long-term sustainability of political and technical systems requires challenging users to expand, rather than protect or contract, their cognitive maps.

As news images and user-generated photos denaturalize participants' experience of local space, disrupting dichotomies of here/ours and there/theirs, these virtual objects operate as forms of graffiti. This characteristic explains why their presence may seem intrusive or even offensive, as some of Karolyn's comments above suggest. As Cresswell (1996) notes, graffiti has political implications in the sense that "if the transgression continues… the place in question will become *their* place" (emphasis original) (p. 60). By incorporating value intentions like wisdom and compassion, effective design leverages this moment of transgression to enable social transformation. Rather than becoming 'theirs' as if by force or threat, spaces of mixed reality experience become 'ours' in a newly expanded and shared sense.

As a defining feature of GIS technologies, layering of the type illustrated in Figures 6.6 and 6.7 allows participants to develop "spatial narratives"—stories about themselves in relation to others in embodied space (Staley, 2007, p. 36). Fittingly, scholars refer to layering as "relational cartography" (Staley, 2007, p. 44), which usually refers to the juxtaposition of different sets of information or data about one geographical area. While layering is possible in analog mapping, GIS augments this type of relational thinking since users can layer an unlimited number of data sets, revealing emergent patterns. From the perspective of cognitive mapping, 'relational cartography' is a process of denaturalizing normative social and political ideologies and re-naturalizing the virtues of wisdom, compassion, and integrity as foundational elements of social reality. Design aesthetics in the Green Zone augment this process by enabling transgressive 'graffiti', making it easier for users to 'read the writing on the wall' with regard to our collective futures.

## Augmenting the 'Presence' of Hope

Phase 2 of the case study, especially Step 7, represents a mixed-reality experience in the proper sense of the term. Whereas commonplace mobile apps tend to foster "a sense of being part of the map" by indicating the users' location in real-time, the special-use Google Earth and ArcGIS applications in Phase 2 create an experience where "symbolic information enters into our visible world"—a design aesthetic which is "in some ways the opposite of seeing ourselves inserted into a screen-based map" (Bolter et al., 2013, p. 39). Building upon the experience in Phase 1, Phase 2 leverages Google Earth and ArcGIS to "locate us 'here and there'" simultaneously (Bolter et al., 2013, p. 44).

In cases where participants are in different locations (e.g. Kevin and Karolyn as described above) participants travel to three destinations at once: physically, to a destination in their local space; virtually, to each other's local destinations and to the corollary destination on the global map. The news images, and the other participant's photos, become virtually present 'here' via the Google Earth and ArcGIS mobile applications. These applications are not merely "a way of finding location-based information," but instead represent "a way for the user to experience the world around her as a mixed and hybrid reality of information on the one hand and physical location and embodiment on the other" (Bolter et al., 2013, p. 44). During their journeys, participants encounter "objects that exist as points on a continuum which cycle between the physical and digital representations" (Cowling et al., 2017, p. 45).

As the most important MR experience in the case study, Step 7 meets several of Murray's (2017) bullet-point characteristics of location-based AR design. It includes a blended experience in which 'real' and 'virtual' elements are closely synced and overlaid. It features multiple "granularities" of augmentation, all of which are "tightly mapped to physical space" (Murray, 2017). It calls attention to spatial details, enticing close-up views and multiple points of view. Further iterations of the exercise, which may include a customized mobile application featuring field-of-view visual overlays, would further enhance users' experience of dramatic agency. Even without the benefit of such extended features, the photo-mapping case study highlights the central importance of social relationships in Green Zone design aesthetics.

Here it is worth exploring the meaning of 'presence' within Green Zone design. In AR and MR research, 'presence' often refers to the technical-visual quality or "reproduction fidelity" of experience within a space, whether objects introduced are real or virtual (Milgram and Kishino, 1994, p. 10). Emphasis on fidelity of this type displaces the central concerns of contemplative design aesthetics, where social presence in a cognitive sense is paramount, and technical reproduction is of secondary importance. JafariMaimi (2015) offers the following distinction:

> The experiences envisioned and fostered by MR cannot be reduced to their material and technological constituents. Neither can they be analyzed solely on qualities of form or methodologies and strategies that bring them to life. Rather, what is most significant for understanding MR are the relationships that it mediates (p. 10).

Murray (2017) likewise argues that "assuming that virtual presence is satisfying in itself" is a design strategy which tends to "undermine immersion" (n.p.). Technical novelties (so-called bells and whistles) which distract us from overarching design goals ought to be avoided. MR can afford "new modes of encounter" which can "challenge common practices or foster critical reflection" (Jafari Naimi, 2015, p.4). These are the primary goals of Green Zone aesthetics.

Beyond creating a sense of physical presence, effective design mobilizes a "rhetoric of presence" to reveal the deeper truth of an experience (Fisher,2019, p. 57). This idea precedes digital technology. In their discussion, Perelman and Olbrechts-Tyteca (1969) insist that "presence, and efforts to increase the feeling of presence, hence must not be confused with fidelity to reality" (p. 118). Whether visual, verbal, or procedural, effective rhetorical strategies can make not only objects but "a judgment or an entire argumentative development" more consciously felt (p. 118).

With ethics as the driving concern, 'presence' refers to the aspirational character virtues of social relationships, such as authenticity, integrity, and compassion. From this perspective, MR applications strive to cultivate not just a sense of physical presence, but an awareness of the possibility of social transformation. As Karolyn (2020) notes in her reflections on Phase 2:

> I am drawn into an emotional place where the flat image on a screen becomes fully humanized not through any change to that image but a change in me—a softening, an opening, and a process of re-seeing and inquiry that moves me from self-centered guilt/shame to connected open inquiry and curiosity.

Whereas the virtuality continuum suggests a goal for users such as: 'I feel your presence here with me because I see a convincing visual, haptic, or auditory simulation of you,' an ethics-driven framework affords a different goal, namely: 'Because I see what you've seen, and what you've created in response to it, I feel a shared presence of compassion and wisdom.' This goal is an aspiration toward ethical or *relational fidelity*, a form of mediated social engagement that is both accurate (informed and knowledgeable) and sincere (empathetic and responsive). This is a mode of engagement described earlier in this chapter in terms of hope, defined not merely as wishful thinking but instead as an imaginative response to clearly-perceived and thoughtfully-understood reality. Hope in this sense is not a fleeting emotion, like the typical "jump scare" moments that drive many commercial AR applications (see Murray, 2017). Instead it is the best form of enchantment that AR and MR applications can provide, since it draws participants into newly transformative ways of thinking and being in the world. The augmentation of hope in this broad sense is the driving goal behind contemplative design aesthetics.

## Conclusion: Mixed Reality as Liminal Space

Given that ethics are a matter of navigating between naiveté and cynicism in our construction of cognitive maps of the world; and given that media technologies are increasingly part and parcel of this process of construction; the central question for ethical MR is, "What kinds of design, development, and use will tend to augment the virtues of wisdom, integrity, and hope, rather than the vices of greed, ignorance, and delusion?" Technical systems that reflect, and therefore tend to augment, these virtues are invaluable in the pursuit of justice and social transformation. Yet such applications tend to be under-funded and under-resourced.

Commercial markets tend to cater to the low-hanging fruit of personal and collective vice represented in Zones 1, 2, and 3. Even in pre-digital eras, most social environments (from communities to nations) encompass multiple subgroups, each of which brings a unique pattern and style to the process of cognitive mapping. As technical systems augment the cognitive ethos of each zone, a dynamic emerges where communication technologies exacerbate differences and fragment populations. Maps diverge, fail to line up, or even fall apart. In various struggles for political and social power, life swings back-and-forth between self-serving illusion and banal complicity with the status quo—a state of affairs that "can be a pretty circular and even nonsensical existence" (Rohr, 2016).

A dysfunctional spiral of this sort has clearly developed in the U.S., where commercial social media platforms have fueled increased levels of political partisanship and regional tensions. Digital capitalism exacerbates the problem, since catering to a niche market in one 'red' zone creates increased demand in the other two. Often, the same commercial entities cater to competing views simultaneously. A case in point is the Russian government's successful strategy to leverage Facebook's algorithms in fueling animosity between rival political groups in the U.S. Notably, Facebook has explicit commercial aspirations in AR and VR development.

While traditional news reporting and social media platforms have failed to provide the kind of civic wisdom that environmental and pandemic crises require, the emerging digital economy has drawn out the worst elements of both—a process of commercially-driven augmentation in which the vices of greed, ignorance, and delusion tend to prevail over the corresponding virtues of integrity, wisdom, and critical hope. An ethical framework of the sort outlined here can help identify design strategies to break this cycle and shift the overall center of gravity into a 'green' zone that is ethically sustainable—stable, yet dynamic in the sense of evolving over time toward greater complexity and inclusiveness.

The coronavirus pandemic has created a moment of increased opportunity and risk. Green Zone applications that leverage arts-based research with contemplative practice may be effective in capturing the opportunities afforded by the current crisis. Contemplative practices allow use to stop and re-assess our understanding of ourselves and our world—a risky endeavor that sometimes leads to what expert practitioners call a 'dark night of the soul,' where the collapse of established cognitive maps, and the perceived lack of their replacement, may cause intense anxiety and depression. Deep practice is not for the faint of heart and amounts to more than mere stress relief since its goal is to dig into the root of stress itself.

The pandemic has forced a kind of de facto moment of collective reflection where, as lockdown and isolation persist, the shadows of our fragmented culture emerge in a moment of challenge and opportunity—a dark night of our collective souls that could alternately portend a propagandist authoritarian state or a wholesale transformation toward economic sustainability. It is no coincidence that sweeping proposals for racial and economic justice, many of which have long suffered from neglect or failure, have in the pandemic context become plausible and, in some cases, quite real.[6]

Richard Rohr, a Franciscan priest and founder of the Center for Action and Contemplation in Albuquerque, New Mexico, eloquently summarizes the challenge that this chapter's proposed ethical framework aims to address. The dysfunction that characterizes today's digital economy, with its vicious cycle of delusion, ignorance, and cynical complicity, requires a radical rethinking of design aesthetics. Rohr's response, which he articulates not as a technologist or researcher but as a philosopher and practitioner, is fitting:

> To get out of this unending cycle, we have to allow ourselves to be drawn into sacred space, in other words, into liminality. All transformation takes place here. We have to allow ourselves to be drawn out of "business as usual" and remain patiently on the "threshold" (*limen*, in Latin) where we are betwixt and between the familiar and the completely unknown. There alone is our old world left behind, while we are not yet sure of the new existence. That's a good space where genuine newness can begin. Get there often and stay as long as you can by whatever means possible (Rohr, 2016).

Liminality here is the unseen, unrecognized opportunity of MR. It is the metaphorical sense of 'nature' alluded to earlier in this chapter. Usually, techniques of augmentation are positioned as tools for enhancing knowledge of a designated space—an additive technology that extends our information about, and knowledge of, the space we inhabit. A robust ethic proposes that we use digital augmentation both as an extension of space (accurate maps anchored in objective reality) and as a disruption of space as we know it (imaginative maps anchored in the pursuit of socio-emotional meaning). Augmentation in these exercises is not additive but transformative. We use MR not to seek our way out of liminal space, but precisely to enter into it.

## Put it into Practice: Contemplative Mixed Reality

Use the ethics heat map to critically evaluate an XR artifact of your choice. First, decide where the artifact falls on the map. Recall that the map can evaluate artefacts

---

[6] Notable in this regard are proposals like guaranteed minimum income, alternative currencies, and bounded investment, which local communities have embraced in response to economic lockdown. Such developments suggest that venture capitalism may give way to more equitable economic systems based on alternative support structures like platform cooperatives, certified benefit corporations (B corps), and low-profit limited-liability companies (L3C) (see Rushkoff, 2017, pp. 118-123), all of which would be more conducive to Green Zone development.

in three main ways: intensity of meditation, complexity of subjective versus objective cognitive heuristics, and severity of ethical concern. Given its position on the map, assess the likely short- and long-term social impact of the artefact. Depending on how far it is from the Green Zone, determine whether the artefact ought to be changed or improved in some way, and how such changes might be implemented. For example, it might need to be more tightly anchored to objective reality. Or conversely, it might need to afford users more creative social-emotional engagement. If the artefact cannot be moved into the Green Zone by such changes, explain why it is so. If necessary, propose a design for a prototype that represents a more balanced or 'contemplative' version of the artifact.

## Acknowledgements

The author would like to thank Karolyn Kinane for her participation in the development of Phase 2 as discussed here, and Michelle Gibbons and Jason Snyder for providing feedback on early drafts of this chapter.

## References

Aubrey, A. (2017). Forest bathing: A retreat to nature can boost immunity and mood. Morning Edition. https://www.npr.org/sections/health-shots/2017/07/17/536676954/forest-bathing-a-retreat-to-nature-can-boost-immunity-and-mood

Babbitt, S.E. (1997). Personal integrity, politics and moral imagination. pp. 107-131. *In*: S. Brennan, T. Isaacs and M. Milde (eds.). *A Question of Values: New Canadian Perspectives on Ethics and Political Philosophy*. Rodopi. Amsterdam.

Barbezat, D.P. and Bush, M. (2013). *Contemplative Practices in Higher Education: Powerful Methods to Transform Teaching and Learning*. John Wiley & Sons, New York.

Beebe, J. (2000). The place of integrity in spirituality. pp. 11-20. *In*: P. Young-Eisendrath and M.E. Miller (eds.). The Psychology of Mature Spirituality: Integrity, Wisdom, Transcendence. Routledge, Philadelphia.

Bennett, J. (2001). *The Enchantment of Modern Life: Attachments, Crossings, and Ethics*. Princeton University Press, Princeton, NJ.

Bolter, J.D., Engberg, M. and MacIntyre, B. (2013). Media studies, mobile augmented reality, and interaction design. *Interactions*, January-February, 36-45.

Cowling, M., Tanenbaum, J., Birt, J. and Tanenbaum, K. (2017). Augmenting reality for augmented reality. *Interactions*, January-February, 42-45.

Cresswell, T. (1996). In Place/Out of Place: Geography, Ideology, and Transgression. University of Minnesota Press, Minneapolis.

Downs, R.M. and Stea, D. (1977). *Maps in Minds: Reflections on Cognitive Mapping*. Harper & Row, New York.

Ellul, J. (1973). *Propaganda: The Formation of Men's attitudes*. Vintage Books, New York.

Engberg, M. and Bolter, J.D. (2014). Cultural expression in augmented and mixed reality. *Convergence*, 201, 3-9.

Engberg, M. and Bolter, J.D. (2020). The aesthetics of reality media. *Journal of Visual Culture*. 19.1, 81-95.

Erikson, E. (1980)[1959]. *Identity and the Life Cycle*. W.W. Norton & Company, Inc., New York.

Fisher, J. (2019). Interactive Non-fiction with Reality Media: Rhetorical Affordances. Dissertation. Georgia Institute of Technology.

Gethin, R. (2011). On some definitions of mindfulness. *Contemporary Buddhism*, 12(201), 263-279.

Gunnlaugson, O., Sarath, E.W., Scott, C. and Bai, H. (2014). *Contemplative Learning and Inquiry Across Disciplines*, SUNY Press, Albany, NY.

Hampden-Turner, C. (1981). Generativity and the life-cycle: Erik Erikson's concept of identity. pp. 132-135. *In*: C. Hampden-Turner (ed.). Maps of the Mind: Charts and Concepts of the Mind and Its Labyrinths. Collier Books, New York.

Harris, T., Weiner, D., Warner, T. and Levin, R. (1995). Pursuing social goals through participatory geographic information systems. pp. 196-222. *In*: J. Pickles (ed.). Ground Truth: The Social Implications of Geographic Information Systems. New York, Guilford Press.

Healey, K. (2013). Contemplative media studies. Paper presented at Association for Contemplative Mind in Higher Education (ACMHE), Amherst, MA.

Healey, K. (2014). Coercion, consent, and the struggle for social media. *Explorations in Media Ecology*. 13, 195-212.

Healey, K. (2015). Contemplative media studies. *Religions*. 6(3), 948-968.

Healey, K. (2018). Being Digital Citizens: Mindful Media from Tweets to Big Data. Conference presentation. Association for Contemplative Mind in Higher Education. Amherst, MA.

Healey, K. (2020). Contemplative photo-mapping. Website. https://arcg.is/0qSD5H

Healey, K. and Stephens, N. (2017). Augmenting justice: The politics of wearable technology from Silicon Valley to Ferguson. *Journal of Information, Communication and Ethics in Society*, 15(4), 370-384.

Healey, K. and Woods, Jr. R.H. (2019). *Ethics and Religion in the Age of Social Media: Digital Proverbs for Responsible Citizens*. Routledge, New York.

Jafari Naimi, N. (2015). MR$^x$ as a participatory platform. *Digital Creativity*, 26.3-4, 207-220.

Kabat-Zinn, J. (1994). *Wherever You Go, There You Are*. Hyperion, New York.

Kirkpatrick, D. (2010). *The Facebook Effect: The Inside Story of the Company That Is Connecting the World*. Simon & Schuster, New York.

Kinane, K. (2013). Contemplative pedagogy, enchantment, and the medieval past. *In*: Mary Dockray-Miller (ed.). Postmedieval Forum IV. https://postmedieval-forum.com/forums/forum-iv-pedagogy/contemplative-pedagogy-karolyn-kinane/

Kinane, K. (2020). Personal communication.

Leavy, P. (ed.) (2018). *Handbook of Arts-based Research*. Guilford Press, New York.

Levinas, E. (1969). Alphonso Lingis trans. *Totality and Infinity: An Essay on Exteriority*. Duquesne University Press, Pittsburgh.

Labouvie-Vief, G. (2002). Affect complexity and the transcendent. pp. 103-119. *In*: P. Young-Eisendrath and M.E. Miller (eds.). The Psychology of Mature Spirituality: Integrity, Wisdom, Transcendence. Routledge, Philadelphia.

Louv, R. (2008). *Last Child in the Woods: Saving Our Children from Nature-Deficit Disorder*. Algonquin Books, Chapel Hill, NC.

Maskey, M., Rodgers, J., Ingham, B., Freeston, M., Evans, G., Labus, M. and Parr, J.R. (2019). Using virtual reality environments to augment cognitive behavioral therapy for fears and phobias in autistic adults. *Autism in Adulthood*, 2. DOI: 10.1089/aut.2018.0019

McHaffie, P.H. (1995). Manufacturing metaphors: Public cartography, the market, and democracy. pp. 113-129. *In*: J. Pickles (ed.). Ground Truth: The Social Implications of Geographic Information Systems. Guilford Press, New York.

Milgram, P. and Fumio, K. (1994). A taxonomy of mixed reality visual displays. *IEICE Transactions on Information Systems*, E77-D(12).

Monmonier, M. (1996). *How to Lie with Maps*. Second Edition. University of Chicago Press, Chicago.

Murray, J. (2017). *Thresholds of Reality: Creating Coherent Enchantment in AR*. AR in Action Leadership Summit. AR in Action (organization). New York, NY.

Newton, C. (2019). Bodies in seats. The Verge. https://www.theverge.com/2019/6/19/18681845/facebook-moderator-interviews-video-trauma-ptsd-cognizanttampa

Nozick, R. (1989). *The examined life: Philosophical meditations*. Simon and Schuster, New York.

Oman, D. (2010). Similarity in diversity? Four shared functions of integrative contemplative practice systems. pp. 7-16. *In*: T. Plante (ed.). Contemplative Practices in Action: Spirituality, Meditation, and Health. Praeger, Santa Barbara, CA.

Perelman, C. and Olbrechts-Tyteca, L. (1969). The New Rhetoric: A Treatise on Argumentation. Trans. J. Wilkinson and P. Weaver. Center for the Study of Democratic Institutions. University of Notre Dame Press, Notre Dame, Indiana.

Pickles, J. (1995). Conclusion. pp. 223-240. *In*: J. Pickles (ed.). Ground Truth: The Social Implications of Geographic Information Systems. Guilford Press, New York.

Pickles, J. (1995). Representations in an electronic age: Geography, GIS, and democracy. pp. 1-30. *In*: J. Pickles (ed.). Ground Truth: The Social Implications of Geographic Information Systems. Guilford Press, New York.

Press, E. (2018). The wounds of the drone warrior. New York Times. https://www.nytimes.com/2018/06/13/magazine/veterans-ptsd-drone-warrior-wounds.html

Rohr, R. (2016). Transformation: week 2 (series: on Liminality). Center for Action and Contemplation blog. https://cac.org/liminal-space-2016-07-07/#gsc.tab=0

Rushkoff, D. (2017). *Throwing Rocks at the Google Bus: How Growth Became the Enemy of Prosperity*. Penguin Books, New York.

Rushkoff, D. (2020). Restoring the Economy Is the Last Thing We Should Want. Medium. https://gen.medium.com/restoring-the-economy-is-the-last-thing-we-should-want-308045d58e0a

Sivek, S. (2018). Both facts and feelings: Emotion and news literacy. *Journal of Media Literacy Education*, 102, 123-138.

Slovic, P., Finucane, M.L., Peters, E. and MacGregor, D.G. (2007). The affect heuristic. *European Journal of Operational Research*, 177, 1333-1352.

Staley, D.J. (2007). Finding narratives of time and space. pp. 35-47. *In*: D. Stuart Sinton and J.J. Lund (eds.). Understanding Place: GIS and Mapping Across the Curriculum. ESRI Press, Redlands, CA.

Stanley, B.J. (2012). The communion of strangers. The Sun. https://www.thesunmagazine.org/issues/436/the-communion-of-strangers

Stevens-Long, J. (2000). The prism self: Multiplicity on the path to transcendence. pp. 160-174. *In*: Polly Young-Eisendrath and Melvin E. Miller (eds.). The Psychology of Mature Spirituality: Integrity, Wisdom, Transcendence. Routledge, Philadelphia.

Stuart Sinton, D. and Lund, J.J. (eds.) (2007). *Understanding Place: GIS and Mapping Across the Curriculum*. ESRI Press. Redlands, CA.

Stuart Sinton, D. and Witham Bednarz, S. (2007). About that G in GIS. pp. 19-34. *In*: D. Stuart Sinton and J.J. Lund. (eds.). Understanding Place: GIS and Mapping Across the Curriculum. ESRI Press. Redlands, CA.

Warf, B. and Arias, S. (2009). Introduction. pp. 1-10. *In*: B. Warf and S. Arias (eds.). The Spatial Turn: Interdisciplinary Perspectives. Routledge, New York.

Warf, B. (2009). From surfaces to networks. pp. 59-76. *In*: B. Warf and S. Arias (eds.). The Spatial Turn: Interdisciplinary Perspectives, Routledge, New York.

Wohlleben, P. (2016). *The Hidden Life of Trees: What They Feel, How They Communicate.* Jane Billinghurst (trans.). First English Language Edition, 8th Printing edition, Greystone Books, Berkeley, CA.

World Health Organization (2019). International classification of diseases for mortality and morbidity statistics 11th Revision. Retrieved from https://icd.who.int/browse11/l-m/en

Zajonc, A. (2014). Contemplative pedagogy in higher education: Toward a more reflective academy. pp. 15-29. *In*: O. Gunnlaughson, E. Sarath, C. Scott and H. Bai (eds.). Contemplative Learning and Inquiry Across Disciplines, SUNY Press, Albany, NY.

# Chapter

# 7

# Life, Liberty, and the Pursuit of Pokémon: The Tension between Free Speech and Municipal Tranquility

**Brian D. Wassom**

Warner Norcross + Judd LLP, 45000 River Ridge Dr., Ste. 300 Clinton Township, MI 48038
Email: bwassom@wnj.com

In 2017, the author[1] had the unique opportunity to file and win the first lawsuit vindicating First Amendment free speech rights in the XR medium (Candy Lab Inc. v. Milwaukee County, 2017). Consistent with the times, the litigants employed the phrase "augmented reality," ("AR") but the judge who decided the case defined this as "the digital enhancement of physical senses, most sight in particular"—a broad understanding that encompasses what today we're more likely to call "XR" (Candy Lab Inc. v. Milwaukee County, 2017). In the course of resolving and, to a modest degree creating this dispute, the author's legal team shined light on the "time, place, and manner restriction" framework that is likely to shape the parameters of XR displays in public places for many years to come (Candy Lab Inc. v. Milwaukee County, 2017).

## Prologue: How the Author Came to Champion XR Free Speech Rights

Before discussing the case itself, this chapter begins with a brief explanation of what led the author—a lawyer in private practice in suburban Detroit—to champion free speech rights in XR. Not only does it provide the background for how the *Candy Lab v. Milwaukee* case came to be, but hopefully it also inspires readers to recognize their own individual agency and the abundance of opportunities available for making a difference in the still-nascent XR space (Candy Lab Inc. v. Milwaukee County, 2017).

---

[1] The views expressed in this article are those of the author only, and are not attributable to his law firm or its clients. The author also thanks Bill K.A. Warners and Brianna Loder for their editorial assistance.

The author's fascination with AR was triggered by a professional milestone. He had spent the first decade of his career under the wing of a partner with a robust media law practice, and whose signature client was the largest newspaper in Michigan. And this was still in the period of time in which people bought newspapers, so the publishers could still afford to hire lawyers and stand up for principle when circumstances warranted it. This provided the opportunity to conduct a great deal of litigation defending against the types of accusations that tend to be leveled against journalists who do their job well—such as in defamation and invasion of privacy cases (Convertino v. Ashenfelter, 2015; State News v. MSU, 2008; Radio One v. Wooten, 2006; Detroit Free Press v. Ashcroft, 2002)—as well as proactive fights to gain access to closed court proceedings and government documents (Convertino v. Ashenfelter, 2015; State News v. MSU, 2008; Radio One v. Wooten, 2006; Detroit Free Press v. Ashcroft, 2002).

By 2010, however, the demise of traditional media formats was already predicted. It would be impossible to build a successful career trying to replicate a newspaper-based practice. At the same time, though, the author had learned to love the First Amendment and the importance of defending its fundamental tenets. Although traditional media was suffering, journalism and free expression would always continue to be vital to our democratic society.

The author set out to discerning which forms of digital media would be most important to society's future. Social media was the first and most obvious answer, since that was precisely the moment in time in which Facebook, Twitter, and the like were just coming into their own. His further speculations on what form future media would take grew organically out of a lifelong enjoyment of science fiction. One aspect of those stories kept coming back time and again—the idea of digital content being liberated from a two-dimensional display screen to occupy three-dimensional space, and becoming part of the landscape or even an object of sorts that humans could perceive from any direction and interact with as if it were tangibly present in our physical reality. Examples of this concept were already present in the on-field graphics in football and other sports broadcasts (Berlin, 2009). They also kept appearing in all sorts of futurist stories such as *Minority Report, Star Wars, Firefly, The Terminator, Iron Man,* and other films (Spielberg, 2002; Lucas, 1977; Whedon, 2002; Cameron, 1984; Favreau, 2008). This concept of engaging with digital content with all the human body senses to perceive reality went from seeming logical to a likely singularity towards which all media was inevitably converging. The author wanted to be a part of shaping the law that would govern this emerging media.

## The Inherent and Inevitable Tension between Free Speech and AR

Despite the breadth and depth of its potential, the AR medium would take much longer to mature than its enthusiasts initially predicted. One of the earliest topics explored in the author's writings was the intersection of First Amendment rights and AR. He was not the first to do so. At least one commentator—John C. Havens, who has gone on to do remarkable work in the development of ethics in digital media—wrote about it in a June 2011 article on *Mashable* (Havens, Who Owns the Advertising Space in an Augmented Reality World?, 2011). This article was one of the first to use the term "virtual air rights" to describe a legal framework for deciding whose digital content would be allowed to occupy which physical spaces. Variations of this phrase soon became commonplace in AR circles (Fairfield, 2012; Havens, Hacking Happiness: Why Your Personal Data Counts and How Tracking It Can Change the World, 2014).

In posts on his *Augmented Legality* blog from 2011 onward, and in his 2015 book *Augmented Reality Law, Privacy, and Ethics*, the author had an issue with this concept of "virtual property rights," and labeled the phrase a misnomer (Wassom, Augmented Reality Law, Privacy, and Ethics: Law, Society, and Emerging AR Technologies, 2014 ). The reason is simple. "Although AR creates the illusion that digital data occupies physical space, it's *not really there*," he wrote in a 2013 post (Wassom, Augmented Reality as Free Speech - A First Amendment Analysis, 2013). "Property law is about the right to exclude others from physical space. But an infinite number of people can each create their own AR layer superimposing digital data over the same physical space without impeding anyone else's ability to do so, and without invading the rights of the real property owner. Therefore, property law doesn't help us think accurately about the AR experience" (Wassom, Augmented Reality as Free Speech – A First Amendment Analysis, 2013).

Instead, when a digital device recognizes a person, place or thing and is triggered to augment one's view of it with digital information, the experience is much more like clicking a hyperlink on a web page – except that the "web page" is the physical world around people, and the hyperlinked "text" is the person, place, or thing that triggered the display. Just as with a web page, there is someone responsible for writing the short piece of link code and for choosing to associate it with that person, place, or thing in the program being run by the digital device. Therefore, "the possibility that an AR coder's choice to associate digital content with a tangible object is itself speech protected by the First Amendment's prohibition of laws that 'abridge … the freedom of speech, or of the press'" (Wassom, Augmented Reality as Free Speech - A First Amendment Analysis, 2013).[2] This fundamental disconnect between digital content and real property law would soon receive far more validation.

## The Pokémon That Broke the Camel's Back

The author had not paid much attention to the buzz building among Pokémon fans throughout the first half of 2016. When the game launched on July 6, 2016 it was an immediate hit. The game quickly became the most popular app in all the major mobile app stores, and forever altered society's relationship with AR. This game

---

[2] Humorously, the author wrote this article with an urgency demanded by his sense that "consumer-level digital eyewear was just around the corner"—a technological milestone that is still rumored to be imminent as these words are being written in mid-2020 (Wassom, Augmented Reality as Free Speech – A First Amendment Analysis, 2013).

was not the first entry in its category and was not even the first one released by its creator, Niantic, a spin-off from Google (Olanoff, 2015). On the contrary, Niantic had released the game *Ingress* a full five years earlier (Rusell, 2014). *Ingress* raised the same novel issues of privacy, property rights, and personal injury concerns that *Pokémon Go* would, and as such had already prompted much discussion on the author's blog (Wassom, Ingress AR Game Impacting Kansas Law Enforcement?, 2014). *Pokémon Go* essentially repurposed the geolocations used in *Ingress* and re-skinned its core functionality with a different intellectual property. This was one reason why the author had not expected the game to materially advance the AR industry, from a legal perspective (Wassom, Ingress AR Game Impacting Kansas Law Enforcement, 2014). However, he was wrong.

Beginning a day after the game's release, the author joined over 30 other adults in befuddlement over the large groups of people—mostly teens, but adults as well—roving the sidewalks while pointing and oddly flicking at their phones. Downtown areas, shopping malls, and public parks known to be quiet were suddenly flooded with crowds. Places dedicated to solemn contemplation—such as the Holocaust Memorial, museums, and churches—began posting signs to keep players away (Peterson, 2016; The Associated Press, 2017).

After digital media professionals tried to spark an interest in XR technologies for countless years, the phrase "AR" suddenly started dominating public conversation—and these conversations were mostly about how to regulate this new phenomenon (Sharma, 2016; Hobson, 2016; Metz, 2015). On July 11, the *Hollywood Reporter* republished the author's blog post about the legal issues raised by AR games (Wassom, How Pokémon GO Players Could Run Into Real-Life Legal Problems, 2016; Wassom, Pokémon Go and the Crisis On An Infinitely Augmented Earth, 2016). In August, the author was contacted to brief the staff of a U.S. Senate committee on AR law, and in December that committee held the first Congressional hearings on AR—with witnesses including the head of AR company Daqri and CEO of "Niantic" John Hanke (Hanke, 2016).

Reaction was swift at the local level as well. Before July 2016 was over, a number of property owners had filed lawsuits against Niantic seeking to hold it responsible for various forms of alleged trespass and nuisance by players (Marder v. Niantic, Inc. et al, 2016). These cases would be consolidated in the US District Court for the Northern District of California, and not resolved until 2019 (In re Pokemon Go Nuisance Litigation, 2019). Municipalities began increasing police presence in public areas and enforcing hours of operation at parks (Pamplin, 2016; Wickliffe, 2016). Still, the tide of players continued to surge.

## What Made Milwaukee Different

Milwaukee, Wisconsin encountered the same issues related to Pokémon Go as every other major municipality in the country (Williams, 2016). Unsurprisingly, the initial reactions of local leaders were mixed, reactionary, and sometimes contradictory (Milwaukee County Board of Supervisors, 2017). Politics often has a way of getting more petty the less there is at stake, and that principle was made evident (Shepherd, 2016). However, the manner in which Milwaukee leadership increasingly focused its attention on the publisher of the game—Niantic—rather than the individuals engaging in unwanted behavior is what distinguished their reaction from other localities (Behm, 2016).

For example, on August 16, 2016, Milwaukee County Parks Director John Dargle, Jr. reportedly sent the following letter to Niantic CEO John Hanke (Wild, Milwaukee County Parks are trying to remove Pokemon Go from Lake Park, 2016). Citing congestion, littering, and trampled flora, the letter demanded the removal of all fixed-location AR content from county parks, particularly Lake Park:

Dear Mr. Hanke,

The Pokémon GO phenomenon is on full display at Milwaukee County's parks, most notably at its beloved and historic Lake Park (National Register of Historic Places #93000339). Indeed, this park is a national treasure, designed by the renowned Frederick Law Olmsted, who once described his park work as a "democratic development of the highest significance." [...] Lake Park has quickly become known as one of the most active Pokémon Go areas in the Midwest.

The Pokémon phenomenon has introduced hundreds, if not thousands, of individuals to our park system and doubtless has resulted in many new positive recreation experiences. The Milwaukee County Parks, Recreation and Culture Department applauds those outcomes. However, there have been other unanticipated and negative consequences from Pokémon-related activities which have caused significant disruption both within Lake Park and in adjacent neighborhoods. These include daily traffic congestion, parking issues, littering, compacted and damaged turf, risks to sensitive flora and fauna habitats, and noncompliance with park system operation hours.

This letter is provided to notify you of the Milwaukee County parks' policy related to virtual geocaches and to require your immediate compliance with that policy, which includes prior written permission before placement of a virtual geocache in any Milwaukee County park. Niantic, Inc. must complete a separate notification placement for each intended Pokémon GO site within the Milwaukee County parks' system [...] As noted, should Niantic, Inc. be granted permission to place Pokémon Go sites within any Milwaukee County park, it will thereafter be responsible for regularly monitoring each cache (4 times per year is recommended) and reporting vandalism or deterioration of property.

Be advised that until such approval is obtained, Niantic, Inc. must deactivate and remove all Pokémon GO sites, including Poke stops and Gyms within Milwaukee County parks, including, but not limited to Lake Park, located between 2900 North Lake Drive and 2800 East Kenwood Drive, Milwaukee Wisconsin (Wild, Milwaukee County Parks are trying to remove Pokemon Go from Lake Park, 2016).

Contemporaneous statements from County officials suggested that, at the time, Milwaukee's Police Department, Sheriff's Department, and Park Rangers had collectively written hundreds of citations to *Pokémon Go* players for such offenses as curfew violations, alcohol use, and bringing dogs into the parks (Mueller, 2016).

In an August 30, 2016, open letter to local *Pokémon Go* players, however, Mr. Dargle walked back this position. Citing "confusion in the community as to Milwaukee County Department of Parks, Recreation & Culture's (DPRC) stance on Pokémon Go," Dargel sought to make "clear, we are not asking for Niantic to remove Pokémon Go sites from Milwaukee County Parks, nor are we asking Pokémon Go players to apply for a permit (Wild, Milwaukee County Parks would like to clear up the "confusion" surrounding Pokemon Go, 2016 ). Rather, we would like to partner with Niantic, celebrating the successes of the game and working together to manage both respect for our parks and neighbors" (Wild, Milwaukee County Parks would like to clear up the "confusion" surrounding Pokemon Go, 2016 ). The letter went on to ask players to abide by park hours, follow existing ordinances against littering, and to respect the plant life (Wild, Milwaukee County Parks would like to clear up the "confusion" surrounding Pokemon Go, 2016 ).

This passive-aggressive approach of playing lip service to the benefits of residents using the park system while at the same time insisting that Niantic bear responsibility for players' behavior continued in a September 7, 2016 public meeting in the Lake Park neighborhood dedicated to the issue (Wild, Lake Park's Pokemon Go Meeting was Boring, Livid, and Gloriously Absurd, 2016). The *Milwaukee Record*, a local alternative news outlet, skewered the event as "the sound of a ridiculous situation taken to its ridiculous extremes (Wild, Lake Park's Pokemon Go Meeting was Boring, Livid, and Gloriously Absurd, 2016). It was the sound of two sides possessing both reasonable concerns and defiant inabilities to listen to one another" (Wild, Lake Park's Pokemon Go Meeting was Boring, Livid, and Gloriously Absurd, 2016). The room was packed out with residents passionate on both sides of the issue. County Supervisor Sheldon Wasserman, whose constituency included the Lake Park neighborhood, "repeatedly stressed that while it was indeed wonderful to see so many people enjoying the park, the area was in the process of being 'loved to death,'" citing trash, parking issues, lack of bathrooms, trampled landscapes, and neighbors "threatened with violence," though tangible examples of the latter were conspicuously absent (Wild, Lake Park's Pokemon Go Meeting was Boring, Livid, and Gloriously Absurd, 2016). "One option, obviously, is to sue Niantic," suggested an unidentified alderman. "Another option is to ask Niantic nicely" (Wild, Lake Park's Pokemon Go Meeting was Boring, Livid, and Gloriously Absurd, 2016).

The more time passed, the more local leadership centered its attention on what it considered the real problem—the publisher of the game. On December 6, 2016, Supervisor Wasserman introduced an ordinance intended to regulate location-based AR games, and to ensure that nothing like the events of Summer 2016 ever happened again. The proposal would declare that "virtual and location-based AR games are not permitted in Milwaukee County Parks except in those areas designated with a permit for such use by the Director of the Department of Parks, Recreation, and Culture." By his own admission, Wasserman had modeled the approach on the County's existing regulation of geocaching, the pastime of hiding small objects that players locate using geo-coordinates.

The author blogged about it the next day, repeating what had become a mantra on the issue: "Here's the problem: AR gaming companies don't 'place things like PokeStops in Milwaukee County parks,' because they're *not actually there*. (An important distinction from the geocaching regulations also referenced in the article.)... They are the creative expression of the game designers who made them. In short, they are *speech*" (Wassom, Milwaukee, Pokemon Go, and the First Amendment, 2016). The remainder of the blog post went on the develop the same arguments that would eventually find their way into our legal briefing against the County. Anticipating that possible outcome, the post ended with, "Perhaps a judge will completely disagree with my perspective. But I doubt it" (Wassom, Milwaukee, Pokemon Go, and the First Amendment, 2016). It was glaringly obvious that the County's proposed ordinance overstepped Constitutional bounds.

## Milwaukee's Ordinance Regulating Location-based AR Games

Milwaukee County did not disappoint. On December 15, 2016, Supervisor Wasserman delivered an impassioned plea to his colleagues to protect his district's parks from rampaging hordes of *Pokémon Go* players (Wassom, No Pokemon For You?, 2017). One of his colleagues, David Sartori, echoed these sentiments, and asked to be added as a co-sponsor. Cooler heads, however, soon prevailed. Several other Board members rose to challenge the ordinance, noting that they'd heard about it from constituents, who were universally opposed. In the end, the Board voted 13-3 to refer the ordinance back to committee for further review.

On February 2, 2017, however, Supervisor Wasserman reintroduced the proposal as Resolution 16-637 (the "Ordinance"). Again, his justification for the measure was the expense of policing and cleaning up after *Pokémon Go* players in Lake Park (Wasserman, 2017). Multiple supervisors spoke against the Ordinance, disputing Wasserman's claims about the game's impact. Said Supervisor West: "the library, the American Legion post, and the Caterpillar Museum are all Pokémon Go spots. We have never had to call the police[…] It was great to see them running and being outside and being together and it was a very diverse group of people[…]I didn't hear about rioting. I didn't hear about people not getting along with each other. And I didn't hear about additional sheriff's deputies being needed. I know that they were patrolling the parks just like they normally do" (Milwaukee County Board of Supervisors, 2017). Supervisor Cullen added: "I didn't think anything that drastic was happening. It looked like a bunch of young people[…]using their free time to be active in the park" (Milwaukee County Board of Supervisors, 2017). One noted that "the Pokémon Go craze is pretty much over," while more than one perceived the true driving force behind residents' complaints to be a self-interested, "not in my backyard" reaction (Milwaukee County Board of Supervisors, 2017). "I don't think because you live across the street from a park that you should expect that you're never going to have people utilizing your park," said West (Milwaukee County Board of Supervisors, 2017).

There were two things that all of the Supervisors appeared to agree on. First was that *Pokémon Go* represented an entire genre of games that would only get more popular going forward. The second was that the Ordinance was designed to make money for the County. For example, Wasserman argued that "this company came in and made all the money off of our citizens. We had no recourse. We paid for it ourselves" (Milwaukee County Board of Supervisors, 2017). Supervisor Nicholson agreed: "I think permitting a company to work within our parks is a great way to raise revenue" (Milwaukee County Board of Supervisors, 2017). Said Supervisor Moore: "I don't have a problem with large companies who make millions of dollars of games having to break us off a piece because they're using our parks" (Milwaukee County Board of Supervisors, 2017). At the end of the day, the Board adopted the Ordinance by a vote of 13-4. On February 20, the Ordinance was published and became effective. The relevant text of the Ordinance read:

(3) *Permits required for location-based augmented reality games.* Virtual and location-based augmented reality games are not permitted in Milwaukee County Parks except in those areas designated with a permit for such use by the Director of the Department of Parks, Recreation, and Culture. Permits shall be required before any company may introduce a location-based augmented reality game into the Parks, effective January 1, 2017. The permitting application process is further described on DPRC's website for companies that create and promote such games. That process shall include an internal review by the DPRC to determine the appropriateness of the application based on site selection, protection of rare flora and fauna, personal safety, and the intensity of game activities on park lands. Game activity shall only occur during standard park hours, unless otherwise authorized by the DPRC Director, who has the authority to designate special events and activities within the Parks outside of the standard operational hours.

The resolution adopting the Ordinance (but not the codified language itself) defines "virtual gaming" as "an activity during which a person can experience being in a three-dimensional environment and interact with that environment during a game, and the game typically consists of an artificial world of images and sounds created by a computer that is affected by the actions of a person who is experiencing it; and[...][further provides that] Pokémon Go fits the characteristics defined by virtual gaming and is considered as such by the standards of the DPRC" (Kozlowski, 2017). The Ordinance does not define what it means by the term "location-based augmented reality games," other than to repeatedly imply that *Pokémon Go* is such a game.

Even though the idea of requiring software publishers to obtain government permission before publishing their speech is inherently offensive to the First Amendment, one could be forgiven for reading this single-paragraph Ordinance and concluding that simply having to ask permission is not much of an imposition (Brown v. Entertainment Merchants Association, 2011). The devil, however, is in the details.

The DPRC website at the time noted that the "Milwaukee County Parks 2017 Special Event Application" ("Permit Application") is required for "virtual gaming," although the website gives software publishers no guidance in finding the Permit Application or in understanding when it is needed (Candy Lab Inc. v. Milwaukee County, 2017). This 10-page document requests a vast amount of information, such as estimated attendance, location in park, event dates and times, site map, whether and how the event will be advertised(Milwaukee County Parks Special Event Application, 2017). It requires detailed plans for garbage collection, on-site security, and medical services, and warns that applicants will be responsible for these services. The Permit Application requires applicants to have liability insurance and make it available on-site for inspection. It also requires payment of several fees, and reserves the limitless discretion to demand more, including "additional information or documentation regarding the applicant, applicant's company, sponsoring company/organization, co-sponsors, event participants, event vendors, event activities or the event itself. Moreover, Milwaukee County Parks may postpone approval of event permit(s) until receipt of additional requested information or documentation. Failure to submit requested information or documentation in a timely manner may be cause for denial of a Special Event Permit." Even after all this, "Submittal of an application does not automatically grant [an applicant] a permit or confirmation to conduct your planned event," according to the Application.

Penalties for violating the ordinance included fines and imprisonment. The Ordinance was codified in Section 47 of the County Municipal Code, which regulates County "Parks and Parkways." Section 47.29(1) specifies that the penalty for "violating any of the provisions of chapter 47... [is] a penalty of not less than ten dollars ($10.00) nor more than two hundred dollars ($200.00), together with the taxable costs in said action, in the discretion of the court, and in default of payment thereof, shall be imprisoned in the county jail or in the house of corrections of the county for a period not to exceed ninety (90) days, in the discretion of the court." In addition, the Ordinance also allows officers to arrest violators, and empowers the DPRC to issue citations in addition to the foregoing penalties.

## How the *Candy Lab AR v. Milwaukee* Lawsuit Came to Be

From the moment the author learned about the potential Ordinance in early December 2016, he began forming the arguments to be used in suing the County. The trouble was, he didn't yet have a client. Obviously, the party most naturally positioned to challenge the Ordinance in court was Niantic, since the measure was overtly intended to regulate *Pokémon Go*. But the company chose not to get the route of litigation. There was a great deal of wisdom in Niantic staying quiet on the issue. It was still a relatively small software company that had gone from obscurity to a worldwide target literally overnight. The company had more than enough on its hands without picking fights over petty municipal measures that had not yet, and may have never been, actually enforced.

Although the Ordinance was inspired by *Pokémon Go*, it targeted the industry as a whole. The author approached his colleagues and clients at AugmentedReality. Org—the leading XR trade association and organizers of the long-running Augmented World Expo ("AWE")—and several companies that often attended the conference. All of them shared the author's concerns, and many were willing to help. Taking the risk of actually stepping up and being the ones to file a lawsuit, however, is a big task. Although the law allows successful civil rights plaintiffs to recover attorneys' fees and costs, no one could guarantee victory. Any legal activity would be a distraction from the business of the company. But the upside was the opportunity to have the company's name repeated every time people discussed the name of the first case to establish free speech rights in AR.

The person who rose to the challenge was Andrew Couch, co-founder and CEO of Candy Lab, Inc., d/b/a Candy Lab AR, a location-based AR technology company incorporated in Nevada and based in Irvine, California. The company had been publishing location-based AR experiences since 2012—the same year Niantic had released *Ingress*. Candy Lab had published an AR game it for attendees of a prior AWE event. And, it so happened that, during the South by Southwest festival in March 2017, the company had just announced its own location-based AR game

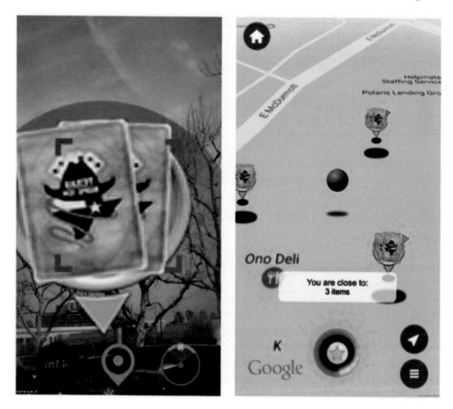

**Figure 7.1:** (QuickSilver Software, Inc., 2015)

called "Texas Rope 'Em" (QuickSilver Software, Inc., 2015). This game functioned much like *Pokémon Go* in many ways. Players needed to visit game stops at designated geographic coordinates in order to collect digital items that they can then use to compete against others. Except here, the items are playing cards rather than Pokémon, and the competition is the Texas Hold 'Em variation of poker (QuickSilver Software, Inc., 2015).

Because *Texas Rope 'Em* was a location-based AR game, it was theoretically subject to Milwaukee's Ordinance. Just to be sure we had no difficulties proving the company's standing in court, however, Candy Lab AR reached out to the County to ask whether it needed a permit to make its game available in Milwaukee. The County said yes. We also made sure to create local waypoints on the game map so that the game was playable in Milwaukee—right in the middle of Supervisor Wasserman's beloved Lake Park.

That, in a nutshell, is how a Michigan lawyer teamed up with a California-based, Nevada-incorporated start-up to use a game about Texas to get a Wisconsin law struck down.

## The Opening Move

The author and Candy Lab filed suit on April 21, 2017, in the US District Court in Milwaukee. Together with the complaint, they filed a motion for preliminary injunction preventing the Ordinance from being enforced. Such immediate legal relief is a severe remedy and is granted only when the Court agrees that the plaintiff is highly likely to win its case as a matter of law.

In support of these pleadings, sworn declarations were filed not only from Mr. Couch, but also from two other giants in the AR field: Ori Inbar, President of AugmentedReality.Org, and Mark Skwarek, a pioneering digital artist who teaches AR at NYU Polytechnic. The declarations were necessary to ensure the court properly understood the technology at issue and depth of its expressive potential. Declarations also have the distinct advantage of not being included within the page limits to which motion papers are subject.

Mr. Inbar's declaration was 38-pages long and peppered with color screen-grabs demonstrating AR's power as a medium of communication—from *Terminator* and *Iron Man* to NFL broadcasts to CNN news reports to numerous AR apps. After summarizing for the Court his own background and qualifications on the topic, Mr. Inbar explained why the issues at stake went far beyond one game and one municipality:

> 2. I submit this declaration in support of Candy Lab's challenge to Milwaukee County's ordinance regulating the publication of location-based augmented reality games. I am gravely concerned that laws like this pose a serious threat to the emerging medium of augmented reality, which promises to be one of the most important and innovative ways that human beings will use to communicate with each other in the 21st Century....

11. It is difficult to overestimate the importance of AR in contemporary society, both now and in the coming years. AR has accurately been called the "Eight Mass Medium" in human history, following the mass media of print, recordings, cinema, radio, television, internet, and mobile devices. It is a platform on which content of any subject matter can be displayed....

20. According to data collected by Greenlight Insights and reported by Upload, venture capitalists invested a total of $1.07 billion in AR companies, which is over four times the total of 2015 investments.[3] But the same report also shows that the majority of investments are small, led by a few very large investments. The spread of large and small investments indicates a young industry that is anticipated to grow rapidly in coming years.

21. There is no shortage of market studies and projections on where the AR industry is headed. The details vary slightly between these reports, but the overwhelming consensus is that AR and related technologies will be a source of enormous revenue in the near future. Digi-Capital, a tech advisor, believes that the combined market for augmented and virtual reality could be $108 billion by 2021. My research and experience suggests this to be a realistic projection.

22. Use cases for AR are already widespread, and are limited only by a developer's imagination. Some of the most compelling use cases to date include:

*Industrial manufacturing and processes*: Employees wearing AR eyewear are using the devices to visualize data, follow guided work instructions, and receive visual cues from subject-matter experts in remote locations.

*Navigation*: AR navigational displays (whether on mobile devices, wearable displays, or windshields) display way-finding data in a three-dimensional, volumetric manner, so that the display appears to be part of the road or walkway in front of the viewer instead of a two-dimensional map. This helps reduce distraction and traffic accidents.

*Health Care*: AR displays have been used to remotely guide the actions of a surgeon wearing AR eyewear by displaying instructions in the surgeon's field of view. Other wearable AR devices use sensors to enhance the appearance of veins, allowing phlebotomists to more accurately deliver injections. AR applications have been used in mental health counseling by exposing patients with phobias to their fears in a realistic, but safe, manner.

*Education and Training*: The ability to display content in three dimensions unlocks a new world of teaching methods for educators, especially for students who are more likely to learn through hands-on applications than through reading or two-dimensional displays. It also allows workers to learn dangerous or complicated new skills (such as welding) by performing them in three dimensions without using up actual physical materials or incurring risk. Moreover, content recorded through an instructor's first-person perspective using wearable devices conveys information in unique ways.

---

3  https://uploadvr.com/ar-smashed-funding-records-2016/

*Art*: Artists have accomplished amazing things in the AR medium, including by overlaying digital content on physical artworks, by painting huge murals that trigger AR experiences; by overlaying digital graffiti on public spaces without physically altering them; by enabling users to create in three dimensions with virtual "brushes," and so much more.

*Entertainment, Storytelling, and Gaming*: As with any expressive medium, some of the most engaging work being done in AR is that which tells stories and interacts with the user. AR applications bring print books and artwork to life, and create immersive fictional worlds that blend with the physical world in new and creative ways.

*Political Speech*: AR has already proven to be an important medium for political expression around the world. For example, artists like Mark Skwarek and others created AR mobile applications related to the "Occupy Wall Street" movement, including apps that allowed users to virtually "protest" in areas they could not physically access, and that displayed political messages when pointed at certain Wall Street buildings. Skawrek also released "The Leak in Your Hometown" in 2011, which superimposed a leaky oil pipe onto BP gas station signs as a means of protesting the Gulf Oil Spill. During the 2012 election, a startup called GoldRun created a feature called "Visualize the Vote" that lets users pose for a picture with their favorite presidential candidate—super imposed over the user's physical location—then share that photo with their friends. Professor BC Biermann and the New York-based Public Ad Campaign launched a project called "AR Ad Takeover," a mobile app that recognized particular print advertisements that were then prominent across New York City and superimposed the artists' own messages on them....

Inbar even described at length forms of XR that enhanced human senses other than sight, in order to capture the breadth and depth of what "augmented reality" was being used to describe. From there, Inbar segued into the specific form of XR in front of the Court—location-based AR gaming—and explained how even this term encompassed a wide variety of expression not easily captured by the clumsy language of Milwaukee's ordinance:

28. Mobile AR games are nothing new. The degree of AR functionality and the nature of the game mechanics vary between applications.

29. The simplest version of mobile AR game is one that uses a device's video camera to locate a pre-determined physical image, or "marker," and then superimposes a digital image on top of the video display of that marker....

30. Other games trigger on-screen gaming options after recognizing a physical marker, or a three-dimensional object (sometimes called "markerless object recognition").

31. Still other mobile games are "location-based." As I use and understand this term, location-based mobile games are those that display digital content in reaction to a device's proximity to specified geographic locations.

32. Not all "location-based" games are "augmented reality" games. The two terms describe different things. Dozens of games available on the market are

location-based—in that they require a user to be physically present in certain geolocations in order to take certain actions or interact with certain content—but are not AR games, because they display their content entirely in a two-dimensional fashion. Popular examples of such games include "TurfWars" (a mobster-themed game) and "QONQR" (a science-fiction game), two GPS-based, multiplayer role-playing games in which players compete with each other to "control" real-world territory and build the strength of their respective "organizations," each in the course of playing out a fictional storyline.

33. Similarly, not all AR games are "location-based" in the sense that they rely on GPS or other sensors to determine a user's real-time physical location and incorporate it into the gameplay, as the term "location-based game" typically indicates. Instead, an AR game may superimpose the same digital content on a device's surroundings regardless of where the device is.

34. Therefore, I use the term "location-based augmented reality game" to mean a mobile game that both incorporates the user's real-time physical location into the gameplay, and that displays content in an AR format. I have often heard the term used in the same manner by others, but I am not aware that the phrase has an officially defined meaning.

35. In a manner of speaking, however, any AR display—whether meant for gaming or any other purpose—is "location-based," and has some relationship to the user's physical location, because AR displays by their very nature are meant to be blended with the user's view of their physical surroundings. With this understanding, even an application that displays the same digital image regardless of physical location could be said to be location-based, in that the location and the image blend to form a unique expression.

Inbar went on to describe at length a number of location-based AR games published before *Pokémon Go*, including several he had created himself, in order to place the Court's understanding of the game in context:

41. Nothing in Pokémon Go—not the gameplay, its location-based features, or the optional AR display—was new or unique in the mobile gaming market. The appeal of these features, the timing of the release, and the popularity of the Pokémon content, however, combined in a serendipitous manner to make Pokémon Go a breakout hit....

44. In sum, it is fair to say that use of mobile devices for location-based and AR gaming purposes is here to stay, and that these experiences will only expand in number and diversity.

With this background in mind, Inbar turned to the Milwaukee ordinance, and how its many flaws threatened not only the mobile games published by Candy Lab and Niantic, but also—if its ideas were deemed lawful—the entire XR ecosystem that he had just so painstakingly laid out for the Court:

55. The text of the Ordinance is incredibly vague, to the point where it is impossible for me to discern what it permits and what it regulates. For example:

a. "Virtual gaming" is defined as "an activity during which a person can experience being in a three-dimensional environment and interact with that environment during a game." Taken literally, this describes *every physical game* in which any person can engage, such as baseball, hopscotch, tag, or even swinging on park swings. The Ordinance goes on to explain that a virtual game "*typically* consists of an artificial world of images and sounds created by a computer that is affected by the actions of a person who is experiencing it," but the word "typically" indicates that this description is not a necessary part of the definition. Running down a sidewalk while wearing an activity tracker such as an Apple Watch or a wearable device like Google Glass can cause those devices to emit both images and sounds. Similarly, two children play-fighting with battery-powered *Star Wars* lightsabers also experience a three-dimensional environment accompanied by artificial images and sounds. Both of these activities appear to fit the Ordinance's definition of "virtual gaming."
b. The term "location-based augmented reality game" is not defined. As used in this context:
i. "location-based" could mean any of the following:
1. Content that is fixed to, and only accessible at, predetermined geographic coordinates, like the game stops used in AR games like NBA: King of the Court, Paranormal Activity: Sanctuary, Ingress, Pokémon GO, and Texas Rope 'Em, as well as in non-AR games such as TurfWars and QONQR, and in non-gaming applications such as Metaio's Timetraveler. (As noted above, this is how I use the term "location-based" as applied to mobile games, but I am not aware of any official definition endorsing this meaning.)
2. Content that is triggered by physical objects regardless of where they are located, such as the Nintendo 3DS, Dos Equis Ring Toss, and Disney Magic Mirror.
3. Content that is dynamically triggered based on the user's proximity to objects that are not fixed in space, such as another person's mobile device.
4. Content that is dynamically assigned to specific geographic locations randomly chosen by an algorithm, such as how digital creatures are generated in Pokémon Go.
5. Content that is assigned to a particular geographic location by a player, such as in Clandestine Anomaly or in Hololens-based games.

ii. The term "augmented reality" is subject to multiple interpretations.
1. Many would argue that even the one example of AR given in the Ordinance—Pokémon Go—is not really an "augmented reality" game, since the AR component of the game is not essential to the gameplay and can be deactivated. Some people accept the static overlay of digital content over a live video feed to be AR, while others use AR to mean digital content that dynamically interacts with physical surroundings in some way.
2. As detailed above, "augmented reality" also describes the digital enhancement of senses other than the sense of sight—i.e., the senses of hearing, touch, taste, smell, and others, which are also means by which people

perceive reality. The Ordinance is entirely unclear as to whether and how it applies to these applications, or as to the circumstances under which digital augmentation of these other senses could be considered "location-based."

iii. "Game" is also undefined. Does it require a defined set of rules? Does it apply to applications that are purely for gaming purposes and no other, or does it include applications that add a game-like incentive system—like Candy Labs' CacheTown, which was described in the press as gamified advertising, or Google's popular navigation program "Waze," which offers users "points" and "badges" for doing things like visiting new locations or reporting traffic incidents? It may also be argued to apply to Yelp's Monocle feature, since Yelp itself allows users to compete with each other to become the "duke" or "duchess" of a particular establishment.

iv. What degree of "location-based augmented reality game" function is required before the game falls under the Ordinance? Would Pokémon Go or Clandestine Anomaly still be regulated if users disabled their AR features?

c. What does "not permitted in Milwaukee County Parks" mean? Does it mean that individuals are not allowed enter the parks carrying devices that have the game installed? If so, does that mean developers are responsible for the actions of each such person (as the Permit Application repeatedly says)? Or does it only mean that developers cannot publish a game containing content specifically designed to be playable in the parks?

d. What does "before any company may introduce a location-based augmented reality game into the Parks" mean?
i. Game developers do not "introduce" software "into" *any* physical location, even if the game is designed to be played in particular places. Rather, developers simply publish the game in app stores for users to download. Even if certain "AR" content is designed to be displayed in a particular geolocation, it *does not actually exist in* that location; rather, it is merely displayed on a mobile device screen. Therefore, the phrase "introduce... into the Parks" is nonsensical as used in this context.

ii. This sentence of the Ordinance applies only to "location-based augmented reality games" and not to "virtual games," a term that is defined much more broadly. To what extent must the developer of a virtual game that is not a location-based augmented reality game obtain a permit?

e. Who is included within the phrase "companies that create and promote such games"? Does it include every business partner that helped Candy Lab create the content in Texas Rope 'Em? Does it include Apple and Google, who "promote'" the game for download in their app stores? Does it include every entity that speaks favorably about the game in social media? Does it apply to Candy Lab when it develops white-label applications for other companies? Does it even apply to nonprofit organizations like AR.Org, which features numerous AR works at its AWE conferences and works to promote the entire industry? After learning about the Ordinance and the anti-AR militancy of those who advocated for it, I am forced to second-guess how far I can safely go in publicly discussing location-based AR games.

f. What does it mean that "Game activity shall only occur during standard park hours"? Does this apply only to players, whose behavior the developer is then responsible? Or does it purport to require developers to somehow determine "park hours" for each location, and then proactively disable the software on every device on which it has been installed outside of those hours? That is a logistically prohibitive, and perhaps impossible, requirement to meet.

56. The text of the Ordinance requires game publishers to apply for a permit that is said to be available on the Parks Department's website. It is remarkably difficult, however, for developers to determine what they are required to do, even if they learn that the Ordinance exists in the first place (which I do not know how they would unless they hear about it second-hand, as I did).

57. I have come to learn of the "Milwaukee County Parks 2017 Special Event Application" (the "Permit Application"). This 10-page document requests a vast amount of information, such as estimated attendance, location in park, event dates and times, site map, whether and how the event will be advertised, plans for garbage collection, and provisions for on-site security and medical services. Much of this information is either inapplicable, or impossible to accurately assess with respect, to a mobile application. For example, mobile games like Texas Rope 'Em do not have "dates" and "times," but rather are always accessible to a user once downloaded to a mobile device. Nor can a game developer reliably estimate the number of people who will both download the application and travel to a specific location (such as Milwaukee County Parks) to play the game. Mobile application developers certainly do not undertake responsibility, much less plan for, the amount of garbage removal, security, medical services, or restrooms that players may require.

58. The Permit Application also "reserves the right to require additional information or documentation regarding the applicant, applicant's company, sponsoring company/organization, co-sponsors, event participants, event vendors, event activities or the event itself. Moreover, Milwaukee County Parks may postpone approval of event permit(s) until receipt of additional requested information or documentation is submitted. Failure to submit requested information or documentation in a timely manner may be cause for denial of a Special Event Permit."

59. It is my perception that Milwaukee County adopted the Ordinance as a knee-jerk reaction to the unexpectedly large number of people who played Pokémon Go in 2016. Having read the "Whereas" clauses contained in the Ordinance, as well as the comments made by County Supervisor Sheldon Wasserman in the course of proposing the Ordinance, only reinforces that understanding. This, in turn, leads me to believe that the County will take every opportunity it can to put hurdles in the way of applicants publishing Texas Rope 'Em and other

location-based games, including by dragging out the permitting process with requests for information and by demanding the payment of exorbitant fees.

60. The Permit Application gives a similar definition of "virtual gaming" as the Ordinance: "An activity during which a person can experience being in a three-dimensional environment and interact with that environment during a game. The game typically consists of an artificial world of images and sounds created by a computer that is affected by the actions of person who is experiencing it."

61. Texas Rope 'Em clearly fits this definition. The augmented reality display of poker cards that a player sees upon reaching designated coordinates is a "three-dimensional environment," and players "interact with that environment during the game." Texas Rope 'Em displays "an artificial world of images and sounds created by a computer [*i.e.*, by the mobile application] that is affected by the actions of person who is experiencing it." At the very least, the user interface of Texas Rope 'Em fits this definition at least as much as does that of Pokémon Go, which the Ordinance was designed to regulate.

62. Moreover, Texas Rope 'Em is a "location-based augmented reality game," at least according to my understanding of that term.

63. The County website also instructs that a Permit Application in connection with "virtual games" is required "for game developers only," and Candy Lab is the developer of Texas Rope 'Em.

64. Therefore, I read the Ordinance (especially the portion regulating the "introduction" of games "into" the Parks), and the Permit Application issued pursuant to the Ordinance, as requiring Candy Lab to submit the Permit Application and receive a Special Event Permit before being allowed under the Ordinance to publish a version of Texas Rope 'Em that allows players to play the game in Milwaukee County Parks.

65. Because Texas Rope 'Em has already been released to the public in beta form, and because that version is playable in a Milwaukee County Park, Candy Lab appears to already be in violation of the Ordinance.

66. Indeed, as I have summarized above, there are dozens, if not hundreds, of mobile games on the market that may fall within the scope of the Ordinance, some of which have been available since 2010—and some of which I have helped create and publish. From the way Milwaukee appears to be interpreting its Ordinance, those who have developed, published, or endorsed any one of these may find themselves subjected to liability.

67. Candy Lab, like the vast majority of companies developing location-based and AR games, is still a modestly sized startup company reliant on a handful of investors. Companies like this simply cannot afford to undertake the process of researching the need to, and undertaking the effort to apply for, permits from municipal governments before publishing the very mobile applications that are the source of the company's revenue. Nor can it afford to pay *any* permitting fees, much less the exorbitant fees contemplated by Milwaukee's Permit Application, to even one municipality, let alone all the others that will follow Milwaukee's example if the Ordinance is upheld.

68. Instead, if these companies were forced to obey the Ordinance, they would simply choose not to publish a game capable of being played in Milwaukee County Parks—which, depending on how the Ordinance is interpreted, could be any game at all. This, in turn, would deprive the developers of the ability to further their business and to engage in the creative use of the augmented reality medium. If the Ordinance and laws like it are allowed to stand, I am certain that many companies that would otherwise publish innovative, creative content in the AR medium would give up or go out of business. And that, in turn, would be incredibly detrimental to the entire AR industry, and consequently to society as a whole, which stands to benefit enormously from the innovations in information-sharing that AR will bring to all aspects of modern life.

69. Never in my entire career have I heard of a governmental unit purporting to regulate the publication of AR content like this. Because location-based mobile gaming was still a relatively novel concept in 2011, I read occasional news reports in the years following the release of Ingress about players who either injured themselves or had run-ins with law enforcement. Things like that will inevitably happen with any new technology. Indeed, we still read news reports of people injuring themselves because they were distracted by mobile applications that have nothing to do with location-sensing or augmented reality. The fact that individual users might do things they shouldn't while playing a game, however, is not a reason to prevent the game from being published, any more than government could or should ban the publication of a map, book, or movie that might encourage people to visit a particular place.

70. Indeed, I am reminded of the closing scene of the 2015 film Star Wars: The Force Awakens. It was filmed on the remote Irish island of Skellig Michael. Tourist demand to visit the island immediately skyrocketed, leading to resistance from conservationists. Regulators responded by enforcing existing limits on the number of daily visitors to the island—not by banning the film or trying to tax its producers.

71. I also fear that, if laws like this Ordinance are upheld, there is no reason to believe they will stop at location-based AR games. If these can be regulated, why expect governments to stop there? They may decide to impose onerous regulations on all AR content for whatever reason, or prevent developers from adding AR content of any type to a particular location. Because all AR content is inherently location-based to some degree, as I explained above, reserving this power to government would devastate the entire AR industry.

72. The very act of a software developer assigning AR content to a particular location is, in and of itself, a creative and expressive choice. This choice can have obvious significance, such as the depiction of the Berlin Wall in Metaio'sTimeTraveler app. Or it may be more subtle, such as the assignment of game stops to particular locations. Either way, if such choices are not dictated by the function of the software, they are inherently creative choices.

73. Indeed, before I learned of the Ordinance, it was my understanding that no government in the United States—let alone a county park department—had

the power to regulate the content of mobile video games, especially not just because they were afraid that too many people might play them. The genuine fear and apprehension I feel over how laws like this could decimate that AR industry to which I have dedicated my career is part of what motivates me to support Candy Lab's stand against this unjust and unlawful Ordinance.

74. The Ordinance does not define what it means by the term "location-based augmented reality games," other than to repeatedly imply that Pokémon Go is such a game. As described above, I certainly have an understanding of what I believe the term to mean, and I believe that Texas Rope 'Em is a "location-based augmented reality game." I do not, however, know the parameters of what Milwaukee County understands the term to mean.

Mr. Skwarek's declaration likewise included examples of the many location-based apps he had created—many of which were used for political expression and activism. The court needed to understand that AR had already proven its potential as an expressive medium, and that it provided to be a revolutionary means of expression—if it was not prematurely regulated by governments:

> 30. The Ordinance is also seriously vague about who it applies to. For example, the popular AR platforms Wikitude and Vuforia offer content-creation tools (called "Software Development Kits" or SDKs) for sale to developers, who then create applications through the software and market them to the public. The end products created with these SDKs are still primarily composed of software authored by the SDK publisher. Does that mean that Wikitude or Vuforia will be subject to regulation by Milwaukee every time one of their customers creates an application that can be played in Milwaukee parks? If so, that prospect would severely disrupt the AR industry. Metaio provided a similar SDK that I used to make many of my apps until the company was purchased by Apple; its sudden disappearance forced me to abandon or completely rewrite the applications I had made with their software.
>
> 31. I also fear that, if laws like this Ordinance are upheld, there is no reason to believe they will stop at location-based AR games. If these can be regulated, why expect governments to stop there? They may decide to impose onerous regulations on all AR content for whatever reason, or prevent developers from adding AR content of any type to a particular location. Because all AR content is inherently location-based to some degree, as I explained above, reserving this power to government would devastate the entire AR industry.

The lawsuit attacked the Ordinance on two primary grounds. First, it challenged the Ordinance as being a "prior restraint" on speech. A "prior restraint" is a rule that restricts expression before it takes place rather than imposing penalties on the expression after it occurs. The elements of a prior restraint are: (1) a person seeking to exercise First Amendment rights is required to apply to the government for permission; (2) the government is empowered to determine whether the applicant should be granted permission on the basis of a review of the content of the proposed expression; (3) approval is dependent upon the government's affirmative action; and (4) approval is not a routine matter, but involves an examination of the facts, an exercise of judgment, and the formation of an opinion. The Ordinance certainly fit this bill, as it imposed a permit requirement "*before* any company may introduce a location-based AR game into the Parks." Prior restraints on speech and publication are the most serious and the least tolerable infringement on First Amendment rights and are presumptively unconstitutional under well-established Supreme Court case law (Near v. Minnesota, 1931). For example, in the 1970s, the Supreme Court refused to enjoin the *New York Times'* publication of the "Pentagon Papers," even though their disclosure was likely to put lives at risk (New York Times Co. v. United States, 1971).

Second, the lawsuit challenged the Ordinance as being unconstitutionally vague. The Supreme Court has condemned as vague broadly worded licensing ordinances which grant such standardless discretion to public officials that they are free to censor ideas and enforce their own personal preferences. The most obviously defective portion of the Ordinance was the phrase "before any company may introduce a location-based AR game into the Parks." Game developers do not "introduce" software "into" any physical location, even if the game is designed to be played in particular places. Rather, developers publish the game in app stores for users to download. Even if certain content is designed to react to, or be displayed in, a particular geolocation, it does not actually exist in that location. It is merely displayed on a mobile device screen.

The Ordinance also failed to define which "games" it regulated. Its preamble and the Permit Application define "virtual gaming" as "an activity during which a person can experience being in a three-dimensional environment and interact with that environment during a game. Taken literally, that could describe any physical game in which any person can engage, such as baseball, hopscotch, tag, or even swinging on park swings. The Ordinance preamble further explains that a virtual game "typically consists of an artificial world of images and sounds created by a computer that is affected by the actions of a person who is experiencing it." But the word "typically" indicates that this description is not a necessary part of the definition. Running down a sidewalk while wearing an activity tracker such as a Fitbit bracelet or Apple Watch can cause those devices to emit both images and sounds. Similarly, two children playing with battery-powered *Star Wars* lightsabers also experience a three-dimensional environment accompanied by artificial images and sounds. Both of these activities literally fit the Ordinance's definition of "virtual gaming," but fall outside its apparent intent. It is impossible to determine whether this conduct is regulated.

The Ordinance singles out AR "games." But that provides no standards to law enforcement officers to decide what a "game" is. As another court presciently mused in a 2000 decision, "Is bicycling a game? Juggling? What about Pokémon? Suppose I am trading Pokémon cards but not trying to beat the other Player?" (Weigand v. Village of Tinley Park, 2000). Similarly, the phrase "location-based augmented reality games" is not self-defining (Weigand v. Village of Tinley Park, 2000). Many would argue that even the example of AR provided in the Ordinance—*Pokémon Go*—is not really an "augmented reality" game, since the AR component of the game is not essential to the gameplay and can be deactivated.

## Public Reaction to the Suit

Feedback from across the XR spectrum, the legal community, and beyond was tremendous. Whether in person or in social media conversations, the words of encouragement and support continued to come, as Candy Lab AR CEO Andrew Couch explained in a June 15, 2017 open letter to the community (Couch, 2017). Inverse wrote that "the future of AR hangs in the balance" with this case, while the influential blog TechDirt wrote "Candy Labs asserts the ordinance is a prior restraint... And it's quite difficult to see how that isn't the case" (Geigner, 2017; Zakarin, The 'Pokemon Go' AR Lawsuit In Milwaukee Is Getting Nastier, 2017). Even the comments sections of the various news articles covering the case have been overwhelmingly agreeable (Geigner, 2017). For example, one commenter argued "This is public land. If there are restrictions on its use, they should in NO WAY be tied to augmented reality games. If they are trying to protect the lawn, put up a "keep off the lawn" sign and enforce the rules for everyone, not just the people playing a game" (Geigner, 2017). Another commenter agreed that the ordinance "might be sound in principle, but they seem to be based on a complete misunderstanding of the mechanics and issues at question" (Geigner, 2017).

## The County's Response to the Suit

Milwaukee attempted to dodge the lawsuit with a curious argument: that its regulation of AR games was fine under the First Amendment because *Texas Rope 'Em* is not speech (Milwaukee County's Motion to Dismiss, 2017). Despite acknowledging Supreme Court precedent that video games are entitled to full First Amendment protection, the County argued that this particular video game was so simplistic as to express no ideas whatsoever. Doubling down on that argument, Milwaukee argued that the game was actually an "illegal lottery," since poker is a gambling game (Milwaukee County's Motion to Dismiss, 2017). It made these arguments both in response to the preliminary injunction motion and in a separate motion to dismiss the case.

It then argued that the Ordinance was a reasonable "time, place, and manner" restriction. The Supreme Court acknowledges that certain types of speech can be limited in this manner if the restrictions are no more burdensome than made necessary by the circumstances and are imposed in a content-neutral manner (Ward v. Rock Against Racism, 1989). This is how permitting schemes for protests or other gatherings in a public park are permissible, because only a certain number of people can occupy the same space at any given time. We pushed back, arguing that even when analyzed under this framework the Ordinance was neither content-neutral nor reasonable.

The County also filed a motion to stay the court's decision on both the preliminary injunction motion and the motion to dismiss, while the County "considered whether" to amend the Ordinance. Although the County suggested its revised version "might" solve the constitutional problems raised by the lawsuit, it couldn't commit to that— or even acknowledge that the problems existed. There was no reason to expect the County to get it right the next time without guidance from the court, especially when they continue to insist on such flawed legal arguments–and when they insist on the ability to continue enforcing the Ordinance against others in the meantime. Every day this Ordinance remained in effect chilled speech across the AR industry and was an affront to the First Amendment.

## The Court's Decision

On July 20, 2017, without hearing oral argument, the Court rendered its decision on all three motions—granting our motion for preliminary injunction and denying both of the County's motions. It was a complete victory.

First, the Court agreed that *Texas Rope 'Em* qualified for First Amendment protection. The threshold here is minimal indeed, and, quoting the Supreme Court, the Court noted that "the basic principles of freedom of speech and the press, like the First Amendment's command, do not vary when a new and different medium for communication appears" (Brown v. Entm't Merchants Ass'n, 2011). The Texas-themed imagery and the animated lasso imagery it used to "grab" playing cards "lend an air of excitement and novelty to a traditional card game. Moreover, what Candy Lab's game lacks in compelling literary tropes, it makes up for by employing features distinctive to the medium (such as the player's interaction with the virtual world)."

This latter observation validated Candy Lab's argument that the game designers' choices in selecting which real-world elements to interact with and what digital content to associate with them were expressive choices in themselves that deserved protection." Indeed, these choices are materially identical to those made by the author of any video game—a medium already recognized by the Supreme Court to merit full First Amendment protection—except that the AR program involves the additional layer of choosing how the game interacts with its physical surroundings. After all, the defining characteristic of the AR medium is that its content appears to be, but is not actually, present in three-dimensional physical space. That effect is accomplished by illusion. And for all the technological know-how that goes into creating the tools that effect the illusion, actually accomplishing it is very much an art. The software designer has a wide palette of options available in order to momentarily convince a user to accept what they see as being "real." The *Pokémon Go* game, for example, has evolved in this respect over time. Its simplest AR mode began, as many similar apps did, by overlaying flat, two-dimensional digital characters on the live video camera feed of the user's mobile device. More recent updates to the game will now use the device's camera to first scan the user's surroundings for a flat surface, then project the creature onto that surface as a sharper, apparently-three-dimensional character, complete with a shadow. Still later updates occlude the character when it walks "behind" a physical object.

Other AR expressions choose less precise, more abstract interactions that may be less convincing but convey more sense of whimsy—such as the oversized poker cards users may "select" in *Texas Rope 'Em*. Still others swing to the opposite end of the spectrum relying on pupil-tracking and even brainwave-reading sensors to convince the user that what they see is absolutely real. And once the manner of display is chosen, there is an entirely separate set of decisions to make about how the user may go about interacting with the displays within the confines of the application. Many of these are expressive, authorial choices that programmers make, and the output that results from the sum of those choices is speech that merits protection.

And despite all the ink the County had spilled on the "contention that Texas Rope 'Em constitutes illegal gambling and is therefore unprotected by the First Amendment," the Court dismissed it with one word: "specious."

Second, and more meaningful, was the Court's application of the First Amendment to the Ordinance. The County scored a few points here. For example, the Court agreed that it was proper to analyze the Ordinance through the lens of a time, place, and manner restriction. And it declined to agree with us that the Ordinance was content-neutral. "The Ordinance imposes restrictions on functionalities of games like Texas Rope 'Em, most importantly the fact that they are location-based. The Ordinance covers such games regardless of their content, be it poker, zombie-killing, or Pokémon-catching. As such, it cannot be said that the Ordinance applies to one game or another because of the topic discussed or the idea or message expressed."

That said, the Court did find "some appeal to Candy Lab's position on this question... that although the Ordinance does not care about the contents of the AR game being played, it is arguably content-based because it is directed at the physical act of game-playing, which is itself a part of the expression." As noted supra, even the act of defining what a "game" is involves some degree of subjectivity and value judgment. One person's game is another's skill-building regimen, physical exercise, or meditative distraction. Wherever the line between "game" and "not game" is drawn, it will divide what the definer considers a serious pursuit from what is considered self-gratifying, if not frivolous. How can that not be a content-based distinction?

"Nevertheless, resolution of that question is not dispositive, as the Ordinance does not pass muster even under the more lenient standards applicable to content-neutral time, place, and manner restrictions. This is because the Ordinance does not employ sufficient procedural safeguards to ensure the protection of First Amendment rights." The Court reached this conclusion because the Ordinance and Permit Application reserved "unbridled discretion" for the County in determining whether or not to issue a permit. The Ordinance indicates that County officials will determine "the appropriateness of the application based on site selection, protection of rare flora and fauna, personal safety, and the intensity of game activities on park lands." Yet the Permit Application is inconsistent with the idea that these criteria will limit a reviewing official's discretion, as it expressly warns that "Milwaukee County Parks in its sole discretion may grant, deny, revoke, or suspend any permit, at any time and for any reason."

"Moreover, even if this discrepancy between the Ordinance and the Permit Application did not exist," the court continued, "the Ordinance's criteria are themselves too vague to afford adequate protection to free speech interests." In other words, what does "site selection" and "safety" mean? "Likewise, upon reading phrases like 'protection of rare flora and fauna' and 'the intensity of game activities on park lands,' how is a developer to know how much flower-trampling is too much, or what plants count as 'rare,' or what 'intense' use of parklands entails?" These abstract considerations provided no guidance to AR game developers, and thus could not pass muster. After all, any restriction on speech is in derogation of the fundamental guarantees of free speech, and are permissible only if "narrowly tailored." Giving the government any degree of subjectivity in defining the parameters of the speech restriction is to abandon any assurance that the restriction will remain a "narrow" one.

Fortunately, the Court did not stop there—or else the County might have gotten away with simply specifying its criteria for how much daisy-trampling is too much. Instead, the Court recognized that punishing a game publisher in order to curb misbehavior by a handful of game players is excessive—what one Supreme Court precedent calls "burning down the house to roast the pig"—and thus cannot be a "narrowly tailored" means to solve the perceived problems:

> The Court observes that the Ordinance suffers from other serious infirmities, most notably that it does not appear narrowly tailored to serve the interests it purports to promote. Here, the Ordinance is revealed for its strangeness and lack of sophistication. The Ordinance treats game developers like Candy Lab as though they are trying hold an "event" in a Milwaukee County park. However, this misunderstands the nature of the problem, since Candy Lab's video game will not be played at a discrete time or location within a park. Requiring Candy Lab to secure insurance, portable restrooms, security, clean-up, and provide a timeline for an "event" is incongruent with how Texas Rope 'Em (or any other mobile game) is played.
>
> Forcing a square peg in a round hole demonstrates a true lack of tailoring, much less "narrow" tailoring designed to address the County's interests as they might be affected by Candy Lab. Rather than prohibit publication of the game itself, the County could address its concerns by directly regulating the objectionable downstream conduct. This might include aggressively penalizing gamers who violate park rules or limiting gamers to certain areas of the park. Such measures would assuage the alleged evils visited upon the parks by gamers while stifling less expression than the Ordinance does.

The County's contention that its Ordinance solves the problems presented by AR games is irrelevant. This misses the operative question: whether less restrictive measures would be inadequate as a substitute.

For all of these reasons, the Court enjoined enforcement of the Ordinance.

## The Aftermath

In most cases, once a defendant loses a preliminary injunction motion, they soon come to accept that they will inevitably lose the case. That was true here as well. Although Supervisor Wasserman initially made noises in the press about continuing the fight, the County soon realized that it would not only fail to defend the Ordinance, but it would ultimately be on the hook for our attorneys' fees as well (Zakarin, Milwaukee's War on 'Pokemon Go' Could Change Tech Forever, 2017). To save face, its lawyers asked for a small discount on those fees—reducing them to just under $100,000—and we agreed. They used this to sell a settlement to the County Board by which it paid us that reduced amount and stipulated to an entry of a permanent injunction striking down the Ordinance. That political process took some time, but the Order was entered on December 29, 2017 (Order of Permanent Injunction, 2017).

When introducing the settlement to the Board for a vote, the County's corporation counsel vowed that a replacement measure intended to address the Court's concerns would be forthcoming. To date, however, no new ordinance has been adopted. The original language, however, remains on the books.

## Epilogue: Where from Here?

As the nuance of the Court's analysis suggested, the blatant violation of the First Amendment in this case was just one battle—not the whole war. As a medium, XR enjoys full First Amendment rights, but those rights are also constrained by the same boundaries and caveats to which all other media are subject. Although this may have been an easy case for the content creators, the next one might not be.

In many circumstances, it may be the rights of others that will and should prevail. For example, the author has had many conversations with private landowners and businesses that oppose the idea of others making augmented content visible on their private property without permission. In many cases, they will likely be powerless to do anything about, for the same reason that motivated the author's opposition to Milwaukee's Ordinance—the content *isn't really there*, so the landowners' real property rights offer them no mechanism to stop its display. That said, certain types of speech—such as defamation, infringements of intellectual property rights, or commercial speech that misleads or confuses consumers—is subject to regulation even in light of the First Amendment. Those same limitations will apply to XR as well. And because many of those laws have yet to be applied in the XR context, the exact parameters of their application have yet to be determined.

One interesting window into what future time, place, and manner restrictions may look like is the February 2019 settlement Niantic reached with plaintiffs in the consolidated cases alleging trespass and nuisance claims (Class Action Settlement Agreement, 2019). Of course, the only reason the case lasted that long was that the court had refused to dismiss the claims as a matter of law, leaving open the question of whether "digitally induced trespass" is a valid legal theory (Nealon, 2019). Under those circumstances, Niantic and the plaintiffs eventually agreed to a framework that the plaintiffs said was designed, "to prevent the future placement of virtual game items on private property, and to promptly address future complaints of trespass and nuisance by Pokémon Go players when they arise." Specifically, Niantic would maintain a form on its website through which property owners can submit complaints "believed" to be related to *Pokémon Go* players, and to request removal of any Pokestops or Pokémon gyms (Class Action Settlement Agreement, 2019). Niantic would then use "commercially reasonable efforts" to respond to such complaints and requests within 15 days, and to comply with removal requests within 5 days thereafter (Class Action Settlement Agreement, 2019). The agreement clarifies that removal may be requested by any single-family homeowner within

40 meters, regardless of whether they've experienced an issue. Niantic would also agree to comply with public parks' requests to shut off access to Pokestops and gyms outside of park hours, and to add additional warnings to players. These terms would all be in place for a period of three years.

These parties cannot force another AR company (such as Microsoft and its *Minecraft Earth*) to abide by this agreement. And notably, the agreement does not even apply to any of Niantic's other games, such as *Ingress* or the newer *Harry Potter: Wizards Unite*. But those who come first tend to chart a path for those who follow. It may become easy for smaller AR companies to point to this agreement as a model, and for aggrieved residents to complain about companies that do not abide by these standards. The more who do so, the easier it will be to support an argument that such rules have become an "industry standard" by which future tort claims can be measured. Even voluntary limits can become enforceable by the Federal Trade Commission and other agencies, if industries agree to them.

For now, though, this is just an agreement between two sides to resolve one lawsuit. The future is still up to us all to shape.

## Putting These Ideas into Practice

*Taking Your Own Stand*

Hopefully, you have taken away from this story ideas that you can put into practice. Do you believe strongly that a particular legal rule or set of ethical norms ought to be applied with respect to XR? Chances are high that others agree with you, and that the question has not yet been authoritatively determined—because so few have at this point. Just like the author did, you too can stand up for what you believe is right. But it won't happen to you accidentally. Give the issue some in-depth, prolonged thought. In what circumstances will the question come up? How can you be prepared to advocate your position? Who are your allies in this fight? Line up as many answers as you can to these questions, and keep your eyes open for the right test case in which to take action.

*Time, Place, and Manner*

The *Candy Lab* case may have been the first case to query what time, place, and manner boundaries should apply to XR displays, but it certainly won't be the last. Spend some time pretending you're wearing XR smart glasses as you go through your day—in the car, in the office or classroom, and out in public. Let your imagination wander to the types of digital displays and interactive features you'd like to see (or would expect to see) in a robust XR ecosystem. Think through why a content provider or developer would put the content there, how people are likely to interact with it, and what the potential downsides of the display would be. Based on these observations, what reasonable boundaries should be placed on the time, place, and manner in which this content is displayed? And it the provider refused to abide by these boundaries, which (if any) of them might be permissible for a government to impose?

*Unauthorized Content*

You operate a business with a physical building on a busy city street. A third party has created AR content that is visible on your property. Under what circumstances would you object to the content? Even if you object, under what circumstances should your interests be legally permitted to override the third party's right to display it?

# References

Behm, D. (2016, August 24). Milwaukee demands permits for Pokemon placement in parks. Retrieved from USA Today: https://www.usatoday.com/story/news/nation-now/2016/08/24/milwaukee-demands-pokemon-placement-permits/89304408/

Berlin, L. (2009, July 11). Kicking Reality Up a Notch. *New York Times*.

Bowens v. ARY, 794 N.W.2d 842 (Michigan Supreme Court March 18, 2011).

Brown v. Entertainment Merchants Association, 564 U.S. 786 (The Supreme Court June 27, 2011).

Brown v. Entm't Merchants Ass'n, 564 U.S. 786 (The Supreme Court 2011).

Cameron, J. (Director) (1984). *The Terminator* [Motion Picture].

Candy Lab Inc. v. Milwaukee County, 266 F. Supp. 3d (E.D. Wis. July 20, 2017).

Class Action Settlement Agreement (2019, February 2). Retrieved from https://www.scribd.com/document/399721150/Pokemon-Go-Nuisance-Complaint-Proposed-Settlement#fullscreen&from_embed

Convertino v. Ashenfelter (6th Circuit July 31, 2015).

Couch, A. (2017, June 15). Dear Friends and Colleagues Across the AR Industry. Retrieved from Linkedin: https://www.linkedin.com/pulse/dear-friends-colleagues-across-ar-industry-andrew-wayne-couch

Detroit Free Press v. Ashcroft, 303 F.3d 681 (6th Circuit 2002).

Encyclopaedia Britannica. (2020, June 26). Pokémon. Retrieved from britannica.com: https://www.britannica.com/topic/Pokemon-electronic-game

Fairfield, J.A. (2012). Mixed reality: How the laws of virtual worlds govern everyday life. *Berkeley Technology Law Journal*, 55-116.

Favreau, J. (Director) (2008). *Iron Man* [Motion Picture].

Geigner, T. (2017, May 3). Game Maker Sues Milwaukee Over Permit Requirement to Make Augmented Reality Games. Retrieved from Techdirt: https://www.techdirt.com/articles/20170421/14432337211/game-maker-sues-milwaukee-over-permit-requirement-to-make-augmented-reality-games.shtml

Hanke, J. (2016, November 16). Exploring Augmented Reality. (S. a. U.S. Senate Committee on Commerce, Interviewer)

Havens, J.C. (2011, June 6). Who Owns the Advertising Space in an Augmented Reality World? Retrieved from Mashable: https://mashable.com/2011/06/06/virtual-air-rights-augmented-reality/

Havens, J.C. (2014). *Hacking Happiness: Why Your Personal Data Counts and How Tracking It Can Change the World.* New York: Jeremy P. Tarcher/Penguin.

Hobson, A. (2016). Reality Check: The Regulatory Landscape for Virtual and Augmented Reality. *R Street Policy Study*, 1-5.

In re Pokemon Go Nuisance Litigation (N.D. California August 30, 2019).

Kozlowski, J.C. (2017, November 1). Park Permit for Location-Based 'Pokémon Go' Games. Retrieved from nrpa.org: https://www.nrpa.org/parks-recreation-magazine/2017/november/park-permit-for-location-based-pokemon-go-games/

Lucas, G. (Director). (1977). *Star Wars* [Motion Picture].

Marder v. Niantic, Inc. et al., 4:16-cv-04300 (California Northern July 29, 2016).

Metz, R. (2015, June 15). Augmented-Reality Glasses Could Help Legally Blind Navigate. Retrieved from MIT Technology Review: https://www.technologyreview.com/2015/06/15/72902/augmented-reality-glasses-could-help-legally-blind-navigate/

Milwaukee County Board of Supervisors. (2017, February 2). Meeting. Milwaukee, Wisconsin, United States of America.

Milwaukee County's Motion to Dismiss. (2017).

Milwaukee County Parks. (2017). *Milwaukee County Parks Special Event Application.*

Mueller, M. (2016, August 24). Pokemon Go (somewhere else): County Parks gets in turf war with viral game. Retrieved from onmilwaukee: https://onmilwaukee.com/buzz/articles/parksvspokemongo.html

Nealon, A. (2019, February 14). Places Where You Must Not Pokemon Go. Retrieved from Patentarcade.com: http://patentarcade.com/tag/class-action

Near v. Minnesota, 283 U.S. 697 (The Supreme Court June 1, 1931).

New York Times Co. v. United States, 403 U.S. 713 (The Supreme Court June 30, 1971).

Nichols v. Moore, 477 F.3d 396 (6th Circuit February 20, 2007).

Olanoff, D. (2015, August 12). Niantic Labs, Maker of Ingress, Spun Out of Google As Its Own Company. Retrieved from Techcrunch: https://techcrunch.com/2015/08/12/niantic-labs-maker-of-ingress-spun-out-as-its-own-company/

Order of Permanent Injunction (2017, December 29). Order of Permanent Injunction.

Pamplin, T. (2016, July 18). 5 ticketed for playing 'Pokemon Go' in local park after hours. Retrieved from Clickondetroit : https://www.clickondetroit.com/news/2016/07/19/5-ticketed-for-playing-pokemon-go-in-local-park-after-hours/

Peterson, A. (2016, July 12). Holocaust Museum to visitors: Please stop catching Pokémon here. Retrieved from The Washington Post: https://www.washingtonpost.com/news/the-switch/wp/2016/07/12/holocaust-museum-to-visitors-please-stop-catching-pokemon-here/

QuickSilver Software, Inc. (2015, January ). Retrieved from QuickSilver Software, Inc.: https://quicksilver.com/wp/texas-rope-em/

Radio One v. Wooten, 452 F. Supp.2d 754 (E.D. Mich. 2006).

Rusell, J. (2014, July 14). Google's Ingress augmented reality game quietly launches for iOS devices. Retrieved from Thenextweb.com: https://thenextweb.com/google/2014/07/14/googles-ingress-augmented-reality-game-quietly-launches-ios-devices/

Sharma, P. (2016, July 10). Virtual and augmented reality need a PG-13 moment. Retrieved from Techcrunch.com: https://techcrunch.com/2016/07/10/virtual-and-augmented-reality-need-a-pg-13-moment/

Shepherd, K. (2016, August 24). Milwaukee County official wants to ban Pokemon Go until it secures proper local permits: report. Retrieved from The Washington Times : https://www.washingtontimes.com/news/2016/aug/24/milwaukee-officials-want-ban-pokemon-go-until-it-s/

Spielberg, S. (Director). (2002). *Minority Report* [Motion Picture].

State News v. MSU, 481 Mich. 692 (Michigan Supreme Court July 16, 2008 ).

The Associated Press (2017, June 11). Russian Who Played Pokemon Go in Church is Convicted of Inciting Hatred. Retrieved from New York Times: https://www.nytimes.com/2017/05/11/world/europe/pokemon-go-ruslan-sokolovsky-russia.html

Ward v. Rock Against Racism, 491 U.S. 781 (The Supreme Court June 22, 1989).

Wasserman, S. (2017, February 2). *Resolution/Ordinance*. Milwaukee, Wisconsin, United States: Milwaukee County Board of Supervisors.

Wassom, B. (2013, April 1). Augmented Reality as Free Speech – A First Amendment Analysis. Retrieved from Wassom.com: https://www.wassom.com/augmented-reality-as-free-speech-a-first-amendment-analysis.html

Wassom, B. (2014 ). *Augmented Reality Law, Privacy, and Ethics: Law, Society, and Emerging AR Technologies.* Rockland: Syngress.

Wassom, B. (2014, January 25). Ingress AR Game Impacting Kansas Law Enforcement?

Wassom, B. (2016, July 11). How Pokémon GO Players Could Run Into Real-Life Legal Problems. Retrieved from Hollywood Reporter: https://www.hollywoodreporter.com/thr-esq/how-pok-mon-go-players-909869

Wassom, B. (2016, December 7). Milwaukee, Pokemon Go, and the First Amendment. Retrieved from Augmented Legality : http://augmentedlegality.wnj.com/?p=6479

Wassom, B. (2016, July 10). Pokemon Go and the Crisis On An Infinitely Augmented Earth. Retrieved from Wassom.com: http://www.wassom.com/6316.html

Wassom, B. (2017, January 12). No Pokemon For You? Retrieved from augmentedlegality. wnj.com: http://augmentedlegality.wnj.com/?p=6495#more-6495

Weigand v. Village of Tinley Park, 114 F. Supp. 2d 734 (N.D. Illinois September 21, 2000).

Whedon, J. (Director). (2002). *Firefly* [Motion Picture].

Wickliffe, G. (2016, July 17). Group charged with misdemeanors for playing Pokemon Go in park after hours. Retrieved from mlive: https://www.mlive.com/news/detroit/2016/07/group_charged_with_misdemeanor.html

Wild, M. (2016, August 30). Milwaukee County Parks would like to clear up the "confusion" surrounding Pokemon Go. Retrieved from milwaukeerecord: https://milwaukeerecord.com/city-life/milwaukee-county-parks-confusion-pokemon-go-thing/

Wild, M. (2016, September 8). Lake Park's Pokemon Go Meeting was Boring, Livid, and Gloriously Absurd. Retrieved from milwaukee record: https://milwaukeerecord.com/city-life/lake-parks-pokemon-go-meeting-was-boring-occasionally-livid-gloriously-absurd/

Wild, M. (2016, August 23). Milwaukee County Parks are trying to remove Pokemon Go from Lake Park. Retrieved from milwaukeerecord: https://milwaukeerecord.com/city-life/milwaukee-county-parks-is-trying-to-remove-pokemon-go-from-lake-park/

Williams, D. (2016, September 13). Public hearing to be held regarding Pokemon Go in parks; parking fees on lakefront. Retrieved from Fox6now: https://fox6now.com/2016/09/13/public-hearing-to-be-held-regarding-pokemon-go-in-parks-parking-fees-on-lakefront/

Zakarin, J. (2017, May 4). Milwaukee's War on 'Pokemon Go' Could Change Tech Forever. Retrieved from Inverse.com: https://www.inverse.com/article/31145-milwaukee-pokemon-go

Zakarin, J. (2017, June 14). The 'Pokemon Go' AR Lawsuit In Milwaukee Is Getting Nastier. Retrieved from Inverse.com: https://www.inverse.com/article/32961-pokemon-go-ar-ordinance-lawsuit-milwaukee-county

# Reconceptualizing Video Games for Community Spaces

**David Antognoli**

916 S. Wabash Ave., Suite 101, Chicago, IL 60605
Email: dantognoli@colum.edu

Experiencing art in a community context changes the character of the experience in beneficial, interesting, and dynamic ways. Video games, an interactive media art, are perhaps the most dominant form of art happening today. Yet, compared to other art forms, video game experiences in community spaces are few and far between. Technical challenges and the stifling economic forces commanding the game industry and game culture can provide explanations for this scenario. These forces have shaped a limited conception of video games that widely dictates the types of games that are developed as well as how and where players consume them. However, while modern mainstream commercial games have largely evolved into a form unsuitable for community spaces, there exists historical and current design paradigms for video games intended for such spaces. In particular, the burgeoning medium of augmented reality (AR) fits naturally into community spaces, as demonstrated in mainstream examples such as Snapchat *ART* and *Pokémon GO* (Constine, 2017; Niantic, 2016). Through examining the qualities of video game formats that succeed in community spaces in contrast to the prototypical format of the home video game, I hope to raise awareness of a broader conception of video games and urge game developers toward applying their craft in more community spaces through emerging media such as AR.

## Defining Video Games in Community Spaces

To understand the desired outcome of more video games in community spaces, some definitions are necessary. "Community spaces," in this context, refers to physical locations shared by community members from multiple households. While this definition includes public spaces, it does not require public ownership or official sanction. For example, both a privately owned bar and a public park can be community spaces.

The physical distinction is important here as well. In this definition I am intentionally excluding virtual communities, such as communities that exist within a mediated experience and those defined exclusively by common participation in a mediated experience. Prominent examples of such communities can be found within video games and social media. The intent of excluding virtual communities is not to discredit or undervalue them. In fact, the label "virtual" itself is perhaps misleading, as it implies not real, and many consider these to be real communities. They are just not linked by in-person interaction and physical space, elements that shape experiences in unique ways. Attracted by monetization potential, game development and social media companies already invest heavily in virtual communities and tools for fostering them (Vivas, 2017). In other words, there are plenty of communities of gamers, but comparatively fewer examples of video games in community spaces.

Within the context of this chapter, a video game in a community space must also include the participation of multiple members of the community. As a result of mobile gaming, including mobile AR gaming, many people play video games while they are in community spaces. However, it is important to distinguish games played in a community space that preclude participation from other members of the community, from games that include participation from multiple members of the community. For example, someone playing *The Legend of Zelda: Breath of the Wild* on their Nintendo Switch in the park would not count as a video game in a community space, as the gameplay is a private experience (Nintendo, 2017).

Likewise, though an AR experience might inherently use the player's physical space within gameplay, it does not fit this definition unless it can engage multiple participants within that space. For example, the AR game *Ghost Detector Radar Camera* involves the player searching their surrounding physical space for virtual ghosts that appear in their device's onscreen camera view (First Class Media B.V., 2017). However, the game does not facilitate interaction with other community members.

This requirement of participation from multiple members of a community space is not limited to synchronous participation. For example, a statue in a park is art in a community space even though the community members that stop and admire it may do so at different times. Likewise, a Nintendo Switch kiosk in a Target store running *Breath of the Wild* is a video game in a community space, even though it is still a single player game. After any given play session, the game remains for the next community member to try. In *Pokémon GO*, players must move physically near virtual gyms that are linked to real world GPS coordinates to interact with them. Though there may be no community members present at that time, players interact asynchronously with previous players who have visited the gym.

Complicated scenarios emerge when considering the case of multiplayer gaming. Two or more physically present players participating in a local multiplayer game in a community space fits this definition of a video game in a community space. It happens in a community space and involves multiple members of that community. For example, two friends playing *Mario Kart 7* together in the park counts as a video game in a community space (Nintendo, 2011). A group of people playing a local multiplayer game in a community space can attract other community members to join. Permanence is not a requirement and an event-based model for video games in community spaces is a viable approach.

On the other hand, a mobile gaming session involving virtual community members connected via an online multiplayer system would not count. For example, one person playing a Snapchat Snappable AR game while waiting for a bus, then sharing it over the Internet with other players who are not physically present, would not fit this definition of a game in a community space (Snap Inc., 2018).

# What Changes When Art Moves into Community Spaces

Virtual communities, despite their merits and the impressive strides of technology, remain lacking in some of the desirable qualities of physical community spaces. The COVID-19 pandemic is a testament to this. Everyone experiencing the pandemic with the privilege of access to virtual communities is surely appreciative of them. But this experience has also punctuated the fact that virtual does not equal physical. Remote work, while quite feasible in many cases, is different from being in the office (*Monster Poll Results from Work in the Time of Coronavirus*, 2020). Remote learning is not the same as in-person school (Boyd, 2020). Zoom happy hour is not the same as meeting up at the local tavern after work. Likewise, listening to an MP3 is not the same as attending a concert, nor is watching a movie at home the same as seeing it in the theater. Mainstream technology has allowed communities to transcend physical distance, which is an amazing feature. However, it has not yet completely duplicated the dynamic elements of communities bound by shared physical locations. Those frustrated with teleconferencing hiccups might understandably suggest that fidelity is the key difference between virtual and in-person experiences. Yet, fidelity is not the only factor. After all, the audio quality of concerts is commonly worse than that of studio recordings, but fans still flock to live performances. Despite our technological advances, there are qualities that are challenging to reproduce virtually.

## Presence

Art in community spaces brings people together. Experiencing art in a community context makes audiences feel like they are a part of something bigger. This can be understood as presence. It adds an element of perceived authenticity. Both the physical world and audiences add presence to an experience, and art in community spaces leverages this. While perhaps related to fidelity, synchronous experience, or liveness, affects our experience of art in community spaces beyond these factors (Auslander, 2008). I have a T-shirt from *AEW Revolution*, a professional wrestling show that I attended in Chicago. The shirt has the name and date of the event, plus the phrase "I was there" printed on the back. This slogan capitalizes on the unique sensation of being present in a community experience. Many others also viewed the event live on pay-per-view and probably had better views of the in-ring action, but they could not join in the electricity of the communal applause, boos, and chants. They were not there.

## Discovery

With the emergence of digital streaming platforms, we live in an era of on-demand art consumption. However, it is difficult to demand something that you do not know exists. This contributes to a discovery problem wherein audiences only experience content and ideas that they already know and like. Thankfully, art in community spaces can foster discovery. A new art installation can capture a passerby's attention. Going to a bar or coffee shop and discovering live music or an open mic night can add an unexpected and dynamic element to the experience. While many concertgoers seek specific acts, a captivating performance by an opening band can mean a new and unexpected addition to the regular playlist rotations. By bringing together community members and giving them something to discuss or participate in together, art in community spaces helps people discover new social connections. In its subversion of the on-demand model of art consumption, art in community spaces exposes people to diverse content and ideas that they might otherwise never have encountered.

## Enchantment

Related to discovery is the sense of enchantment. Consider the sense of mystery and wonder of exploring a place for the first time, showing up on the first day of school, or going on a first date. As we prolong our exposure to new elements, we naturally map and rationalize them. Through this process we more narrowly define what's possible, dispelling the sense of enchantment. The dynamic and unpredictable possibilities of art in community spaces elevate their vibrancy and raise an air of enchantment. Stumbling across a street performance or discovering a newly painted mural can pleasantly interrupt a person's highly mapped and efficient routes through everyday life.

In contrast, experiences that exist outside of community spaces are often dictated by intentionality and control. Behavior outside of the parameters of user expectations is considered a defect. A chance conversation with a random bystander at a bar is sociable, but an uninvited participant in a Zoom meeting is an offense (Meadows, 2020). When we engage in a virtual community, we expect a high measure of control. I can choose who to follow and who to mute. The same forces of intentionality and control that dictate virtual communities are characteristic of art experiences that occur in private. I choose what music to listen to, show to watch, or game to play. I control the timing of these activities, the environment they take place in, and who is among the audience.

While intentionality and control in some contexts are clearly desirable, such as in the realm of business productivity, they minimize organic discovery and the enchanting feeling of unlimited possibilities. As Sue Ding puts it in her thesis on enchantment and location-based media, "In the constant push for efficiency and discipline, our world is disenchanted of magic and mystery." (Ding, 2017). Art in community spaces enhances everyday life by imbuing presence, discovery, and enchantment into our environments.

# The Lack of Video Games in Community Spaces

According to the Entertainment Software Association:

> More than 214 million people in the United States today play video games one hour or more per week. 75% of all U.S. households have at least one person who plays. In sum, 64% of U.S. adults and 70% of those under 18 regularly play video games (Entertainment Software Association, 2020).

Revenue from gaming has surpassed all other entertainment media categories (OppenheimerFunds, 2018). However, despite their popularity and commercial dominance, there is a lack of video games in community spaces. Video games almost exclusively happen on personal screens. Players purchase video games and play them on their TV, computer monitor, mobile device, or VR headset. Opportunities to engage with video games outside of this model are relatively uncommon. While game-centric events exist, most are essentially professional trade shows designed to market the biggest commercial games, as opposed to community art exhibitions. In contrast, consider the local music scenes that thrive in many metropolitan areas. In such areas, at least prior to the COVID-19 pandemic (and who knows what the future holds), community members could attend shows featuring local musicians daily. Shows could take place in a public street or park, in a restaurant or bar, or at a dedicated music venue. Consider visual arts, where opening receptions invite community members to gather over discussions of new art; or restaurants and coffee shops host walls featuring rotating displays from local artists. There are few parallels for video games. Game industry economics and the related social construct of the "gamer" have shaped our cultural conception of video games as a form that is largely incompatible with community spaces.

## The Commoditization of Video Games

The development budget required to create a mainstream game has skyrocketed to tens of millions of dollars and continues to rise. While improved and cheaper development tools like Unity, Unreal Engine, ARKit, and ARCore have proliferated, the increased fidelity and scale made possible by such tools and related technological innovations have led to an arms race of complexity in game content. This, in turn, has led to ever-increasing consumer expectations in the amount and type of content in games. Additionally, the greater accessibility of increasingly powerful development tools has created crowded market conditions that drive a parallel marketing arms race as publishers and independent developers compete for the attention of consumers (Koster, 2018).

Considering the scale of investment necessary to develop a game in this environment, the conservative gatekeeping of publishers should come as no surprise. Sequels or clones of successful games make for safer investments as marketers can leverage existing fan bases. Creating annual editions of sports games and other franchises allows developers to save money by reusing existing art, sound, and code assets. In this way, though gamers might complain about the lack of original IP and concepts in games, consumer demand for games to include more and higher fidelity content has directly contributed to this dearth of originality.

Further, the crowded market has caused consumers to adopt more stringent criteria for filtering what they invest their time and money in, thus framing questions about what to play as economic decisions. Game journalism fuels this commoditization of games by distilling criticism down to a question of whether a game is worth buying. If you ask someone if they would recommend a game, it is not uncommon to hear, "It's fun, but not worth the full price." Pick a game on Steam and read the user reviews. Inevitably there will be some version of this cost-benefit analysis. As competitive market forces have driven prices down and the length of games has increased, players compile vast backlogs of games to play. As a result, audiences increasingly consume only the games packaged in the formats that yield the most fun per dollar investment (or, as prices approach zero, per unit of time) (Portillo, 2014). This leads to consumers being less willing to risk investing in genres of games outside of what they have enjoyed in the past. Distribution platforms have keyed in on this, creating recommendation algorithms that simultaneously feed on and accelerate this trend (Robertson, 2019). These forces limit audiences to experience only (what publishers—or algorithms—perceive as) the most commercially viable games existing within the parameters of what players are known to enjoy. While video games are an art, this intense capitalistic framing of games as commodities clearly stifles creative diversity and the artistic expression of game developers. This system has narrowed the popular conception of video games as a commodity incongruent with community spaces.

## The Gamer Metanarrative

In Western culture, a dominant metanarrative has emerged that has cleft a perceived division between "gamers" and "non-gamers." Despite statistics indicating that over 50% of US adults regularly play video games, only about 10% self-identify as gamers (Duggan, 2015). There is an aging stereotype that gamers are "isolated, pale-skinned teenage boys [...] hunched forward on a sofa in some dark basement space, obsessively mashing buttons" (Williams, 2005). The gamer stereotype reflects the narrow conception of video games and contributes to the relative lack of video games in community spaces.

Many who identify with the gamer label interpret the culturally dominant form of the commercial video game as the superior and true representation of interactive media art as opposed to casual, educational, or so-called "serious" games, for example (Vanderhoef et al., 2013). Meanwhile, attitudes about video games by those who *do not* consider themselves gamers, again largely inspired by the most visible commercial video games, have led some to dismiss video games as an art form or even blame them for societal problems (Ebert, 2010; Morin, 2019).

In a culture where work ethic is a key value, the word "game" denotes frivolity to those who believe video games are for children. It is easy for Western culture to understand a sculpture within the context of public art, but it relegates video games as children's diversions. The early marketing of video games toward young boys (e.g. Game Boy) helped instill a lasting conception that only young boys can or should enjoy them (Lien, 2013). In this way, the gamer metanarrative hampers diversity both in the types of video games that are created and the audiences that experience them. This in turn has a dampening effect on the diversity of game developers, as the gamer metanarrative's myopic conception of video games shrouds the possibilities of the medium from potential creators.

There is not an intrinsic quality of video games that alienates people[1]. Nor does it make any sense to binarily sort people with the culturally loaded term "gamer." Given the growing ubiquity of games, this is as absurd as sorting people into "music listeners" and "non-music listeners" and judging them across a variety of unrelated categories. Commoditization drives commercial games to have complex control schemes and long-term time commitments, as well as extensive marketing campaigns featuring stereotypical tropes. This ostracizes unfamiliar audiences and adds to the social construction of the gamer metanarrative, which contributes to the myopic conception of video games that keeps them out of community spaces.

It is noteworthy that the conceptions of who gamers are and what content is acceptable in games have been increasingly called into question in the wake of more ubiquitous game platforms (such as mobile devices), Gamergate, and the social justice movements of the early 21st century. Publishers are realizing that a more diverse audience might buy games, too (Alexander, 2014; Sheffield, 2013). However, despite evolving demographics and attempts to reach them with more diverse content, rigid conceptions about the formal elements of video games and the spaces they should inhabit have remained largely unchanged. In other words, *The Last of Us Part II*, possibly the game industry's biggest release in 2020, may feature a gay female protagonist, but you still play it on a screen in your house with a gamepad (Naughty Dog, 2020; Sherr, 2020).

# Formats for Video Games in Community Spaces

Beyond the economic and cultural obstacles facing video games in community spaces, designers must consider formal challenges. Special hardware is required, which can limit creators and audiences to those with financial privilege and specialized technical expertise. On the other hand, a viewer can admire a sculpture in a gallery, field, or town square with no need for power, far less vulnerability to weather, and no hardware or training requirements.

Analysis of the suitability of existing formats for video games in community spaces illuminates these challenges as well as strategies for overcoming them. Accordingly, video games in community spaces must present two qualities to be effective: access and attraction.

## Criteria for Analysis

These criteria are multifaceted and intertwined. They play key roles in a video game's ability to evoke the elements of presence, discovery, and enchantment that characterize art in community spaces.

---

[1] It is some of the adopted conventions of the game industry such as long play times, byzantine rules, and a lack of diverse content that are alienating.

## Access

Access describes how easily audiences can access an experience. In the context of games in community spaces, access relates specifically to existing community members. A game designed for a specific community space does not need to be accessible to audiences outside of the community space.

Presence cannot happen without access. While physical access to a video game in a community space is clearly essential, players must also be able to easily access its core functionality and essence in order to truly experience it. This means interactions must be clear and highly usable. Further, it is important to evaluate access from the perspective of how easily creators can author experiences. Ideal formats are not limited to those creators who can afford immense budgets.

## Attraction

Attraction is the ability to catch the attention of passersby and compel them to participate. In this way, attraction is an essential element for discovery. Successful attraction can draw a crowd. In her essay about media of attraction, Rebecca Rouse describes attraction as "the inciting of wonder or astonishment" in the spectator (Rouse, 2016). This description draws clear connections to enchantment. Media of attraction are better suited for imbuing environments with a sense of enchantment.

# The Home Video Game Format

The current home video game format is the result of the commoditization of video games and the gamer metanarrative. It can work in community spaces, but it wasn't designed for them. It is included here as a point of departure and to help explain why its design paradigm is not suited for community spaces. That said, it still occasionally occurs in community spaces, such as museums, coffee shops, and game industry event show floors.

## Access

With the proliferation of home video game consoles in the 1980s, game design began to increase in complexity and shift away from a pay-per-play session model. As a result, both the total playtime of games and the length of the typical gameplay session have increased. In 2019, the average video game play session was 1 hour and 22 minutes (*Market Research: The State of Online Gaming – 2019*, 2019). In a community context, players may not have anticipated encountering the game to begin with, so the cost of playing (in time *and* money) should be kept low to encourage new players to try. Extended gameplay sessions afford steeper learning curves and dedicated tutorials. This requires players to play even longer before accessing a game's essential experience. Further, in scenarios where only a limited number of players can play at once, long play sessions can block new players from participating as earlier players occupy the experience.

For creators, while console game development is expensive and closely gate kept, developing a home video game for the PC can be relatively accessible. It can be done with standard PC hardware and there are numerous tools and tutorials available freely online. However, deploying PC games in community spaces faces logistical challenges. They require a power supply and shelter from weather. They cannot be left unattended, as the general public could steal or damage the relatively delicate hardware.

## Attraction

Game developers are very adept at creating attraction within the virtual worlds of their games, but the external, physical presence of home gaming hardware is not inherently designed for attraction. When combined with large TV screens and loudspeakers (elements not baked into the format), the compelling graphics and sound design of home video games can create attraction. However, when left unattended between play sessions, these games appear stagnant and boring. They do not restart themselves and may be left in states especially inhospitable to new players. Imagine a player quitting on a difficult part of a game that they could not get past and then leaving it as the starting point for the following player. As a result of more complex designs, many home video games require spectators to have experience with the game to fully appreciate what is happening on screen. Watching an esports broadcast of a game that you have never played immediately illustrates this issue (Marshall, 2017).

Because video games are developed and tested using personal computers, it can be simplest for developers to showcase their work using the natural interface of the PC: a mouse and keyboard. But these devices were created for typing and navigating desktop productivity software, not playing video games. The multitude of buttons on a keyboard without any intuitive natural mapping to the in-game actions they correspond with can intimidate or confuse uninitiated users. For some, the interface of the keyboard and mouse represents work or official business and has an air of privacy that does not invite public use. A gamepad is better. It has fewer buttons and thus fewer controls to learn. The ergonomic shape of gamepads invites users to pick them up. They are specifically associated with games. But the modern gamepad reflects the complexity of modern console game design. While a gamepad has fewer buttons than a keyboard, it still harbors enough complexity to confuse new players. The gamepad is meant to universally support any game. While intuitive patterns do exist (such as the analog stick controlling character movement), control schemes are not standard across all titles. Further, there is no standard gamepad. While Nintendo, Microsoft, and Sony each use similar controller layouts and shapes, button labels are different for each console vendor.

## The Arcade Game Format

The arcade game cabinet is the classic form of presenting video games outside of the home, and in arcade games we can see an example of more accessible video game design. Arcade hardware is designed to withstand the abuse and wear and tear of prolonged public use. The presentation, control schemes, and game mechanics of arcade games are designed to maximize approachability and minimize learning curves.

## Access

Arcade games represent the genesis of commercial video games, and early arcade games such as *Pac-Man* were not designed for extended play sessions (Namco, 1980). After all, a long play session means slower monetization, as typical arcade games charge players per play session. If an experience is intended to welcome unfamiliar players rather than intimidate them, players must be able to learn how to play as quickly as possible—perhaps in a matter of seconds. Short play sessions help accommodate busy schedules.

Arcade games, with their intuitive designs, can be more accessible for non-gamer audiences than typical video games designed for play at home. However, some of the same reasons that make them so suitable also render them impractical as an accessible format for creators. Arcade cabinets' bulk and durability, while great for standing up to abuse, also makes them expensive and difficult to deploy or relocate. This makes arcade cabinets less desirable for one night only shows. Their custom interfaces are intuitive but prohibitively expensive and difficult to fabricate. In addition, while arcade cabinets are more durable than home gaming formats, they must still be sheltered from weather and require a power supply, restricting the spaces they can be deployed in.

## Attraction

Arcade games are designed for attraction, competing with one another in rooms lined with arcade cabinets. Unlike home video games, they evolved under separate economic forces where attraction defined success. Their physical forms, augmented with lights, speakers, and moveable parts, are designed to catch attention. When arcade games sit idle, they enter into an "attract mode" designed to showcase their gameplay and lure in passersby.

While a given home video game might be designed intuitively and may only use two buttons, the gamepad interface still has many buttons, labeled generically as A, B, X, Y (among others) to support many possible games. In contrast, arcade game cabinets typically house a single game, and their interfaces are designed specifically for that game. As a result, an arcade game can label buttons as "Jump," "Shoot," or any other gameplay function and leave out any extraneous buttons. These simpler appearances are more attractive for new players.

However, many arcade games eschew such abstract control schemes altogether in favor of more intuitive and exciting metaphors. For example, driving games employ steering wheels and pedals. Shooting games employ gun-shaped controllers that the player aims at in-game targets and shoots by pulling a trigger. Dance arcade games are controlled by dancing on a platform. There is even a Japanese arcade game about flipping tables, *Cho Chabudai Gaeshi!*, that uses a flat table-shaped surface attached to a hinge as a controller (Taito, 2009). In the game, the player flips the hinged surface to simulate the act of flipping a table. The spectacle of these interfaces attracts audiences.

Some arcade games employ additional screens that show off gameplay to attract bystanders. For example, the VR arcade game *Virtual Rabbids: The Big Ride* uses a large screen above players to showcase the experience that the players are witnessing in their head-mounted displays (LAI Games, 2017). *Mario Kart Arcade GP* employs cameras to superimpose photographs of players over their avatars for one another to see (Namco, 2005). This use of mixed reality (MR) enhances immersion, creating attraction for spectators and players alike.

## The Bar Trivia Format

Anyone who has been to a restaurant or bar with video trivia has witnessed an implementation of the bar trivia format. While it might not be what someone thinks of first when imagining a video game, it is an effective format for video games in community spaces. The essential elements of this format are distributed interfaces for participants and a centralized communal output source (usually a TV) for facilitating the game. Some non-trivia examples fit this format as well. The Jackbox Games series of party games, where players use their mobile devices for input and share a TV to facilitate the game, when deployed in a community space, fall under this umbrella (Jackbox Games, 2014). The game *Johann Sebastian Joust* provides another interesting example of the format. This no-graphics game uses PlayStation Move controllers as distributed input devices and uses music for communal output.

### Access

These games are typically easy to play with short and intermittent play sessions, opening them up to a greater number of players. Distributed input devices open the format up to as many players as there are devices. If a given community space, such as a bar, had greater occupancy than the number of devices, access could be problematic. Allowing users to use their own mobile devices can open the experience more broadly and offset some of the costs for the operator. However, this subjects the experience to the inequity of the digital divide. This format also requires at least one communal screen or another output device oriented such that all players can see (or hear) it, as well as a computer to drive the output device and synchronize the experience between the distributed input devices. These elements have associated costs and logistical challenges from weather, required power supply, and the need for a space that promotes access to as many users as possible.

### Attraction

The bar trivia format is an example of what Rouse describes as unassimilated media, which she contends is an essential quality for media of attraction.

> […] they are not part of the fabric of everyday life, retain some novelty, and often have no formal, codified training for associated practitioners. Unassimilated media are not restricted to new technologies; assimilated technologies may be combined in new ways to create convergent media artefacts that also lack assimilation (Rouse, 2016).

Through its novelty, this unassimilated format evokes attraction. Witnessing a group of players stalking one another in *Johann Sebastian Joust* demonstrates the attractive nature of unassimilated media.

Additionally, specific formal elements of the bar trivia format generate attraction. If the distributed input devices are left on restaurant tables or spread out visibly throughout a community space, they can attract players. If players' own mobile devices are used as input devices, information about how to join the game can be physically distributed throughout the community space, or perhaps announced by a host. The communal output device that facilitates the game is an essential element for attraction in this format. A communal screen can catch the attention of spectators, attracting them to become participants. Allowing players to enter a name, which is then broadcast to the occupants of the community space via a screen, is a compelling feature. The knowledge that others will witness a player's actions adds presence and validates the experience.

## Augmented Reality

Since AR is inherently connected to physical space, it is a natural format for video games in community spaces. While AR comes in many forms, the prevalence of AR mediated by mobile devices, as popularized by the likes of *Pokémon GO* and Snapchat, makes this format immediately viable for game developers.

Some AR is designed for any space, such as Snapchat filters that overlay animal features over users' faces; while other AR is location specific, such as the gyms in *Pokémon GO.* While either modality, in the right conditions, can technically satisfy the requirements established in this chapter for games in community spaces, AR anchored to specific locations is a closer match to examples of more traditional art in community spaces. The genre of location-specific AR can be even further subdivided into two categories: AR designed so contextually that its meaning only works in a specific location, such as adding virtual labels beside each president's image on Mt. Rushmore, and AR arbitrarily linked to a specific location, like a gym in *Pokémon GO* linked to a McDonald's restaurant. The presidential labels only make sense in the context of Mt. Rushmore. However, the Pokémon gym could be anywhere the game designers see fit (in this case, driven by paid sponsorship). Both subcategories can work well for games in community spaces and impact access and attraction (Sharma et al., 2017).

### Access

Mobile AR uses a more embodied interface than traditional video games, with a combination of the touch screen, motion control, GPS, and camera hardware. The intuitive metaphors of physically aiming a mobile device's camera to control a view of the world or moving through physical space to move an avatar make the fundamental AR experience easy to learn.

The spatial possibilities of AR affect access. With mobile AR, while the experience can still be spatially connected to a community space, the computing power and hardware required to host the experience are moved to end users' mobile devices. This drastically expands the spaces capable of hosting an AR experience. As smartphones are battery powered, the host space no longer requires a power supply. Further, since the smartphones are not permanently fixed in the host location, they do not require weatherproofing. With smartphone-based AR, installations can become nimbler with no physical footprint. For example, a physical mural is a great example of the enchantment of community art, but it requires its own wall to inhabit.

Yet, even when a physical area becomes constrained, AR allows an infinite number of possible experiences to occupy that same space. In addition, the scale of an AR installation can range from as small as the face of a playing card to encompassing an entire city. Installations can be designed to scale with player participation. For example, with AR, a player could build a virtual sculpture that grows as other players add to it. In contrast to street art like graffiti, unsanctioned AR is more difficult to detect and prohibit. This raises complicated ethical questions. For example, it may take extra elbow grease to remove a physical graffiti tag, but the means for removing it and understanding its removed status are clear cut. Removing an AR installation can be less straightforward (Wadhwa, 2016). Regardless of such issues, AR clearly makes a greater range of community spaces accessible to game developers.

The minimum cost of creating an installation falls without the requirements of physical installations, custom hardware, and custom physical interfaces. There are increasingly powerful tools available to developers—such as ARKit, ARCore, and Unity MARS—that simplify the complexities of AR development. These factors open the format to a greater number of creators. Professors John T. Murray and Emily K. Johnson write more about this in their chapter for this book, *XR Content Authoring Challenges: The Creator-Developer Divide.*

In the wake of COVID-19, AR provides a model for video games in community spaces that requires no shared hardware. However, it is important to consider the impact of limiting access to only those with capable smartphones with specific apps installed and the related ethical issues of the digital divide (Hurley, 2016; Marín-Díaz, 2018). Ideally, public art should not have a price of admission. However, as the cost of such devices falls, AR-capable technology is becoming more ubiquitous, and the tradeoffs could make sense.

## Attraction

Attraction in mobile AR is less clear cut than it is with arcade games or traditional art forms. This stems from the fact that the virtual elements of a mobile AR experience overlaid on the physical world are invisible without a mediating mobile device that has a specific app open. This raises two key challenges to attraction: first, the way in which players discover the app on the marketplace; and second, the way in which they discover the location-based experience once the app is downloaded.

Generally, the first issue of discovering the app is subject to the same crowded market conditions of home video games. However, the premise of hosting a game in a community space provides additional avenues for attraction and solving the discovery problem. If the game experience is linked to a specific event, the host of the event can provide details for how to obtain the app. This relates to Rouse's concept of seamed media, which she establishes as a quality of media of attraction.

> The role of the film narrator highlights early film's lack of "narrative self-sufficiency" by emphasizing the seam between physical and mediated modes of performance. Many of today's MR [mixed reality] works are similarly seamed, and likewise not self-sufficient narratively. They require ancillary

materials, explanations, and even live performers or guides. But it is through this exposure of seams that the audience to media of attraction is made explicitly aware of the technology itself. If leveraged well, this awareness can operate to allow audiences to take meta-pleasure in the mediation presented, in addition to the feeling of immersion. This double sense of wonder at both the mastery of the designer, as well as the wonder or astonishment at the effect of the illusion itself, is at the core of media of attraction (Rouse, 2016).

If the experience is embedded in a public place, the players themselves become a force of attraction. Evidence of the attractive power of AR can be seen in the roving assemblies inspired by *Pokémon GO*. If the game experience is asynchronous and location-based, physical signs can be added to the environment to call out the experience and provide instructions for participating. For example, the *Yellow Arrow* project issued yellow arrow stickers that could be placed in the physical world and linked to virtual messages (Ding, 2017).

There is a strong potential for synergy between street and public art and AR. Players passing by initially notice the public art which can include instructions for further engagement via a mobile device. This attraction synergy can be seen in the *Statue Stories* project in Chicago, where curious passersby can scan QR codes displayed near the statues to hear the figures "talking" as mediated through their mobile device (Kogan, 2017).

## Conclusion

Video games in community spaces can weave presence, discovery, and enchantment into our environments—far beyond the possibilities of home video game formats. The commoditization of games and the gamer metanarrative have restricted our conception of video games to a form largely incompatible with community spaces. Through the examination of the game formats above, developers and players can see new avenues for integrating games into community spaces. Expanding the presence of video games in community spaces can subvert and dismantle the restrictive conception of video games. This might seem like an unwinnable scenario where the solution to the problem is blocked by the problem itself. However, game developers and gamers latently understand the promise of games in community spaces. A kindling is there, waiting for sparks. Adventuresome venues, event organizers, and independent game developers must be the ones to take on this mantle. The brutal market conditions of the game industry mean most independent developers will have difficulty reaching audiences through the home video game format. As game developers and designers, we need to create opportunities for experiencing video games in community spaces like those that exist for other media. Let us enchant our communities!

## Put it into Practice: An AR Game for a Community Space

Come up with an idea for an AR game hosted in a specific community space. This doesn't necessarily need to be a wholly original game concept, just one that is not currently associated with your chosen community space. Summarize the concept and describe the community space. Why would this game work well in your chosen space? Evaluate the concept in terms of access and attraction. How could this concept create opportunities for presence, discovery, and enchantment for community members?

# References

Alexander, L. (2014). "Gamers" don't have to be your audience. "Gamers" are over. Gamasutra. https://www.gamasutra.com/view/news/224400/Gamers_dont_have_to_be_your_audience_Gamers_are_over.php

Auslander, P. (2008). *Liveness: Performance in a Mediatized Culture*. Routledge.

Boyd, R. (2020). *Zoom and Gloom: Universities in the Age of COVID-19*. Los Angeles Review of Books. https://lareviewofbooks.org/article/zoom-and-gloom-universities-in-the-age-of-covid-19/

Constine, J. (2017). Snapchat to launch augmented reality art platform tomorrow. TechCrunch. https://techcrunch.com/2017/10/02/snapchat-art/amp/?guccounter=1

Ding, S. (2017). Re-Enchanting Spaces: Location-Based Media, Participatory Documentary, and Augmented Reality. Diss. Massachusetts Institute of Technology.

Duggan, M. (2015). Which Americans play video games and who identifies as a "gamer." Pew Research Center. https://www.pewresearch.org/internet/2015/12/15/who-plays-video-games-and-identifies-as-a-gamer/

Ebert, R. (2010). Video games can never be art. RogerEbert.Com. https://www.rogerebert.com/roger-ebert/video-games-can-never-be-art

Entertainment Software Association. (2020). 2020 Essential Facts About the Video Game Industry. https://www.theesa.com/esa-research/2020-essential-facts-about-the-videogame-industry/

First Class Media B.V. (2017). *Ghost Detector Radar Camera*. First Class Media B.V.

Hurley, A. (2016). Chasing the frontiers of digital technology: Public history meets the digital divide. *Public Historian*, 38(1), 69-88. https://doi.org/10.1525/tph.2016.38.1.69

Jackbox Games. (2014). *Jack Box Party Pack*. Jackbox Games.

Kogan, R. (2017). Revising Statue Stories: They're still talking and still worth hearing. Chicago Tribune. https://www.chicagotribune.com/entertainment/ct-statue-stories-kogan-sidewalks-ent-0606-20170605-column.html

Koster, R. (2018). The cost of games. Venture Beat. https://venturebeat.com/2018/01/23/the-cost-of-games/

LAI Games. (2017). *Virtual Rabbids: The Big Ride*. LAI Games.

Lien, T. (2013). No girls allowed. Polygon. https://www.polygon.com/features/2013/12/2/5143856/no-girls-allowed

Marín-Díaz, V. (2018). The relationships between augmented reality and inclusive education in higher education. *Bordon, Revista de Pedagogia*, 69(3), 125-142. https://doi.org/10.13042/bordon.2017.51123

Market Research: The State of Online Gaming – 2019. (2019). Limelight Networks. https://www.limelight.com/resources/white-paper/state-of-online-gaming-2019/

Marshall, C. (2017). *Spectating Is Key to a Successful Esports Title*. Redbull.Com. https://www.redbull.com/ca-en/spectating-esports-titles-accessibility

Meadows, J. (2020). Zoom-Bombing Teams Cause Chaos, Confusion in Lake County Courts.

Yahoo News. https://news.yahoo.com/zoom-bombing-teams-cause-chaos-210114496.html

Monster poll results from work in the time of coronavirus (2020). Monster. https://learnmore.monster.com/poll-results-from-work-in-the-time-of-coronavirus

Morin, A. (2019). The Harmful Effects of Too Much Screen Time for Kids. Verywellfamily. Com. https://www.verywellfamily.com/the-negative-effects-of-too-much-screen-time-1094877

Namco (1980). *Pac-Man*. Namco.

Namco (2005). Mario Kart Arcade GP. Namco.

Naughty Dog (2020). The Last of Us Part II. Sony Interactive Entertainment.

Niantic (2016). Pokémon GO. Niantic.

Nintendo (2011). Mario Kart 7. Nintendo.

Nintendo (2017). The Legend of Zelda: Breath of the Wild. Nintendo.

OppenheimerFunds. (2018). Investing in the Soaring Popularity of Gaming. Reuters. https://www.reuters.com/sponsored/article/popularity-of-gaming

Portillo, E. (2014). The pricing game and its current effects on the video game industry. GameZone. https://www.gamezone.com/originals/the-pricing-game-and-its-current-effects-on-the-video-game-industry/

Robertson, A. (2019). Steam's new Interactive Recommender is built for finding 'hidden gems.' The Verge. https://www.theverge.com/2019/7/11/20690231/valve-steam-labs-interactive-recommender-game-recommendation-machine-learning-tool

Rouse, R. (2016). Media of attraction: A media archeology approach to panoramas, kinematography, mixed reality and beyond. *Lecture Notes in Computer Science (Including Subseries Lecture Notes in Artificial Intelligence and Lecture Notes in Bioinformatics), 10045 LNCS*, 97–107. https://doi.org/10.1007/978-3-319-48279-8_9

Sharma, H.N., Alharthi, S.A., Dolgov, I. and Toups, Z.O. (2017. A Framework Supporting Selecting Space to Make Place in Spatial Mixed Reality Play. https://doi.org/10.1145/3116595.3116612

Sheffield, B. (2013). Let's retire the word "gamer." Gamasutra. https://www.gamasutra.com/view/news/192107/Opinion_Lets_retire_the_word_gamer.php

Sherr, I. (2020). The Last of Us Part 2 sells 4M, becomes fastest-selling Sony game for PS4 ahead of Spider-Man. Cnet. https://www.cnet.com/news/the-last-of-us-part-2-sells-4m-becomes-fastest-selling-sony-game-for-ps4-ahead-of-spider-man/

Snap Inc. (2018). Introducing Snappables. Snap.Com. https://www.snap.com/en-US/news/post/introducing-snappables/

Taito (2009). Cho Chabudai Gaeshi! Taito.

Vanderhoef, J. (2013). Casual Threats: The Feminization of Casual Video Games. *Ada: A Journal of Gender, New Media, and Technology*, 2. https://doi.org/10.7264/N3V40S4D

Vivas, R. (2017). Game devs: Build your community as you build your game. Venture Beat. https://venturebeat.com/2017/11/13/game-devs-build-your-community-as-you-build-your-game/

Wadhwa, T. (2016). Who Do You Complain To When Your House Becomes A Pokémon GO Gym? Forbes. https://www.forbes.com/sites/tarunwadhwa/2016/07/14/who-do-you-complain-to-when-your-house-becomes-a-pokemon-go-gym/#6b8d3d47673e

Williams, D. (2005). A Brief Social History of Game Play. DiGRA '05 – Proceedings of the 2005 DiGRA International Conference: Changing Views: Worlds in Play. http://www.digra.org/wp-content/uploads/digital-library/06278.32314.pdf

# Part 3

# The Augmented City
## for Education

# Chapter
# 9

# Reflecting in Space on Time: Augmented Reality Interactive Digital Narratives to Explore Complex Histories

**Hartmut Koenitz**

P.O. Box 94323, 1090 GH Amsterdam
Email: h.a.koenitz@uva.nl

## Introduction: The Ubiquity Moment of Augmented Reality

Augmented Reality's (AR) breakthrough as a ubiquitous technology is near. Important milestones on the way are hardware products like Google Glass and Magic Leap, but also content-products like Ingress and Pokémon Go. The latter in particular changed the perception of AR and has shown the technology's potential to enable novel kinds of experiences paired with global commercial success. Before, the technology was known to a tech-savvy minority, yet ever since, AR—not necessarily by that name, but as a concept—has reached widespread awareness, which is an important step towards ubiquity.

Amongst the large technology companies, Apple[1] in particular has emphasized the importance of the technology for several years now and in mid-2020 speculations about an upcoming Apple-brand of AR glasses runs high, having a fully integrated display in a frame nearly indistinguishable from normal glasses.

However, as the case of Virtual Reality (VR) has shown, technological potential alone is not a guarantee for compelling products and mass market success. Therefore, the speculated advancements in hardware which will probably differentiate Apple's offering from Google's earlier attempt might be considered to be of lesser importance, and the more significant change could be that Apple in 2020 is also a media production company, investing considerable sums in building up a catalog

---

[1] Tim Cook, CEO of Apple discussed the importance of AR in several interviews and public appearances.

of content for its TV platform. For an upcoming release of Apple AR glasses, the availability of content could be the deciding factor for the product's success in the market. In other words—if Apple can build a library of high-quality content (either in-house or in collaboration with its developers and creative partners), and offer a good enough hardware platform, AR could have its "ubiquity moment", similar to how the introduction of the iPhone in 2007 marked the breakthrough for multi-touch technology and mobile devices.

Ultimately, the question is not about any single company or product. AR is poised for ubiquity in the very near future, regardless of which company will take the lead and thus the question becomes how we—as scholars and designers—should analyze and use the technology. In this article, I position AR as a platform for public education and discourse, as a means to 'reflect in space on time', to connect past, present and speculative futures. To that end I will start discussing historical predecessors and the current state of AR before considering the question of complex histories as a problem of AR. While that aspect has been discussed previously (Engberg, 2017; Graham, Zook and Boulton, 2012; Swords et al., 2020), this paper adds a perspective on interactive digital narratives (IDN) as a means to enable complex representations in AR. Specifically, I will emphasize the need for narrative as a sense-making function, which in the context of AR means interactive digital narrative (IDN), due to the systemic and dynamic nature of the medium as well as its participatory aspect.

To further illustrate this point, I will provide a description of a complex historical situation and use this example to detail a pre-production design process aimed at deciding on a suitable type of IDN for a work which invites reflection on a complex situation.

## Foundational Considerations

### Augmented Reality is an Age-old Human Concept

Before starting to discuss digitally augmented reality, it is useful to take a step back and realize that augmenting reality is a deeply-rooted human activity. Seen in a more abstract way, the building of the first dwelling at the dawn of humanity can be described as "augmenting reality". Closer to today's sense of AR are later efforts at Trompe-l'œil effects in architectural paintings (for example, paintings on walls that create the illusion of non-existent architectural structures or fake see-through-effects) and landscape gardening (for example, the hidden fence, a trench invisible from the main vantage point to create the illusion of an unbroken landscape extending into the distance, or the optical illusion of making a distant river appear to be flowing through a park by means of a cleverly placed pond which appears as a river bend in the distance etc.) as well as a building in a theatrical setting. In that sense, count Potemkin's infamous non-existent villages can be described as a non-digital AR representation. The reason I am invoking this sense of AR is to remind us that in the very strictest sense such manifestations are 'lying', since they can be characterized as falsifying reality. This is a danger we should be aware of—as AR scholars, creators and consumers—especially with the continuously increasing fidelity of AR representations. In this regard, Marcus Carter and Ben Egilston provide a good overview of ethical considerations concerning 'mixed reality' technologies in a recent report (Carter and Ben Egliston, 2020).

In addition, we should be aware of the military lineage of AR technology. Arguably the most direct technical predecessor of today's AR technology was the "reflector gun sight", a technology invented in the early 20th century and in wide use by WW2, where aiming markings were projected over the optical image of the real world. The next step in development was the head-up display (HUD), introduced first by the Royal Air Force in WW2 in order to show radar information in the direct line of sight of fighter pilots.

## The State of AR

Pokémon Go amply demonstrated the advantages of AR–with global market saturation of smartphones, the necessary technology is now widely available almost anywhere and thus the potential audience can be counted in billions. Conversely, Pokémon Go is testimony to the wide acceptance of augmentation, of content that adds to and blends in with real environments. Additionally, the game showed that many players are willing to supply user-generated content in the form of pictures and locations of actual landmarks, re-cast as "Pokestops". In that way, players extend a project and thus provide resources beyond the means of a single developer. Arguably, this aspect was a major factor in helping make a relatively small developer's project a world-wide phenomenon. In addition, this customization function allowed players to visibly express themselves and made them perceive the project as their own. Finally, Pokémon Go displayed a capacity often associated with artistic works–the ability to make the familiar unfamiliar and thus interesting. Many players (re-)discovered their actual surroundings on foot, as movement any faster than walking was detected by the program and prohibited interaction. In this sense, AR has the potential to create positive health effects, even while reports of accident by distracted players might paint the opposite picture.

However, the quick drop-off in player numbers and the considerably reduced success of follow-up products like "Wizards Unite" also make clear that the ubiquity moment of AR is not quite there yet. Currently, AR is still more of an 'extra function' than a standard feature. For example, Google Maps supports a "Live view" AR function since 2019, yet, at the time of writing this article, the feature is not prominent (as evidenced by numerous internet guides explaining how to even find it) and only available for navigation on foot. Similarly, Apple's efforts have led to AR-based measurement tools for DIYers, furniture catalogues which allow the placement of products in user's homes and games which extend onto tables and floors. All useful functionality, but not ubiquitous yet.

In sum, the current state of AR is characterized by the following five conditions:

1. Near universal availability of necessary technology.
2. Wide acceptance of augmentation through digital devices.
3. Willingness of interactors to supply user-generated content, thus extending and customizing AR projects.

4. AR can make the familiar unfamiliar (an important function of art in general) and thus has demonstrated a potential to create behavioral change.
5. The ubiquity moment of AR—where the technology becomes an expected standard feature—is not quite there yet.

## The Challenge of Complexity in Historical Context

AR so far exists in the form of overlays, visible on a screen that also shows a camera image of the real world. As soon as we start augmenting this already mediated reality with navigation signs and more complex depictions (e.g. of a historical building which stood at a spot a hundred years ago), we enter a complex space where history-making, ideology, and personal interpretation meet. A given experience might appear free of ideology at first sight, but this just means that its ideological layers are more hidden. For example, a game like Pokémon Go embeds an ideology of hierarchies, segregated groups, constant growth, competition through measurement matrices and direct fights.

However, things get even more problematic when it comes to AR works with a closer relation to past, present and future realities (for example, in the form of a historical guide or an AR depiction of a new construction project). The danger with simple overlays is in the potential for problematic simplifications of a complex social history context. Therefore, at its most extreme, AR might be used to support dubious claims about national or private ownership of historical landmarks or landscapes. This could happen deliberately or due to an overly naïve approach to the works' design.

In the Americas, perspectives influenced by European colonialism could ignore native American populations and for example depict the great plains as empty prior to the arrival of the Europeans or ignore native American monuments. In Europe, an additional issue arises: modern conceptions of nation states could be projected on monuments from the middle ages where such notions did not yet exist. For example, would the inhabitants of the North German city of Lübeck during the 16th century understand themselves as Germans in the same way we understand citizenship and national belonging nowadays? Or would they rather have seen being German as secondary to their identity as Lübeck citizens and as belonging to a city that at the time was a leading member of the Hanseatic League and thus a prosperous trade hub? And, how should we consider a Scandinavian monument from the time of the Kalmar Union (1397-1523), under which Denmark, Sweden, Norway and Finland were governed by a single crown? Are monuments from these times Danish, Swedish, Norwegian, or Finnish? Or, do they rather belong to a shared "Kalmar" history, which is not entirely compatible with later notions of statehood. Furthermore, while these two examples might create mostly mild-mannered discussions, how about the many contested monuments and borders on the grounds of the former republic of Yugoslavia?

I can illustrate these issues even more clearly with the help of my own family history and the difficulties in depicting parts of it in AR. With this aim in mind, I will provide a short historical overview of a particular complex part of European history in the following section. The scope of this description is to consider the complexity of a historical situation, and how to approach it in the AR context. A full historical account is beyond the scope of this chapter.

## A Concrete Example for a Complex History

On my father's side my family comes from what was once known as the "Freie Stadt Danzig"—the Free City of Danzig, a problematic construct created by the victorious nations of WW I as a part of the Versailles Treaty in 1919, which was organized as a protectorate under the League of Nations (the predecessor to the United Nations). This particular construct aimed to solve two issues: The newly founded Republic of Poland (Poland did not exist as a country between 1795 and 1919, since in 1795 the remainder of historic Poland had been partitioned between Russia, Austria-Hungary and Prussia) had been promised full access to the sea and been given a short coast line, but was missing a port for import and export of goods. At the same time, the majority of Danzig citizens were ethnic Germans (over 90% according to official censuses during the time) and thus making the city and its trade port a full part of the new Polish Republic was deemed not feasible.

The Free City had most of the characteristics of an independent state: a democratically elected parliament and government, its own civil administration, including a police force, as well as its own currency and postal and customs administration. However, the Polish Republic was given the right of military administration and was later allowed to install an ammunitions depot in the harbor of Danzig. Poland was also guaranteed free access to the harbor as well as given the right to operate its own customs procedures (a customs union between the Free City and the Polish Republic was mandated by the Versailles Treaty) and postal system. A High Commissioner was appointed by the League of Nations as their representative in the Free City and as a first instance to moderate in possible disputes between the Free City and Poland. Finally, for a child born in Danzig, an "options model" was devised, allowing its parents to choose between Danzig, German, and Polish Citizenship.

This construction resulted in two decades of constant conflict in the inter-war years 1919-1939 between the Polish Republic, the Free City, Germany, and the League of Nations. Put simply, the Polish state felt it had been unduly denied full control of the city and especially its port vital for the country's international trade, while the large majority of the Danzig population felt betrayed by decisions without their consent (being severed from Germany as well as in regards to the considerable rights given to Polish authorities on Danzig grounds). It should be noted that this construction was neither a Polish nor a German idea—rather, these two sides had to live with its consequences.

Especially in the pervasive climate of nationalism at the time, and the high level of distrust between German and Polish sides, conflict was all but inevitable. What ensued was essentially a small-scale cold war, in which the Polish government implemented what appeared as a strategy aimed at taking over the city with measures like regularly blocking transport of people, goods, and mail into the city from

Germany, increasing its military presence beyond the agreed number of soldiers and attempting to take over all customs operations. Several complaints lodged by the Free City's government to the League of Nations against the Polish government's measures were mostly ineffective. The Weimar Republic at the same time understood itself as the proper representative of the Danzig people and attempted to aid the Free City as well as it could. At the same time, the Polish minority in the Free City was heavily discriminated against, with its members being effectively treated as representatives of hostile occupants no matter what their personal perspectives were.

Realizing that control over Danzig might after all be elusive, the Polish government's strategy followed a dual approach–while keeping up the pressure on the Free City, the Polish Republic started to build its own international seaport in the neighboring village of Gdynia starting in 1920. By the mid-1930s, Gdynia had become a major international hub and consequently the Polish Republic's dependence on the Free City's port was considerably reduced. Yet the conflict remained, fueled in part by the nationalistic interests of both Polish (under authorian rule since a coup in 1926) and German governments (under Nazi rule since 1933). The Nazi party had also won elections in the Free City and became its governing political group in June of 1933, however, its influence was somewhat diminished by the Free City's special status. The Jewish population faced increasing discrimination and consequently many Jewish Danzigers emigrated, with only a small part remaining by the beginning of WW2 and about 500 (out of 12,000 in 1925) were murdered in the holocaust. In the period immediately before WW2, the Nazi propaganda machine used the conflict for their purposes in an attempt to build up a pretense for war. Indeed, WW2 started with a German battleship shelling the Polish ammunitions depot in the Free State's harbor. During WW2, Danzig was re-integrated into Germany, while the Polish population was driven out of the city, and pressed into slave work for German industry and agriculture, or taken to concentration camps, one being Stuthoff, erected on the grounds of the former Free City. At the end of WW2, most of the old town burned down. In the post-war period, the ethnic German population had to leave the city. For the most part (85% according to statistics), the city was repopulated with Polish citizens from former eastern Polish provinces, which after 1945 had become part of the Soviet Union. Stalin had moved Poland to the west and compensated the country with former east German provinces including Danzig. This also means that a large part of the population of present day Gdańsk has no direct connection to the history of the city. The main part of the old city quarter was beautifully reconstructed from the ruins in a massive effort. Some claims exists that the reconstruction emphasized architecture from before the 1795 partition of Poland.

## A Wider Context

If this stub description of Danzig history appears complex, we should be aware that it only covers a part of the first half of the 20th century. It does not even start to engage with the eventful history of a once mighty capital of trade which gained, lost, regained and defended autonomy status during much of the Middle Ages and early modern times, under different powers such as the Polish King and the Teutonic

Nights Order. Nor does it cover the events in the now polish city of Gdańsk that led to the founding of the Solidarność trade union in 1980 under the leadership of Gdańsk native Lech Wałęsa, and ultimately to the fall of the communist regime in Poland. Nor does it cover a recently growing interest in Gdańsk to learn more about the city's pre-war history. For example, there is a bilingual website "history teller" (http://www.opowiadaczehistorii.pl/) covering daily life in the period before 1945, sponsored by the city, and in addition city libraries have made efforts to digitize German documents to make them widely accessible (for example, population registers).

What does all of this mean for AR depictions? This example evokes the question of how we can present this and similarly rich and complex histories to audiences in AR. More concretely, we need to consider the question of realizing a project which invites reflection on the historical period of the Free City with all its different perspectives in AR while walking around in the old city part of Gdańsk today.

In order to address this question, in the next section, I will first position AR as platform for novel forms of narration, for interactive digital narratives (IDN). Then, I will describe the specific advantages of IDN for the representation of complex topics, before outlining a multi-step design approach.

## Augmented Reality as Interactive Digital Narrative

Narrative is central to human sense-making and self-construction (Ricoeur, 1991)— we remember, communicate and transfer knowledge by using narration. Consequently, Kurt Ranke (1967) and Walter R. Fisher (1984) have independently from each other proposed to understand our species as "homo narrans", the narrative human. More recently, advancements in cognitive sciences have led to a new understanding of a narrative as a function of our brains, a "flexible, forgiving cognitive frame for mentally projected worlds" (Herman, 2002) in the words of David Herman, a leading figure of the 'cognitive turn' in narratology.

Importantly, this perspective does not mean that everything is a narrative to start with, nor that all narratives take the forms commonly understood to be narratives such as print literature, movies, or oral storytelling events. The brain might understand music, a painting, or an elaborate meal as narrative. In addition, it is important to realize that narrative is not restricted to Eurocentric perspectives on structure such as the 'three-act story arc' or the supposedly universal 'hero's journey' (Campbell, 1949). In fact, many alternative structures exist the world over. Narrative comes in many forms, ranging from cyclical narratives in some variants of African oral storytelling forms to Japanese Kishotenketsu, a narrative form without conflict, tension build-up or climax in the Eurocentric sense (Koenitz et al., 2018).

This also means that novel forms of narrative are possible and that the digital medium presents an opportunity for such expressions in the form of interactive digital narratives (IDN). AR is thus a platform for IDN.

In her seminal book *Hamlet on the Holodeck* (Murray, 1997), Janet Murray has identified specific characteristics of the digital medium pertinent to interactive digital narrative. She identifies affordances (procedural, participatory, spatial and encyclopedic) and specific aesthetic qualities (immersion, agency and transformation). For Murray, interactivity is the product of the computer's ability to independently execute a series of commands (procedural) and its capacity to wait for the input of its audience (which Murray calls "interactor") and react to it (participatory).

In order to describe IDN artefacts, I have developed a model for IDN influenced by Roy Ascott's earlier understanding of cybernetic art on the basis of Murray's work (Ascott, 1964; 1968). The SPP model distinguishes *system*, *process*, and *product* (Koenitz, 2015). System is the dynamic artefact which contains a protostory—a term which depicts all potential narratives in a given IDN work. Process describes the interactive engagement of an interactor with the system, while product is the recording of a playthrough. Two aspects are crucial in the current context: first, that an IDN work can contain many different (and potentially conflicting) narratives, and secondly that they need instantiation, meaning once an interactor engages they are caused to happen.

These characteristics give IDN particular advantages in depicting complexity, which can be summarized thusly: an IDN work can represent a complex situation in its system and at the same time provide its audience with a comprehensible, expressive and quintessential human communicative form–narrative–emerging during the audience's own interactions with the system in an interactive process. At every step of the way, a temporary reduction of complexity occurs by means of the choices taken, aiding in the process of sense-making and comprehension. Conversely, an awareness of complexity through choices not taken occurs—even if an interactor only experiences a single traversal, they know that there is additional material to engage with. Better still, audiences can revisit their choices through replay and thus deepen their engagement and understanding. Unlike in earlier fixed mediated forms, the reduction to a single linear flow of events in a narrative product is not permanent, as many more narrative products can be instantiated from the same IDN work.

AR adds embodiment to the experiential dimensions of IDN, situating the interactor in a concrete space and time of a real-life environment and thus increasing the quality of the artwork Walter Benjamin has termed "aura" (Benjamin, 1963), as Jay Bolter reminds us (Bolter et al., 2006).

## An Approach for Depicting Complex Histories

Given the potential of IDN to represent complex topics, how can we apply it in a concrete design? I propose a multi-step process which starts with a collection of assets and complications. Based on this material, the second step identifies what mechanism(s) contributes to the complexity and potential conflicting narratives. The third step is to consider which forms of IDN can be used to address these mechanism(s) while representing a complex history and inviting audiences to reflect on it. Technically, this process covers the pre-design phase, leaving creative license for the actual implementation.

## Step 1: Assets and Complications

In this step, assets (positive aspects and available content) as well as complications (issues creating complexity, conflicting perspectives, unavailable content) are collected. In the case of a potential Gdańsk/Danzig history project, here are the lists:

*Assets*:

- There is an exceptionally rich and varied history to draw from.
- In its heydays, the city was one of the most powerful and rich trade capitals in Europe.
- For much of its history, Danzig's is an example of economic success and political independence.
- The Free City of Danzig provides a microcosm for a reflection on world history post WW1, especially on the ambition of creating a lasting peaceful world order and the ultimate failure of this order.
- The city's old town has been beautifully reconstructed and well maintained after WW2 and is now a tourist destination.
- There is a fair share of famous people from Danzig/Gdańsk who could be used to exemplify and personalize history. Some examples are the philosopher Schopenhauer, the scientist Fahrenheit (who invented the temperature scale still used in the US and some other countries), the actor Klaus Kinski, and two Nobel prize winners, Günther Grass (for literature, much of which describes Danzig during the Free City period) and Lech Wałęsa (Peace prize), leader of the Polish opposition movement during the 1980s and later Polish president.
- Plenty of historical material exists and is accessible, both in Polish and German archives, as well as on sources like YouTube and Google image search.
- There are signs of a growing interest in the current population for the pre-1945 history.

*Complications*:

- There is a complex history.
- There are differing, conflicting understandings of historical events, coinciding with different national perspectives.
- The conflict does not fit into more common approaches aimed at decolonizing history.
- Many of the buildings in the old city were reconstructed during the 1950s and 1960s and often differed from earlier versions (see Figure 9.1), and some of the changes might have been motivated by the wish to emphasize the Polish influence on the city.
- In addition, the street layout was changed.
- The population was exchanged after WW2 and most of the current inhabitants are not directly connected to the city's history, instead, they have been moved there without consent from formerly Eastern Polish regions.
- Some historical documents have been lost over time, especially in the last days of WW2 and the intermediate aftermath.

**Figure 9.1:** Danzig buildings in 1900 (left) and today (right)—notice the changed roof of the rebuilt structure to the right (Krantor) as well as the difference in the wooden structure in the front of it and the differences in the row of houses to the left of the Krantor

What these two lists show us is that many good assets exist, along with considerable complications. The challenge is to make use of the assets without losing the complex context. The next step is identifying the mechanism or mechanisms that contribute to the complexity and potential conflicting narratives.

## Step 2: Mechanism(s) of Complexity

In order to find the mechanism(s) of complexity, I propose to start with a series of questions:

- "What makes this history complex?"
- "Do different perspectives exist?"
- "Are these perspectives individual or shared by a group?"

If a group exists in the context of a project, the next question would be: "Can we broadly identify one or more groups"? The nature of the identified group will then be a key to identifying the underlying mechanism, for example, if the group is a political party, the underlying mechanism might be ideology. In the concrete example, we can answer the questions as follows:

*"What makes this history complex?"*

- It is a long history, reaching into the middle ages.
- The city was the location of a twenty-year conflict in the first half of the 20th century.
- Different rulers and nations have laid claim to the city.
- The city was ruined and rebuilt – many buildings are not original.
- The city population was exchanged almost entirely post WW2 with most newcomers having their own roots in former eastern Polish provinces.

*"Do different perspectives exist?"*

- Yes, different perspectives can be identified.

*"Are these perspectives individual or shared by a group?"*

- Different perspectives are shared by large groups

*"Can we broadly identify one or more groups?"*

- Yes, it is broadly possible to identify a Polish and German perspective where differences exist.

Given that the groups we can identify are nations, nationalism is an important mechanism leading to complexity in this example. This means, on a more abstract level, the conflicting histories are due to nationalistic lenses. However, there are two different effects of this mechanism. The ideological aspect of the nationalistic German and Polish lenses aim at the reduction of the other side's influence on Danzig/Gdańsk's history which leads to a binary extreme: Danzig was always German, Gdańsk was always Polish. It is quite clear that these extreme forms are wrong, and a more realistic perspective can be found at a middle ground between them. However, an additional factor is also important: the ahistorical nature of nationalistic lenses. A nationalistic perspective on history is a modern understanding of nationhood projected onto earlier times, which ignores the fact that nation states simply did not exist during the middle ages,  and were a gradual development afterwards which reached different regions at different times. In the concrete case of Danzig, during the times before the development of nation states reached the region, it was entirely possible to have a German-speaking city swearing allegiance to a Polish King in exchange for far-reaching autonomy. It also means that the German-speaking city of Danzig might not have welcomed the occupation by the equally German-speaking Teutonic knights order as it meant losing a considerable portion of their autonomy. Both cases do not fit well into later nationalistic frameworks.

## Step 3: Choice of Type of IDN

Given the assets, complications and mechanisms identified in the previous steps, what form of IDN can we choose to represent the complex history and simultaneously invite reflection on the problematic ideological and ahistorical mechanism of nationalism? Established forms of IDN targeting complex issues can be categorized as follows:

### Parallel Perspectives

In a parallel perspective IDN, two or more perspectives are presented alongside each other, often allowing the interactor to change between the conflicting narratives at pre-defined moments. A typical example is the award-winning interactive documentary *The Last Highjack Interactive* (Duijn, Wolting, & Pallotta, 2014), in which the complex topic of piracy in Somalia is represented through parallel narrative threads of a pirate, a ship's captain and intermediaries negotiating the release of a captured ship. For the current topic, a parallel perspective IDN could represent the Free City of Danzig Period through Polish and German characters providing personal voices to the conflicting views, potentially sourced from actual historical diary entries.

### Stakeholder

This kind is similar to type 1 (Parallel Perspectives), yet applies accumulation of perspectives, from the voices of different stakeholders presented in shorter statements in contrast to the extended narratives of parallel perspectives. An example is the interactive documentary *Fort McMoney* (Dufresne, 2013), which depicts the complex situation of the real-life Canadian town Fort McMurray, which became a boom town after massive oil sand deposits had been found there. A complex situation ensued which included environmental protection issues, massive population growth and the resulting urban planning challenge, as well as conflicts between newcomers to the town and the existing population. *Fort McMoney* conveys these issues mostly through stakeholders, which the interactor can interview or visit and thus learn about the complex situation. An IDN project in the current context could accumulate different voices from the period of the Free City, and in this way invite reflection.

### Alternate or Fictional Realities

This type of IDN creates a fictitious setting in order to enable reflection on a complex topic. A prominent example is the narrative video game *Papers, Please!* (Pope, 2013) which invites reflection on complicity in an oppressive state by putting the interactor into the role of a customs officer who needs to feed his family and is faced with ever-changing regulations and difficult moral decisions leading to potentially dire consequences (for example, letting an assassin into the country and being responsible for the ensuing murders). An alternate reality version inviting reflection on the Free City of the Danzig period could be named "The Monaco of the Baltic" and depict a current city which has embraced a model similar to the city state of Monaco and its relationship with the surrounding country of France. The connection to that model is strengthened with an emphasis on Zopot, a famous seaside resort, spa and casino town on the grounds of the Free City, which became popular in the 19th century and today features several five-star hotels.

### Decision Maker

This kind of IDN puts the interactor in the position of decision maker in a complex situation. Simulations games like SimCity (Maxis, 1989) and The Sims (Wright, 2000), in which the interactors control a city's or virtual characters' fates through their decisions are examples of this category. PeaceMaker (Sweeney, Brown and Burak, 2007), a game in which the interactor attempts to find a peaceful solution to the Arab-Israeli conflict is another example. An IDN inviting reflection on the Free City period could put an interactor into different roles, such as Danzig president, High Commissioner, Polish President, or German Chancellor in a simulation of the year 1926, facing pressing issues of that period.

### Data Narrative

This type of IDN puts a narrative interface on big data and uses elements such as real-time data visualizations to make data comprehensible. An example project for this type of IDN is The Industry (Duijn, 2018), an award-winning work, which depicts the illegal drugs industry in the Netherlands. The work contains several years' worth of data from the Dutch police on drug-related incidents and allows interactors to input their zip code and see all illegal activity in the vicinity of their homes. The work also features diagrams of relationships between "employees" of the industry as well as audio interviews with them. A data narrative on the Free City period could be realized through the digitization of existing records, and then would allow the visualization of population movements, building activities, flow of goods, voting behavior and many other aspects.

*Behind the Scenes*

This type of IDN invites reflection by offering interactors an 'inside view' of the mechanics of a complex situation. An example includes the Dutch project *The Asylum Machine* (Blankevoort and van Driel, 2015), which lets the interactor explore the inner workings of the process for asylum seekers in the Netherlands in great detail. Every step of the process is depicted and the interactor is invited to reflect on the bureaucracy and idiosyncrasies of the process. This reflection is encouraged through built-in questions, which ask the audience to propose improvements to the process. This type of IDN is difficult to apply to historical settings, as it requires access to details no longer accessible from a historical distance. It is listed here for the sake of completeness.

# Choice of Interactive Digital Narrative Type

The choice of IDN type for a concrete project depends on many factors including audience type, production budget and available material. As the previous section has shown, there are a range of possible choices in the context of representing the complex historical situation of the Free City of Danzig in AR.

The resulting AR interactive narratives would make use of IDN's specific simultaneous abilities to represent complex situations and provide a temporary reduction of complexity, which is key in enabling understanding.

Different forms of Immersive technology use embodiment as a crucial addition to the digital experience. Not so long ago, the digital medium was mostly confined to a stationary screen, cut off from 'real world'. In this regard, AR provides a specific advantage, as the experience occurs in the actual space emphasizing the connection to a real location and its history. The specific aura, the authority of a space in time, further enhances the experience.

Considering these conditions, a personal favorite of this author amongst the different types of IDN for the current project would be the alternate history version, as it would enable a playful reflection that escapes the prevailing binary opposites of the historical situation. Instead it could consider issues befitting a tax haven and glitzy, upscale seaside resorts, such as the discussion surrounding the building of yet another skyscraper on the Speicherinsel (stockhouse island) for the ever growing Bank of Danzig and its employees managing countless tax-free anonymous accounts. Seeing these imagined additions to the city's skyline in AR would make the ramifications of actual history palatable, and also enhance the understanding of potential alternatives. Inviting such reflections means to apply the potential of AR interactive digital narratives.

# Conclusion

In this paper, I have described the state of AR and positioned the technology as a platform for the representation of complex histories by means of interactive digital narratives, creating memorable embodied experiences in a real-life space.

Using the example of a complex historical situation, I have detailed a multi-step pre-production design process to help identify assets and complications, but also the dominant mechanisms which create the complexity of the situation. In the design process, this insight is connected to the choice of IDN type for a concrete work intended to address the identified mechanism and invite reflection on the complex historical situation.

The ubiquity moment of AR is near and as scholars and designers we should be ready to analyze and apply the technology's potential. There is are a particular opportunity to apply this potential for positive social impact in AR IDN projects depicting complex issues.

# Put it into Practice: Choosing an IDN Type for AR

- Consider the aim of the project (e.g. make the audience reflect on an aspect of history).
- Consider the context of the proposed work in terms of target audience and required resources.
- Select from the following types:
  1. Parallel Perspectives
     Two or more perspectives are presented alongside each other, often allowing the interactor to change between the conflicting narratives at pre-defined moments.
  2. Stakeholder
     Similar to Nr. 1 (Parallel Perspectives), applies accumulation of perspectives, of the voices of different stakeholders presented in short statements.
  3. Alternate or Fictional Realities
     This type of IDN creates a fictitious or alternate history setting in order to enable reflection on a complex topic, divorced from the restrictions of actual situations.
  4. Decision maker
     This kind of IDN puts the interactor in the position of the decision maker in a complex situation, and thus enables a reflection on its politics.
  5. Data Narrative
     This type of IDN puts a narrative interface on big data and uses elements such as real-time data visualizations to make data comprehensible. This type requires access or the creation of considerable amounts of viable data.
  6. Behind the Scenes
     This type of IDN invites reflection by offering interactors an 'inside view' of the mechanism of a complex situation.
- Implement the selected type.

# References

Ascott, R. (1964). *The Construction of Change*. Cambridge Opinion.

Ascott, R. (1968). The Cybernetic Stance: My Process and Purpose. *Leonardo*, 1(2), 105. http://doi.org/10.2307/1571947

Benjamin, W. (1963). Das Kunstwerkim Zeitalterim Zeitalter seiner technischen Reproduzierbarkeit. Frankfurt/Main: Surhkamp.

Blankevoort, E. and van Driel, E. (2015). *The Asylum Machine*. The Hague. Retrieved from http://asielzoekmachine.nl

Bolter, J.D., MacIntyre, B., Gandy, M. and Schweitzer, P. (2006). New Media and the Permanent Crisis of Aura. *Convergence: The International Journal of Research Into New Media Technologies*, 12(1), 21-39. http://doi.org/10.1177/1354856506061550

Campbell, J. (1949). *The Hero with a Thousand Faces*. New York, NY: Harper & Row.

Carter, M. and Ben Egliston (2020). Ethical Implications of Emerging Mixed Reality Technologies. pp. 1-39. Sydney: University of Sydney.

Dufresne, D. (2013). Fort McMoney. National Filmboard of Canada &Arte. Retrieved from http://www.fortmcmoney.com

Duijn, M. (2018). The Industry. Amsterdam: Submarine Channel. Retrieved from https://theindustryinteractive.com/

Duijn, M. and Wolting, F. (2014). Co-Director Documentary, and Pallotta, T., Co-Director Documentary. Last Hijack Interactive. Amsterdam: Submarine Channel.

Engberg, M. (2017). Augmented and Mixed Reality Design for contested and challenging histories. pp. 1-8. Presented at the MW 2017. Retrieved from http://mw17.mwconf.org/paper/augmented-and-mixed-reality-design-for-contested-and-challenging-histories-postcolonial-approaches-to-site-specific-storytelling/

Fisher, W.R. (1984). Narration as a human communication paradigm: The case of public moral argument. *Communication Monographs*, 51(1), 1-22. http://doi.org/10.1080/03637758409390180

Graham, M., Zook, M. and Boulton, A. (2012). Augmented reality in urban places: Contested content and the duplicity of code. *Transactions of the Institute of British Geographers*, 38(3), 464-479. http://doi.org/10.1111/j.1475-5661.2012.00539.x

Herman, D. (2002). Story Logic. Lincoln, NE: U of Nebraska Press.

Koenitz, H. (2015). Towards a specific theory of interactive digital narrative. In Interactive Digital Narrative: History, Theory, and Practice. New York.

Koenitz, H., Di Pastena, A., Jansen, D., de Lint, B. and Moss, A. (2018). The Myth of "Universal" Narrative Models. pp. 107-120. *In*: R. Rouse, H. Koenitz and M. Haahr (eds.). Interactive Storytelling: 11th International Conference for Interactive Digital Storytelling, ICIDS 2018. Cham: The 3rd International Conference for Interactive Digital Storytelling. Retrieved from https://doi.org/10.1007/978-3-030-04028-4_8

Maxis (1989). Sim City. Redwood Shores, CA: Maxis.

Murray, J.H. (1997). Hamlet on the Holodeck: The Future of Narrative in Cyberspace. New York: Free Press.

Pope, L. (2013). Papers, Please. 3909 LLC.

Ranke, K. (1967). Kategorienprobleme der Volksprosa. *Fabula*, 9(1-3), 4-12. http://doi.org/10.1515/fabl.1967.9.1-3.4

Ricoeur, P. (1991). Narrative identity. *Philosophy Today*, 35(1), 73-81. http://doi.org/10.5840/philtoday199135136

Sweeney, T., Brown, E. and Burak, A. (2007). Peace Maker. Impact Games. Retrieved from http://peacemakergame.com

Swords, J., Nally, C., Rogage, K., Watson, R., Charlton, J. and Kirk, D. (2020). Colliding epistemologies, productive tensions and usable pasts in the generation of heritage-led immersive experiences. *International Journal of Heritage Studies*, 48(13), 1-14. http://doi.org/10.1080/13527258.2020.1780462

Wright, W. (2000). The Sims (video game). Redwood City, CA: Electronic Arts.

# Chapter
# 10

# Augmented Reality, Aura, and the Design of Cultural Spaces

**Hank Blumenthal[1] and Joshua A. Fisher[2]**

[1] Bowling Green State University, 369 Sycamore Glen Drive, Miamisburg, OH 45342
Email: hankblumenthal@gmail.com
[2] Columbia College Chicago, 916 S Wabash, Chicago, IL 60605
Email: jofisher@colum.edu

The use of Augmented Reality (AR) technologies in museums and cultural locations has accelerated (Hammady, 2016, Haahr, 2017). Early AR technology implemented decades ago (Blair MacIntyre et al., 1993) has given way to new tools for experiencing cultural heritage sites. AR enthusiasts see cultural heritage spaces as playgrounds for experimentation (Mäyrä, 2016; Choudary et al., 2009; Vlahakis et al., 2001). These experiments include, but are not limited to, *Jerusalem Awakes* at the 2000 year old Tower of David Museum (Blum, 2017) and The Smithsonian's AR exhibition of art from Burning Man that toured the United States ("Intel Is Bringing the Smithsonian's Burning Man Exhibit to Snapchat Using AR" 2018; Motsinger, 2019). However, these designers do not consider how adding AR media to a space might be changing the space's aura.

Aura, first defined by Walter Benjamin, is a unique phenomenological experience attached to perception and embedded within media artefacts. In the moment an artist perceives their subject and begins to mediate it through paints, clay, or any other medium they attempt to capture their subject's essence. This essence is connected to the artist's perception, mode of representation, and aesthetic inclination. Further, this act of representing a subject is situated within a specific time and place that can be felt by the artist and later by a viewer. In his initial discussion of aura, Benjamin relates this anecdote about being on top of a mountain, "If, while resting on a summer afternoon, you follow with your eyes a mountain range on the horizon or a branch which casts its shadow over you, you experience the aura of those mountains, of that branch (Benjamin, 1968)". An artist, sketching this same scene, attempts to represent this aura. Further, the act of sketching the subject of the mountain range or branch, creates an aura by itself. Attempting to represent aura is auratic in its own right. This has particular consequences for AR in relation to cultural heritage sites (Benjamin, 1968). As designers and developers attempt to use AR on site, they alter the aura of that site through a user's mediated visit and the situated AR content.

Pokémon Go is an illustrative, and at this point canonical example, of AR's capacity for altering a public space's aura by situating location-based AR gameplay. The utilization of the physical and communal space to create a Pokémon Go hotspot, known as a gym, connects with Benjamin's warning, "Every day the urge grows stronger to get hold of an object at very close range by way of its likeness, its reproduction (Benjamin 1968)." In line with his observation, the authors recognize that through the reproduction of historical sites or moments in AR, designers and developers claim that the technology brings us closer to the past or makes the past more current. However, the authors are in agreement with other scholars who have noted that this fundamentally changes the aura of these spaces (Bolter et al., 2008; MacIntyre, Bolter and Gandy, 2004; J. Fisher, 2019). Once digital material is situated within these cultural places their originating aura is negotiated by the users onsite, the designers and developers offsite, as well as the historicity and physical materiality of the space. A grave site might be turned into a place to catch a Pokémon, a dangerous biking path may become a gamified race, and a historical financial district may become a protest site. The mediation and subsequent mechanical reproduction of the spaces is their transformation from historical, culturally critical spaces for the public into art or artefacts for consumption. However, since aura is a design affordance of AR, it can be plied by developers in a way that is not detrimental to a cultural heritage site.

By examining various design strategies, the utility of AR for aura in public spaces can be uncovered. Different spaces and artefacts require designs respectful of an originating aura, but these methods vary depending on the considerations and content of the space. There is an inherent paradox expressed between the aura in the mechanically generated reproduction of a space as public art and its historical aura. Aura in AR design utilizes duality as a framing paradox. That is, the negotiation of an aura occurs through AR content and the original aura of a space. What results in the tension between the two is a negotiated aura that can be explored, designed, and critiqued through design methods.

## Augmented Reality's Problematic Connection to Aura

Walter Benjamin's use of the term aura signified cultural infusions into an artefact beyond its material or aesthetic qualities to establish the primacy of the original. He declared:

> Even the most perfect reproduction of a work of art lacks in one element: its presence in time and space, its unique existence at the place where it happens to be. This unique existence of the work of art determined the history to which it was subject throughout its existence. This includes the changes that it may have suffered in physical condition over the years and the various changes in its ownership. The traces of the first can be revealed only by chemical or physical analyzes which it is impossible to perform on a reproduction; changes of ownership are subject to a tradition which must be traced from the situation of the original.

The original piece's perceived authenticity, cultural value, and political considerations are part of its aura. An example for Benjamin was a statue of Venus that had changed in meaning and value since antiquity when it was first created. In his time, it was mass produced. Each mechanically reproduced version of Venus lacked the verve of the original and it seemed divorced from its sculptor's hand. Benjamin suggested that technologies used by artists for creation were becoming a wedge between them and their works. He believed that in this way technologies of reproduction and distribution were changing the field of art. The reproduction of art through printing, reproductions, and cinema was exasperating for Benjamin. He believed that in each reproduced artefact, the reality of the original interpretation was at stake and this had social and ideological consequences. With this in mind, this essay celebrates what Benjamin said, "The presence of the original is the prerequisite to the concept of authenticity."

Regarding ruins and historical sites, how AR can add meaning or expand the aura of a space is complicated. Greek and Roman ruins, which are in fragments and lacking their colors, are often barren of context though still redolent with aura. When originally discovered without paint, an aesthetic of whiteness and purity was extolled by scholars and tourists until the existence of color-detection methods revealed the structures' original vivid colors and changed our modern view of them (Panzanelli et al., 2008). AR, as a technology, can change our perspectives in similarly unexpected ways. For example, take the famous Percy Shelley poem *Ozymandias*:

I met a traveller from an antique land
Who said: Two vast and trunkless legs of stone
Stand in the desert. Near them, on the sand,
Half sunk, a shattered visage lies, whose frown,
And wrinkled lip, and sneer of cold command,
Tell that its sculptor well those passions read
Which yet survive, stamped on these lifeless things,
The hand that mocked them and the heart that fed:
And on the pedestal these words appear:
'My name is Ozymandias, king of kings:
Look on my works, ye Mighty, and despair!'
Nothing beside remains. Round the decay
Of that colossal wreck, boundless and bare
The lone and level sands stretch far away.

The emotional impact of Shelley's poem is situated within the absence of Ozymandias' empire. It is not there—it has been buried by sand. The ravaging effects of time on the imagined empire are presented for the reader. Ozymandias' inscription "Look on my works, ye Mighty, and despair!" rings tragically in the empty desert. This fictional space has a strong aura, one that can be felt in any ruin of a cultural site that has been touched by time and altered. This aura has cultural and historical value. However, if an AR reconstruction of Ozymandias' "works" was rendered on site, in front of the viewer, the aura of the space would be altered. Whether or not a user would "despair" more or less upon seeing the original space is debatable and worth greater exploration.

Looking at specific use cases at museums and public cultural heritage sites provides insights on how aura is already being modified. For example, in a museum, visitors listen to taped information about an artist and his painting. Their experience of the painting is altered and so too is its aura. Aura becomes mediated between the painting's original aura, the user's perception of that piece, and how that perception is altered by the synthesis of the audio narration. Another example, the Roman Forum, might have its aura enhanced or diminished—its historical aesthetic of ruins—once it is enmeshed with technological and contemporary cultural forces. The cultural heritage site might have its aura bolstered by the real time rendering of intact structures and past peoples' actions. The aesthetic and design choices that impact aura are complex and their consequences not immediately perceptible.

## Existing Discussions of Aura and Augmented Reality

Professors Jay Bolter and Blair MacIntyre of the Georgia Institute of Technology examined and applied auratic thinking to guide their AR research over a decade before the technology was readily available. In 2004, they began to explore aura as a design affordance while building a prototype for the famous Oakland Cemetery in Atlanta, Georgia (MacIntyre et al., 2004). The experience allowed users to tour the cemetery and see the historical connections of the spaces through stories retold by historical characters superimposed on the spaces. They asserted that "An [Mixed Reality] application can exploit aura to make the user's experience more compelling or educationally rewarding." The experience retains its uniqueness and presence. They noted, "First, aura arises from the significant historical, cultural and personal aspects of a place or object, in contrast to the more generic social and cultural constructions associated with all instances of the place or object. Second, aura is a relationship between a person and the place or object—media experiences do not in general have aura, but can leverage or enhance the aura a person feels (MacIntyre et al., 2004)." In these ways AR can complement and enrich users' responses.

In the article *Crisis of AR*, Bolter and MacIntyre delve into the complexity and evolution of the term and how it applies to AR and mediation in general (Bolter et al., 2008). They noted that "In digital media, like film and television, the aura has become a design parameter. Designers can decide whether to cast a certain experience as auratic or not (Bolter, 2006)." However, they point out that this overlay of mechanical and reproducible technologies can both destroy aura, or enhance it as Benjamin proposed. "New media maintain aura in a permanent state of oscillation or crisis, and this crisis is a key to understanding it." The understanding of this crisis was the tension felt between the physical aura of the space and the augmented aura onsite. They do not place value to the design choice in this crisis but instead elevate its neutrality. Bolter and MacIntyre recognize that the preservation or decay of a physical space's aura is a unique design decision, which AR designers and developers must engage in to the experience's advantage. The pursuit of either the originating aura or an augmented one is an aesthetic decision.

In previous work, Joshua A. Fisher believes that such aesthetic choices have ethical consequences. He has discussed the preservation, decay, and alteration of aura in relation to dark tourism sites through XR with Jay Bolter and Sarah Schoemann (Joshua A. Fisher and Schoemann, 2018; J.A. Fisher and Bolter, 2018). In the paper with Bolter, Fisher discusses this in relation to the ethical use of AR on site. In relation to AR, where the spectacle of the medium may literally occlude the original site, Fisher and Bolter encourage the use of,

> two design strategies, which the authors have called 'transparency' and 'hypermediation'. Transparency enhances aura by making the interface of AR as inconspicuous as possible; hypermediation calls aura into question by emphasizing the mediated nature of the experience. This dual nature of aura is also discussed in regards to dark tourism sites. These places are particularly auratic due to the tragic uniqueness of calamity. As such, there is an understandable sensitivity to facilitating tours at all.

They conclude their paper by suggesting that there are some sites where the use of AR is generally not culturally or socially acceptable. Fisher and Schoemann address how the aura of dark sites is often conspicuously absent from experiences in VR. Fisher uses the strategies of transparency and hyper mediation here as well but recognizes that they have different consequences.

> In VR, a user's perception of a place's aura is mediated by strategies of transparency and hypermediation. Transparency enhances aura by removing the interface of VR. Certainly, the darker tourism trips to concentration camps and other sites rely on transparency to enhance the aura for the user. Hypermediation on the other hand, calls into question the VR dark site by emphasizing the mediated nature of what the user is experiencing. […] In VR, the use of hypermediation strategies may result in billboards, games, offensive content or even advertisements. These will alter the perceived aura of the site, perhaps belittling it.

In the co-author's previous work, Fisher drew attention to two broad design strategies and how they might be used to ethically integrate XR into the site. However, he did not put forward models for the utility of aura for other designers. Instead, in both papers, he and his colleagues only presented general ethical guidelines for XR. Accordingly, three different strategies for constructively using the crisis of aura with AR are now put forth. In cultural spaces, AR can facilitate either reenactments or performances to enhance information and promote engagement. This may be information that diminishes the sense of aura, or it could be part of a narrative situated within the space that can strengthen it.

## Design Models for the Constructive Use of AR and Aura at Historical Sites

Building upon the work of Bolter, MacIntyre, Fisher, and Schoemann the following design models are put forward: reconstructions, historical overlays, and interactive storytelling. These design models are not inclusive of every potential AR experience but address many of their foundational features. Each of these models can be used synchronously.

## Augmented Reality Reconstructions

Reconstructions of architectural objects that no longer exist, exist partially, or can be better envisioned with additional augmented photos or videos can enrich the cultural space by showing their historical context. Further, other historical perspectives that may have been lost can be presented. Just as history is negotiated and tied to politics, so too are architectural reconstructions of ruins and lost spaces. Critically, this means that these AR reconstructions do not restore a lost aura but present a contemporary and constructed representation as having a historical aura. Due to the temporal and spatial constraints of Benjamin's aura, the past aura is always unattainable. However, AR designers can rhetorically use the physical ruins of a space to claim the restoration of an aura.

For an AR experience at Fort Meigs Historic Site in Ohio, developed with the Virtual and Augmented Environments Lab at Bowling Green State University, a reconstruction method was used. This is shown in Figure 10.1. Seeing parts of the fort in operation complements the aura of the place. Some examples, such as the reconstructions in Jerusalem of two-millennia old and destroyed buildings, can have a powerful auratic affect. The JFK Museum created an AR app that worked at the museum and off site as well to show the size of the Apollo rockets and their journey to the moon ("JFK Library Launches AR Recreation of Apollo 11 Mission in Celebration of 50th Anniversary of Moon Landing | JFK Library" n.d.). None of these recreate the lost aura of the space or objects in their own situated historical moment but frame a contemporary aura as historic.

**Figure 10.1:** A historical reconstruction of Fort Meigs' Barracks in augmented reality

## Historical Augmented Reality Overlays

Historical Overlays provide a greater depth of information that help define the cultural space. At Gettysburg, amateur AR apps show,the movement of military forces throughout the battle in large primitive blocks ("R/USCivilWar – Gettysburg Augmented Reality Tour App Available" n.d.; *Gettysburg Augmented Reality Mobile Tour* 2019). The crude abstractions employed can interfere with the historical aura but are valued by some users for their explanatory utility. This visualization is equivalent to the graphics superimposed on the field during a football game. The graphics can be very informative at home but are not welcomed by viewers of the game where the aura of attendance is critical to the aesthetic enjoyment of the experience.

Historical overlays can add to the feeling of place and immersion through the integration of historicity. However, linking information to physical spaces can break the sense of place through hypermediation. Each new level of information, design, and visualization interferes with immersion. It may be fascinating to see the abstract movement of forces and the biographies of individuals on the battlefield of Gettysburg, but it interrupts the space's aura with data visualizations. However, artistic expressions can incorporate informational elements into a coherent narrative.

## Interactive Storytelling with Augmented Reality

An evolving use of AR for historical and cultural locations is to create a narrative that explains what has happened at that site (Hammady, Ma and Temple, 2016; "Holocaust Memorial Museum Uses Augmented Reality to Make History Visceral", 2018; Haahr, 2017). Sometimes those narratives are about historical characters or past events (Haahr, 2015). These interactive storytelling experiences might adhere to a dramatic telling model, whether journalistic or otherwise, for a specific application (Azuma, 2015). It can either enhance or disrupt the aura of the space, depending on the application and its design.

While cultural locations are socially viewed as static artefacts, they are full of implicit historical stories and social connections that create their aura. AR can make the aura manifest for the users through a narrative structure, with its story, characters, events, and drama. It can be structured to engage an audience emotionally. Storytelling can be used as a memory construct to enhance retention and aura. In the Oakwood Cemetery project discussed earlier, the AR was animated by the stories of deceased individuals.

# Examples of AR Applications Engaging with Aura

Experimentation with AR for historical spaces to communicate narrative and historical context through visual and aural mediations are now commonplace. Examples include the Westwood Project, Wither et al. (2010), Bram Stoker's Vampires (Haahr, 2017), The Oakwood Cemetery (Bolter et al., 2008), and others.

## The Westwood Experience: Reconstructions, Historical Overlays, and Interactive Narrative

The Westwood Experience (Wither et al., 2010) was a narrative AR project told from the perspective of the mayor of Westwood. The experience was run in 2009 and 2010 using mobile computers to merge video and other assets with real locations to give a culturally informative and entertaining tour. The presence of the spaces was maintained while actors provided context.

Starting at a theater, the users meet an actor portraying the mayor who introduces them to a story told along a journey. Users are presented with visualizations and auditory augmentations at historical locations they visit. They are introduced to a mysterious character central to the story's unfolding in 1949. Along the journey, they stop at augmented locations that are significant to the mysterious person's life. For example, a ring is purchased and a taxi is seen disappearing with the character alive for the last time (Azuma, 2015).

This revelation occurs at the final location. Users finish the tour at the resting place of Marilyn Monroe, at her crypt, a place of aura. The final narration knits feeling, place, and augmented aura into a personal introduction:

> She became what she said she would, a movie star...In the end, Norma came back to Westwood too. She's between engagements now, 'resting' as actors sometime say. She's not alone, but among many others, some who lived their lives as publicly as she did, many of their names once as familiar as hers. I come to see her every so often, as many others do. I'm taking you to her now. I know you'll be mindful of the customs proper to the place we find her, a place of real people and real endings (Azuma, 2015).

This project illustrated how the technical affordances of AR and a compelling narrative can be intertwined to produce a very positive response in audiences.

## Historical Reconstructions

Visual reconstructions of historical buildings were used to superimpose static outlines of older images on the present space. Videos also mediated the environment. The Westwood project prototyped different types of media in a narrative story. Different forms of media, such as still imagery versus video, had unique impacts on the aura of spaces.

## Historical Overlays

Historical overlays were limited to audio and some visualizations of the location. These overlays animated ordinary places that did not have an obvious aura, with the exception of Monroe's crypt, and some locations that were historically significant because they still existed in a changing city. The additional information expanded the sense of aura by providing access to a greater depth of knowledge. It elevated the unique details of the tour stops in a temporal and cultural context.

## Interactive Narrative

The AR narrative is a significant design element that leverages physical space (H. Blumenthal and Xu, 2012; H. Blumenthal, 2016). The added production quality of audio narratives encouraged the creation of a mythic web that constituted an aura through an effective narrative strategy. As the story converges around Marilyn Monroe and her crypt, the aura of the narrative and the physical locations fall into synch. This interactive approach with virtual overlays and characters amplifies the aura of a place through enriched, situated interactions that are connected to narrative emotions.

## Bram Stoker's Vampires: Historical Overlays and Interactive Storytelling

Bram Stoker's Vampires (Haahr, 2017) was a project by Mads Haahr and other researchers using an AR platform they created at Trinity College called Haunted Planet (Haahr, 2017). They developed the platform to engage in research using AR to enhance cultural places around the college and the city of Dublin (Nisi et al., 2006). These areas already have a rich history. Haunted Planet published three games exploring the relationship between cultural heritage and AR experiences. Touring around historic districts allowed a GPS navigation system to recognize a spot and trigger a video, audio, or game experience. Each asset was part of a narrative that was culturally informational. The locations were spaces that have historical significance and aura. *Bram Stoker's Vampires* won multiple game industry awards and showed how audience engagement through mediated dual presence was enhanced (Haahr, 2017). Not surprisingly, the design of appropriate interactions situated onsite through AR was a significant design consideration. The need to, "explore the best design practices for locative games that can help create a feeling of immersion into a site's cultural content without losing a sense of presence in the cultural space (Haahr, 2017)" was realized. The additional cultural content is the AR and the presence, or aura, resides in the physical location.

### Historical Overlays

*Bram Stoker's Vampires* was an AR game that involved a nonlinear narrative tour around spots where Bram Stoker was known to visit when he was a student. At the same time the narrative focused on interacting with the fictional characters of Stoker's book and not his historical personage. The historical presence of Bram Stoker at the game site, Trinity College, added to the aura already present and reified.

### Interactive Storytelling

The additional layer of fictional aura sets up a new way to explore these design characteristics of aura. The paradox of the invoked physical and narratological auras presents a unique potential crisis of AR's superimposition on a cultural location. This is not a narrative reinforcement of nonfiction and historical content as reviewed previously in the Westwood Project with Marilyn Monroe. *Bram Stoker's Vampires* uses an AR that inserts an aura of fictional provenance as a way of creating an incentive to take a tour of historical locations. In turn, the balance between cultural heritage site and site as an artefact for the consumption of entertainment is blurred. This is a negotiation of the site's aura that does not expand the historicity of it, while not diminishing the physical space.

## The Holocaust Museum Memorial Uses Historical Overlays and Interactive Storytelling

The U.S. Holocaust Memorial Museum launched an Aurasma based AR app that provided visitors with additional information about a wall of photographs ("Holocaust

Memorial Museum Uses Augmented Reality to Make History Visceral", 2018; "Aurasma", 2019). By launching the Holocaust Museum's branded app in a specific exhibit after downloading it, the application could recognize photos as markers and trigger additional information.

Most of the additional information was biographical and text based. The AR included names, dates, and personal stories connected to pictures of victims and survivors. "This initiative aims to make Holocaust history relevant, engaging and personal for visitors, especially youth who are developing different expectations for their Museum visit compared to other generations," said Michael Haley Goldman, the museum's director of future projects, in a statement. "We're exploring how to use this technology appropriately in a memorial and a museum such as ours that deals with a difficult history. We're also interested in whether participants think this is a worthwhile addition to their visitor experience ("Holocaust Memorial Museum Uses Augmented Reality to Make History Visceral", 2018)."

As Fisher has noted, this experience is a form of Dark Tourism that is removed from the physical location of death, suffering, and tragedy. As such, it does not contain the originating and historical auras of concentration camps and other dark sites across Europe. That said, the Holocaust Museum in D.C., like so many others, attempts to recreate these sites within its walls in order to present the scale and tragedy of the genocide. The intention is not to create a memento mori, but instead a moment for collective remembrance. This communal effort is auratic in its own right even as it is disconnected from the originating sites of pain and suffering.

### Historical Overlays as Interactive Storytelling

The D.C. exhibit was almost all AR overlays of text. The physical aspect, and the photos had some aura insomuch as they were connected to a real historical tragedy that occurred. The vast number of photos displayed had an aura collectively, but not as individual artefacts. The textual augmentation of names, and the act of naming, brought the power of aura to the individual humanity of each person which was rectified. Second level interactions told a brief history of the person. The AR application created aura where there was very little through the layering of historical biographical information. No longer a set of photos, the AR biographical information creates a set of historical people who lived, suffered, and had their lives tragically cut short. Through the AR app, users were invited to fill that space with a richer meaning and consequently a stronger aura.

## The Fort Meigs Project Uses Interactive Storytelling, Historical Overlays, and Reconstructions

The Fort Meigs AR experience was a prototyping project worked on at Bowling Green State University as part of a Virtual and Augmented Environments Lab and a few students in an AR/VR course over two years. Several versions of the project were done on multiple AR platforms, including HP Reveal/Aurasma, Blippar, and Unity. Special historical reenactment events occurred twice a year at the fort and the

AR technology allowed for an engagement with rich media, storytelling, and greater depth of resources that sought to enhance those experiences. The entire experience was meant to consist of 15 to 25 AR scenes.

In this instance, the design for the specific site attempted to convey current historical understandings without adopting an ideological or a critical analysis of the site. This is not to say these sites are not redolent with cultural discourses related to often inaccurate historical stories, mythic constructions, and contemporary social bias. In the case of Ft. Meigs and other notable battles in the region with the Native Americans, many of the towns, streets, and malls are named after battles and individuals. However, understanding the historical significance of these names is lost along with their aura. This project sought to engage and elevate the historical aura through AR design considerations.

### Interactive Storytelling

At various locations within the fort, details of its construction and the personal stories of soldiers were meant to be presented by an augmented character. The main narrator of the experience was supposed to be Eleazar Wood, who was the engineer overseeing the construction of Fort Meigs. This narrative was constructed to add aura to the experience. The character is derived from nonfiction material and data instead of a mythology. This design choice was made to establish the historicity of the experience.

Both officers' and soldiers' tents on site provided insight into the daily lives of both groups. In a soldiers' tent, the AR experience was meant to describe the cramped conditions and the daily routine of the men regarding camp work and drilling. Additional details, such as how a man's wife, if accompanying her husband, would have to share the same tent with her husband's bunkmates, was also meant to be presented. This is a new aura that conflicts with existing understanding of life at the fort. There are stories that are only now beginning to be told. Their inclusion in reenactments changes the aura through new perspectives. AR afforded an efficient means to expand the aura of the existing locations even as they changed.

AR allowed for a broader perspective by showing what is invisible to visitors or only available on specific days. It provides additional historical context that enhances aura even in the presence of reproduction. Each individual can shape his or her perspective by interacting with the experiences in uniquely. Different paths are available through the fort, and a diversity of points of view can be accommodated. Each of these unique user flows creates its own aura at the site. They become active in their creation of belief and understanding of the site's history.

### Historical Overlays

One student designed a tour focused on the site's contemporary Veterans Memorial and its construction. This set of videos and illustrations educates visitors on the topic of stone crafting. Stone monuments are a specific tool to unite memory and place in a permanent and enduring aura. This prototype illustrated that monument aura can be maintained through AR even as it diminishes over time. The medium facilitates an enriched memory and reinforces political significance.

Other students focused on visualizing the battle. Some of the amateur work that has been done at Gettysburg shows the deployment and movement of troops. Since the battle is the primary interest for some visitors, an interactive AR experience, or one that links to other more detailed information on that topic, is compelling.

### Historical Reconstructions

One historical reconstruction was an AR video of a reenactor's setup of a tent line at the Fort; it includes information on the everyday experience of the common soldier. This everyday soldier experience threaded through the augmented reconstruction to create an aura of an ordinary serviceman.

In another section, earthworks were meant to be recreated in AR. During the First Siege of Fort Meigs, British artillery continuously bombarded the fort for five days. The earthworks visitors see are remnants of fortifications created by the soldiers to protect themselves and the camp from this bombardment. The earthworks have been wearing down over the past two centuries and have not been rebuilt to their full height. In some areas, the earthworks measured nearly twenty feet high ("Fort Meigs" n.d.). Seeing earthworks at scale in AR instead of in their reduced situation is more impressive than accurate. However, the reconstruction can improve the sense of place even if it smudges the historical aura.

## Conclusion: Future of Augmented Reality in Cultural Locations

AR is being applied and prototyped increasingly by museums and other cultural locations. The presented models are foundational to how designers and developers can engage with the aura of these places. The models place a burden on the designer to understand how they are using or changing auratic engagement in ideological or cultural ways on the site. Recognizing the phenomenological crisis that occurs as designers displace the physical world with a mediated overlay is a caveat to the perceived technological and financial imperative to add media to museums and cultural institutions. The goal is to engage with a site's aura without diminishing its historical and cultural relevance.

## Putting it into Practice: Designing for Aura

Designing for aura at a historical or cultural location is a multi-step design process. First you need to do your research. This means more than consulting histories and individuals—you need to discover new perspectives and also assess how the aura of the location has changed over time. The Ft. Meigs structure has been rebuilt twice and while the location is original little else is. The greater the aura, the more care needs to be shown not to block that original experience. Once you have collected enough historical and nonfiction material about the site, consider the tactics of transparency and hypermediation through the models of historical overlays, reconstructions, and interactive stories on site. Find ways to balance a respect for the originating historical aura and the augmented one. Use insights based on the examples presented in this paper to frame your work.

# References

Aurasma (2019). *In*: Wikipedia. https://en.wikipedia.org/w/index.php?title=Aurasma&old id=920724441.

Azuma, Ronald (2015). Location-Based Mixed and Augmented Reality Storytelling. *Fundamentals of Wearable Computers and Augmented Reality*, 2nd Edition. pp. 259-276. CRC Press.

Benjamin, Walter (1968). *Illuminations*. 1st ed. New York: Harcourt, Brace & World.

Blair, MacIntyre, Jay David Bolter, Emmanuel Moreno and Brendan Hannigan (1993). Augmented Reality as a New Media Experience. pp. 197-206. *In*: Proceedings IEEE and ACM International Symposium on Augmented Reality. 10.1109/ISAR.2001.970538.

Blum, Brian (2017). Ancient and Augmented Reality Meet in Jerusalem. ISRAEL21c. October 24, 2017. https://www.israel21c.org/ancient-and-augmented-reality-meet-in-jerusalem/.

Blumenthal, H. and Xu, Y. 2012. The Ghost Club Storyscape: Designing for Transmedia Storytelling. *IEEE Transactions on Consumer Electronics*, 58(2), 190-196. https://doi. org/10.1109/TCE.2012.6227412.

Blumenthal, Henry (Hank). 2016. Storyscape, a New Medium of Media. March. https:// smartech.gatech.edu/handle/1853/54989.

Bolter, Jay David (2006). New Media and the Permanent Crisis of Aura. *Convergence*, 12(1), 21-39.

Bolter, Jay David, Blair MacIntyre, Maribeth Gandy, Petra Schweitzer and Jürgen Müller (2008). Benjamin's Crisis of Aura and Digital Media. pp. 87–99. Nodus Publikationen.

Choudary, Omar, Vincent Charvillat, Romulus Grigoras and Pierre Gurdjos (2009). MARCH: Mobile Augmented Reality for Cultural Heritage. *In*: Proceedings of the 17th ACM International Conference on Multimedia, 1023-1024. MM '09. New York, NY, USA: Association for Computing Machinery. https://doi.org/10.1145/1631272.1631500.

Fisher, J.A. and J. David Bolter (2018). Ethical Considerations for AR Experiences at Dark Tourism Sites. 2018 IEEE International Symposium on Mixed and Augmented Reality Adjunct (ISMAR-Adjunct), 365-369.

Fisher, Joshua (2019). Interactive Non-Fiction with Reality Media: Rhetorical Affordances. https://doi.org/10.13140/RG.2.2.30163.63527.

Fisher, Joshua A. and Sarah Schoemann (2018). Toward an Ethics of Interactive Storytelling at Dark Tourism Sites in Virtual Reality. pp. 577-590. *In*: Rebecca Rouse, Hartmut Koenitz and Mads Haahr (eds.). Interactive Storytelling. Cham: Springer International Publishing.

Fort Meigs. n.d. Accessed August 10, 2020. http://touringohio.com/history/fort-meigs-history. html.

*Gettysburg Augmented Reality Mobile Tour*. 2019. https://www.youtube.com/watch?v=a4akH zNQjB8&feature=youtu.be.

Haahr, Mads (2015). Literary Play: Locative Game Mechanics and Narrative Techniques for Cultural Heritage. https://doi.org/10.1007/978-3-319-19126-3_10.

Haahr, Mads (2017). Creating Location-Based Augmented-Reality Games for Cultural Heritage. *In*: MacIntyre, Blair, et al. Augmented reality as a new media experience. Proceedings IEEE and ACM International Symposium on Augmented Reality. IEEE, 2001. Serious Games: Third Joint International Conference, JCSG 2017, Valencia, Spain,

November 23-24, 2017, pp. 313-318. Valencia, Spain. https://doi.org/10.1007/978-3-319-70111-0_29.

Hammady, Ramy, Minhua Ma and Nicholas Temple (2016). Augmented Reality and Gamification in Heritage Museums. pp. 181-187. *In*: Tim Marsh, Minhua Ma, Manuel Fradinho Oliveira, Jannicke Baalsrud Hauge and Stefan Göbel (eds.). *Serious Games*. Cham: Springer International Publishing.

Holocaust Memorial Museum Uses Augmented Reality to Make History Visceral (2018). *Venture Beat* (blog). August 31, 2018. https://venturebeat.com/2018/08/31/holocaust-memorial-museum-uses-augmented-reality-to-make-history-visceral/.

Intel Is Bringing the Smithsonian's Burning Man Exhibit to Snapchat Using AR (2018). August 24, 2018. https://www.adweek.com/brand-marketing/the-smithsonian-is-bringing-its-burning-man-exhibit-to-snapchat-with-an-augmented-reality-tour/.

JFK Library Launches AR Recreation of Apollo 11 Mission in Celebration of 50th Anniversary of Moon Landing | JFK Library. n.d. Accessed August 5, 2020. https://www.jfklibrary.org/about-us/news-and-press/press-releases/jfk-library-launches-ar-recreation-of-apollo-11-mission.

MacIntyre, Blair, Jay David Bolter and Maribeth Gandy (2004). Presence and the Aura of Meaningful Places. *In*: 7th Annual International Workshop on Presence (Presence 2004) Proceedings Presence 2004, 36-43.

Mäyrä, Frans (2016). Pokémon GO: Entering the Ludic Society. *Mobile Media & Communication*, 5(1), 47-50. https://doi.org/10.1177/2050157916678270.

Motsinger, Carol (2019). Burning Man Exhibit May Be the Most Jaw-Dropping Show at the Cincinnati Art Museum. *The Enquirer*. May 22, 2019. https://www.cincinnati.com/story/entertainment/2019/04/22/burning-man-cincinnati-art-museum-why-to-go/3522633002/.

Murray, Janet H. (1998). *Hamlet on the Holodeck: The Future of Narrative in Cyberspace*. Cambridge, Mass: MIT Press.

Nisi, Valentina, Ian Oakley and Mads Haahr (2006). Inner City Locative Media: Design and Experience of a Location-Aware Mobile Narrative for the Dublin Liberties Neighborhood. *Intelligent Agent*, 6.

Panzanelli, R., Schmidt, E.D., Lapatin, K.D.S., Brinkmann, V., Paul Getty Museum, J., Ostergaard, J.S., Getty Research Institute, Collareta, M. and Potts, A. (2008). *The Color of Life: Polychromy in Sculpture from Antiquity to the Present*. J. Paul Getty Museum. https://books.google.com/books?id=2gQesgryr8oC.

R/USCivilWar - Gettysburg Augmented Reality Tour App Available. n.d. Reddit. Accessed August 11, 2020. https://www.reddit.com/r/USCivilWar/comments/b65nnl/gettysburg_augmented_reality_tour_app_available/.

Vlahakis Vassilios, John Karigiannis, Manolis Tsotros, Michael Gounaris, Luis Almeida, Didier Stricker, Tim Gleue, et al. 2001. Archeoguide: First Results of an Augmented Reality, Mobile Computing System in Cultural Heritage Sites. *Virtual Reality, Archeology, and Cultural Heritage* 9(10.1145): 584993-585015.

Wither, J., Allen, R., Samanta, V., Hemanus, J., Tsai, Y., Azuma, R., Carter, W., Hinman, R. and Korah, T. (2010). The Westwood Experience: Connecting Story to Locations via Mixed Reality. 2010 IEEE International Symposium on Mixed and Augmented Reality – Arts, Media, and Humanities, 39-46.

# Chapter

# 11

# Building a Virtuous Cycle of Activism Using Art and Augmented Reality: A Community of Practice-Based Project

**Janíce Tisha Samuels[1] and Kelvin Ramirez[2]**

[1] Pepperdine University Graduate School of Education and Psychology,
6100 Center Drive, Los Angeles, CA 90045
Email: janice@nationalyouthartmovement.org
[2] Lesley UniversityDepartment of Expressive Arts Therapies, 29 Everett Street,
Cambridge, MA 02138
Email: kramirez@lesley.edu

## Introduction

The concept of holding space has multiple connotations. In a physical sense, it means to literally be present in a space. Conversely, in the field of Psychology, the space in reference is the mind and the act of holding, a suspension of judgement paired with the willingness to be a compassionate witness to the needs of others (Flax, 2011; Kim, 2019). In either of these contexts, holding space is critical to marginalized groups. Mixed reality (MR) technologies uniquely provide emerging affordances for holding space in both a physical and mental context that can benefit marginalized groups (Fisher et al., 2018; Marín Diaz, 2017; Poretski et al., 2019).

Marginalization is an oppressive practice that relegates a person or group of people to a position of powerlessness within society. When a population is marginalized, they are "systematically prevented from accessing opportunities and resources that are normally available to others, and critical for them to reach their full potential and become contributing members of society" (Iwasaki et al., 2014, p. 317).

A number of social justice projects have used MR technologies to bring the issues of the marginalized to the mainstream and to incite social change in collaboration with marginalized communities (Ferilli et al., 2016; Graham et al., 2013; Hidalgo, 2015; Marin Diaz, 2017; Skwarek, 2018; Thiel, 2004). Notable among these projects is Mark Skwarek's use of Augmented Reality (AR) to circumvent a blockade by police to place thousands of protestors in front of the New York Stock Exchange for an Occupy the Wall Street protest. It was a crucial moment for the movement and its members who claimed economic oppression by the 1% who possess a significant percentage of the world's wealth (Massey and Snyder, 2012; Skwarek, 2018). Also, using MR technology to place people in critical spaces, Tamiko Thiel's "Beyond Manzanar," a virtual reality historical re-enactment of becoming imprisoned in the U.S. in a Japanese Internment camp, created an interactive learning experience at the Museum of Art in San Jose, California that gave visitors the space to fully imagine the personal and cultural impact of state-sanctioned violence on people of foreign descent in the U.S. (Gessner, 2016; Smith, 2010; Thiel, 2004). Furthermore, Leigh Anna Hidalgo integrated the interactivity of AR into the Latino cultural phenomena of fotonovelas, a long-held tradition of translating popular films (and later original content) into printed pamphlets (Hidalgo, 2015; Hidalgo, 2017). Like Thiel's "Beyond Manzanar," Hidalgo's Augmented Fotonovelas provide a counter-narrative to mainstream perspectives of minority cultures. Hildalgo has intentionally collaborated with the Latino community to develop these narratives to protest legislation that supports racial-profiling (for example, Arizona State Bill 1070) and to inform the community and the public of unequal access to formal banking institutions in Latino communities (Hidalgo, 2011; Hidalgo, 2015). In their use of MR technologies to hold space for marginalized groups, all of these projects provide an entry point into a kind of public pedagogy of the oppressed, which re-envisions the artists as educators and their art as sociopolitical tools for a process of place-making that demands the recognition of the marginalized and that offers a shared and/or collaborative learning experience that is liberarory (Freire, 1970; Schuermans et al., 2012).

Also centered on liberatory forms of social engagement and public acts of resistance through tech-enabled learning experiences, the focus of this chapter is on the development and implementation of the National Youth Art Movement Against Gun Violence (NYAM) project, an out-of-school-time program (OST program) developed in Chicago whose mission is to raise marginalized youth to the position of thought leaders on gun reform using art and AR. Youth under the age of 18 are a marginalized population due to state and federal laws and institutional rules that limit their autonomy, which contributes to a lack of legitimate recourse and vulnerability for youth to social and political injustices (Besley, 2010; Giroux, 2009; Simpson, 2018). Prior to the Black Lives Matter and March for Our Lives movements, the marginalization of youth at state and national-levels of leadership for gun reform, largely rendered this population silent and dependent on adults (Cottle, 2018; Parsons et al., 2018). Stereotypes of youth legitimize their marginalization as leaders and treatment as a population in institutional governance practices and policies (Giroux, 2009; Simpson, 2018; Youth Speak Out Coalition, 2007). NYAM challenges mainstream perceptions of youth and gun violence by using their art and AR experiences to create physical and virtual sites of interactive informal learning that provide counter-narratives. Unfettered by the oppressive structures of traditional education, as an OST program, NYAM provides youth with the freedom to take on new identities as leaders of a public pedagogy (Sandlin et al., 2011).

# Background

NYAM was designed as an OST program because the marginalization of youth begins in the education system. The governance structures of schools and school systems in the US have a continuing legacy of perpetuating inequality among students (Morgan, 2000; Stoll, 2013). This is because the public school experience in the US is not a universal one, but one that varies based on the income-levels of residents within a school district. Public education, which by law is compulsory for youth under the age of 18, "is paid for with the amount of money available in a district, which doesn't necessarily equal the amount of money required to adequately teach students" (Semuels, 2016, para 5). So, while youth below the age of 18 are required to attend school, state and local funding schemes for public schooling do not allow for equitable experiences. As a result of this variance, youth in low-income communities tend to be more marginalized than those from high income communities (Bloome et al., 2018). Research has shown that social economic status (SES) is a major predictor of educational success because of its correlation with the types of resources, opportunities, and even disciplinary measures experienced by students in schools (Garcia & Weiss, 2017).

Schools are not holding space for low-income students and youth of color (Giroux, 2009). Instead, these youth are disproportionately disciplined and continuously removed from schooling due to zero tolerance policies (Reyes, 2006; United States Commission on Civil Rights, 2019). Zero tolerance policies were initially developed and implemented in the 1980s to eliminate the use and fear of guns in schools, but later became applied at the discretion of administrators to anything deemed to be a weapon and for general issues of disobedience (American Psychological Association Zero Tolerance Task Force, 2008; Triplett et al., 2014). The implementation and expansion of zero tolerance policies in schools over the decades has had a continuing detrimental effect on the lives of students, and youth of color, in particular, who are disciplined in greater numbers, due to a lack of teacher preparation in classroom management (Vavrus and Cole, 2002), lack of training in culturally competent practices (Ferguson, 2001; Townsend, 2000), and an over reliance on disciplinary practices that conform with concepts of racial stereotyping (Bargh and Chartrand, 1999; Graham & Lowery, 2004).

Institutionalized inequities in governance has led schools to perform more like carceral spaces, for example, extensions of the prison industrial complex, rather than places of learning and growth (Meiners, 2010; Wun, 2018). When schools function as carceral spaces, punishment is prioritized over learning and youth are displaced from classrooms into the streets and the juvenile justice system. Youth who are displaced from schools and become justice-involved[1] experience higher rates of unemployment, higher levels of income inequality, and increased issues with mental and physical health over their lifetimes (Mendelson et al., 2018).

Research shows that when youth are included in governance decision-making in their classrooms and in their schools the use of disciplinary action and truancy is

---

[1] A person with a history of juvenile or adult offences within the criminal justice system.

reduced (McCluskey, 2012; Rennie Center for Education and Research Policy, 2019; Virginia Department of Education, 2005). However, despite the findings, instances of distributed leadership between youth and adults in school governance are few, especially at a systemic level (McCluskey, 2012). Beliefs about youth that are based on stereotypes contribute to their marginalization in governance structures (Giroux, 2009; Simpson, 2018). Stereotypes that youth are lazy, apathetic, needy and selfish abound in popular culture, the media, and in adult circles (Giroux, 2009; Simpson, 2018). These beliefs have been codified in governance structures at all levels, from the federal government to local organizations. The result is that youth are one of the most vulnerable and marginalized groups in the US due to a lack of representation in most governance structures and an inability to vote on representation at the federal level (Tilton, 2010). The right to vote and to be represented within the political system are part of the main privileges of US citizenship. While over the years the formerly enslaved, indigenous groups, and women have been extended these privileges, youth have never been considered full citizens due to age-restrictive policies that project youth as citizens in the making (Coady, 2014; Hart, 2008; Sarrica et al., 2010). The concept of youth as "citizens in the making" marginalizes and demeans their contributions to and capacity for impacting society at any age (Coady, 2014; Hart, 2008; Kennelly, 2011; Offerdahl, 2014; Tsekoura, 2016).

## From Marginalization to Youth Leadership

In and out of schools, youth are afforded limited pathways to legitimate leadership. In the same vein that youth are seen as "citizens in the making," leadership programs for youth are often created to support their development as "future leaders" (Camino and Zeldin, 2002; Charteris and Smardon, 2019; Iwaski et al., 2014; Kirshner, 2008; Mortensen et al., 2014). As such, youth leadership programs and opportunities have tended to provide superficial or practice-oriented activities, rather than providing youth with a platform for broad-based influence and decision-making power. "In a society where adults hold legitimate power and are ultimately responsible for decisions and actions, creating equitable power-sharing within the contexts of youth empowerment programs is a challenge" (Jennings et al., 2006, p. 44). This is particularly true within formal institutions like schools, whereas, more dynamic youth-adult partnership (Y-AP) models have grown in popularity in OST programs (Larson et al., 2005; Zeldin et al., 2013; Wu et al., 2016).

OST programs are educational programs that occur before and after school hours and during the summers. OST programs provide a mix of formal and informal learning opportunities for children and youth that are generally more youth directed and driven than classroom-based programming (Fredricks, 2011; Toldson and Lemmons, 2015; Youth Speak Out Coalition, 2007). Of these programs, social justice and participatory action research programming that fosters youth adult partnerships and the empowerment of youth voice are particularly centered on the development of authentic leadership pathways for youth (Carlson, 2005; Livingstone et al., 2014; London and Chabrán, 2004; Perri, 2007; Ross, 2017; Suess and Lewis, 2007; Wright, 2007).

As an OST program, NYAM sees its role as raising marginalized youth to the position of thought leaders on gun reform. NYAM's strategy for gun violence reduction is to strengthen youth capacity for activism and to bring youth influence to bear on perceptions of gun violence. To this end, NYAM selected five African American and Latino youth artists from a city-wide call for art in Chicago to create and broadcast their perspectives on the issue of gun violence in the form of 16 interactive artworks placed on commercial billboards. The billboard artworks were distributed across neighborhoods on the south and north west sides of the city and were interconnected into an experiential walking tour experience using the GPS-enabled storytelling app, Vamonde, which featured AR technology (Proboscis, 2019). NYAM utilized the immersive quality of AR to strengthen public connection to and understanding of the socio-political messaging within the artwork.

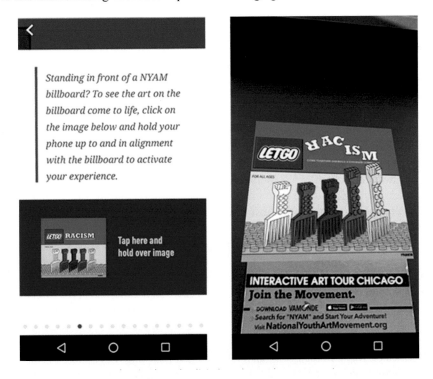

**Figure 11.1:** NYAM's In-App Augmented Reality directions and sample in-motion image[2]

# Education Workshops and Leadership Opportunities

In the spring of 2017, NYAM distributed a call-for-art to middle schools, high schools, colleges, and community groups in Chicago. The 200+ middle schools and high schools selected were participants in the Chicago Public Schools Department of

---

[2] *Letgo Racism* Artwork by Franco

Arts Education Art Liaisons program. Colleges and community groups who received the call-for-art were selected at random. NYAM received close to 50 submissions to their call-for-art. The submissions included both an original artwork and an essay by each youth artist explaining their intended message. The submitted artwork was evaluated by a small panel of judges (NYAM's executive director, its lead artist, and a college-enrolled art student) based on its use of color and symbols, creativity, public impact, technicality, and its ability to develop a meaningful and coherent narrative. The final selection of the artists to participate in the NYAM project were made based on their artwork being ranked as one of the highest scoring artworks among multiple judges' selections.

Youth whose artwork was selected were invited to become members of NYAM's Cohort 1, which required a two-year commitment to participating in educational and leadership opportunities and creating artwork for the purpose of promoting gun violence prevention. Cohort 1's work with NYAM kicked off with a series of five weekend workshops to prepare for the interactive art tour that provided formal learning opportunities in art technique and a study of the news media's depictions of gun violence in Chicago. Interpretation and analysis of news stories on gun violence provided a critical understanding of mainstream depictions of firearm-related homicides in different parts of the city (Leonard, 2016; Martin, 2013). These analyses led to intense discussions on bias and discrimination in depictions of gun violence in the media (Gruenwald et al., 2011; Johnson, 2009; Parham-Payne, 2014; Ross, 2019). As heavy consumers of media, it is important to "develop young people's critical awareness of how all authored texts (print, visual, and oral) situate them as readers, writers, and viewers within particular cultural and historical contexts," especially in the context of transformational learning (Alvermann, 2004, p. 78; Rogers, 2016).

To strengthen the learning, the workshops, and the entire NYAM project, were designed as a community of practice, a concept developed by educational theorists Jean Lave and Etienne Wenger that theorizes that when learning is situated within a community of practitioners, the learners advance in their expertise in the domain of interest as a result of "legitimate peripheral participation" (LPP) (Lave and Wenger, 1991). LPP occurs dynamically as newcomers to a community of practice are drawn deeper into a group's culture and engage in a process of co-construction in increasingly sophisticated ways. In their seminal book, *Situated Learning: Legitimate Peripheral Participation*, they note that traditional education espouses that the teacher bestows knowledge on the learner, but in their observations the process of learning is socially constructed, and, as such, often negotiated and mediated through the tools, practice, and collaboration of a community (Lave and Wenger, 1991).

Using the community of practice model, NYAM's youth artists were intentionally selected to be diverse in age, with participants ranging from 16 to 27 years-old, and to range in levels of experience with art activism. Additionally, the community of practice model was chosen for NYAM's program design to give space for adult/expert guidance as part of the community learning experience. As such, the workshops were also supported by Max Sansing, a well-known Chicago artist and prolific muralist, and Susy Shultz, then the President of Public Narrative, a Chicago non-profit organization that connects marginalized community organizations with the media. Max informally supported the youth artists during their art creation sessions by making himself available to them for expert advice on art techniques, and by sharing his journey with them as an artist and his experience with gun violence in the city. Susy Schultz presented a customized presentation for the group on storytelling, which she developed specifically to support their development of visual narratives for the billboards.

While a mix of formal and informal learning strategies were offered to the youth artists, no learning objectives were imposed. The only goal presented was the responsibility of the youth artists to create a large-scale public art campaign to influence a diversity of people all across the city to become involved in gun violence prevention. The workshops were not hierarchical, but collaborative, so while teaching happened, the youth artists learned from each other and the adults, and were empowered to integrate the lessons that they felt best served their purpose. The first two workshops were open discussion sessions where the facilitators and youth shared: (1) when and what led them to start practicing art; (2) what their art practice meant to them; (3) what made them engage in the NYAM project and what they hoped to achieve; (4) what their previous experience with activism and/or art activism was; (5) what they knew about gun violence; and (6) who in the media spotlight they saw as peers that they looked up to as leaders and why. During those initial sessions, several newspaper articles from local newspapers with distinct styles and viewpoints on gun violence in Chicago were also shared and discussed. The last three meetings were dedicated to workshopping the individual art submissions as a group, learning narrative art techniques for further development of their submissions, and time and space for art creation and revision.

Ben Kirshner (2015), Director of Colorado University's Community Based Learning and Research program, who has worked with scores of youth in a multitude of settings, notes, "Empowerment is not an entity that can be handed over to a person, ready-made. It requires the young person to exercise agency; to take risks and try out new practices" (p. 107). As a community of practice, NYAM is built on that notion and so extends the work of activism beyond the canvas for its participants. In addition to the development of the interactive art tour, NYAM's youth were encouraged to seek influence on gun violence prevention by drawing attention to their artwork and their stories at a Chicago press conference on proposed firearm legislation. This was done by developing and giving out protest posters of their artwork at the DC and Chicago March for Our Lives, and participating in demonstrations of their interactive artwork at the Human Factors in a Computing conference in Montreal, in addition to performing at a Nobel Peace Prize Forum peace concert in Minneapolis and a live painting event during a peace concert at a local Chicago high school. While three out of the five artists in NYAM Cohort 1 had used their art for activism in the past, none had previously participated in a project of this scale where they served as leaders.

# From Artist to Activist

Within the NYAM community of practice, the process of learning from each other and leaning on each other to create art and to take risks as activists had an impact. The project director collected and thematically coded interviews with the youth artists, their submitted writings, and notes on their interactions over the two-year period of the NYAM pilot intervention that revealed that as a result of their work with the group, a shift in the youth artists' art practices occurred over time, which had an impact on their self-concepts, namely their self-identities. Lave and Wenger found that within a group process of co-construction the identity of a learner moves incrementally over time from newcomer to old-timer and from novice to expert (Lave and Wenger, 1991).

Due to the limitations of the data collected (some participants did not provide written feedback when requested), the stories that emerged from studying the findings focus on only three of the five participants of NYAM Cohort 1: Millie, 16; Daria, 17; and Liz, 27.

Millie described herself at the outset of her two-year tenure with NYAM as being new to art: "I'm only 16 years-old, so I'm not exposed to that much yet. I've just started working as an artist." Although she publicly referred to herself as an artist, her tone in expressing this to the group during her first NYAM meeting was hesitant. Growing up in a family with several older siblings with established interests and art practices, Millie personally saw herself as dabbling in art in comparison to them. Like 4 out of 5 of her peers in Cohort 1, she admitted that her initial impetus for creating art was for "escape" and for "self-healing." She said, "It's a hobby, but it's also a way for me to be able to communicate without words, and also a way of healing. Whenever I'm down, or something, I use painting as a distraction."

Daria never hesitated to refer to herself as an artist. In her family, the visual arts were an interest and a creative expression unique only to her. Like Millie, however, she also began drawing and painting for self-healing or what she referred to as "coping." In describing her affinity to art, she said, "I'm an artist because I use it to communicate the feelings that I am not able to express verbally."

Liz, more than ten years older than Millie and Daria from the outset of her tenure with NYAM, was completely comfortable with describing herself as a portrait artist having honed her craft at a local amusement park in her teens and then as a student of art in college. While her work continues to focus on portraiture, she uses this medium now to better represent the underrepresented (particularly women) by telling their stories in visual narratives. "I'm an artist because I enjoy telling others' stories as well as telling my own and having a way of writing my own narrative and other's narratives in a way that I feel people have not been represented, especially those of color, women in particular." Like the younger members of Cohort 1, Liz turned to art to deal with life challenges when she was younger. She also saw art as a means of healing, which, she as a mature artist shares with the women whose portraits she paints: "Healing is a big part of my practice. The act of looking at yourself and being able to perceive what you want, how you see yourself, what's important to you, how you want others to see you, and why. I feel like my [art] practice gives people an area where they can actually ask those things."

Although Millie and Daria's purpose for creating art prior to NYAM had been largely self-focused, they also had aspirations of being of help to others as part of their future professions. A rising senior in high school, Daria hoped to become an art therapist and was looking into colleges with art and psychology programs. Contemplating her future, Millie stated, "I like helping people. I like making people feel better...that's why [becoming] a doctor wouldn't be so bad." As a junior in high school, still in the process of figuring out what she wanted to study in college and to "become" as an adult, it was in fact her compulsion to be of service and her interest in art that led her to NYAM. She shared in an interview with NYAM's director that it was her teacher who encouraged her to submit an art piece. They discussed how the mission of the NYAM project aligned with her personal goals to help people and seeing that connection, prompted Millie to try making art for a social cause and to say, "Hopefully, I got the chance."

While the opportunity to create art for NYAM began Millie's shift in self-concept from making art as a hobby to making art to help others, it was NYAM's curriculum focus and revision process in the workshops that profoundly changed how both Millie and Daria understood audience resonance with and interpretation of images. During the workshops, in preparing the youth for creating narrative artworks meant to convey a message and a call-to-action for mass public consumption—two main concepts were addressed: the use of symbols and color in media. For both concepts, the group looked across their collective artwork to dissect and discuss how they were using symbols and color and if their intended messages were clearly being communicated in the artworks they submitted.

In reviewing her own work while taking part in discussions with her peers as part of the revision process, Millie noted that "Now, I realize even the smallest choice of color can represent something or the smallest choice in a shape or a painting can also mean something." This lesson was distinctly illustrated in the changes Daria made to her submitted artwork following its work shopping.

Daria submitted to NYAM a watercolor image of a child with a gun and an American flag to his head. She explained during the workshops that the intention of her submitted artwork was to show that she felt that politicians were holding young people of all races in America hostage to gun violence by not passing

**Figure 11.2:** Daria Velazquez submitted artwork        **Figure 11.3:** Daria Velazquez revised artwork

firearm legislation to protect them. Discussion of her submitted artwork led her to a revelation: Her artwork was being interpreted as making a statement about police shootings because the blue sleeve and the pale white hand holding the gun triggered familiar images of police officers for the group. Becoming aware of the unrealized psychological effect of the color blue in the context of her painting, Daria honed the messaging in her artwork by replacing the blue sleeve for a black suit jacket, which produced greater resonance for the group with a politician.

The subject of Daria's artwork arose from her personal experience with gun violence. Daria grew up in two vastly different Latino neighborhoods in Chicago at different points in her childhood: one of them a quiet community in the far north side of the city, and the other, on the west side of the city, a community that struggled with increasing levels of crime and shootings. She spoke of hearing gun shots from her bedroom at night when living in Chicago's west side and of friends who had been arrested because of guns.

Personal stories like these were what drove each of the youth artists to create their art, but it was in the group, through their analyses, that they refined their understanding of what their art could do for others. For Millie, this meant developing the sense that art actually touches people's lives, "Being a growing artist, I definitely learned a lot [about] how a simple painting or a sketch could mean so much to someone else."

And, it was in the implementation of their art in acts of activism, that they experienced a shift in what they saw as possible with their art. Reflecting on seeing her art displayed on the college campus of Augsburg University in Minneapolis, MN as a component of the 2017 Nobel Peace Prize Forum, Daria divulged:

> ..when I was standing on the field where my art was being displayed in front of hundreds...my heart was racing and my body felt ecstatic...I never thought that I would ever have a voice, especially a voice so big that hundreds of people in a whole other state would be able to hear, but after being with the National Youth Art Movement Against Gun Violence, I realized how my art was able to give me the voice I was never able to use.

Previous to this experience, Daria noted that due to incidents like bullying that she had endured in her childhood she "never thought that anybody would be interested in what [she] had to say." After seeing her artwork displayed in Chicago and Minneapolis, Liz described her shift in self-concept in this way:

> [NYAM] has given me a chance to think bigger because this project is not only about women, but it's about all types of families, all different ages, all different individuals throughout Chicago and in the cities in general.

She noted that the change in her self-concept also resulted in a shift in her art practice because it provided a path for her to merge her interests into a singular vision: "[Prior to NYAM] I was stuck in the space between artist and activist with no clear way to fuse the two worlds in an action-oriented way."

For Liz, NYAM provided a model for art activism. "The whole experience taught me a lot about each of our potentials and how they magnify together" Liz said at the end of her 2nd year with NYAM.

**Figure 11.4:** Liz Gomez Photo in Chicago Sun Times

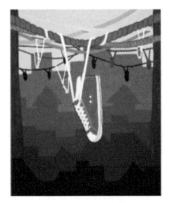

**Figure 11.5:** Millie Martinez submitted artwork

**Figure 11.6:** Millie Martinez revised artwork

Captivated by the possibilities for influencing change as an artist, Liz is now leading the charge for her own large-scale art intervention: The Divine Gratitude Self-Portrait Movement whose goal is to honor people who are working to reduce fear and division in their communities. Two years after her tenure with NYAM, Daria is now a sophomore art education major in college.

**Self-Concept and Gun Violence:** Although close in age, Daria's experience with gun violence was much different than Millie's, which is reflected in the subject and point of view expressed in each of their artworks. Unlike Daria, Millie's whole childhood was spent in a northwest neighborhood in Chicago that historically has had lower levels of firearm-related injuries and homicides than the west and south sides of the city. Millie explained that it wasn't until she joined NYAM that her perception of gun violence in the city changed: "When I came into these workshops and I talked to everybody else, I realized "Wow, this is a huge issue." Her shift in perspective on the scale of the issue is visually represented in the changes in her artwork.

In the essay that she submitted to NYAM with her original image, Millie explains the intention of her artwork:

> I got a symbol that reminded me of the city—the shoes hanging. You hear so much about what that means, but no one really knows the true significance of it. That's how I feel about gun violence among youths in general—I don't know that much about it, but you know it's there and you don't really notice it until it happens to you.

Millie changed the focus of her image from a kind of mythology of gun violence, which was indicative of her previous perception of the issue, to illustrate the reality that she came to discover in participating in the group that: Not only is gun violence a genuine problem, it is one that is taking the lives of thousands of her peers. Her revised artwork depicts a Chicago skyline filled with the sneakers missing of its missing youth. In describing the revision, she said: "With the shoes in the background, I wanted to spread awareness of the mass quantities of people who are victims to this [gun violence] everyday."

Millie's increased understanding of gun violence motivated her to take an activist stance on the issue. "Hearing all these stories about tragic events that have happened to my peers is very upsetting. I felt lucky about where I live, but at the same time I felt guilty because I shouldn't be labeled safe or feel lucky because of the neighborhood I'm in." In that statement, Millie is expressing her recognition of the unfair circumstances that are leading to the violent deaths of her peers. She adds, "While it is upsetting to see my peers go through so much at such a young age, I was more upset when I realized that there were more people like me who weren't aware of how serious gun violence is or [who don't] acknowledge the issue because it's not happening to them, and that's why I decided to get involved."

At the conclusion of the workshops, Millie reflected on working with her peers to develop artwork on gun violence and expressed feeling an internal change by the experience: "I feel like you can do a lot with art, and this organization, especially now... I can kind of call myself an activist now, because I'm doing something for the better and I'm using my art."

## Holding Space with Public Art and Augmented Reality

Understanding that youth have wisdom to share and build on, NYAM encourages its youth artists to unpack the deeply layered ways that violence or the fear of violence has affected their lives, and to turn their knowledge and experience into artworks that spur engagement within the broader public for the purpose of intergenerational coalition building for gun violence prevention. To this end, in 2017, NYAM developed an interactive art tour in Chicago showcasing the artwork of the city's youth and three adult allies using commercial billboards in seven northwest and southside neighborhoods.

This interactive public display of youth artwork on billboards is a unique and essential component of NYAM because it provides an active resistance to the marginalization of youth and the silencing of youth voice on an issue that deals with the life and death consequences of political decisions made by adults on behalf of this vulnerable population.

> "Cultural production is a critical site for challenging dominant narratives and articulating alternative identities and forms of social relations. As such, youth media can be a form of cultural activism, enabling youth to visibly 'put forth critique and analysis of urban social inequality, as well as posit potential solutions to these problems'" (Ferman and Smirnov, 2016, p. 185).

While NYAM was the first youth-led art activism campaign to use AR on commercial billboards in Chicago and in the U.S., its use as a large-scale tool for social change has been growing since the Occupy Wall Street movement emerged in 2011 (Skwarek, 2018). Mark Skwarek, a New York University professor of art and an activist against financial inequality and corporate greed, was one of thousands who planned to protest in front of the New York Stock Exchange (NYSE) on Sept. 17, 2011 but was pushed back by police to stage the protest at the nearby Zuccotti Park instead.

The imagery of protestors in front of the NYSE was critical to the Occupy movement, so undeterred, Skwarek put out an international call for photos, and an AR protest filling the streets of the financial district with supporters from far and wide which was fully realized. He transported the bodies, signs, determined and concerned expressions and voices of thousands of protestors in real time and placed all this against the backdrop of the NYSE using AR (Skwarek, 2018).

Holding space is critical to marginalized groups; it means that they are not invisible. The Occupy movement held space for economic injustice by physically taking over parks and college campuses throughout the country. It is for this reason that NYAM not only virtually augments reality with an app but places large-scale artefacts of the unseen struggles of youth in areas that challenge passersby.

**Figure 11.7:** Chantala Kommanivanh's *Loco Boyz* artwork and Augmented Reality overlay

This placement in public space helps to connect disparate members of a community (Schuermans et al., 2012; Mathew, 2015) like those who have lost loved ones to violence and those who have not, by making the invisible visible such as in the artwork "Loco Boyz," a mixed-media painting by Chantala Kommanivanh. Chantala, NYAM's 2017–18 lead artist, depicts a group of faceless young brown-skin men whose bodies blend and even disappear into their environment like the ubiquity of graffiti on an urban landscape; the image subtly challenges the viewer to see beyond the surface in order to acknowledge that these young men are going missing and no one is paying attention. The AR for this piece superimposes tombstones where these young men once stood and asks the question: "What do we choose to ignore?"

Millie and Daria, like Chantala, use their art to expose what's missing. For Daria, what's missing is a universal understanding that gun violence does not discriminate and that politicians who choose to oppose gun laws are holding young people hostage. To bring this message home to viewers, the AR for Daria's piece rotates through a variety of ethnicities by morphing the skin and hair color of the profile of the young boy from blond and blue-eyed to dark-skin and black hair. At the end of this rotation, the stars and stripes drop off the American flag being held by the politician (who is also holding a gun to the child's head), revealing it to be a white flag of surrender. Her AR vignette ends with the question, "What do we assume?"

**Figure 11.8:** Daria Velazquez *You or Me America* artwork and Augmented Reality overlays

For Millie, what's missing is a real awareness of how many young people are victims to gun violence. The AR for her piece brings to life how, sneakers are added in memoriam for her peers over time in block after block in the city. Her AR vignette starts with a single sneaker moving in the breeze on a telephone line and then quickly multiplies into a skyline overwhelmed with the shoes of scores of missing children; an image that begs the question of all who are witness, "For whom are we responsible?"

Each AR vignette in the NYAM interactive art tour experience ends with a reflective question as a means of intentionally asking the viewer to consider the messages presented in the artwork personally. This interactive component shifts the viewer experience from disconnected voyeur to responsible witness. Rabbi Josh Feiglsen, Executive Director of the nonprofit Ask Big Questions, who helped NYAM to formulate the questions for the art tour, believes that reflective questions not only help people to share and listen better, but also to clarify their values and beliefs (Maclin, n.d.). Responses to gun violence are uniquely tied to culture in America, which stem from long held beliefs about freedom and people of color (Metzl, 2019; Parker, 2017). Chantala, Daria, and Millie's artwork asks viewers to look past any preconceived notions and consider the human impact of gun violence.

## Gun Violence, Trauma and Public Spaces

To connect viewers to the human experience of gun violence, NYAM's artists visually and experientially, through AR, laid bare the sociopolitical trauma that inspired their artistic expressions. From a liberation psychology perspective, the impact of oppression and disenfranchisement is a form of sociopolitical trauma (Quiros and Berger, 2015; Karcher, 2017; Gupta, 2018a, b) whereby traumatic symptomology can emerge among the marginalized community members who have experienced chronic and sustained systemic discrimination (Martin-Baro, 1994; Duran and Duran, 1998; Watkins and Shulman, 2010). Many scholars have documented the impact of sociopolitical traumas on the health of urban populations in public health literature (Centers for Disease and Prevention, 2012; Jenkins et al., 2009; Nugent et al., 2012; Parto et al., 2011; Rich, 2009; Roberts et al., 2011; Smith, 2014; Thompson, 2009; Zinzow et al., 2009).

Public art is a platform through which community healing for these sociopolitical traumas can occur. Rayner (2005) noted that "psychological trauma takes control away from victims; it is the lack of control that leads to someone being unable to escape from a traumatic situation." Punamäki et al. (2004) documented "ample evidence that trauma victims tend to distort, narrow, and repress their memories of painful and often shameful scenes." Wilkie (2018) affirmed that through art therapy, mural making can bring a traumatized community together through the collective healing process. Not only does mural making benefit the creators through the process of creation, the product can enhance public space, contribute to a community's connection to the space and create opportunities of open discussion with its audience (Stevenson, 2016).

Gun violence produces a traumatic relationship with public spaces that makes reclaiming them for healing all the more necessary, especially when how these acts of violence often become publicly memorialized is considered (Doss, 2006; Senie, 2016). Dell Aria (2020) presents the case in her article "Loaded objects: Addressing Gun Violence Through Art in the Gallery and Beyond," that makeshift memorials placed at the sites of the deaths of loved ones after violent acts creates a kind of "symbolic cemetery" that mirrors the stalemate in our political dialogue as these memorials offer little more than "thoughts and prayers." The emotional catharsis of these memorials, frozen in time and circumstance, become daily reminders of grief and loss in communities that compounds the trauma from the initial act of violence (Dell Aria, 2020; Doss, 2006).

As such, in an attempt to transcend and transform the grief that emerges from gun violence into something that can serve the community and its residents rather than entrench it in ongoing victimization, Dell Aria (2020) asks several key questions:

1. How can art generate experiences for viewers that allow for a more complex consideration of gun-related violence than the cycle of grief seen in immediate and permanent memorials?
2. How can artworks model a form of engagement within the public sphere that mobilizes rather than entrenches through affect?

For Rosetto (2012), the answer to those questions comes back to community mural making, which has a long and storied tradition in a variety of cultures. Rossetto (2012) points out that, "the subtle power of art and community involvement allows participation in both the critique of cultural systems and the creation of new cultural values" (p. 24). Creation, in this way, moves individuals past creating art as "thoughts and prayers" to creating it to stimulate active participation in co-creating change within communities. According to Wilkie (2018) engagement in these creative cultural practices can help community members strengthen and deepen their relationship with society and their community while concurrently engaging in social action. With these murals, "the image can serve as a call for individual and collective action to address marginalized aspects of human potential" (Hocoy, 2005, p. 8).

For NYAM, supporting the development of persons and communities in creating alternative futures that transcend current social ills through public art is integral to its mission. This is why the billboard artwork in its interactive art tour was intentionally designed by the city's youth who represent, by age and ethnic backgrounds, the population most victimized and vulnerable to gun violence and in need of gun safety legislation (Development Services Group, 2016). NYAM's interactive art tour experience is centered on the concept of enablement, which espouses the activist stance of "facilitating and developing opportunities for people to fulfill their potential and to develop their own capacity" (Dombrowski et al., 2016). The development of artwork for the interactive art tour for the youth artists is a process of making meaning on the issue of gun violence. In that process they ask themselves, "What role can my personal experiences play in my art practice and for what purpose?" This contemplation and decision by the artist is what gives strength to the artwork because it is developed for a specific purpose: to use what they have as artists to create a change in the world, which was exemplified in the descriptions of Chantala, Daria and Millie's contributions to the interactive art tour (Foth et al., 2013; Stetsenko, 2014).

B'Rael Ali Thunder, a 25 year-old with NYAM who grew up on the South Side of Chicago, contributed a piece called "Guns and Roses" to the interactive art tour that incorporated a public memorial in its imagery. In Chicago, the south and west sides of the city are heavily impacted by gun violence; public memorials for loved ones lost in these tragic incidents are common. With the mission to create billboard art that inspires social action, the group decided that art works placed in communities struggling with gun violence should challenge viewers in a different way than those placed in other neighborhoods. As a result of this collective intention, B'Rael's artwork, which was placed in the South Side Chicago neighborhood of Auburn Gresham, illustrated a black mother actively fighting to not let her family succumb to the fate of another public memorial and the real-world reality of the possibility of yet another family broken as a result of gun violence.

With Guns & Roses, B'Rael paints a powerful image of the mother as a superhero protecting her family from the bullets of strangers and the AR demonstrates the dark side of what happens if a mother goes missing due to gun violence. This combination of art and media asks the question, "When do you take a stand?" and asserts the

**Figure 11.9:** B'Rael Ali Thunder's *Guns & Roses* artwork and Augmented Reality overlay

fact that the viewers have a choice: to proactively defend families and communities against gun violence or to let this victimization, which ultimately impacts children, continue. Its display in Auburn Gresham, which persistently has some of the highest rates of gun violence in Chicago, makes public the personal and familial outcomes of gun violence that are not addressed in the mainstream news media (Center for Illinois Politics, 2020; Gallardo, 2020). It also attempts to move victims of gun violence and the community beyond "thoughts and prayers" into taking action (Dell Aria, 2020).

Similarly, 25 year-old Leah LaQueens' "Hands Up," another artwork in the NYAM interactive art tour, publicly reveals the personal struggles of victims of gun violence. Using a simple silhouette to draw attention to the dehumanizing nature of mainstream news media coverage of black victims, Hands Up alludes to the issue of police violence (Dukes, 2017; Gruenewald, 2009). Its AR animation, brings attention to the contrasting imagery in the foreground of the piece, which presents symbols of academic achievement on the left juxtaposed with symbols of a life gone awry on the right, and in the middle, the question, "What will be our legacy?" appears imploring viewers to see this choice as their own, to hold space for this reality in their consciousness. A reality where an encounter with law enforcement can have grave consequences (Alang et al., 2017; Edwards et al., 2019; Peeples, 2020; Smiley and Fakunle, 2016).

Placed in the once thriving African American enclave of South Shore Chicago, Leah's artwork spoke to the traumas that have perpetuated a social and economic downward trend in predominantly African American communities across Chicago and across the US (Bergen et al., 2017). Its question of legacy, however, pointedly seeks to move residents and passersby beyond the traumas to reclaim their power of choice and change.

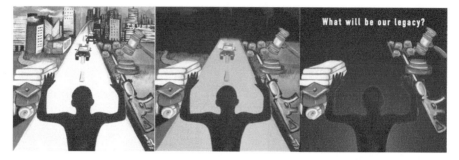

**Figure 11.10:** Leah LaQueens' *Hands Up* Artwork and Augmented Reality overlays

## A Virtuous Cycle

As much as NYAM is an art activism project for social justice, its intentional placement of artwork in neighborhoods across Chicago and its use of geolocation using the Vamonde app for its AR experiences, also made its interactive art tour across the city a spatial-justice project. Spatial justice is a dimension of the field of social geography that analyzes the interactions between space and society revealing how social relations within geographic contexts produce inequities (Lupton, 2009; Soja, 2010). Inequities within geographic spaces have much to do with the power dynamics between people, which impacts their access to resources and influences public and private concepts of individual and collective identity (Soja, 2010). What this means is that who we are is not only a product of the spaces we come from, but that the spaces themselves are a product of social relationships well beyond the bounds of the block we live in and the neighborhood that surrounds it. Institutional systems, social networks, and media representations are at play in the milieu that constitutes these spaces we call communities. In addition, if this is true, no community stands on its own, but is part of an interconnected web of realities pushing and pulling against the other to share or dominate space and resources to signify value or lack thereof as part of that negotiation (Sundstrom, 2003).

In an attempt to make the issue of gun violence a valued collective concern for all residents of Chicago, rather than a neighborhood specific issue, NYAM's artwork and AR experiences were placed in beleaguered communities on the south side and in less violence prone communities like Bucktown and Wicker Park on the north west side of the city. Solo walking tours were a part of the geolocating functionality of the Vamonde app, but guided group walking tours of the artwork led by an artist and gun violence survivor, were also offered. The intention of the walking tour aspect of the interactive experience on the northwest side of the city was to bring awareness to the startling and vulnerable aspects of public violence on city streets to residents unfamiliar with gun violence.

In reaction to that aspect of the tour one participant said, "The tour was very impactful. I would say being forced to walk in the streets and go to different spots in particular. You know the violence is happening on the streets, so when you are walking from place to place on the tour and you're thinking about these kids who are also going around the city and they're just trying to live."

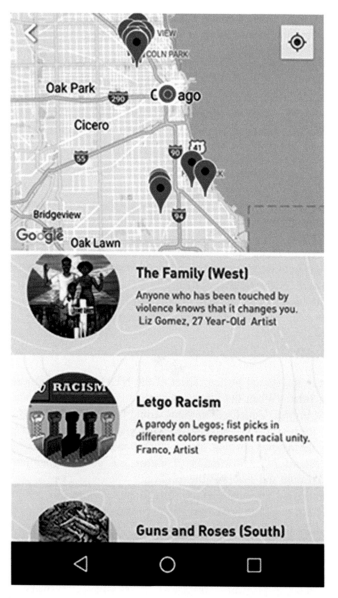

**Figure 11.11:** NYAM's In-App view of geolocated artworks in Chicago

Another tour participant, who grew up in the suburbs of Chicago, noted that the tour provided context to gun violence that had been missing for him—a personal connection.

"Through the tour you were able to meet and actually talk to people who [gun violence] had been affected by. I think that talking to someone who has been affected by gun violence and not just reading it in the news has helped me process everything that has been going on with a real world example."

Several participants said that hearing the story of a gun violence survivor among the images and AR of the tour was powerful for them because the three-dimensional quality of the experience stood in such contrast to their childhood memories.

"Just hearing that personal story, seeing the images that were produced by children who are living in fear of gun violence, on a level that, you know, I never knew as a kid. It was touching."

These types of reactions also had a positive effect on both the gun violence survivor and the artist who led the group. Both shared feelings of elation with the project director after leading a group because of the positive reactions to the artwork and the empathy expressed during conversations in between tour stops. Comments that this was "good work" abounded.

While several guided tours were held, only participants from one group of four Chicago residents took part-in follow-up interviews. As such, these comments are not representative of the reactions of all tour participants. However, the interviews that were held do offer some insight into the tour experience and indicate a need for comprehensive data gathering following the tours in the future.

## Conclusion

With respect to the spatial justice aspect of the NYAM art tour, Andrew Hickey's 2010 chapter titled "When the Streets Become a Pedagogue" is an apt description of the NYAM project. Equally as apropos would be to substitute "the streets" with "our youth" to describe the project as "when our youth become a pedagogue," emphasizing the unique position of the city's youth as educators to adults. Both descriptions, signifying a disruption of norms and power dynamics that places marginalized people and spaces in the forefront.

Our youth using the streets as an instructional platform for community-based learning is a form of public pedagogy. Public pedagogy is a conception that expands the education landscape by legitimizing learning as occurring beyond the walls of formal educational institutions (Sandlin et al., 2011). Its roots generated from a desire to compel a more civic-minded body politic to achieve a public aligned in values and collective identity (Sandlin et al., 2011). For NYAM, the hope for this work is to compel each adult, regardless of their place of residence, to feel accountable to the larger community and to stop ignoring the problem and/or making assumptions about gun violence, its victims, and its perpetrators. And, instead, take a stand fully knowing that a decision for action or inaction against gun violence determines the city's legacy—the future of its people.

Mixed reality technologies capacity to connect liberatory frames of thinking and being into spaces unrestrained by tradition and unshackled by oppression provides the marginalized with tools for change. The true power of these tools, however, is only emerging and yet to be fully realized as is the power of youth and their pursuit for justice in this digital age.

# Putting it into Practice: Using AR in a Youth Movement

Using the lessons from the above chapter, envision working with youth to create a public art project with AR.

## Project Guide:

1. Identify a youth group or a community organization with young leaders to lead this project. Consider reaching out to the National Youth Art Movement for guidance and to add your group to their youth leadership network at nationalyouthartmovement.org.
2. Discuss and select an issue with this group of young leaders that has meaning within the group's community, and that has neglected including youth voices in the mainstream media.
3. Create a call for art to address the issue from the perspective of youth.
4. Engage the artists who respond to the call for art in participatory workshops to develop the artwork to tell stories about the issue.
5. Situate the work as a public pedagogy and community activist effort.
6. Explore news articles, statistics, research papers, and interviews in the workshops with a diversity of community members on the issue to inform the art creation.
7. Collectively choose public spaces in which to "hold space" for youth voices on the issue using the resulting artwork.
8. Digitize the artwork and use an accessible and democratic AR platform to deepen engagement with the messaging within the artwork.
9. Develop a campaign to convey the intended message(s) about the issue to the public and to get the public to engage with the art and AR.

The following is suggested to enrich and support the art creation for the purpose of public pedagogy:

- Find and assess both historical and current information on the selected issue in news articles, statistics, and research papers. Is there a consistency to the findings?
- Consider the intersectionality of other issues with the selected issue. What makes the intersections significant or insignificant?
- Connect the findings from the research to the actual lived experiences of people in the community through interviews. Do the readings and other media match up with the lived experiences and perspectives of people in the community? If not, why?
- Illustrate the nuances and/or dichotomies discovered in your research in narrative artwork. How can the combination of art and AR not only encourage critical thinking, but community action too that brings people together on an issue rather than divide them?

**Table 11.1:** Project Rubric

| | Below Expectation | Emerging/Developing | Meets Expectation |
|---|---|---|---|
| Youth Voice | The AR experience did not elevate youth voice, agency, or action. | The AR experience to some extent elevates youth voice, agency, or action. | The AR experience elevated youth voice, agency, or action. |
| Intersectional Exploration | The AR experience lacked a clear exploration of the intersectional issues that compound the selected issue. | The AR experience provided a clear exploration of the intersectional issues that compound the selected issue. | The AR experience provided a creative and concise exploration of the intersectional issues that compound the selected issue. |
| Augmented Reality Experience | The AR experience failed to move the viewer through the complexities explored within the community space in a thoughtful and sensitive fashion. | The AR experience moved the viewer through the complexities explored within the community space but did not thoughtfully and/ or in a sensitive fashion connect the space to the selected issue. | The AR experience moved the viewer through the complexities explored within the community space in a thoughtful and sensitive fashion that connected to the selected issue. |
| Ability to create dialogue or action | The AR experience did not provide a mechanism to contribute to the conversation on the selected issue to take appropriate action. | The AR experience somewhat provided a mechanism to contribute to the conversation on the selected issue and to take appropriate action. | The AR experience provided a mechanism to contribute to the conversation and to take appropriate action on the selected issue in a way that enriched each viewer and the surrounding community. |

# References

Alang, S., McAlpine, D., McCreedy, E. and Hardeman, R. (2017). Police brutality and black health: Setting the agenda for public health scholars. *American Journal of Public Health*, 107(5), 662-665. https://doi.org/10.2105/AJPH.2017.303691

Alvermann, D.E. (2004). Media, information communication technologies, and youth literacies: A cultural studies perspective. *American Behavioral Scientist*, 48(1), 78-83. doi: 10.1177/0002764204267271

American Psychological Association Zero Tolerance Task Force (2008). Are zero tolerance policies effective in the schools?: An evidentiary review and recommendations. *American Psychologist*, 63(9), 852-862. https://doi.org/10.1037/0003-066X.63.9.852

Bargh, J.A. and Chartrand, T.L. (2000). The mind in the middle: A practical guide to priming and automaticity research. pp. 253-285. *In*: H.T. Reis and CM. Judd (eds.). Handbook of Research Methods in Social and Personality Psychology. Cambridge University Press.

Besley, T. (2010). Governmentality of youth: Managing risky subjects. *Policy Futures in Education*, 8(5), 528-547. http://dx.doi.org/10.2304/pfie.2010.8.5.528

Bergen, K., Caputo, A. and Lee, W. (2017). South Shore, once thriving, struggles amid economic erosion and crime. Chicago Tribune. https://www.chicagotribune.com/news/breaking/ct-south-shore-profile-met-20170428-story.html

Bloome, D., Dyer, S. and Zhou, X. (2018). Educational inequality, educational expansion, and intergenerational income persistence in the United States. *American Sociological Review*, 83(6), 1215-1253. https://doi.org/10.1177/0003122418809374

Camino, L. and Zeldin S. (2002). From periphery to center: Pathways for youth civic engagement in the day-to-day life of communities. *Applied Developmental Science*, 6(4), 213-220. https://doi.org/10.1207/S1532480XADS0604_8

Carlson, C. (2005). Youth with influence: The youth planner initiative in Hampton, Virginia. *Children, Youth and Environments*, 15(2). www.jstor.org/stable/10.7721/chilyoutenvi.15.2.0211

Centers for Disease Control and Prevention (2012). Youth Violence: Facts at a Glance. https://www.cdc.gov/ViolencePrevention/pdf/yv-datasheet-a.pdf

Center for Illinois Politics (2020). We've got the rap of being one of the most violent cities in the nation. Here's a detailed look at why, and our best way out. https://www.centerforilpolitics.org/articles/weve-got-the-rap-of-being-the-most-violent-city-in-the-nation-heres-a-detailed-look-at-why-and-our-best-way-out

Charteris, J. and Smardon, D. (2019). Student voice in learning: Instrumentalism and tokenism or opportunity for altering the status and positioning of students? *Pedagogy, Culture & Society*, 27(2), 305-323. https://doi.org/10.1080/14681366.2018.1489887

Coady, M.M. (2015). Citizenship: Inclusion and exclusion. *In*: Wyn J. and Cahill H. (eds.). Handbook of Children and Youth Studies. Springer. https://doi.org/10.1007/978-981-4451-15-4_63

Cottle, M. (2018). How the Parkland students changed the gun debate. The Atlantic. https://www.theatlantic.com/politics/archive/2018/02/parkland-students-power/554399/

Dell'Aria, A. (2020). Loaded objects: Addressing gun violence through art in the gallery and beyond. *Palgrave Communications*, 6(1), 1-11. https://doaj.org/article/9569a0b10d4b4c7b8eef73aa4c96667a

Development Services Group (2016). Literature review: Gun violence and youth. United States Office of Juvenile Justice and Delinquency Prevention. https://www.hsdl.org/?view&did=834045

Dombrowski, L., Harmon, E. and Fox, S. (2016). Social justice-oriented interaction design: Outlining key design strategies and commitments. *In*: Proceedings of the

2016 ACM Conference on Designing Interactive Systems (DIS '16), 656-671. doi: 10.1145/2901790.2901861

Doss, E. (2006). Spontaneous memorials and contemporary modes of mourning in America. *Material Religion*, 2(3), 294-318, doi: 10.1080/17432200.2006.11423053

Dukes, K.N. and Gaither, S.E. (2017). Black racial stereotypes and victim blaming: Implications for media coverage and criminal proceedings in cases of police violence against racial and ethnic minorities. *Journal of Social Issues*, 73(4), 789-807. doi: 10.1111/josi.12248

Duran, E., Duran, B., Brave Heart, M.Y.H. and Yellow Horse-Davis, S. (1998). Healing the American Indian soul wound. pp. 341-354. *In*: Y. Danieli (ed.). International Handbook of Multigenerational Legacies of Trauma. Plenum Press.

Edwards, F., Lee, H. and Esposito, M. (2019). Risk of being killed by police use of force in the United States by age, race-ethnicity, and sex. Proceedings of the National Academy of Sciences. Aug 2019, 116(34), 16793-16798. doi: 10.1073/pnas.1821204116

Ferguson, D.L., Kozleski, E.B., Smith, A. and Education Development Center, N.M.N.I. for U.S.I. (2001). On...Transformed, Inclusive Schools: A Framework to Guide Fundamental Change in Urban Schools. https://files.eric.ed.gov/fulltext/ED460172.pdf

Ferilli, G., Sacco, P.L. and Blessi, G.T. (2016). Beyond the rhetoric of participation: New challenges and prospects for inclusive urban regeneration. *City, Culture and Society*, 7(2), 95-100.

Ferman, B. and Smirnov, N. (2016). Shifting stereotypes and storylines: The personal and political impact of youth media. *In*: Conner, J. and Rosen S. (eds.). Contemporary Youth Activism: Advancing Social Justice in the United States. Praeger. https://publisher.abc-clio.com/9781440842139/196

Fisher, J.A., Shangguan, L. and Crisp, J.C. (2018). Developing a platform for community-curated mixed reality spaces. *In*: Extended Abstracts of the 2018 CHI Play Conference on Human Factors in Computing Systems (CHI '18,) October 28-31, 2018, Melbourne, VIC, Australia.

Flax, M. (2011). A crisis in the analyst's life: Self-containment, symbolization, and the holding space. *The Psychoanalytic Quarterly*, 80(2), 305-336. doi: 10.1002/j.2167-4086.2011.tb00088.x

Foth, M., Parra-Agudelo, L. and Palleis, R. (2013). Digital soapboxes: Towards an interaction design agenda for situated civic innovation. *In*: Canny, J.F., Rekimoto, J. and Langheinrich, M. (eds.). UbiComp '13 Adjunct: Proceedings of the 2013 ACM Conference on Pervasive and Ubiquitous Computing Adjunct Publication. Association for Computing Machinery, United States of America, pp. 725-728. http://dx.doi.org/10.1145/2494091.2495995

Fredricks, J.A. (2011) Engagement in school and out-of-school contexts: A multidimensional view of engagement. *Theory into Practice*, 50(4), 327-335. doi: 10.1080/00405841.2011.607401

Freire, P. (1970). *Pedagogy of the Oppressed*. Continuum International Publishing Group.

Gallardo, M. (2020). Auburn Gresham neighbors try to overcome violence amid rise in homicides. ABC7.com. https://abc7chicago.com/auburn-gresham-tries-to-overcome-violence-amid-rise-in-homicides/6329985/

Garcia, E. and Weiss, E. (2018). Education inequalities at the school starting gate: Gaps, trends, and strategies to address them. Economic Policy Institute, September 2017. https://www.epi.org/publication/education-inequalities-at-the-school-starting-gate/

Gessner, I. (2016). Tamiko Thiel's virtual reality installations as sites of learning in and beyond the museum. *Studies in the Education of Adults*, 48(2), 155-176, doi: 10.1080/02660830.2016.1229849

Giroux, H. (2009). *Youth in a Suspect Society*. Palgrave MacMillian: New York.

Graham, S. and Lowery, B.S. (2004). Priming unconscious racial stereotypes about adolescent offenders. *Law and Human Behavior*, 28(5), 483-504. http://www.njjn.org/uploads/digital-library/resource_248.pdf

Graham, M., Zook, M. and Boulton, A. (2013). Augmented reality in urban places: Contested content and the duplicity of code. *Transactions of the Institute of British Geographers*, 38(3), 464-479.

Gruenewald, J., Pizarro, J. and Chermak, S.M. (2009). Race, gender, and the newsworthiness of homicide incidents. *Journal of Criminal Justice*, 37, 262-272, doi:10.1016/j.jcrimjus.2009.04.006

Hart, R.A. (2008). Stepping back from 'the ladder': Reflections on a model of participatory work with children. *In*: Reid, A., Jensen, B.B., Nikel, J. and Simovska, V. (eds.). Participation and Learning. Springer. https://doi-org.lib.pepperdine.edu/10.1007/978-1-4020-6416-6_2

Hickey, A. (2010). When the streets become a pedagogue. pp. 161-170). *In*: J. Sandlin, B. Schultz and S. Burdick (eds.). Handbook of Public Pedagogy: Education and Learning Beyond Schooling. Routledge.

Hidalgo, L. (2011). Predatory, financial, legal, and political land-scapes in Phoenix. AZ: A fotonovela. http:// www.calameo.com/read/000553314050ed3a3eff4

Hidalgo, L. (2015). Augmented fotonovelas: Creating new media as pedagogical and social justice tools. *Qualitative Inquiry*, 21(3), 300-314. https://doi.org/10.1177/1077800414557831

Hidalgo, L. (2017). Predatory landscapes: Pedagogical and social justice tools to uncover the racist nativism in the spatial dimensions of economic exclusion. pp. 67-87. *In*: D. Morrison, S. Annamma and D. Jackson (eds.). Critical Race Spacial Analysis: Mapping to Understand and Address Educational Inequity. Stylus Publishing: Sterling, VA.

Hocoy, D. (2005). Art therapy and social action: A transpersonal framework. *Journal of the American Art Therapy Association*, 22(1), 7-16. https://files.eric.ed.gov/fulltext/EJ682608.pdf

Iwasaki, Y., Springett, J., Dashora, P., McLaughlin, A.M., McHugh, T.L. and Youth 4YEG Team. (2014). Youth-guided youth engagement: Participatory action research (PAR) with high-risk, marginalized youth. *Child & Youth Services*, 35(4), 316-342.

Jenkins, E.J., Wang, E. and Turner, L. (2009). Traumatic events involving friends and family members in a sample of African American early adolescents. *American Journal of Orthopsychiatry*, 79, 398-406. doi:10.1037/a0016659

Jennings, L.B., Parra-Medina, D., Hilfinger-Messias, D.K. and McLoughlin, K. (2006). Toward a critical social theory of youth empowerment. *Journal of Community Practice*, 14(1-2), 31-55. doi: 10.1300/J125v14n01_03

Johnson, J.D., Olivo, N., Gibson, N., Reed, W. and Ashburn-Nardo, L. (2009). Priming media stereotypes reduces support for social welfare policies: The mediating role of empathy. *Personality and Social Psychology Bulletin*, 35(4), 463-476. https://doi.org/10.1177/0146167208329856

Karcher, O.P. (2017). Sociopolitical oppression, trauma, and healing: Moving toward a social justice art therapy framework. *Art Therapy*, 34(3), 123-128. doi: 10.1080/07421656.2017.1358024

Kennelly, J. (2011). Understanding youth political engagement: Youth citizenship as governance. *In*: Citizen Youth. Education, Politics, and Public Life. Palgrave Macmillan. https://doi.org/10.1057/9780230119611_2

Kim, J. (2019). What does it mean/look like to hold space for someone?: A crucial tool for life coaching and relationships. *Psychology Today*. https://www.psychologytoday.com/us/blog/the-angry-therapist/201910/what-does-it-meanlook-hold-space-

someone#:~:text=Holding%20space%20means%20to%20be,no%20matter%20what%20
they%20are.

Kirshner, B. (2008). Guided participation in three youth activism organizations: Facilitation, apprenticeship, and joint work. *The Journal of the Learning Sciences*, 17(1), 60-101. https://doi.org/10.1080/10508400701793190

Kirshner, B. (2015). Youth activism in an era of education inequality. *NYU Press*. www.jstor. org/stable/j.ctt17mvk9f

Larson, R., Walker, K. and Pearce, N. (2005). A comparison of youth-driven and adult-driven youth programs: Balancing inputs from youth and adults. *Journal of Community Psychology*, 33(1), 57-74. doi: 10.1002/jcop.20035

Lave, J. and Wenger, E. (1991). *Situated Learning: Legitimate Peripheral Participation*. Cambridge University Press.

Leonard, D.J. (2017). Illegible black death, legible white pain: Denied media, mourning, and mobilization in an era of "post-racial" gun violence. *Cultural Studies ↔ Critical Methodologies*, 17(2), 101-109. https://doi.org/10.1177/1532708616664234

Livingstone, A., Celemencki, J. and Calixte, M. (2014). Youth participatory action research and school improvement: The missing voices of black youth in Montreal. *Canadian Journal of Education /Revue Canadienne De L'éducation*, 37(1), 283-307. www.jstor.org/ stable/canajeducrevucan.37.1.283

London, J. and Chabrán, M. (2004). Youth-led rep: Building critical consciousness for social change. *Practicing Anthropology*, 26(2), 45-50. www.jstor.org/stable/24791129

Lupton, R. (2009). Area-based initiatives in English education: What place for space and place? pp. 111-23. *In*: Education and Poverty in Affluent Countries. C. Raffo, A. Dyson, H. Gunter, D. Hall, L. Jones and A. Afrodit (eds.). Routledge.

Maclin, A. (n.d.). 32 big questions that spark personal growth. Oprah.com. http://www.oprah. com/inspiration/josh-feigelson-ask-big-questions-iniative

Marín Díaz, V. (2017). The relationships between Augmented Reality and inclusive education in Higher Education. *Bordón*, 69(3). 125-142. doi:10.13042/Bordon.2017.51123.

Martin, D.G. (2000) Constructing place: Cultural hegemonies and media images of an inner-city neighborhood. *Urban Geography*, 21(5), 380-405. doi: 10.2747/0272-3638.21.5.380

Martín-Baró, I. (1994). *Writings for a Liberation Psychology*. Harvard University Press.

Massey, J. and Snyder, B. (2012, September). Occupying Wall Street: Places and spaces of political action. *Places Journal*. https://doi.org/10.22269/120917

Mathew A.P. (2015). Urban Research Machines: Engaging the Modern Urban Citizen through Public Creativity. *In*: Araya D. (ed.). Smart Cities as Democratic Ecologies. Palgrave Macmillan, London. https://doi.org/10.1057/9781137377203_5

McCluskey, G. (2014). "Youth is present only when its presence is a problem:" Voices of young on school discipline in school. *Children & Society*, 28(2), 2-11. doi:10.1111/J.1099-0860.2012.00450.x

Meiners, E.R. (2010). *Right to be Hostile: Schools, Prisons, and the Making of Public Enemies*. Routledge.

Mendelson, T., Mari, K., Blum, R.W., Catalano, R.F. and Brindis, C.D. (2018). Opportunity youth: Insights and opportunities for a public health approach to reengage disconnected teenagers and young adults. *Public Health Reports*, 133(1_suppl), 54S-64S. https://doi. org/10.1177/0033354918799344

Metzl, J.M. (2019). What guns mean: The symbolic lives of firearms. *Palgrave Commun.*, 5(35). https://doi.org/10.1057/s41599-019-0240-y

Morgan, J. (2000). Critical pedagogy: The spaces that make the difference. *Pedagogy, Culture and Society*, 8(3), 273-289, doi: 10.1080/14681360000200099

Mortensen, J., Lichty, L., Foster, F.P., Harfst, S., Hockin, S., Warsinske, K. and Abdullah,

K. (2014). Leadership through a youth lens: Understanding youth conceptualizations of leadership. *Journal of Community Psychology*, 42(4), 447-462. https://doi.org/10.1002/jcop.21620

Nugent, N.R., Koenen, K.C. and Bradley, B. (2012). Heterogeneity of posttraumatic stress symptoms in a highly traumatized low income, urban, African American sample. *Journal of Psychiatric Research*, 46(12), 1576-1583. https://doi.org/10.1016/j.jpsychires.2012.07.012

Offerdahl, K., Evangelides, A. and Powers, M. (2014). Overcoming youth marginalization: Conference report and policy recommendations. Columbia Global Policy Initiative, June 2014. https://www.un.org/youthenvoy/wp-content/uploads/2014/10/Columbia-Youth-Report-FINAL_26-July-2014.pdf

Parham-Payne, W. (2014). The role of the media in the disparate response to gun violence in America. *Journal of Black Studies*, 45(8), 752-768. https://doi.org/10.1177/0021934714555185

Parker, K., Horowitz, J., Igielnik, R, Oliphant, B. and Brown, A. (2017). *America's Complex Relationship with Guns*. Pew Research Center, June 2017. http://www.pewsocialtrends.org/2017/06/22/americas-complexrelationship-with-guns/

Parsons, C., Thompson, M., Vargas, E.W. and Rocco, G. (2018). America's youth under fire. Center for American Progress. https://www.americanprogress.org/issues/guns- crime/reports/2018/05/04/450343/americas-youth-fire/

Parto, J.A., Evans, M.K. and Zonderman, A.B. (2011). Symptoms of posttraumatic stress disorder among urban residents. *Journal of Nervous Mental Disorders*, 199, 436-439. doi:10.1097/NMD.0b013e3182214154

Peeples, L. (2020, June). What the data say about police brutality and racial bias—and which reforms might work. Nature.com. https://www.nature.com/articles/d41586-020-01846-z

Perri, M. (2007). Vaughan youth cabinet: Youth participation in community planning and design. *Children, Youth and Environments*, 17(2), 581-593. www.jstor.org/stable/10.7721/chilyoutenvi.17.2.0581

Poretski, L., Arazy, O., Lanir, J., Shahar, S. and Nov, O. (2019). Virtual objects in the physical world: Relatedness and psychological ownership in augmented reality. *In*: Proceedings of 2019 CHI Conference on Human Factors in Computing Systems (CHI 2019), May 4-9, 2019, Glasgow, Scotland, UK. https://doi.org/10.1145/3290605.3300921

Proboscis (2019). Vamonde (Version 4.1.0) [Mobile application software]. https://apps.apple.com/us/app/vamonde-travel-like-a-local/id1015489274

Punamäki, R.L., Komproe, I., Qouta, S., El-Masir, M. and de Jong, J.T.V.M. (2005). The deterioration and mobilization effects of trauma on social support: Childhood maltreatment and adulthood military violence in a Palestinian community sample. *Child Abuse & Neglect*, 29(4), 351-373. doi:10.1016/j.chiabu.2004.10.011

Quiros, L. and Berger, R. (2015). Responding to the sociopolitical complexity of trauma: An integration of theory and practice. *Journal of Loss and Trauma*, 20(2), 149-159. doi:10.1080/15325024.2013.836353

Rayner, L. (2005). Ecological collapse, trauma theory and permaculture. Resilience.org. https://www.resilience.org/stories/2005-10-29/ecological-collapse-trauma-theory-and-permaculture/

Rennie Center for Education Research & Policy (2019). Student Voice: How Young People Can Shape the Future of Education. Boston, MA: Rennie Center for Education Research & Policy. https://files.eric.ed.gov/fulltext/ED594109.pdf

Reyes, A.H. (2006). *Discipline, Achievement, and Race*. Rowman & Littlefield Publishers.

Rich, J. (2009). *Wrong Place, Wrong Time: Trauma and Violence in the Lives of Young Black Men*. Johns Hopkins University Press.

Roberts, A.L., Gilman, S.E., Breslau, J., Breslau, N. and Koenen, K.C. (2011). Race/ethnic differences in exposure to traumatic events, development of post-traumatic stress disorder, and treatment-seeking for post-traumatic stress disorder in the United States. *Psychological Medicine*, 41, 71-83. https://doi.org/10.1017/S0033291710000401

Rogers, T. (2016). Youth arts, media, and critical literacies as forms of public engagement in the local/global interface. *Literacy Research: Theory, Method, and Practice*, 65(1), 268-282. https://doi.org/10.1177/2381336916661519

Ross, K. (2017). Engaging in social change: Motivations, inspirations, and action. pp. 94-119. *In*: Youth Encounter Programs in Israel: Pedagogy, Identity, and Social Change. Syracuse University Press. doi:10.2307/j.ctt1pk86gm.10

Ross, T. (2019). Media and Stereotypes. *In*: Ratuva S. (eds.). The Palgrave Handbook of Ethnicity. Palgrave Macmillan, Singapore. https://doi.org/10.1007/978-981-13-0242-8_26-1

Rossetto, E. (2012). A hermeneutic phenomenological study of community mural making and social action art therapy. *Art Therapy*, 29(1), 19-26. doi: 10.1080/07421656.2012.648105

Sandlin, J.A., O'Malley, M.P. and Burdick, J. (2011). Mapping the complexity of public pedagogy scholarship: 1894-2010. *Review of Educational Research*, 81(3), 338-375. https://doi.org/10.3102/0034654311413395

Sarrica, M., Grimaldi, F. and Nencini, A. (2010). Youth, citizenship and media: An exploration from the social representations perspective. *Revue internationale de psychologie sociale, tome* 23(4), 37-62. https://www.cairn.info/revue-internationale-de-psychologie sociale-2010-4-page-37.htm.

Schuermans, N., Loopmans, M. and Vandenabeele, J. (2012). Public space, public art and public pedagogy. *Social & Cultural Geography*, 13(7), 675-682. doi: 10.1080/14649365.2012.728007

Semuels, A. (2016). Good school, rich school; bad school: The inequality at the heart of America's education. *The Atlantic*. https://www.theatlantic.com/business/archive/2016/08/property-taxes-and-unequal-schools/497333/

Senie, H.F. (2016). *Memorials to Shattered Myths: Vietnam to 9/11*. Oxford University Press.

Simpson, G. (2018). The missing peace – Independent progress: Study on youth, peace and security. United Nations Population Fund and Peacebuilding Support Office, 2018. https://www.youth4peace.info/system/files/2018-10/youthweb-english.pdf

Skwarek, M. (2018). Augmented reality activism. pp. 3 - 40). *In*: V. Geroimenko (ed.). Augmented Reality Art: From an Emerging Technology to a Novel Creative Medium, 2nd edition. https://doi.org/10.1007/978-3-319-69932-5_1

Smiley, C. and Fakunle, D. (2016). From "brute" to "thug": The demonization and criminalization of unarmed Black male victims in America. *Journal of Human Behavior in the Social Environment*, 26(3-4), 350-366. doi:10.1080/10911359.2015.1129256

Smith, M. (2010). Liquid walls: The digital art of Tamika Thiel. *PAJ: A Journal of Performance Art*, 32(3), 25-34. www.jstor.org/stable/40856575

Smith, S.S. (2014). Traumatic loss in low-income communities of color. *Focus*, 31, 32-34. https://www.irp.wisc.edu/wp/wp-content/uploads/2019/04/foc311j.pdf

Soja, E.W. (2010). *Seeking Spatial Justice*. University of Minnesota Press.

Stetsenko, A. (2014). Transformative activist stance for education: The challenge of inventing the future in moving beyond the status quo. pp. 181-198). *In*: Corcoran, T. (ed.). Psychology in Education. Brill Sense.

Stevenson, S. (2016). Transforming a community: A collaborative group art therapy mural. *The Journal of Art for Life*, 8(5), 1-22. file:///Users/samuelsjanice/Downloads/87258-Article%20Text-114911-2-10-20161215.pdf

Stoll, L.C. (2013). *Race and Gender in the Classroom: Teachers, Privilege, and Enduring Social Inequalities*. Lexington Books.

Suess, G. and Lewis, K.S. (2007). The time is now: Youth organize to transform Philadelphia high schools. *Children, Youth and Environments*, 17(2), 364-379. www.jstor.org/stable/10.7721/chilyoutenvi.17.2.0364

Sundstrom, R.R. (2003). Race and place: Social space in the production of human kinds. *Philosophy & Geography*, 6(1), 83-95, doi: 10.1080/1090377032000063333

Thiel, T. (2004). Beyond Manzanar: Creating dramatic structure in ergodic narrative. *In*: Göbel, S. et al. (eds.). Technologies for Interactive Storytelling and Entertainment. TIDSE 2004. Lecture Notes in Computer Science, vol. 3105. https://doi.org/10.1007/978-3-540-27797-2_32

Thompson, S.N. (2009). Coping styles of African American youth living in poverty: Understanding the role of coping in resiliency. College of Liberal Arts & Social Sciences Theses and Dissertations. https://via.library.depaul.edu/etd/2

Tilton, J. (2010). What is "the power of the youth"? pp. 191-228. *In*: Dangerous or Endangered?: Race and the Politics of Youth in Urban America. NYU Press. www.jstor.org/stable/j.ctt9qfgp9.13

Toldson, I.A. and Lemmons, B.P. (2015). Out-of-School time and African American students: linking concept to practice (editor's commentary). *The Journal of Negro Education*, 84(3), 207-210. doi:10.7709/jnegroeducation.84.3.0207

Townsend, B.L. (2000). The disproportionate discipline of African American learners: Reducing school suspensions and expulsions. *Exceptional Children*, 66(3), 381-391. https://doi.org/10.1177/001440290006600308

Triplett, N.P., Allen, A. and Lewis, C.W. (2014). Zero tolerance, school shootings, and the post brown quest for equity in discipline policy: An examination of how urban minorities are punished for white suburban violence. *The Journal of Negro Education*, 83(3), 352-370. doi:10.7709/jnegroeducation.83.3.0352

Tsekoura, M. (2016). Spaces for youth participation and youth empowerment: Case studies from the UK and Greece. *Young*, 24(4), 326-341. https://doi.org/10.1177/1103308815618505

United States Commission on Civil Rights (2019). Beyond suspensions: Examining school discipline policies and connections to the school-to-prison-pipeline for students of color with disabilities. Briefing before the United States Commission on Civil Rights, July 2019, Washington, DC. https://www.usccr.gov/pubs/2019/07-23-Beyond-Suspensions.pdf

Vavrus, F. and Cole, K. (2002). "I didn't do nothing": The discursive construction of school suspension. *The Urban Review*, 34(2), 87-11.

Virgina Department of Education (2015). Improving School Attendance: A resource guide for Virgina Schools. https://www.iirp.edu/images/conf_downloads/yepHFO_improving_school_attendance.pdf

Watkins, M. and Shulman, H. (2010). *Toward Psychologies of Liberation*. Palgrave Macmillan.

Wilkie, S. (2018). An exploration of community mural making in the context of art therapy and social action: A literature review. Lesley University expressive therapies capstone theses. https://digitalcommons.lesley.edu/expressive_theses/71

Wright, D. (2007). ¡Escuelas, Si! ¡Pintas, No! (schools, yes! prisons, no!) connecting youth action research and youth organizing in California. *Children, Youth and Environments*, 17(2), 503-516. www.jstor.org/stable/10.7721/chilyoutenvi.17.2.0503

Wu, H.C.J., Kornbluh, M., Weiss, J. and Roddy, L. (2016). Measuring and understanding authentic youth engagement: The youth-adult partnership rubric. *Afterschool Matters*, 23, 8-17. https://files.eric.ed.gov/fulltext/EJ1095954.pdf

Wun, C. (2018). Angered: Black and non-Black girls of color at the intersections of violence and school discipline in the United States. *Race Ethnicity and Education*, 21(4), 423-437. doi: 10.1080/13613324.2016.1248829

Youth Speak Out Coalition and Zimmerman, K. (2007). Making space, making change: Models for youth-led social change organizations. *Children, Youth and Environments*, 17(2): 298-314. www.jstor.org/stable/10.7721/chilyoutenvi.17.2.0298

Zeldin, S., Christens, B.D. and Powers, J.L. (2013). The psychology and practice of youth-adult partnership: Bridging generations for youth development and community change. *American Journal of Community Psychology*, 51, 385-397. https://doi-org.lib.pepperdine.edu/10.1007/s10464-012-9558-y

Zinzow, H.M., Rheingold, A.A., Hawkins, A.O., Saunders, B.E. and Kilpatrick, D.G. (2009). Losing a loved one to homicide: Prevalence and mental health correlates in a national sample of young adults. *Journal of Traumatic Stress*, 22, 20-27. doi: 10.1002/jts.20377

# Part 4
# Preparing the Augmented Citizen

# Chapter
# 12

# XR Content Authoring Challenges: The Creator-Developer Divide

**John T. Murray[1] and Emily K. Johnson[2]**

Games and Interactive Media, University of Central Florida P.O. Box 163121,
Orlando, Florida 32816-3121
[1] Email: jtm@ucf.edu;
[2] Email: ekj@ucf.edu

## Introduction

Computer media has expanded from screen-based interfaces, including smartphones and personal computers, to encompass an emerging focus on spatial and reality media. These new affordances derive from advances in algorithms, hardware, and general computing, but their real impact is on how they redefine our relationship with computing. The technologies reside under a number of umbrella terms, specifying immersive media, such as virtual reality (VR) and mixed reality (MR), devices that have spatial awareness and overlay graphics through augmented reality (AR), and the more catch-all term "eXtended Reality" (XR). These technologies have been examined through many lenses, with most of the societal impact work being speculative in nature (Carter and Egliston, 2020). Carter and Egliston review ethical issues surrounding AR and VR as related, though their focus is more on the technology writ large and specific commercial examples of its impact on society. At the center of the technology, and yet largely missing from academic discussions, is XR content and the platforms used to produce it. By understanding the choices and the forces shaping these important pieces of software, we can better understand how to broaden participation in this important new medium.

This chapter develops a framework for understanding authoring platforms with a focus on XR and argues that traditional taxonomies of technical capabilities and features should be joined with studies of the assumptions and context of these important software tools. Authoring platforms are defined as software tools that primarily aid in the creation and testing of content for a given computational medium. They play a critical role in who participates in the content ecosystem.There are few available studies that examine how existing authoring platforms and paradigms encode problematic assumptions that turn off novices. For instance, Mercan and

Durdu evaluate a set of tasks using Unity by both novice and experienced users and cite the cryptic error messages as one major barrier to use (Mercan and Durdu, 2017), while Good and Howland evaluate the use of natural language in aiding novice programmers and alleviate some of the same barriers by providing additional descriptions of what is happening alongside the code interface (Good and Howland, 2017). Alongside studies of novices, there are several low or no-code editors that offer the marketing promise of a solution that can appeal to 'nontechnical' users with 'no technical expertise required[1],' allowing the creation of apps 'without writing code.'[2,3] All of these indicate a strong distinction in the industry and the authoring platforms between developers and creators, and technical and non-technical authoring. Authoring platforms are distinct from programming languages, user interfaces, and software development, though their effectiveness and critiques are necessarily entangled with them. While individual companies may produce authoring systems, each often shares more in common than marketing materials would suggest. This chapter uses a close analysis of current authoring platforms and a set of case studies of challenges encountered during the production of XR projects to develop an agenda for the field and to situate it in relation to existing work on platform studies and digital humanities.

The ethical issues that are entangled with XR are well described by Carter and Egliston and are worthy of additional attention (Carter and Egliston, 2020). Carter and Egliston accurately survey the studies that chart the accessibility of XR experiences, including how they might not be equally available through interface decisions or assumptions to all potential users. This includes women and persons with disabilities, two populations disproportionately affected by simulator sickness, sexual harassment and assault, and a general lack of representation—all of which results in a lack of participation in the creation and testing of XR works among disadvantaged populations more generally. There are also the dangers inherent in collecting personal and potentially revealing data about users by virtue of the interface fidelity, which can even include eye tracking. These challenges are posited as responsibilities of the technology owners and developers to overcome, as at least some of these issues are solvable through software implementation. Another common thread in their work is the necessity of including a variety of users in the development process. The relationship between authoring paradigms and potential users is the primary topic of this chapter and can have an outsized impact on who creates XR content by directly using the available tools. Improving authoring platforms would also benefit the design and development of educational XR for a broader set of users. This would broaden the options for engaging learning opportunities and help close some of the achievement gaps created by underlying and systemic issues facing K-12 education.

---

[1]  https://zap.works/designer/ZapWorks Designer
[2]  https://bubble.io/ No-code platform
[3]  https://www.yoyogames.com/gamemakerGameMaker

# Authoring Platforms

Platform studies were proposed by Ian Bogost and Nick Montfort as a "set of approaches which investigated the underlying computer systems that support creative work" (Bogost and Montfort, 2009). The approach was used in a series by the same name published by MIT, which included a series of studies of hardware (and software) platforms. Apperley and Parikka draw the necessary connection between the enterprise of platform studies and media archaeology (Apperley and Parikka, 2015). They observe that the study of a platform depends on a "variety of materials to place the platform at the center of a materially grounded discourse." This methodology proves challenging for *authoring platforms*, which have been previously considered alongside the other elements of software platforms. Murray and Salter make the argument that the affordances of the Flash authoring tool, particularly in its earlier incarnations, gave rise to the unique constituency of its community of creators and the types of aesthetic artifacts produced (Salter and Murray, 2014). These were due to not only the accessible authoring tool that empowered creators to draw interactive works using metaphors from paint and illustration programs, but also the portability of the resulting artifacts due to the then-popular Flash browser plugin.

These authors propose focusing on "authoring platforms" as a related but distinct concept from the "platform" of platform studies to highlight the interplay between:

1. **Behaviors,** including authoring scripts and specifying interactions and relationships.
2. **Configuration**, such as placement of assets and assigning of values and behaviors.
3. **Workflow**, evaluation and how and when changes are made.
4. **Information management**, or support for persisting and sharing data
5. **Conceptual metaphors**, such as the object-component model, or object-oriented methodologies.

These concerns form a framework that prioritizes authoring over the underlying data formats and engine and/or hardware features. The study of authoring platforms necessarily builds on both platform and software studies but offers a unique lens on the intermediary stages of development and the implications of authoring platform design decisions for both users and content.

The obvious modern instances of authoring platforms for XR include Amazon Sumerian, Unity and Unreal. These software packages solve several common problems in production. They share enough features and purpose in common to be considered different implementations of the same authoring platform paradigm, which separates 3D content and behaviors. The fact that each can be chosen for a similar end and by a similar user helps to describe the position of these software platforms in a way that is not possible when comparing them using the traditional approach taken by platform studies: the unique affordances of a platform define the software that runs on it, as Montfort and Bogost argue in Racing the Beam (Montfort and Bogost, 2009).

Besides tutorials intended for beginners, a variety of artifacts and "paratexts" (blog posts, publications, etc.) pertaining to authoring tools are not available. The development process (especially for commercial games) and intermediary source files, outside of academic contexts, are not normally published. Focusing on the unique problems that authoring platforms solve is worth the effort however. These problems collectively act as a gatekeeper, both for the structure of content produced and variety of users able to learn and utilize the tool.

Authoring platforms each have assumptions and intended users that shape their use and utility. These have implications for the first encounter of a neophyte and the work of an expert alike. Despite efforts to promote computational literacy and programming through various efforts and programs, it is clear that there is a need to invite and support new authors in creating XR literacy that does not necessitate becoming a computer scientist. This participatory stance on authoring is important, as the past two decades have seen advances in the underlying technology that makes these types of experiences possible, but many of the consequences of the designs were not apparent to their creators. For instance, it was not a foregone conclusion that the structure underlying computer graphics, that of a tree, would be the primary design metaphor used to organize content in the interface. For instance, industry standard graphics software, such as Photoshop[4], a popular design tool used by illustrators and graphic designers, prioritizes named "groups" of visual shapes and elements and uses a different conception of "layers" that describe relationships between elements visually, offering a means of comparing alternatives or reusing elements in different compositions. In Unity, the same term, "layer," is used to describe a set of objects that have varying degrees of separation from one another in terms of the simulated physics system. It has nothing to do with the visual relationships that layers in Photoshop refer to, which instead pays attention to the layers of transparency used in animated films, where different compositions could be made using the same shapes and features. Grouping elements in Unity takes place through a more symbolic "tag" concept, which assigns a single label to every object in the scene and does not function like tags in other media, like blogs. The relationship between the position in 3D space and through parent-child relationships, is controlled through a special component called a "Transform," very familiar to those who have worked with tree structures. The transform is a thin layer on top of the linear algebra used to position the element within the scene graph. While each of these choices to adopt common terms alone may seem benign, they represent a degree of cognitive interference between common concepts used by designers in other media. These decisions have accumulated in the software versions and have become integrated into the general skills of working in this domain, becoming de facto standards in similar interactive media authoring tools.

Recent companies and products have emerged to address the growing need to make these technologies available to a broad set of users through tools that offer a different approach to the challenge. These XR authoring tools can be divided into two categories: professional, and amateur-oriented. Professional-oriented tools

[4] https://www.adobe.com/products/photoshop.html

include Unity MARS, Unreal VR Mode, Adobe Aero, and Zappar. Amateur-oriented tools target creators who are not professional developers or designers, and include Zoe, Enklu, and Neos VR (Karbotte, 2016).

Content creation tools, including programs, languages, and data formats for interactive media can be understood by examining the history of screen-based authoring platforms. First, the target users for these new technologies are limited by the maturity of authoring metaphors to groups with the corresponding technical knowledge, including advanced knowledge of a supported programming language and familiarity with the libraries that coordinate events and user input. The complexity of both the possible input and the possible states of the system are both substantial opportunities over the controlled context of a screen-based program. However, these additional dimensions require conceptual innovation in addition to library and software development. For a review of standard development and the implications for making XR a platform for the web, see MacIntyre and Smith's description of the efforts (MacIntyre and Smith, 2018).

Interactive media that targeted the web took off when tools such as Flash made it possible to work with the materials more directly and preview the output. Flash provided just such an authoring experience, enabling its users to manipulate animations through a visible timeline and associate events with visible boxes that represented frames (Salter and Murray, 2014). The tool hid much of the complexity of the program away from its dominant content genre: web-based interactive animations. It had a key advantage over competing beginner-friendly programming environments such as Processing in that it enabled instant publication without installing software, and without writing a single line of code. This aversion to authoring programs through textual coding will be revisited later, but it is worth noting that the virtue is almost universal in authoring tools marketed toward amateurs.

## Evaluating Authoring Platforms

While every authoring tool espouses an easier authoring experience, each tool prioritizes different users and different end goals. This chapter draws attention to the divide between technical and non-technical, using the marketing materials of the *what* developers should prioritize in the development of future platforms, in order to maximize access to this new medium. While each authoring platform originated to serve the entertainment and gaming markets, they have become the de facto standard tools for creating content for other purposes, including non-commercial and community-oriented works.

Below are key questions that assist in evaluating authoring platforms, and which are useful to identify which features require improving versus which features might require replacing.

### How Much Knowledge is Required for Which Types of Experiences?

Producing a program requires varying levels of skill based on the affordances of the interface. An excel program, for instance, requires some familiarity with the equations and references to relative cell position, whereas IFTTT (derived from If

This, Then That) is a cloud service founded in 2010 by Tibbets and Jesse Tane that supports authoring cloud-based condition and action programs without writing a single line of source code using "recipes" (Finnegan, 2019; Ur et al., 2016). This model builds on the idea that most end-user programs rely on similar simple patterns and that an interface can highlight where these patterns, such as data sources or endpoints, differ.

For the professionally oriented content authoring platforms, such as Unity or Unreal, a programming language is necessary for anything more than non-trivial relationships. Both have adopted visual scripting languages to attempt easing this knowledge burden, including Bolt which was recently acquired by Unity (Desatoff, 2020) and Blueprints, Unreal's solution to the same problem, but the node and wire representation still requires familiarity with the underlying object-oriented architecture and the related concepts of events, variables, and functions. Both Blueprints and Bolt are not true flow-based visual scripting, however, as they rely on the same underlying representations as the text-based programming languages for each platform.

Another trend in addressing the knowledge requirement is the use of block-based programming languages, which remove the barrier of entering syntactically correct instructions, but which suffer from limitations on the complexity and target platforms (Mason and Dave, 2017).

### What Contexts can the Work be Published in?

The potential audience for a work directly depends on whether the work can be distributed or if it requires that users download the work or a runtime in order to be experienced. This is a limitation of many platforms designed to teach computer languages, such as Minecraft: Education Edition[5], where it is difficult for an author to publish work outside of walled gardens. Many authoring tools for interactive narratives offer options to publish works in formats suitable for distribution via traditional app stores, such as Ren'Py, though with Ink[6] and Twine[7], an intermediate step is required.

### How are the Burdens of the Underlying Technology Borne by the Tool?

These burdens include, but are not limited to, managing the memory limitations of the hardware, such as in mobile devices or all-in-one VR headsets, and dealing with noisy data that can result from modern spatial tracking systems, such as AR Core, ARK it and the depth-sensing camera input from XR Headsets. Unity MARS, an AR-specific unity authoring add-on, is one solution to the problem, whereas Unity Remote, an app that can be downloaded from various app stores, was a previous solution for rapidly testing Unity applications on mobile devices, though it did not support camera input or AR features. Both Magic Leap and Microsoft HoloLens

---

[5]  A voxel-based learning environment based on popular IP. https://education.minecraft.net
[6]  A choice-based interactive narrative language and runtime. https://www.inklestudios.com/ink/
[7]  A hypertext interactive narrative authoring platform. https://twinery.org/

offer a feature that supports streaming output from authoring tools such as Unity or UE4 to the device, though this also requires switching back and forth from the editing environment to the device for evaluation. An ideal tool would provide authoring-time assistance with managing these issues or execution-time behavior to handle common challenges without requiring the author to understand the underlying algorithms or hardware limitations at a technical level.

## What is the Conceptual Distance Required to Implement an Idea?

This chapter defines the "conceptual distance" as the number of steps and translations required to implement an intended effect through an authoring platform. For instance, in order to author a behavior in Unity, one must first identify or create a script to execute the behavior, then add the requisite code which requires referencing the underlying engine architecture, and reframing the desired behavior in terms of the authoring platform's ontology. This would involve identifying and referencing the related Game Objects through variables in C#, modifying or translating their properties, such as their position and relation using the command Transform data structure, and, if necessary, provide event handlers that interface with the systems that manage interactions between either objects (the physical system) or the user's input (the input system). All of these steps require additional working memory and knowledge of the target system's nomenclature and affordances which can only be acquired through practice, and which is not related to the domain being authored. All experiences must be translated into more programming-centric view of content. This is distinct from the authoring experience in Ink, for example, where text is both the input and output and where the domain-specific language specifically supports that of choices and paths through syntax that leaves the text as the primary authoring interface.

These questions represent a neglected goal that is distinct from usability (Roberto et al., 2016) or authorial leverage (Chen et al., 2009) which have previously been the focus of research of the authoring software. Instead, the questions move research towards developing a framework of authoring experience for these platforms, analogous to other efforts to examine and understand programmer and player experience.

While player experience has been a topic long understood by game developers, such as examining the combination of factors that game designers consider when shaping a rule system (Hunicke et al., 2004) or adventure game (Fernández-vara, 2008), it has recently been a focus of the human-computer interaction community (Zammitto et al., 2014). Some important work on articulating and identifying authoring challenges for augmented and virtual reality has also become a focus, especially by Billinghurst et al. (Billinghurst, 2020; Billinghurst et al., 2011; Lee et al., 2005).

At the current time, XR is a challenging content category to author, and it is primarily being developed in professional contexts for advertising, training, industrial use cases, and entertainment. More specialized tools are being developed and deployed to address the unique challenges of the content. The next section examines several contemporary XR authoring platforms and is followed by a section analyzing specific cases where the authors are familiar with the experience of developing a project with novices.

# Contemporary XR Authoring Platforms

Authoring for XR has a lot of commercial value. Between the success of Pokémon GO and the documented benefits of AR in education and advertising, many companies, both new and established, have invested in creation of authoring platforms that address the key pain points. This section describes current platforms common to XR authoring challenges, using the framework from the questions posed from the previous section.

Despite advances in certain XR authoring challenges, however, creating content that meaningfully interacts with users for either Unity or Unreal still requires knowledge of coding languages (C# for Unity, C++ for Unreal) or an equivalent visual scripting language such as Bolt (Unity) or Blueprints (Unreal). There are three authoring platforms that depart significantly from the choices made by Unity and Unreal. These include Neos VR, a virtual world that is reminiscent of Second Life, Enklu Cloud, a start-up which is focusing on head-mounted XR authoring, and Zoe, an ed-tech startup with a focus on authoring interactive content for VR.

## Zappar

Founded in 2011, Zappar[8] is one of the larger AR cloud platforms. According to the page's marketing materials, "whether you're a Fortune 500 company, a creative agency, or a hobbyist exploring AR content creation for the first time, the ZapWorks toolkit has everything you need to succeed." The authoring platforms they offer are ZapWorks Studio and ZapWorks Designer. ZapWorks Designer provides a simple content model which attaches 3D models, videos, images and animations to ZapCodes (markers that allow users to launch an experience from the Zappar mobile app), whereas ZapWorksStudio has a lot in common with Unity's authoring interfaces and orientation toward professional use cases.

## Unity MARS

Unity recently released its MARS addition to Unity that specifically targets XR content development pain points. The software is priced at $50/month or $600 a year at the time of writing. The system leverages companion apps to collect and store environmental data which can make authoring on a traditional mouse and keyboard interface easier. From their blog:

> We are trying to create workflows that are accessible to nontechnical users but still familiar to Unity developers. You edit the same scene, with the same assets, using tools that share terminology and, interaction patterns where it makes sense (Schoen, 2020).

---

[8] https://www.zappar.com/

Here the priority for opening up the creation of XR experiences to "nontechnical" users retains the caveat that the workflow be familiar to "Unity developers." This represents one of the forces that prevents more radical changes to the authoring workflow, the need to satisfy the existing user base and to retain the value of the legacy of the Unity authoring platform license model. Based on the use cases and clients described in its marketing material, Unity MARS seems to be targeted at advertising and larger productions, such as Dr. Seuss's ABC AR (Chacko, 2020). The product landing page even emphasizes "Professional-grade workflows for AR development," highlighting the value offered. The initial templates emphasize industrial use cases such as training and games, along with a tabletop scenario. The conceptual organization overlays Unity concepts, adding in the notion of proxies (stand in for encountered real-world tracked objects), semantic tags (describing traits of those objects), conditions (properties that can be the basis of behaviors) and a querying system to author how content gets rendered or how it interacts with the detected environment.

## UE4 VR Mode

The idea of creating VR experiences within VR is an attractive one. One early representation is the 2007 short film "World Builder" (Branit, 2007), or the lure of Minecraft (Kuhn, 2017) as a platform for creating interest in STEM. The main disadvantage of this addition to the Unreal Editor is the lack of any behavior authoring within the mode, which makes it closer to Microsoft Maquette (Lang, 2019) and Google Blocks (Gonzalez, 2017) than to the other XR authoring tools in this section. A user must use C++ or Blueprints to author behaviors.

## NeosVR

Of the currently available authoring platforms, NeosVR is probably the most unique. It is a virtual world platform that includes a full-fledged content authoring platform inside, allowing multiple users to co-create content together in real-time in the same context where it will be published. Founded in 2014, the virtual world follows in the footsteps of Second Life in its ambition to create not just a virtual world, but a virtual economy based on its own cryptocurrency (Karbotte, 2016). The *in situ* authoring tool enables users to author behaviors and place content in their own scenes, using a node and wire based metaphor that visualizes the same object-component model that Unity uses. The primary differences are the lack of a play and edit mode, and the ability to manipulate many facets of the simulation through drag and drop interactions with VR controllers. There is, in fact, no way to author or experience the authored content outside of NeosVR, which limits the possible opportunities for engagement for created content.

## Enklu Cloud

A relatively new company, Enklu focuses on in-situ content creation targeting the Microsoft Hololens, with an emphasis on live events and performances. It was founded in 2016 by Ray Kallmeyer, with a focus on location-based works, developing some of the first AR experiences for brands such as Mercedes Benz and installation "The Unreal Garden" in San Francisco (Stone, 2018).

The shortcomings of adapting a screen-based development environment for XR content development have not been lost on the market. This section describes two products being actively developed to target amateur content creation with an emphasis on education and teaching opportunities.

## Zoe

The major challenge with creating content using the professional tools described above is the level of knowledge necessary to begin. This, coupled with the inherent attraction of VR for educational purposes, were the inspirations behind Zoe, a product built on top of Unity that transforms the platform's authoring capabilities. Zoe is being developed by Apelab, a startup founded by Emilie Joly, Maria Beltran and Sylvain Joly in 2014 (Benzakein, 2016). It is the successor to Spatial Stories, the company's first released XR authoring tool. Like other in-situ creation tools, such as Microsoft Maquette (Lang, 2019) and Google Blocks (Gonzalez, 2017), Zoe supports static asset placement and manipulation, though currently it only supports models from the 3D model cloud service Google Poly[9]. However, Zoe includes *in situ* behavior authoring which is unique among the previously described platforms. The model adopted is conceptually similar to IFTTT, using author-defined conditions that trigger certain actions on other objects in the scene. This has a limitation on dealing with complex relationships, as only a single relationship can be edited at one time but is considerably simpler in terms of conceptual distance between idea and implementation.

**Table 12.1:** XR authoring platform comparison

| Authoring Platform | Modality | Behavior | In situ | Publishing | Knowledge Requirements | Target Market |
|---|---|---|---|---|---|---|
| ZapWorks Studio | AR | Event-Action | No | Platform | None | Pro |
| ZapWorks Designer | AR | Tap-Action | No | Platform | None | Pro |
| Unity MARS | MR | Condition-Constraint | Yes | Multi | Unity | Pro |
| Unreal VR Editor | VR | None | Yes | Multi | Unreal | Pro |
| NeosVR | VR | Object-Component | Yes | NeosVR | None | Amateur |
| Enklu | MR | Scripting (JS) | Some | Export to Unity | None | Mixed |
| Zoe | VR | Event-Action | Yes | Zoe/Unity | None | Education |

---

[9]  https://poly.google.com/

Table 12.1 summarizes the authoring tools and their unique features. It is worth noting that almost every authoring tool requires some programming knowledge to author simple behaviors, with Zoe and NeosVR being the two exceptions. In the next section, we will discuss a set of projects that exemplify the issues that some of these authoring platforms attempt to solve, and further enrich the framework with the addition of the complexities of project management outside a professional context.

## Case Studies

In order to understand the role of platforms on the issue, it is important to examine how work is currently being produced and published. While there are many reports on work produced as part of an academic study, works produced outside the ambit of traditional research contexts are less well documented in how they were authored.

These include location-specific works (such as The Unreal Garden) and performance pieces, such as The Under Presents: Tempest (Melnick, 2020), independent works shared outside of traditional app stores, including Mez Breeze's *V[R]ignettes: A Microstory Series*, which was published using the Sketchfab[10] platform as a series of collaborations that include a collage of 3D models, text and sound with a guided path that incorporates work from different collaborators (*V[R] Ignettes | @MezBreezeDesign*, n.d.). The use of a 3D model sharing platform to publish and distribute a VR work is one way artists and creators have found to circumvent the traditional app store models, but unlike previous amateur web-based outlets such as New Grounds, there are no established publication platforms for such works. Many of these works are recognized and republished in other contexts, such as the VR 2020 Electronic Literature Organization Conference and Media Arts Festival[11] inside of virtual worlds such as AltspaceVR[12].

*The Ice-Bound Compendium* is an iPad app that uses AR to tell a story that requires interacting with a print book (Reed et al., 2014). The app won the "Best Story/World Design" award at IndieCade (2014), but had a dependency on Metaio, a commercial AR SDK that was acquired by Apple (Miller and Constine, 2015). The app was removed from the Apple App store, representing a major challenge creators faced with charting not only how to create new XR works, but how to ensure they remained accessible in a changing ecosystem.

The following sections describe three projects using popular XR authoring software that one of the authors (Johnson) has been involved in creating, highlighting major challenges encountered, and the workarounds or compromises that were needed to overcome them.

### ELLE the EndLess LEarner (ELLE)

The goal of this interdisciplinary project is to create a customizable and engaging learning game in VR (Johnson et al., 2020). The collaborating faculty and staff team

---

[10] https://sketchfab.com/
[11] https://elo.cah.ucf.edu/
[12] https://altvr.com/

had very little experience with VR programming platforms (Unity and Unreal) and had no funding. Therefore, this project relied on a group of undergraduate computer science students in a two-semester capstone course. The course is designed so that interested faculty, staff, and people in the industry (ranging from startups to NASA) come to class and pitch an idea to the students. The students then rank the projects they would like to work on, and the professor puts them in small project groups. With the guidance of their computer science instructor and their industry sponsor, students spend the first semester researching the problem and the second semester developing their solution.

Johnson pitched ELLE as a VR endless-runner language-learning game connected to a database and a user-friendly website where language professors could add new words and create downloadable game modules—sets of terms grouped by chapter, part of speech, or any organization the professor desired. A student group was assigned, and ELLE was born—to some extent. The group never quite got the game to connect to the database, and the sponsors were left with a game that included a total of 10 words hard-coded into the game that they lacked the ability or skill to update.

After several iterations of the project with four different student groups, ELLE had become a suite encompassing nine unique games playable on four different platforms (VR, AR, PC, and mobile), using two different authoring tools (UE4 and Unity), connected to three different databases, summarized in Table 12.1. Each group had solved a specific problem for their course project, but these solutions often came at the expense of other aspects of the game. Students typically prefer to create their own games from scratch and are resistant to working with prior groups' codes, so each new game that was developed to fix a problem in a previous version and often focused on solving only that problem without replicating the other aspects of the prior versions that were effective.

**Table 12.2:** The different versions of ELLE listed in chronological order

| Project | Authoring Platform | Target Platform |
|---|---|---|
| ELLE VR 1.0 | UE4 | VR |
| ELLE PC Over-the-shoulder view | UE4 | PC |
| ELLE PC Side-scroller view | UE4 | PC |
| ELLE mobile 2D graphics | Unity | mobile |
| ELLE mobile 3D graphics | Unity | mobile |
| ELLE AR | Unity | Mobile-AR |
| ELLE Speech | Unity | mobile |
| ELLE VR 2.0 | UE4 | VR |
| Project ELLE | UE4 | PC |

The group that created Project ELLE was actually assigned to join all three databases to as many of the existing games as possible, allowing for software decay.

They were specifically instructed not to create a new game. However, this group had a member who was so intent on making a new game that he shirked the backend work the group leader assigned him and instead created an entirely new game in UE4 on his own, creating extra work for the other group members and lowering their ability to successfully complete the assigned database task. This demonstrates another potential hazard of relying on undergraduates with specialized knowledge to develop educational XR work: they can lack the maturity to stay focused on the primary goal of the project.

Admittedly, the database element of this project added greatly to its complexity and required additional specialized knowledge. This complexity necessitated another layer of interdisciplinary support. However, if the language professors had access to a user-friendly tool that would allow them to author their own experiences, the need for a database to house terms could be negated, and the time and effort spent mentoring the computer science students could be more effectively applied to creating robust, meaningful, course-appropriate learning games.

## Middle Passage Experience (MPE)

Another project Johnson is involved in is a VR simulation of the Middle Passage (Pineda et al., 2020; Pineda and Johnson, 2019). This experience was designed to increase the participant's historical knowledge of the transatlantic slave trade as well as empathy for the people who had to live and die in these harsh conditions. The project PI teaches Brazilian history and sought a more engaging way to help her students understand how this journey contributed to the dehumanization of African captives without focusing on hyperviolence like many Hollywood depictions of slavery.

This project was also unfunded and designed with subject matter experts (in this case, History and Africana Studies) not familiar with Unity or UE4, and so had to rely on the computer science capstone students. This pitch was surprisingly well-received, and the sponsors were lucky enough to get an excellent group with a mature understanding of the project's purpose. The development of this simulation had to be done in a careful manner, and the student in charge of the storyline in the simulation met with the history professor for at least one hour a week throughout the two semesters. The history professor had to spend time teaching the computer science students the content of the simulation and provide them with a plethora of historical documents and images to ensure the accuracy of the final experience.

It took one additional group to work out a few technical issues and finish the initial narrative, but all of this work did result in a functional prototype that could be reliably demonstrated at events and classes—a huge success. However, because the faculty sponsors were still unable to edit even small things in the simulation (even just adjusting the wording on the informational displays on the ship remained outside their expertise), they pitched two additional semesters to the capstone course without any luck. Students are already reluctant to take on a project that another group has started, plus, the addition of the serious and distinctively not fun VR experience of the transatlantic slave trade is rarely a popular topic among undergraduates.

If the history professor had access to a user-friendly authoring tool, she could create and modify these experiences herself and not rely on finding the rare computer science undergraduate who happened to be passionate about history. Challenges this project encountered were due to the gatekeeping nature of the platforms where the sponsor team lacked the programming expertise to fully understand design limitations that the software would present—not knowing how much time and effort any given design feature might require, sponsors often restrict the design unnecessarily and are also hesitant to request changes, constraining the entire project. Additionally, difficulties were encountered throughout the design of the ship's three locations: boarding the ship, the living quarters below deck, and above deck on the slave ship. Overarching these concerns was the struggle with process and workflow. The student in charge of the narrative was meeting regularly with the history professor, but the in-progress VR portion was only demonstrated to the sponsors a few times during the duration of the project. This acted to limit the number and type of modifications the sponsor team could request.

## Sherlock's Riddles of Biblical Archaeology (SherBA)

One digital game that Johnson designed, Sherlock's Riddles of Biblical Archaeology (SherBA), is played on a personal computer and, though immersive, does not fall under our definition of XR. Its creation, however, aptly demonstrates the same issues encountered with the two prior XR projects, as it uses the same authoring tool, Unity.

SherBA was the brainchild of another history professor who wished to create more engaging activities to accompany his theatrical, documentary-style video lectures. In a way that is careful not to promote or condemn any religion, SherBA asks players to gather archaeological evidence by viewing the professor's documentary lectures, which drop down at specific timestamps when the video mentions them. Then, the player must act like Sherlock and engage in critical thinking skills by evaluating archaeological evidence to label artifacts as (A) supporting the historicity of the Bible, (B) refuting its historicity, or (C) irrelevant to the argument.

The proof-of-concept was developed as an independent student's project for a game design course. This student was able to use Unity to create a video player that allowed artifacts to appear at specified timestamps in the video, and then tag and sort them. Unfortunately, after the project was submitted for the game design course, the professor was left with a placeholder video and artifacts that he was unable to change.

The next semester, Johnson was able to hire a work-study student to make a playable build with the proper video and artifacts which was presented at a conference (Johnson et al., 2017). However, the artifacts' accompanying written clues were small and difficult to read, and the history professor wanted to create additional videos and games. He was unable to do so because of the gatekeeping barrier of Unity.

With hopes of alleviating the authoring difficulties for the history professor, Johnson pitched a complex project to the capstone course students, asking them to create both an updated student build and a user-friendly application that the history professor himself could operate to create new student builds. This group created an innovative solution: a build that creates builds. The professor-facing Unity build allows the professor to upload videos, artefact images and new maps to create a new level (city to explore), or even an entirely new game, and this build would create a new student-facing build. This solution's only downfall is currently prohibiting it from being used by the professor and his students: it is not compatible with Apple products. The professor cannot require the use of an educational tool that will not operate on 50% or more of the students' devices. This solution, once functional, remains specific to this single game in this single course. If a more user-friendly tool existed, the professor himself could design and create a variety of engaging games to accompany his ambitious video lectures without going through the convoluted effort of developing single-solution platform creators.

# Discussion

Though it may be tempting to assume that there are few humanities centric XR experiences because scholars lack interest in emerging technology, these case studies are evidence that the interest is there. The problem is the additional hurdles that scholars in this discipline face because their expertise does not lie in computer science. They are subject matter experts in their respective fields, not C#. This work suffers from design limitations, communication issues, and development challenges.

## Design Limitations

The deficient level of programming knowledge within these interdisciplinary faculty and staff sponsor teams actively limited the design of the educational games and simulations. This lack of an in-depth understanding of what the platforms could do, or how easy or difficult any given mechanic or design choice would be to a program meant that the sponsor teams often had to rely on suggestions for design from the student development team. Without a strong commitment by the sponsor teams to push the students to ensure that the final product aligns with the core vision, the project faces the danger of losing its meaning and becoming ineffective for teaching the intended content.

Additionally, both Unity and Unreal Engine 4 (UE4) are primarily intended to design for PC platforms (Evain, 2017; Hilliard, 2020). They have attained compatibility with Apple products only recently. Additional steps requiring even more specialized knowledge and equipment are required to make builds playable on Apple devices, slowing and complicating the XR projects.

## Communication Issues

Likewise, the communication between the designers and the student developers required a great deal of effort and time. The sponsors had to teach each student group the content of each simulation or game—the Portuguese language, the Middle Passage, and biblical archaeology, respectively—before the design discussions could even begin. Even then, sponsors had to keep circling back to the key objectives because of how easily undergraduate students can get distracted by new mechanics or attempts to emulate aspects of their favorite AAA entertainment games.

## Development Challenges

Just as this lack of specialized programming knowledge interferes with the initial design and development of XR creation, it prohibits iterations. In the cases described above, after the computer science students submitted their games, the sponsors were unable to make any changes to them. This destroys the iterative process that is so key to developing effective games and simulations (Hunicke et al., 2004; Schreiber and Brathwaite, 2008). In addition, when iterations are attempted, it becomes a struggle to convince undergraduates to apply them to a prior group's work. Students prefer to conceptualize their own version and start completely over—something that rarely happens in the industry (Parberry et al., 2005).

Additionally, the need to rely on student groups with specialized knowledge to create XR experiences about difficult topics such as slavery can compound other challenges. Though efforts such as Computer Science for All[13] to broaden the participation of minority populations in computer science have been somewhat successful, they still have a long way to go (Cuny, n.d.). The authors continue to pitch projects to capstone computer science classes with a noticeable majority of white male students. Even if the sponsors are successful in convincing some of them to work through the tension they feel while working on a game about race, there is much extra work to be done in order to educate the students about difficult history that is often glossed over in K-12 education.

Despite the above challenges, many faculty and staff members who are not computer scientists are eager to incorporate XR into their courses and research. Countless professors already create and use innovative role-playing games and other engaging activities in their courses that require little or no technology. Public-facing groups, as well, such as museums, libraries, and other nonprofits are also motivated to include XR exhibits to engage the community in a variety of topics. XR holds great promise for augmenting these activities to increase their learning efficacy—that is, if the creation tools can be used effectively by everyone who knows the content best to create custom experiences.

The above challenges make it increasingly more difficult for non-programmers to design and develop XR content. Programs such as Unity and Unreal, while an important step toward a more diverse set of designers and developers act as gatekeeping mechanisms, and maintain the fallacy that only a certain type of person is capable of creating XR. These barriers have been described as illustrations of this gatekeeping behavior to call for the creation of more accessible XR authoring tools.

## Conclusions

This chapter presents a framework for understanding authoring platforms and their design in order to evaluate their claims for utility in non-professional use cases and their appeal to non-technical creators. It analyzes a set of existing XR authoring

---

[13] https://www.csforall.org/

tools based on their common features and uses these features to evaluate a set of case studies of XR content produced by the authors.

In spite of the intense interest and development in novice and non-technical creation in XR, a number of barriers remain that prevent it from being a broadly used medium. When subject matter experts untrained in computer science attempt to create a meaningful XR experience that describes the content of a humanities subject, they face additional obstacles like design limitations, communication issues, and development challenges.

It should be noted that several of the challenges described in the case studies with the computer science student groups are typical of any novice group designing a game or simulation for the first time. Students gravitate to the game genres, mechanics, and styles that they have experience playing, and need direct guidance to create an XR simulation or game that differs from what they know. This is addressed by game design courses that are not part of the required computer science curriculum, and as such, this work often falls to the sponsor teams in addition to the other work that the projects entail for the faculty and staff members in this role.

Authoring platforms are an important part of the ecosystem of XR content production and consumption and deserve additional attention. The framework presented here addresses key questions that probe beyond usability using existing authoring platforms as a guide. Future work should include more detailed investigations of each of the components of an authoring platform. As is the case with Unity MARS, researchers and platform developers should decide whether to build on existing platforms or to explore new paradigms and approaches. That tool solves specific technical and professional problems without opening up the field to newcomers and non-professionals through its dependency on expertise in Unity. The development of more user-friendly XR authoring tools can democratize content creation of XR and foster the creation of a more diverse range of environments.

# Put it into Practice: Envisioning User-friendly Authoring Platforms

Consider the forces shaping XR authoring platforms described in this chapter, and how various interface decisions can influence both who is invited into becoming an XR experience creator as well as the types of content that are "easier" than others based on examples and platform affordances. Unity, for instance, has a very powerful physics simulation system that privileges projectiles and collision-based interactions. In a classroom setting, invite your students into a discussion on the processes by which platforms are shaped and how they might join the conversation by critically assessing them.

For instance, have your students choose an XR creation tool to critique based on either its popularity or its use in the course. Look at both the interface (using videos, tutorials, or even directly interacting with the authoring tool) and the marketing provided by the company that produces it. Identify characteristics of the intended audience and assumptions about what the typical users value, using concrete examples from the manual or interface. Who is being excluded or limited? What features prioritize some uses over others? Encourage them to compare the tools to other software tools, both mundane (Microsoft Word) or more "Creative" (Snapchat), and encourage them to draw from tools they are familiar with. The resulting analysis can take the form of a short presentation intended for the audience of the platform developers on the importance of a set of used cases, or it could be an imaginary feature request that would improve the usability of creating content for an XR platform.

For courses that emphasize critical making, there is an opportunity to have students prototype authoring interfaces and tools that explore different methods for both behaviors and assets used in XR experiences. Current systems share the approach of exposing the graphics API or lower-level tracking capabilities. As a result, such companies and products may be less likely to take risks in exploring creative approaches to XR-specific content, and so would value prototypes and studies that evaluate alternatives. Encourage your students to think about how authoring techniques evolve and how their work may influence future authoring platforms. One way of doing this is to document the work in a video demonstration or even releasing it as an extension of existing editors.

# References

Apperley, T. and Parikka, J. (2015). Platform Studies' Epistemic Threshold. *Games and Culture*, 1-22. https://doi.org/10.1177/1555412015616509

Benzakein, D. (2016, March 7). Apelab, a Swiss interactive studio ready to take on Hollywood. Imm3rsive. https://imm3rsive.com/en/2016/03/07/apelab-a-swiss-interactive-studio-ready-to-take-on-hollywood/

Billinghurst, M. (2020). Rapid prototyping for AR/VR experiences. Extended Abstracts of the 2020 CHI Conference on Human Factors in Computing Systems, 1-4. https://doi.org/10.1145/3334480.3375065

Billinghurst, M., Langlotz, T., MacIntyre, B. and Seichter, H. (2011). Authoring solutions for augmented reality. 2011 10th IEEE International Symposium on Mixed and Augmented Reality, 1-1. http://portal.acm.org/citation.cfm?doid=1228175.1228259

Bogost, I. and Montfort, N. (2009). Platform studies: Frequently questioned answers. Proceedings of the Digital Arts and Culture Conference.

Branit, B. (2007, February 28). *World Builder* [Sci-Fi, Romance].

Carter, M. and Egliston, B. (2020). *Ethical Implications of Emerging Mixed Reality Technologies*. https://doi.org/10.25910/5ee2f9608ec4d

Chacko, P. (2020, June 8). *Introducing Unity MARS – A first-of-its-kind Solution for Intelligent AR*. https://blogs.unity3d.com/2020/06/08/introducing-unity-mars-a-first-of-its-kind solution-for-intelligent-ar/

Chen, S., Nelson, M., Sullivan, A. and Mateas, M. (2009). Evaluating the Authorial Leverage of Drama Management. Proceedings of the AAAI 2009 Spring Symposium on Interactive Narrative Technologies II, 20–23. http://www.aaai.org/ocs/index.php/AIIDE/AIIDE09/paper/viewPDFInterstitial/816/1054

Cuny, J. (n.d.). US NSF - CISE - Calling all schools: Why you need rigorous and engaging computer science courses. National Science Foundation. Retrieved July 8, 2020, from https://www.nsf.gov/cise/news/csed-perspective.jsp

Desatoff, S. (2020, May 4). Unity Technologies acquires Bolt from Ludiq. GameDaily.Biz. https://gamedaily.biz/article/1729/unity-technologies-acquires-bolt-from-ludiq

Fernández-vara, C. (2008). Shaping player experience in adventure games: History of the adventure game interface. pp. 210–227. *In*: O. Leino, H. Wirman and A. Fernandez (eds.). Extending Experiences: Structure, Analysis and Design of Computer Game Player Experience. Lapland University Press.

Gonzalez, R. (2017, July 6). With Blocks, Google Helps Solve One of VR's Biggest Problems | WIRED. Wired. https://www.wired.com/story/google-blocks-vr/

Good, J. and Howland, K. (2017). Programming language, natural language? Supporting the diverse computational activities of novice programmers. *Journal of Visual Languages & Computing*, 39, 78-92. https://doi.org/10.1016/j.jvlc.2016.10.008

Hunicke, R., LeBlanc, M. and Zubek, R. (2004). MDA: A Formal Approach to Game Design and Game Research. *In:* Proceeding of the AAAI Workshop on Challenges in Game AI. 4(1), 1722.

Johnson, E.K., Giroux, A.L. Merritt, D., Vitanova, G. and Sousa, S. (2020). Assessing the impact of game modalities in second language acquisition: ELLE the EndLess LEarner. *Journal of Universal Computer Science*. 26(8), 880-903.

Karbotte, K. (2016, October 1). NeosVR Lets You Build Virtual Worlds With Others, Remotely And In Real Time | Tom's Hardware. https://www.tomshardware.com/news/neosvr-world-building-engine-devlog,32792.html

Kuhn, J. (2017). Minecraft: Education Edition. *CALICO Journal*, 35(2), 214-223. https://doi.org/10.1558/cj.34600

Lang, B. (2019, January 16). Microsoft Reveals "Maquette", a VR Tool for Spatial Ideation and Design. Road to VR. https://www.roadtovr.com/microsoft-reveals-maquette-a-vr-tool-for-spatial-ideation-and-design/

Lee, G.A., Kim, G.J. and Billinghurst, M. (2005). Immersive authoring: What you experience is what you get (WYXIWYG). *Communications of the ACM*, 48(7), 76-81. https://doi.org/10.1145/1070838.1070840

MacIntyre, B. and Smith, T.F. (2018). Thoughts on the Future of WebXR and the Immersive Web. *2018 IEEE International Symposium on Mixed and Augmented Reality Adjunct (ISMAR-Adjunct)*, 338-342. https://doi.org/10.1109/ISMAR-Adjunct.2018.00099

Martin, J.A. and Finnegan, M. (2019, January 31). What is IFTTT? How to use If, This, Then That services. Computerworld. https://www.computerworld.com/article/3239304/what-is-ifttt-how-to-use-if-this-then-that-services.html

Mason, D. and Dave, K. (2017). Block-based versus flow-based programming for naive programmers. *2017 IEEE Blocks and Beyond Workshop (B B)*, 25-28. https://doi.org/10.1109/BLOCKS.2017.8120405

Melnick, K. (2020, July 7). "The Under Presents" Hosting Live Theatrical Performances of Shakespeare's "Tempest" On Oculus Headsets. *VRScout*. https://vrscout.com/news/the-under-presents-vr-theater-tempest/

Mercan, Ş. and Durdu, P.O. (2017). Evaluating the usability of unity game engine from developers' perspective. *2017 IEEE 11th International Conference on Application of Information and Communication Technologies (AICT)*, 1-5. https://doi.org/10.1109/ICAICT.2017.8687303

Merritt, D., Johnson, E.K. and Giroux, A.L. (2017). ELLE the EndLess LEarner: Exploring Second Language Acquisition Through an Endless Runner-style Video Game. Proceedings

From Digital Humanities 2017. Digital Humanities 2017, Montreal, Canada. https://dh2017.adho.org/program/abstracts/

Miller, R. and Constine, J. (2015, May 28). *Apple Acquires Augmented Reality Company Metaio | TechCrunch*. https://techcrunch.com/2015/05/28/apple-metaio/

Montfort, N. and Bogost, I. (2009). *Racing the Beam: The Atari Video Computer System*. MIT Press.

Parberry, I., Roden, T. and Kazemzadeh, M.B. (2005). Experience with an industry-driven capstone course on game programming: Extended abstract. Proceedings of the 36th SIGCSE Technical Symposium on Computer Science Education - SIGCSE '05, 91. https://doi.org/10.1145/1047344.1047387

Pineda, Y. and Johnson, E. (2019). The value in using virtual reality immersion to teach the historical middle passage from the perspective of a historian and game researcher. *Faculty Focus* (Spring, 20191), http://fctl.ucf.edu/Publications/FacultyFocus/content/2019/2019_april.pdf

Pineda, Y., Johnson, E.K., Giroux, A.L. and Gordon, F (2020). The Middle Passage Virtual Reality Experience Demo. Electronic Literature Organization Conference 2020, Orlando, Florida, July 2020.

Reed, A., Garbe, J., Wardrip-Fruin, N. and Mateas, M. (2014). Ice-bound: Combining richly-realized story with expressive gameplay. FDG '14: Proceedings of the 9th International Conference on the Foundations of Digital Games.

Roberto, R.A., Lima, J.P., Mota, R.C. and Teichrieb, V. (2016). Authoring tools for augmented reality: An analysis and classification of content design tools. pp. 237-248. *In*: A. Marcus (ed.). Design, User Experience, and Usability: Technological Contexts. Springer International Publishing. https://doi.org/10.1007/978-3-319-40406-6_22

Salter, A. and Murray, J. (2014). *Flash: Building the Interactive Web*. MIT Press. http://books.google.com/books?hl=en&lr=&id=hhJmBAAAQBAJ&pgis=1

Schoen, M. (2020, April 23). Unity MARS Companion Apps—Unity Technologies Blog. Unity Blog. https://blogs.unity3d.com/2020/04/23/mars-companion-apps/

Schreiber, I. and Brathwaite, B. (2008). *Challenges for Game Designers*. Charles River Media.

Stone, Z. (2018, November 11). The Unreal Garden is San Francisco's selfie museum for the burning man generation [News]. Forbes. https://www.forbes.com/sites/zarastone/2018/11/11/the-unreal-garden-is-san-franciscos-selfie-museum-for-the-burning-man-generation/#1de38bb1422d

Ur, B., Pak Yong Ho, M., Brawner, S., Lee, J., Mennicken, S., Picard, N., Schulze, D. and Littman, M.L. (2016). Trigger-action programming in the wild: An analysis of 200,000 IFTTT recipes. Proceedings of the 2016 CHI Conference on Human Factors in Computing Systems, 3227-3231. https://doi.org/10.1145/2858036.2858556

V[R]ignettes | @MezBreezeDesign (n.d.). Retrieved July 8, 2020, from http://mezbreezedesign.com/vr-literature/vrignettes/

Zammitto, V., Mirza-Babaei, P., Livingston, I., Kobayashi, M. and Nacke, L.E. (2014). Player experience: Mixed methods and reporting results. *CHI '14 Extended Abstracts on Human Factors in Computing Systems*, 147-150. https://doi.org/10.1145/2559206.2559239

# Chapter
# 13

# Motivation Enhancement Methods for Community Building in Extended Reality

**Stylianos Mystakidis**

School of Natural Sciences, University of Patras, Greece
Museum of Science and Technology, Rion Achaia, GR-26504, Greece
Email: smyst@upatras.gr

## Introduction: Extended Reality and Immersive Education

Virtual Reality (VR) has been a part of human experience since the cradle of the history of our species (Blascovich and Bailenson, 2011). Oral storytelling and cave drawings were the first media used to capture and immortalize identity-defining experiences, memorable achievements and communal stories. Theater in ancient Greece was a catalyst of social change and democratic political discourse. Theatrical plays such as tragedies and comedies transported temporary audiences in virtual, mythical or historical, contexts to trigger reflective and cathartic experiences for Greek city-states civic community. Ever since, many invented technologies such as books, photography, radio and cinematography have demonstrated their power to transfer us to remote or imaginary environments based on mediated information received. Current applications of Virtual Reality primarily based on computer-generated three-dimensional spaces and head-mounted displays have the capability to immerse us not just psychologically and socially but also through multiple sensory (multimodal) channels in completely different, synthetic environments cutting us off from our actual physical surroundings. Augmented Reality (AR) adopts a gentler approach towards reality; it embeds digital inputs, and virtual elements into the physical environment. The end-outcome is a spatially projected layer of digital artefacts mediated by devices, e.g. smart phones, tablets, glasses, or other transparent surfaces. Mixed reality (MR) represents an advanced iteration of Augmented Reality in the sense that the physical environment interacts in real time with the projected digital data. For instance, a scripted non-player character in a game would recognize the physical surroundings and hide under a desk or behind a couch.

Exponential technologies and trends transform work and economy and lead to a profound systemic change termed fourth industrial revolution (Schwab, 2016). In this context, Augmented, Mixed and Virtual Reality constitute the crests of the 4th technological innovation wave in the world of computing (Digi-Capital, 2016). The previous three platform waves had a profound impact on every-day life, society and economy by introducing personal computers, the Internet and mobile phones (Schwab, 2016). The umbrella term that embraces all immersive technologies is called Extended Reality (XR). In all instances of XR humans observe and act in a partially or fully digital technology-created environment.

The application of XR for teaching and learning purposes is called Immersive Education. Immersive Education has the potential to enhance student learning, motivation, engagement and performance as it emulates the feeling of co-presence in a physical space through live interactions with peers in remote, virtual environments. Early immersive educational experiences in social Virtual Reality environments can provide valuable insights for flexible, distributed XR community building.

## Learning and Communities

Humans are socially curious beings. Human learning is considered to occur mostly within and through social interaction with others (Ataizi, 2012). Thus, learning is considered to be a cultural and social process. It occurs in the context of human relationships and activities rather than just in the minds of individual learners. Hence the socio-cultural context affects what is learnt and how people learn. Deep learning is characterized by the inherent interest in and active engagement with a discipline in a quest to grasp its underlying principles and associate it with existing concepts and knowledge (Mystakidis et al., 2019a).

The feeling of belonging in a community is vital for learning (Rogoff et al. 1996). Once every participant feels accepted, respected, safe and an equal member in a group educational environment, he or she can build emotional relationships, set personal aims and embark upon a journey of empowerment, discovery and mastery. However, online communities are fundamentally different from those in physical spaces. E-learning extends its affordances in terms of spatial limitations, resource use and implementation time as it features a different mode of transactional distance (Moore, 1997). Gilbert (2005) argues pragmatically that gaining knowledge in this digital age is not an object but a process, initiated in interpersonal interactions. Also, e-learning promotes a more democratic, less hierarchical relationship between learners, teachers and knowledge that allows new ways of organizing learning unrestrained by institutional boundaries (Bonk, 2012).

In our networked era, especially in the context of pandemics, social distancing and emergency remote teaching, two models are of particular interest for distributed communities in XR platforms: community of inquiry and community of practice. The community of inquiry was developed to guide computer-assisted distance teaching and learning towards high quality, deep and meaningful learning (Garrison et al., 2010). Deriving from a social constructivist background, its empirically supported premise it that successful online learning experiences resulting in the formation of active groups combine three elements: teaching, cognitive, and social presence. The teaching presence consists of the responsibilities and actions of tutors such as design, facilitation and direct instruction. Cognitive presence is defined as "the extent to which the participants in any particular configuration of a community of inquiry are able to construct meaning through sustained communication" (Garrison et al., 1999). Social presence signals the shared social identity in a trusting environment where students can communicate purposefully.

A community of practice is formed by people who share a common domain of activity (Lave and Wenger, 1991). When people pursue an interest, a passion, a concern or a craft, they seek like-minded people to learn, share, communicate and improve their competence, in short they build a community around the shared practice. In a community of practice, groups of learners learn from each other by adopting new roles, offering multiple perspectives, becoming peer tutors, and taking on projects and tasks that would be difficult or impossible for a single learner (Dickey, 2005). People can enter, participate in various degrees, congregate and leave structured or spontaneous communities around a shared subject. They learn the common terminology, concepts, norms, values, axioms, processes, experiences and challenges that drive members' activity. All these elements are facets of an identity, professional or of some other nature. In sum, in communities of practice, members learn to know, to do, to be and to become. Communities of practice exist everywhere, inside businesses and organizations but also across regions and countries. Networked technologies have enabled the creation of online, virtual communities of practice (Bronack et al., 2008).

Both presented community-centered constructs have similarities and correspondences. Beyond their shared epistemological background, they both advocate a student-centered transformation of learning; empowered, motivated participants should be at the epicenter of attention and co-decide education action. In that notion, the community becomes a live curriculum where peer interactions play a central role. Building and maintaining online communities of inquiry and practice facilitates learner motivation (Bonk and Khoo, 2014). Hence, the establishment and maintenance of a sense of social presence in a community of inquiry or practice, where learners can build and navigate personal connections (Burgess et al., 2010) is an essential factor associated with deep and meaningful learning in distance education settings (Mystakidis, 2019).

## Motivation

Motivation is one of the most important affective aspects of learning because it influences the cognitive processes of learning (Schiefele, 1991). Motivation in the context of education is defined by Wentzel and Wigfield (2009) as "the energy learners bring to educational tasks, the beliefs, values, and goals that determine which tasks they pursue and their persistence in achieving them, and the standards they set to determine when a task has been completed".

Motivational factors include goal orientation, interest and self-efficacy beliefs (Eccles and Wigfield, 2002). Humans can have multiple goals and motives of an extrinsic or intrinsic different nature in parallel (Covington and Müeller, 2001). Learners with an extrinsic goal orientation engage learning for external incentives such as passing an exam, getting a high grade, material rewards or avoiding a negative consequence (Mystakidis et al., 2019a). Extrinsic motivation is associated with surface learning, anxiety and high drop-out rates (Rothes et al., 2017). Learners with autonomous, intrinsic motives and goals are driven by the practice of learning itself. The Self-determination Theory (SDT) is a theoretical framework that studied motivation from a psychological point of view to determine how, why and what motivates learners (Ryan and Deci, 2000). SDT postulates that intrinsically motivating actions can be enacted in learning environments that exhibit choices, direct feedback, optimal challenges, mastery of meaningful tasks, self-directed interaction and social connectedness (Ryan and Deci, 2008; Mystakidis and Herodotou, 2016). Ryan and Deci (2000)define intrinsic motivation as "the inherent novelty to seek out challenges, to extend or exercise one's capacities, to explore, and to learn". Intrinsic motivation is associated with deep learning, high performance and learning resilience (Zainuddin, 2018; Mystakidis et al. 2019a). Motives are linked to desired identities under construction in particular contexts especially in learning communities (Nolen et al., 2015). Hence, teachers designing learning environments with appropriate cultural norms and values, can support identification with a social practice and change individuals' motives for learning.

## Motivation Enhancement Methods and Games

The complexity of learners' emotions and motivations are often neglected in learning. One potential answer to tackle this deficiency is the purposeful focus, nurturing and enhancement of learners' motivation directed at cultivating a learning atmosphere conducive to intrinsic motivation. An e-learning environment and a shared ethos supporting students' needs for autonomy, competence and relatedness, has a higher probability for recording increased satisfaction, engagement and achievement (Chen et al., 2010). These three components of SDT are inherent characteristics of games (Salen and Zimmerman, 2004). There is a great deal of commonality between the characteristics of games and those of effective learning experiences such as challenges, goals, outcomes, interactions, explorations and safe environments (Mystakidis and Herodotou, 2016).

Game design, mechanisms, processes and effects are proposed foci of study for all education professionals so as to derive useful conclusions on practical ways to enhance and facilitate learning by increasing students' intrinsic motivation (Gee, 2004). Game-based learning strategies include playful design, gamification and serious games. Game-based motivation amplification strategies have been applied in education and e-learning, and are at the epicenter of interdisciplinary research and business development. Next, we will present each method in an increasing degree of design complexity and implementation.

## Playful Design (Playification)

Play has fundamental differences as compared to a game. A game has rules, boundaries and organizes participants' activities towards specific objectives by exercising strategy, skill and effort. Play on the other hand is the free, improvised expenditure of energy for its own sake and is not moderated. Playful design is the simplest way to integrate the enjoyable element of fun in a 'serious', non-gaming context (Borges et al., 2014). One example of playful design in the field of web design is the use of a clever graphic image or text message in an otherwise mundane, indifferent webpage. For example, an error page (Ferrara, 2012). In online education, playful design can be expressed in the aesthetics of a virtual environment. For instance, course curriculum can be described playfully with appropriate linguistic metaphors and aesthetic elements (Mystakidis, 2010). The application of playful design principles in an external context can also be called playification.

One advanced playful design technique is to create a background story and adding a layer of narrative in the educational programme. Humans have always used words and actions interactively to depict elements and images of plots that elicit imaginative responses in a social setting. Stories combine several pedagogical advantages that make them a powerful method in education. When we share stories within a community, members learn from each other without suffering the consequences of the actual experience (Van Eck, 2007). Digital storytelling can be used to design playful and creative teaching or active learning in individual or group projects (Mystakidis and Berki, 2018).

## Gameful Design (Gamification)

Gamification or gameful design is the application of game-based dynamics to an educational endeavour (Kapp, 2012). Gamification adds a new informational and operational layer on top of an existing activity or system that helps administrators and managers turn it into a game. Gamified systems are designed to encourage repeatable actions and reward desirable behaviors. Adding gamification on learning elements in a mechanistic way does not guarantee a lasting positive effect on learning (Sanchez et al., 2019). Extra effort is required to create a compelling experience with sufficient variability and progress so as to maintain a constantly high level of motivation and engagement.

Various gamification methods have been applied in formal education. One game-based systematic strategy in formal and informal attendance-based and distance education is the gamification of curriculum activities. Sheldon proposed the creation of multiplayer classrooms adopting techniques from Massively Multiplayer Online Games involving game mechanics such as avatars, points, levels, badges and leader boards (Sheldon, 2011). Haskell and Dawley developed a quest-based learning management system to support and organize class learning activities (Haskell and Dawley, 2013). In gamified curricula, coursework is re-arranged as a game where students earn points as they choose and complete online and offline learning activities organized around various roles and skills (Sheldon and Seelow, 2017). Assignments in gamified educational programmes become quests and students become fictional or existing role-playing characters. This way, activities are tied to the story; learners are no longer passive recipients of a rigid curriculum but active participants with agency, vested in the final outcome. Starting from zero, the accumulated points determine the earned student grade based on an already known scale.

## Serious Games

Serious or epistemic games comprise a set of meaningful choices in a restrictive context with a primary educational purpose (Michael and Chen, 2005). Serious games invite players to adopt a new identity, to become active actors, interact with peers and the game, and to receive immediate or automated feedback. Serious games prompt learners to think, analyze problematic situations, formulate hypotheses, take decisions, test and experiment, explore, fail in a safe way, reflect, adapt, converse and keep learning by doing. Serious games are structured around the following basic components: (i) an entertaining plot involving a fictional character, (ii) visual aesthetics and artistic elements, (iii) game mechanics implemented in a technical, software programming system, and (iv) a pedagogical approach that links the conceptual representation of specific skills and competencies in a field or discipline with learning outcomes through specific game challenges and activities (Zyda, 2005). Serious games can be used as appropriate learning experiences that allow players to enter their zone of proximal development (Vygotsky, 1978; Lambropoulos and Mystakidis, 2012); learners engage with academic and disciplinary content and competences of appropriate complexity just beyond their current ability levels.

## Social Virtual Reality

Social Virtual Reality (SVR) comprises three-dimensional computer-generated synthetic spaces that facilitate the social or psychological immersion of participants (Mystakidis et al., 2017a). SVR can be accessed either by a desktop or laptop computer. Some SVR platforms can also be experienced using other devices such as mobile phones or a head-mounted displays (HMD).

SVR features a set of affordances that open new horizons of learning enhancement in comparison to 2D virtual synchronous and asynchronous learning platforms. First, they feature a superior sense of self since the participant controls his or her embodied representation, the avatar in the form of a digital persona or agent (Hinrichs and Wankel, 2012). The Avatar's characteristics can be customized and modified in great detail to reflect each learner's preferences of self-expression; they can appear in human-like or completely fictional form. The identification with one's avatar in a virtual environment can have a profound psychological impact on behavior and learning; embodied experiences as avatars in virtual reality spaces have a direct influence on human behavior and transferred to the physical world (Yee and Bailenson, 2007).

The embodied digital identity, and the ability to engage with the environment and virtual objects with multiple points of view, such as a third-person perspective, creates the psychological sense of being in a space, experiencing presence. Presence is the perceptual illusion of non-mediation (Lombard and Ditton, 1997). This feeling is extended though the social communion with other people (Casanueva and Blake, 2001). Although real-time interactions in physical contexts carry a great pedagogical value that is difficult to replicate in online environments, SVR offers a rich alternative; when meeting other avatars synchronously in the same 3D virtual space and acknowledging the persons behind the personas leads to experiencing a prevalent power of co-presence.

Avatar nuanced interactions can be organized in persistent, complex, simulated or completely synthetic environments of high fidelity (Dalgarno and Lee, 2010). 3D environments can be responsive through programming the dynamic behavior of virtual objects under certain conditions and states. In 3D environments avatars can engage in rich, embodied, interpersonal interactions. Students and educators can communicate not just in voice and text modes (for example, private, public and group voice or text chat messages) but also through non-verbal channels such as movement, gestures and virtual body language. Further, virtual reality environments allow the exercise of agency; avatars are free to move and navigate in the virtual space.

SVR enables educators to enhance both face-to-face teaching and distance education by applying creative and innovative instructional methods; for instance, approaches with a socio-constructivist or connectivist epistemological background, where the focus is the activity of the student and the formation of communities of inquiry and practice. These methods include situated, contextual, collaborative, cooperative and experiential learning (Dede and Dawley, 2014) and also virtual coaching, mentoring and apprenticing.

SVR combines a series of affordances that make them an effective technological medium for all, close- or open-ended game-based methods for motivation enhancement; playful design, gameful design and serious games (Christopoulos et al., 2018; Pellas and Mystakidis, 2020). First, SVR supports the development of playful design approaches, environments and activities (Warburton, 2009). Second, SVR is based on advanced technical systems and programming features that allow the implementation of complex gaming mechanics to accommodate gameful design (Mystakidis, 2020), interactive simulations and serious games (de Freitas and Dunwell, 2011; Fragkaki et al., 2020). SVR platforms are mature systems for the development and deployment at a scale of complex immersive experiences such as multiplayer role-playing simulations and games with the help of artificial intelligence, chatbots and non-player characters (Leigh et al., 2012; Mystakidis et al., 2019b, 2020).

# Game-based Motivation Enhancement Methods for Community Building with Social Virtual Reality

Under the following headings we present four implementations of game-based motivation enhancement methods in social Virtual Reality (SVR) that can be useful for community building across the XR spectrum.

## Playful Design and Collaborative Storytelling

A series of publications explored the effect of Storytelling using 3D immersive learning environments in a playful learning experience offered to primary and secondary school students by the University of Patras, Greece (Mystakidis et al., 2014; Mystakidis and Berki, 2018). The hypothesis was that playful, game-informed learning experiences in 3D Virtual Immersive Environments, a type of desktop-based SVR, when enriched with (digital) storytelling and problem-focused education concepts can have a positive impact in facilitating primary education students' learning.

The author designed and implemented the pilot educational program *"From the Ancient to the Modern Tablets"*, featuring immersive multimedia learning experiences about the book history. The pilot program consisted of three stages: a playful library tour, followed by an interactive game-based digital storytelling activity with playful elements, and a collaborative, creative, reflective hands-on activity. Utilizing the avatar power psychology, the visualization and simulation affordances of SVR and the appeal of storytelling and game-based learning, the gamified blended narrative on book evolution enabled learning as problem-focused, embedded and context-generated.

This informative educational student-centered programme has been popular among schools. The programme's high engagement level created enthusiastic student responses and positive learning behaviors. This project also became known and well-accepted among teachers. More than 1,500 students have participated in innovative learning ways and advanced their knowledge and skills through active edutainment (education + entertainment).

Teachers' perceptions regarding the effectiveness of the 3D Virtual Immersive Environments were very positive. They agreed that learners acquired new skills. They also affirmed that the learning experience added to the students' positive mentality towards books and reading. 3D Virtual Immersive Environments were regarded very useful for recalling facts and understanding history. Teachers also noted the high emotional involvement of students; the experience captivated their attention and evoked high levels of interest that lead to high engagement and performance in the final collaborative activity. The overall result was high satisfaction levels, and positive motivation towards book reading, learning, and literacy.

## Playful Open Online Learning Community

In the University of Patras an innovative, motivation-enhanced Massive Open Online Course (MOOC), the first of its kind in Greece to the best of our knowledge, was organized with the title "Open Workshop on Information Literacy" (Kostopoulos et al., 2014; Mystakidis et al., 2017b). The instructional approach was based on Problem-Focused Education (PFE) and Game-Based Learning (GBL). PFE is a variation of Problem-Based Learning. During the course, over three hundred thirty participants acquired information literacy skills using web-based open learning platforms and a SVR platform.

It was hypothesized that a motivation-enhanced 3D immersive learning environment would have a positive effect on completion rates and the quality of learning in a MOOC. The study focused on the experience of using 3D immersive learning environments or SVR environments for synchronous formal and informal collaborative learning in an innovative Open Online Course. Open Education is a distance learning approach that has been strategically proposed well before the covid-19 outbreak to encourage cost-effective training, upskilling and reskilling of large population groups and workforce with speed and flexibility.

MOOC participants achieved sustainable high completion rates, namely over thirty percent, three times higher than the average MOOC. This result is comparable to empirical evidence from a MOOC with a different motivation-enhancement method, namely a serious game demonstrating that the novel pedagogical model deployed with motivation enhancement methods was able to address and overcome common pitfalls of MOOCs, such as anonymity, learner isolation and lack of feedback (Thirouard et al., 2015).

In the virtual space each participant had an individual and representative presence, thus breaking the anonymous, distant, isolated feeling of participants in MOOCs. Therein instructors and tutors appeared as "equals", and they did not have visible privileges over course participants; sometimes tech-savvy participants often assisted the instructors. Additionally, the pervasive character of the environment, the fact that they could enter, leave and move in the virtual space created enhanced the sense of agency. SVR enhanced the live participants' interactions and user experiences beyond the standard classroom experience, through the availability of multiple communication channels such as voice, private voice sessions, public and private chat, movement, apparel and gestures of the avatar.

As a result, participants achieved their set learning outcomes, experienced a community of practice atmosphere, expressed high degree of satisfaction and appreciated the variety of active learning methods. The open publication mode of most learning activities facilitated social agency that lead to increased motivation. The course demonstrated that the effective use of SVREs for rich, synchronous learning, both formal and informal, can significantly enhance Open Online Courses.

## Gamification in Distance Education

When asked to design, organize and teach as a tutor in the distance education postgraduate module "Artificial Intelligence, Bots and Non-Player Characters" at a UK university, the author opted to introduce a gamified curriculum structure, a quest-based layered course over a duration of nine to twelve weeks (Mystakidis, 2020).

The gamified structure was based on the following game mechanics: story, points, levels, quests, classes, badges, achievements. Participants were challenged to assume a professional role and set personal goals; plan and personalize their learning path by choosing quests that best fit their interests and skills. Specifically, starting from the rank of Rookie Cadet, students were invited to rise and reach twelve levels (for example, Senior Designer, NPC Master). Students rose in ranks once they amassed sufficient experience points (XP). Points could be earned by completing quests. Quests were learning activities of three different types: solo, raid or guild corresponding to individual, group or class tasks respectively. The game was organized around three-character classes which were linked with distinct learning objectives.

Within the constraints of the gamified curriculum, one immediate observation was that the playful characters and objects of virtual environment and appealed to participants and evoked feelings of enjoyment and relaxation. Next, students identified conceptual cases and reflected on practical methods to adapt and experiment with AI products and bots in virtual worlds to synthesize novel solutions to achieve specific learning objectives. In the macro-conceptual discourse, students were able to synthesize information demonstrating critical and literate thinking.

Moreover, student work analysis revealed high levels of equal creative thinking and innovative adaptation. Students felt comfortable to not just set personal goals but also propose ideas for additional, voluntary activities beyond the constraints of the compulsory and optional curriculum tasks for incoming students within the wider educational context. Excitement, initiative, innovation and sustained interest to experiment and adapt technology-based solutions are evidence of higher-order levels of engagement associated with self-regulated interest and critical engagement. Findings concluded overall that participants were able to reach high levels of engagement and empathy towards community members.

## Mini Serious Games with Visual Metaphors

Two mini serious games were designed and deployed for a Cybersecurity postgraduate course in a US university (Endicott-Popovsky et al., 2013; Mystakidis et al., 2017a). These social learning experiences were constructed taking into account various game mechanics and components designed to increase their appeal to most game player types and styles (explorers, achievers, socializers). The games featured narrative, rules, team collaboration, competition, challenges, achievements, surprises, levels, rewards, choice, feedback, scoring, time-pressure, exploration.

Assuming that game-based learning in SVR can have a positive impact on the quality of learning, we inquired if online learning can be enhanced using serious games and playful elements. What would be the reaction of postgraduate students, accustomed to traditional e-learning platforms when exposed to a new environment with game-based learning activities? Our research aim was to capture their level of satisfaction of all components of the course as a means to evaluate the pedagogical potential and effectiveness of the employed instructional method.

The participants in this distance education course thought that playful experiences in 3D social virtual reality were beneficial for their learning. They also valued learning activities based on active participation and social interaction. The immersion into a virtual environment and the ability to be embodied in a moving avatar and occupy a virtual space were the most valued components of the virtual environment. Some participants reported that the game had a positive effect on their learning. They noted that the game was a memorable experience, that, it stimulated their senses and emotions and enhanced their learning. Several also noted that they were motivated to experiment with these characteristics.

SVR enabled educators to create interactive exhibits and 3D content as well as entertaining social experiences of learning value to illustrate and visualize real Cybersecurity practices. Programming in virtual reality environments helped participants experience intangible notions such as malware and behavioral patterns with the help of storytelling and visual metaphors. We also confirmed that the steep learning curve of new users in 3D virtual immersive environments are an obstacle for learning that needs to be addressed meticulously. Results revealed the emergence of two user groups called techno-enthusiasts and techno-challenged. The first group participated smoothly and valued the experience. The second group faced serious technical issues in technology access or software use and this fact had a negative impact on their overall experience.

SVR platforms, especially when interconnected or part of a larger, open-ended virtual world, can be environments where students can feel ownership. They can be given the opportunity to have an impact and contribute to the construction of the learning environment—on an equal footing with their educators—or at least have a collective space with the freedom to take initiatives, experiment and express their agency. Also SVR offers visual and auditory representative fidelity that evokes genuine feelings of immersion. There they can meet people and collaborate with peers from all over the world, share thoughts and demonstrate the product of their work and creativity. Hands-on training activities that might be too hazardous, costly, unethical or inconvenient to orchestrate in the physical world can be replicated with great detail in the virtual. Abstract concepts, notions and environments of the micro- or macrocosm can be visualized and experienced for the first time. The participants of this case study appreciated the variety of active learning modes and acquired new skills for virtual team work. The course demonstrated that the effective use of SVR for rich, synchronous formal and informal learning can enhance distance education.

The findings of this study showed that participants valued learning activities which were based on social interaction and active participation. Game users can experience an essential impact on their social development which can have a positive impact on the quality of learning. By embedding social content within the games, such as caring for something or someone, through characters, plots and themes, players can experience decision making with real consequences. By presenting a system of rules and acting on them, such as facing an ethical dilemma, can have a positive influence upon players' social development and learning. In addition, discussing and debating about the game and its content online and offline can have a positive impact on developing players' argumentation, elaboration and reasoning.

## Conclusion

Communities are essential for knowledge, skills and competence in formal and informal learning settings. XR platforms combining VR, AR and MR applications will enable flexible online community building across geographical and cultural boundaries with unique, spatial and embodied presence, superior in comparison to previous computing systems. One promising technology that has addressed social and emotional aspects of learning in open distance learning by transcending limitations of 2D web-based interfaces is social Virtual Reality (SVR). SVR technical features such as cross-platform compatibility of open 3D resources enable educators to support the application of teaching and learning methods that amplify learners' motivation. Motivation enhancement methods can be structured with the appropriate adoption and adaptation of game design principles and elements. Game-based motivation enhancement methods in SVR such as playful design, gamification and serious games can facilitate human connections for the creation of an inclusive, communal learning atmosphere and identity.

Playful design elements and stories create relaxed, humorous, aesthetically pleasing environments inducing positive feelings of enjoyment, satisfaction and reinforcement. When executed appropriately, this strategy does not subtract the seriousness of learning, and on the contrary deepens motivation by liberating students' locus of control, freedom, initiative and creativity. Self-contained immersive gaming experiences and simulations in the form of serious games can supplement learning and bring excitement through game dynamics such as cooperation, competition and conflict. Fully gamified experiences turn the whole learning process into a game experience where participants are the protagonists who script their own heroic journey towards mastery through virtual and cognitive apprenticeships. In this way, gamification shifts their focus from completing a course to actual positive feelings and cognitive satisfaction gains of learning by engaging within the learning community. In this atmosphere, students are encouraged to exit their comfort zone, and expand their knowledge and skills by purposefully accepting new challenges of gradually increasing difficulty or complexity.

Recommendations on the effective use of game-based instructional approaches such as serious games, gamification and play in SVR for community building include the following; Game-based learning experiences should be crafted in close conjunction with the course's learning outcomes. A course-wide narrative can help overall participants' engagement and content retention. The thinking styles of the participants and their learning preferences should also influence rapid tweaking of game parameters in programming and general curricula design decisions in order to accommodate epistemological needs and particular knowledge desires. Games and simulated experiences can help students transfer conceptual understanding and skills to real situations in their future professional roles. SVR enables educators to create interactive exhibits and 3D content in order to illustrate and visualize abstract concepts, tacit knowledge and practices. Learning by doing, with others and through problem finding as well as resolving can be considered as benefits of games. One related challenge is the democratization of immersive education and make game-based methods in XR environments an attainable aim for educators from all fields and levels, without special technical skills. In conclusion, SVR adds a new dimension to e-learning community building with increased degrees of teaching freedom, learning flexibility and creativity. SVR can facilitate superior self-expression, agency, formal and informal genuine peer communication and cooperation in the frame of active, personalized, authentic, motivating, community building experiences.

## Curriculum Design Activity

Interested educators and practitioners seeking to build XR communities should start reflecting collectively on how they can accommodate the cultivation of positive emotions through the use of technology. Elements that can be influenced can be organized in the following layout:

a. Community identity, aims and values (why)
b. Structure, operation and processes (how)
c. Aesthetics (what)

Aims and values should constitute a clear vision and raison d'être, the ethical and motivational compass and identity of the community. The structure of the community, the roles, offices, bodies and groups involved should be part of a plan and roadmap towards the common goals. The roadmap should comprise several processes and activities for and by members that shape the communal ethos. The third layer consists of aesthetics expressed in components such as the attributes of the 3D space, special features or accessories in the appearance of avatars, and even in the language of communications.

It is recommended that all three layers should be aligned to promote member autonomous agency and action towards growth and mastery connected to each other and the communal aims. In this context, community leaders should consider if and how playful and gameful elements can facilitate the common vision, in the micro and macro level of a community taking into account the characteristics of the participants. Can an assignment be renamed and linked to a shared cultural reference? Can a course be organized as a story with multiple episodes or a game with levels and missions? Where will meetings take place, in a virtual amphitheater or around a beach camp fire? Practitioners are especially encouraged to also think of concrete ways to foster ownership of the space to students allowing them to gradually become co-creators and active contributors.

## References

Adaval, R. and Wyer, Robert S.J. (1998). The role of narratives in consumer information processing. *J. Consum Psychol*, 7, 207-245. https://doi.org/10.1207/s15327663jcp0703_01

Anderson, T. and Dron, J. (2011). Three generations of distance education pedagogy. *Int. Rev Res Open Distance Learn*, 12, 80-97.

Ataizi, M. (2012). Situated learning. pp. 3084-3086. *In*: Seel, N.M. (ed.). Encyclopedia of the Sciences of Learning. Springer US, Boston, MA.

Begg, M., Dewhurst, D. and Macleod, H. (2005). Game informed learning: Applying computer game processes to higher education. https://www.innovateonline.info/?view=article&id=176

Blascovich, J. and Bailenson, J. (2011). *Infinite Reality: Avatars, Eternal Life, New Worlds, and the Dawn of the Virtual Revolution*. Harper Collins.

Bloom, A. (1991). *The Republic of Plato*. Basic Books, New York.

Bonk, C.J. (2012). *The World is Open: How Web Technology is Revolutionizing Education*. Jossey-Bass, San Francisco, CA.

Bonk, C.J. and Khoo, E. (2014). *Adding Some TEC-VARIETY: 100+ Activities for Motivating and Retaining Learners Online*. CreateSpace Independent Publishing Platform.

Borges, S., Durelli, V., Reis, H. and Isotani, S. (2014). A systematic mapping on gamification applied to education. pp. 216-222. *In*: Proceedings of the ACM Symposium on Applied Computing. ACM, New York.

Bronack, S., Sanders, R., Cheney, A. et al. (2008). Presence pedagogy: teaching and learning in a 3D virtual immersive world. *Int J Teach Learn High Educ*, 20, 59-69. https://doi.org/10.1016/S0749-5978(02)00001-8

Bruner, J. (1991). The narrative construction of reality. *Crit. Inq*, 18, 1-21. https://doi.org/10.1086/448619

Burgess, M.L., Slate, J.R., Rojas-LeBouef, A. and LaPrairie, K. (2010). Teaching and learning in second life: Using the Community of Inquiry (CoI) model to support online instruction with graduate students in instructional technology. *Internet High Educ*, 13, 84-88. https://doi.org/10.1016/J.IHEDUC.2009.12.003

Casanueva, J. and Blake, E.H. (2001). The effects of avatars on co-presence in a collaborative virtual environment. pp 19-28. *In*: Annual Conference of the South African Institute of Computer Scientists and Information Technologists (SAICSIT2001). Pretoria.

Chen, K.C., Jang, S.J. and Branch, R.M. (2010). Autonomy, affiliation, and ability: Relative salience of factors that influence online learner motivation and learning outcomes. *Knowl Manag E-Learning*, 2, 30-50.

Christopoulos, A., Conrad, M. and Shukla, M. (2018). Interaction with educational games in hybrid virtual worlds. *J Educ Technol Syst*, 46, 385-413. https://doi.org/10.1177/0047239518757986

Cole, M.S., field, H.S. and Harris, S.G. (2004). Student learning motivation and psychological hardiness: Interactive effects on students' reactions to a management class. *Acad Manag Learn Educ*, 3, 64-85. https://doi.org/10.5465/amle.2004.12436819

Covington, M.V. and Müeller, K.J. (2001). Intrinsic versus extrinsic motivation: An approach/avoidance reformulation. *Educ Psychol Rev* 13, 157-176. https://doi.org/10.1023/A:1009009219144

Dalgarno, B. and Lee, M.J.W. (2010). What are the learning affordances of 3-D virtual environments? *Br J Educ Technol*, 41, 10-32. https://doi.org/10.1111/j.1467-8535.2009.01038.x

de Freitas, S. and Dunwell, I. (2011). Understanding the representational dimension of learning: The implications of interactivity, immersion and fidelity on the development of serious games. pp. 71-90. *In*: Cai, Yiyu (eds.). Interactive and Digital Media for Education in Virtual Learning Environments. Nova Science Publishers, New York.

Dede, C. and Dawley, L. (2014). Situated learning in virtual worlds and immersive simulations. pp. 723-734. *In*: Spector, J., Merrill, M., Elen, J., Bishop, M. (eds.). Handbook of Research on Educational Communications and Technology. Springer, New York.

Dickey, M.D. (2005). Three-dimensional virtual worlds and distance learning: Two case studies of Active Worlds as a medium for distance education. *Br J Educ Technol*, 36, 439-451. https://doi.org/10.1111/j.1467-8535.2005.00477.x

Digi-Capital (2016). Virtual, augmented and mixed reality are the 4th wave. https://www.digi-capital.com/news/2016/07/virtual-augmented-and-mixed-reality-are-the-4th-wave/. Accessed 17 Jun 2020

Downes, S. (2007). What connectivism is. *In*: Half An Hour. https://halfanhour.blogspot.com/2007/02/what-connectivism-is.html. Accessed 10 Jun 2019

Eccles, J.S. and Wigfield, A. (2002). Motivational beliefs, values, and goals. *Annu Rev Psychol*, 53, 109-132. https://doi.org/10.1146/annurev.psych.53.100901.135153

Endicott-Popovsky, B., Hinrichs, R.J. and Frincke, D. (2013). Leveraging 2nd life as a communications media: An effective tool for security awareness training. pp 1-7. *In*: IEEE International Professonal Communication 2013 Conference. IEEE.

Ferrara, J. (2012). *Playful Design: Creating Game Experiences in Everyday Interfaces.* Rosenfeld Media.

Fragkaki, M., Mystakidis, S., Hatzilygeroudis, I. et al. (2020). TPACK Instructional Design Model in Virtual Reality for Deeper Learning in Science and Higher Education: From "Apathy" To "Empathy." *In*: 12th Annual International Conference on Education and New Learning Technologies (EDULEARN20) Proceedings. https://doi.org/10.21125/edulearn.2020.0943

Garrison, D.R., Anderson, T. and Archer, W. (2010). The first decade of the community of inquiry framework: A retrospective. *Internet High Educ*, 13, 5-9. https://doi.org/10.1016/j.iheduc.2009.10.003

Garrison, D.R., Anderson, T. and Archer, W. (1999). Critical inquiry in a text-based environment: Computer conferencing in higher education. *Internet High Educ* 2, 87-105. https://doi.org/10.1016/S1096-7516(00)00016-6

Gee, J.P. (2004). *What Video Games Have to Teach Us About Learning and Literacy.* Palgrave Macmillan.

Gilbert, J. (2005). *Catching the Knowledge Wave?: The Knowledge Society and the Future of Education.* NZCER Press.

Haskell, C. and Dawley, L. (2013). 3D GameLab: Quest-based pre-service teacher education. pp. 302-340. *In*: Baek, Y. and Whitton, N. (eds.). Cases on Digital Game-Based Learning: Methods, Models and Strategies. IGI Global, Hershey, PA.

Herodotou, C. and Mystakidis, S. (2015). Addressing the Retention Gap in MOOCs: Towards a Motivational Framework for MOOCs Instructional Design. *In*: 16th Biennial EARLI Conference for Research on Learning and Instruction Proceedings. Limassol, Cyprus

Hickey, D.T. (1997). Motivation and contemporary socio-constructivist instructional perspectives. *Educ Psychol*, 32, 175-193. https://doi.org/10.1207/s15326985ep3203_3

Hinrichs, R. and Wankel, C. (2012). *Engaging the Avatar: New Frontiers in Immersive Education*. IAP, Charlotte, NC.

Kapp, K.M. (2012). *The Gamification of Learning and Instruction*. Pfeiffer.

Kop, R. and Hill, A. (2008). Connectivism: Learning theory of the future or vestige of the past? *Int Rev Res Open Distance Learn*, http://www.irrodl.org/index.php/irrodl/article/view/9.3.4

Kostopoulos, K.P., Giannopoulos, K., Mystakidis, S. and Chronopoulou, K. (2014). E-learning through Virtual Reality Applications. *Int J Technol Learn*, 21, 57-68. https://doi.org/10.18848/2327-0144/CGP/v20i01/49125

Lambropoulos, N. and Mystakidis, S. (2012). Learning Experience+ within 3D Immersive Worlds. pp. 857-862. *In*: Federated Conference on Computer Science and Information Systems (FedCSIS) 2012. IEEE.

Lave, J. and Wenger, E. (1991). *Situated Learning: Legitimate Peripheral Participation.* Cambridge University Press, New York, NY, USA.

Leigh, E., Courtney, N. and Nygaard, N. (2012). The coming of age of simulations, games and role play in higher education. pp. 1-22. *In*: Simulations Games and Role Play in University Education. Libri, Farringdon Oxfordshire.

Lombard, M. and Ditton, T. (1997). At the heart of it all: the concept of presence. *J Comput Commun*, 3. https://doi.org/10.1111/j.1083-6101.1997.tb00072.x

McAdams, D.P. (2006). The redemptive self: Generativity and the stories Americans live by. *Res Hum Dev*, 3, 81-100. https://doi.org/10.1080/15427609.2006.9683363

Mennecke, B.E., Triplett, J.L., Hassall, L.M. et al. (2011). An examination of a theory of embodied social presence in virtual worlds. *Decis Sci*, 42, 413-449.

Michael, D.R. and Chen, S.L. (2005). *Serious Games: Games That Educate, Train, and Inform*. Muska & Lipman/Premier-Trade.

Mimirinis, M. and Bhattacharya, M. (2007). Design of virtual learning environments for deep learning. *J Interact Learn Res*, 18, 55-64.

Moore, M.G. (1997). Theory of transactional distance. pp. 22-38. *In*: Keegan, D. (ed.). Theoretical Principles of Distance Education. Routledge, London, UK.

Mystakidis, S. (2010). UOC CDT4 E-learning Action Course. https://www.youtube.com/watch?v=4G2DpCsIC_o. Accessed 10 Jul 2019

Mystakidis, S. (2019). *Motivation Enhanced Deep and Meaningful Learning with Social Virtual Reality*. University of Jyväskylä

Mystakidis, S. (2020). Distance education gamification in social virtual reality: A case study on student engagement. *In*: Proceedings of the 11th International Conference on Information, Intelligence, Systems and Applications (IISA 2020). https://doi.org/10.1109/IISA50023.2020.9284417

Mystakidis, S., Lambropoulos, N., Fardoun, H.M. and Alghazzawi, D.M. (2014). Playful blended digital storytelling in 3D immersive e-learning environments. pp. 97-101. *In*: Proceedings of the 2014 Workshop on Interaction Design in Educational Environments - IDEE '14. ACM Press, New York, New York, USA.

Mystakidis, S. and Herodotou, C. (2016). OpenQuest: Designing a motivational framework for MOOCs instruction. pp. 141-145. *In*: MOOCs in Europe. European Commission.

Mystakidis, S., Berki, E. and Valtanen, J. (2017a). Toward successfully integrating Mini Learning Games into Social Virtual Reality Environments – Recommendations for improving Open and Distance Learning. pp. 968-977. *In*: 9th Annual International Conference on Education and New Learning Technologies (EDULEARN17) Proceedings. Barcelona, 3-5 July 2017. https://doi.org/10.21125/edulearn.2017.1203

Mystakidis, S., Berki, E. and Valtanen, J. (2017b). Designing and implementing a big open online course by using a 3D virtual immersive environment – lessons learned. pp. 8070-8079. *In*: 9th Annual International Conference on Education and New Learning Technologies (EDULEARN17) Proceedings. Barcelona, 3-5 July 2017. https://doi.org/10.21125/edulearn.2017.0487

Mystakidis, S. and Berki, E. (2018). The case of literacy motivation: Playful 3D immersive learning environments and problem-focused education for blended digital storytelling. *Int J Web-Based Learn Teach Technol*, 13. https://doi.org/10.4018/IJWLTT.2018010105

Mystakidis, S., Berki, E. and Valtanen, J. (2019a). The Patras Blended Strategy Model for deep and meaningful learning in quality life long distance education. *Electron J e-Learning*, 17, 66-78. https://doi.org/10.34190/JEL.17.2.01

Mystakidis, S., Cachafeiro, E. and Hatzilygeroudis, I. (2019b). Enter the Serious E-scape Room: A cost-effective serious game model for deep and meaningful e-learning. *In*: Proceedings of the 10th International Conference on Information, Intelligence, Systems and Applications (IISA 2019). IEEE, Patras, 15-17 July 2019. https://doi.org/10.1109/IISA.2019.8900673

Mystakidis, S., Fragkaki, M. and Hatzilygeroudis, I. (2020). Stairway to heaven: Instructional design alignment in a serious game for experiential religious education in virtual reality. *In*: 12th Annual International Conference on Education and New Learning Technologies (EDULEARN20) Proceedings. https://doi.org/10.21125/edulearn.2020.1246

Nolen, S.B., Horn, I.S. and Ward, C.J. (2015). Situating motivation. *Educ Psychol*, 50, 234-247. https://doi.org/10.1080/00461520.2015.1075399

Paris, S.G. and Turner, J.C. (1994). Situated motivation. pp. 213-237. *In*: Student motivation, cognition, and learning: Essays in honor of Wilbert J. McKeachie. Lawrence Erlbaum Associates, Inc, Hillsdale, NJ, US.

Paulus, T. and Scherff, L. (2008). Can anyone offer any words of encouragement? Online Dialogue as a Support Mechanism for Preservice Teachers. *J Technol Teach Educ*, 16, 113-136.

Pellas, N. and Mystakidis, S. (2020). A systematic review of research about game-based learning in virtual worlds. *J Univers Comput Sci*, 26, 1017-1042.

Rhoads, R.A. (2015). MOOCs, *High Technology, and Higher Learning*. Johns Hopkins University Press.

Rogoff, B., Matusov, E. and White, C. (1996). Models of teaching and learning: Participation in a community of learners. pp. 388-414. *In*: The Handbook of Education and Human Development. Wiley Online Library.

Rosenzweig, E.Q. and Wigfield, A. (2016). STEM motivation interventions for adolescents: A promising start, but further to go. *Educ Psychol*, 51, 146-163. https://doi.org/10.1080/00461520.2016.1154792

Rothes, A., Lemos, M.S. and Gonçalves, T. (2017). Motivational profiles of adult learners. *Adult Educ Q*, 67, 3-29. https://doi.org/10.1177/0741713616669588

Ryan, R.M. and Deci, E.L. (2000). Self-determination theory and the facilitation of intrinsic motivation, social development, and well-being. *Am Psychol*, 55, 68-78. https://doi.org/10.1037/0003-066X.55.1.68

Ryan, R.M., Rigby, C.S. and Przybylski, A. (2006). The motivational pull of video games: A self-determination theory approach. *Motiv Emot*, 30, 347-363. https://doi.org/10.1007/s11031-006-9051-8

Ryan, R.M. and Deci, E.L. (2008). A self-determination theory approach to psychotherapy: The motivational basis for effective change. *Can Psychol Can*, 49, 186-193. https://doi.org/10.1037/a0012753

Salen, K. and Zimmerman, E. (2004). *Rules of Play: Game Design Fundamentals*. MIT Press, Cambridge, Mass.

Salen, K. (2017). Designing a place called school: A case study of the public school quest to learn. *She Ji J Des Econ Innov*, 3, 51-64. https://doi.org/10.1016/J.SHEJI.2017.08.002

Sanchez, D.R., Langer, M. and Kaur, R. (2019). Gamification in the classroom: Examining the impact of gamified quizzes on student learning. *Comput Educ*. https://doi.org/10.1016/j.compedu.2019.103666

Schiefele, U. (1991). Interest, learning, and motivation. *Educ Psychol*, 26, 299-323. https://doi.org/10.1080/00461520.1991.9653136

Schiefele, U. (1992). Topic interest and levels of text comprehension. *In*: Renninger, A., Hidi, S. and Krapp, A. (eds.). The Role of Interest in Learning and Development. Hillsdale, NJ, US, pp. 151-182.

Schunk, D.H., Meece, J.L. and Pintrich, P.R. (2014). *Motivation in Education: Theory, Research, and Applications*. Pearson.

Schwab, K. (2016). *The Fourth Industrial Revolution*. World Economic Forum.

Sheldon, L. (2011). *The Multiplayer Classroom: Designing Coursework as a Game*. Cengage Learning PTR.

Sheldon, L. and Seelow, D. (2017). The multiplayer classroom: The designer and the collaboration. *Int J Innov Online Educ*, http://www.itdl.org/Journal/Jan_05/article0.1.htm

Siemens, G. (2005). Connectivism: A learning theory for the digital age. *Int J Instr Technol Distance Learn*, http://onlineinnovationsjournal.com/streams/course-design-and-development/2589574144889286.html

Thirouard, M., Bernaert, O., Dhorne, L. et al. (2015). Learning by doing: Integrating a serious game in a MOOC to promote new skills. pp. 92-96. *In*: Proceedings of the European MOOC Stakeholder Summit 2015. Mons.

Van Eck, R. (2007). Building artificially intelligent learning games. pp 271-307. *In*: Gibson, D., Aldrich, C. and Prensky, M. (eds.). Games and Simulations in Online Learning. IGI Global.

Vygotsky, L.S. (1978). *Mind in Society: The Development of Higher Psychological Processes*. Harvard University Press.

Warburton, S. (2009). Second Life in higher education: Assessing the potential for and the barriers to deploying virtual worlds in learning and teaching. *Br J Educ Technol*, 40, 414-426. https://doi.org/10.1111/j.1467-8535.2009.00952.x

Wentzel, K. and Wigfield, A. (2009). *Handbook of Motivation at School*. Routledge, New York, NY, USA.

Williams, J.J., Paunesku, D., Haley, B. and Sohl-Dickstein, J. (2013). Measurably increasing motivation in MOOCs. *In*: Proceedings of the 1st Workshop on Massive Open Online Courses at the 16th Conference on Artificial Intelligence in Education. Memphis, TN.

Yee, N. and Bailenson, J. (2007). The proteus effect: The effect of transformed self-representation on behavior. *Hum Commun Res*, 33, 271-290. https://doi.org/10.1111/j.1468-2958.2007.00299.x

Zainuddin, Z. (2018). Students' learning performance and perceived motivation in gamified flipped-class instruction. *Comput Educ*, 126, 75-88. https://doi.org/10.1016/j.compedu.2018.07.003

Zyda, M. (2005). From visual simulation to virtual reality to games. *Computer (Long Beach Calif)*, 38, 25-32. https://doi.org/10.1109/MC.2005.297

# Index